PROFESSIONAL LEARNING: GAPS AND TRANSITIONS ON THE WAY FROM NOVICE TO EXPERT

Innovation and Change in Professional Education

VOLUME 2

Series Editor:
Wim Gijselaers, *Department of Educational Development and Educational Research, University of Maastricht, The Netherlands*

Associate Editors:
LuAnn Wilkerson, *Center of Educational Development and Research, University of California, Los Angeles, CA, U.S.A*
Henny Boshuizen, *Educational Technology Expertise Center, Open University Nederland, The Netherlands*

Editorial Board:
Howard Barrows, *Professor Emeritus, School of Medicine, Southern Illinois University, IL, U.S.A.*
Edwin M. Bridges, *Professor Emeritus, School of Education, Stanford University, CA, U.S.A.*
Thomas M. Duffy, *School of Education, Indiana University, Bloomington, IN, U.S.A.*
Rick Milter, *College of Business, Ohio University, OH, U.S.A.*

SCOPE OF THE SERIES

The primary aim of this book series is to provide a platform for exchanging experiences and knowledge about educational innovation and change in professional education and post-secondary education (engineering, law, medicine, management, health sciences, etc.). The series provides an opportunity to publish reviews, issues of general significance to theory development and research in professional education, and critical analysis of professional practice to the enhancement of educational innovation in the professions.

The series promotes publications that deal with pedagogical issues that arise in the context of innovation and change of professional education. It publishes work from leading practitioners in the field, and cutting edge researchers. Each volume is dedicated to a specific theme in professional education, providing a convenient resource of publications dedicated to further development of professional education.

The titles published in this series are listed at the end of this volume

Professional Learning: Gaps and Transitions on the Way from Novice to Expert

Edited by

HENNY P.A. BOSHUIZEN
Open Universiteit Nederland,
Heerlen, The Netherlands

RAINER BROMME
Westfälische Wilhelms-Universität,
Münster, Germany

and

HANS GRUBER
University of Regensburg,
Germany

KLUWER ACADEMIC PUBLISHERS
DORDRECHT / BOSTON / LONDON

A C.I.P. Catalogue record for this book is available from the Library of Congress.

ISBN 1-4020-2066-X (PB)

ISBN 1-4020-2065-1 (HB)
ISBN 1-4020-2094-5 (e-book)

Published by Kluwer Academic Publishers,
P.O. Box 17, 3300 AA Dordrecht, The Netherlands.

Sold and distributed in North, Central and South America
by Kluwer Academic Publishers,
101 Philip Drive, Norwell, MA 02061, U.S.A.

In all other countries, sold and distributed
by Kluwer Academic Publishers,
P.O. Box 322, 3300 AH Dordrecht, The Netherlands.

Printed on acid-free paper

© 2004 Kluwer Academic Publishers
No part of this work may be reproduced, stored in a retrieval system, or transmitted
in any form or by any means, electronic, mechanical, photocopying, microfilming, recording
or otherwise, without written permission from the Publisher, with the exception
of any material supplied specifically for the purpose of being entered
and executed on a computer system, for exclusive use by the purchaser of the work.

Printed in the Netherlands.

Contents

Contributing Authors — ix

Preface — xxi

Acknowledgments — xxiii

Part 1: INTRODUCTION — 1

INTRODUCTION: ON THE LONG WAY FROM NOVICE TO EXPERT AND HOW TRAVELLING CHANGES THE TRAVELLER — 3
HENNY P. A. BOSHUIZEN, RAINER BROMME AND HANS GRUBER

Part 2: INITIAL EDUCATION: ACQUIRING KNOWLEDGE TO BECOME AN EXPERT — 9

THE ROLE OF EXPERIENCE IN PROFESSIONAL TRAINING AND DEVELOPMENT OF PSYCHOLOGICAL COUNSELLORS — 11
JOSEF STRASSER AND HANS GRUBER

THE CASE OF PLANT IDENTIFICATION IN BIOLOGY: WHEN IS A ROSE A ROSE? — 29
RAINER BROMME, ELMAR STAHL, TOBIAS BARTHOLOMÉ AND STEPHANIE PIESCHL

OVERCOMING PROBLEMS OF KNOWLEDGE APPLICATION AND TRANSFER ROBIN STARK, HANS GRUBER, LUDWIG HINKOFER AND HEINZ MANDL	49
Part 3: GAPS AND TRANSITIONS: ACCUMULATING EXPERIENCE TO BECOME A PROFESSIONAL	71
DOES PRACTICE MAKE PERFECT? HENNY P. A. BOSHUIZEN	73
FOSTERING MANAGERIAL PROBLEM-SOLVING JOS A. R. ARTS, WIM H. GIJSELAERS AND MIEN S. R. SEGERS	97
FROM THEORY TO PRACTICE IN MEDICAL EDUCATION KATINKA J. A. H. PRINCE AND HENNY P. A. BOSHUIZEN	121
EMBEDDING AND IMMERSION AS KEY STRATEGIES IN LEARNING TO TEACH HARM H. TILLEMA	141
Part 4: WORKPLACE AND ORGANISATION: ENCULTURATION TO BECOME AN EXPERT PROFESSIONAL	157
TEACHING EXPERTISE EERO ROPO	159
PROFESSIONAL LEARNING: DELIBERATE ATTEMPTS AT DEVELOPING EXPERTISE MARGARETHA W. J. VAN DE WIEL, KIM H. P. SZEGEDI AND MATHIEU C. D. P. WEGGEMAN	181
LEARNING PROFESSIONALS: TOWARDS AN INTEGRATED MODEL P. ROBERT-JAN SIMONS AND MANON C. P. RUIJTERS	207
FROM INDIVIDUAL COGNITION TO COMMUNITIES OF PRACTICE ANNELI ETELÄPELTO AND KAIJA COLLIN	231
COMPETENCE-SUPPORTING WORKING CONDITIONS CHRISTIAN HARTEIS AND HANS GRUBER	251

Contents vii

NETWORK TIES, COGNITIVE CENTRALITY, AND TEAM
   INTERACTION WITHIN A TELECOMMUNICATION
   COMPANY 271
   TUIRE PALONEN, KAJ HAKKARAINEN, JAANA TALVITIE AND
   ERNO LEHTINEN

Index 295

Contributing Authors

Jos A. R. Arts
Faculty of Economics and Business Administration, Department of Educational Development and Research, University Maastricht, PO. Box 616, 6200 MD Maastricht, The Netherlands. A.R.M.Arts@tue.nl or Arts@educ.unimaas.nl

Jos Arts works in the field of educational development at University Maastricht, Department of Educational Development and Educational Research, and at Eindhoven Technical University, the Educational Service Centre. His research interests are problem solving abilities, reasoning during problem solving, knowledge use during solving problems, evaluation and design of student-centred education. He earned his master degree in educational technology in 1991 (Twente University). He is preparing his Ph.D. thesis on 'knowledge use and reasoning during managerial problem solving in a student-directed learning environment', expected spring 2004, University Maastricht.

Tobias Bartholomé
Psychologisches Institut III, Westfälische Wilhelms-Universität Münster, Fliednerstraße 21, D-48149 Münster, Germany. tbartho@psy.uni-muenster.de

Tobias Bartholomé is a researcher at the University of Münster, Germany, Department of Educational Psychology. He received his diploma in psychology with a thesis on the perception of facial attractiveness in 2001. Since 2002 he is holder of a scholarship in the virtual Ph.D.-program 'Knowledge Acquisition and Knowledge Exchange with New Media'. In his Ph.D. project he focuses on the effects of new media on the acquisition and use of robust and flexible conceptual knowledge. His current research interests comprise knowledge acquisition through learning with multiple representations, development and evaluation of interactive learning environments as well as help seeking within interactive learning environments.

Henny P. A. Boshuizen
Educational Technology Expertise Centre, Open Universiteit Nederland, PO Box 2960, 6401 DL Heerlen, The Netherlands. els.boshuizen@ou.nl

Henny Boshuizen is a full professor of education and educational technology at the Open University of the Netherlands, Educational Technology Expertise Centre (OTEC), where she a member of the management team and director of the (post)graduate study programmes on educational technology. Her research interests concern learning and expertise development in professional domains (such as medicine, law, education, accountancy and management), learning from experience and communication and learning in (distributed) multi-professional teams. Furthermore, she has done research on the effects of activating educational strategies, such as problem-based learning. She studied psychology at the University of Amsterdam where she received her MSc degree in 1979; her Ph.D. thesis dealt with expertise development in medicine, University Maastricht, 1989. She received a post-graduate Spencer grant by the U.S. National Academy of Education. She co-chairs the EARLI (European Association for Research on Learning and Instruction) Special Interest Group 'Learning and Professional Development' (since 1999).

Rainer Bromme
Psychologisches Institut III, Westfälische Wilhelms-Universität Münster, Fliednerstraße 21, D-48149 Münster, Germany. bromme@uni-muenster.de

Rainer Bromme is a full professor of educational psychology at the Department of Psychology at the University of Muenster. He studied psychology at the University of Münster (Diplom Degree 1975), achieved a doctor's degree at the University of Oldenburg (1979) and the 'Venia Legendi' for psychology (habilitation) at the University of Bielefeld. His research interests are cognition and teaching/learning processes, especially related to the communication and cooperation between experts and laypersons, development of professional expertise, learning with new media, and the development of knowledge and understanding in science and mathematics. He is a faculty member of the virtual Ph.D.-program 'Knowledge Acquisition and Knowledge Exchange with New Media', funded by the German Research Foundation (DFG).

Kaija Collin

Institute for Educational Research, FIN-40014 University of Jyväskylä, PO Box 35, Finland. kaija.collin@ktl.jyu.fi

Kaija Collin is a Ph.D. student preparing her dissertation in adult education. She is working as a researcher in the Institute for Educational Research at the University of Jyväskylä. Her current work is funded by Academy of Finland in the project of 'Learning and the Development of Expertise in the Interaction between Higher Education and Working Life' directed by Professor Päivi Tynjälä. Collin's research interest focuses on learning in the workplace from the employees' point of view. She approaches workplace learning as shared practice.

Anneli Eteläpelto

Department of Education, FIN-40014 University of Jyväskylä, PO Box 35, Finland. anneli.etelapelto@edu.jyu.fi

Anneli Eteläpelto is a full professor of educational psychology in the Research Centre for Educational Psychology at the University of Helsinki. She received her Ph.D. degree in psychology from the University of Jyväskylä. Eteläpelto has researched professional learning and developing professional expertise in schooling and working life environments, and learning professional competencies in design, programming, and teaching. She is a founding member and present co-chair of the EARLI-SIG 'Learning and Professional Development'. She is the vice-president of the Finnish Educational Research Association. From the beginning of the year 2004 Anneli Eteläpelto is a full professor of adult education at the Department of Education at the University of Jyväskylä, Finland. Her recent research interest additionally address themes on developing professional identities in small-group-based learning communities.

Wim H. Gijselaers

Faculty of Economics and Business Administration, Department of Educational Development and Research, University Maastricht, PO. Box 616, 6200 MD Maastricht, The Netherlands. w.gijselaers@educ.unimaas.nl

Wim Gijselaers is a full professor of education at University Maastricht, The Netherlands. He is interested in various aspects of problem-based learning, cognition and instruction, and educational measurement. His current research focuses on the instructional design of powerful learning environments, expertise development in management education, and shared cognition in teams. Over the past 15 years, he was one of the persons responsible for the implementation and further development of problem-based learning in the economics and international business programs at this university. As a consultant he was involved in the implementation of curriculum reform at several institutions in higher education adopting problem-based learning as leading educational principle. He chaired the executive board of EDiNEB, an international network of innovative educators, for a period of eight years. He received his Ph.D. degree (1988) in education from University Maastricht. Currently he serves the positions of Director of the Graduate Program of International Business, and chair of the department of Educational Development and Educational Research at the Faculty of Economics and Business (University Maastricht).

Hans Gruber
Institute for Education, University of Regensburg, Universitätsstraße 31, D-93040 Regensburg, Germany. hans.gruber@paedagogik.uni-regensburg.de

Hans Gruber is a full professor of education (learning and instruction) and Dean of the Faculty of Philosophy II (Psychology, Education, and Sports) at the University of Regensburg, Germany. He studied psychology at the University of Munich, Germany. He was the recipient of a dissertation grant from the Max-Planck-Institute for Psychological Research. He did his Ph.D. in psychology, education, and German literature. He received the 'venia legendi' for psychology and empirical education (habilitation) from the University of Munich. His current research topics are expertise (domains under investigation: counselling, music, sports, medicine); professional experience; complex learning environments in professional domains; epistemological beliefs; further learning at universities. He is founding member of the EARLI Special Interest Group 'Learning and Professional Development' and co-chaired it for four years (1999 – 2003).

Kai Hakkarainen
Department of Psychology, PO Box 9, FIN-00014 University of Helsinki, Finland. kai.hakkarainen@helsinki.fi

Kai Hakkarainen is working as a research fellow of the Academy of Finland. Currently he is the Director of the Centre for Research on Networked Learning and Knowledge Building at the Department of Psychology, University of Helsinki. He investigates socio-cognitive aspects and theoretical foundations of computer-supported collaborative learning and working. His research interests focus on dynamic theories of learning and inquiry that help to understand and explain knowledge-creation processes. He is particularly interested in empirically and theoretically analysing complex reciprocal relations between individual, socially distributed and cultural-historical cognitions. He received his MA degree in 1989, University of Helsinki, Finland, and his Ph.D. degree in 1998, University of Toronto, Canada.

Christian Harteis

Institute for Education, University of Regensburg, Universitätsstraße 31, D-93040 Regensburg, Germany. christian.harteis@paedagogik.uni-regensburg.de

Christian Harteis holds a full position as research assistant at the Department for Research on Learning and Instruction (Prof. Dr. Hans Gruber) at the Institute for Education of the Regensburg University. Main topics of his research are workplace learning, development of professional competence, vocational education and training, personnel and organisational development, and constructivism. He earned both his diploma in education (Dipl.-Päd.) and his Ph.D. degree at the Regensburg University in 2002.

Ludwig Hinkofer

Department of Psychology, Institute of Educational Psychology, Ludwig-Maximilian-University Munich, Leopoldstraße 13, D-80802 München, Germany. hinkofer@edupsy.uni-muenchen.de

Ludwig Hinkofer is a research collaborator and scientific assistant at the Ludwig-Maximilian-University of Munich, Institute of Educational Psychology. His research interests are learning with worked-out examples, instructional measures to foster knowledge construction and transfer, e-learning and didactics of multimedia. In 1997 he received his degree in Business Administration at the University of Applied Sciences in Munich (main focus on tourism, personnel development and human behaviour). He earned his Ph.D. in education and psychology in 2003 at the University of Munich.

Erno Lehtinen

Department of Teacher Education, FIN-20014 University of Turku, Finland. Erno.lehtinen@utu.fi

Erno Lehtinen is a full professor of education and vice-rector of the University of Turku. He graduated in educational science in 1977 at the University of Turku and received his Ph.D. from the same University. He has been a visiting research scholar at the universities of Bern, Edinburgh, and Pittsburgh. His scientific interests focus on research on learning environments, educational technology, and the development of expertise in various contexts. He has studied the development of networked working practices, computer supported collaborative learning and is currently studying processes of conceptual change in learning advanced mathematics. Lehtinen was the president of the EARLI in 2001-2003.

Heinz Mandl

Department of Psychology, Institute of Educational Psychology, Ludwig-Maximilian-University Munich, Leopoldstraße 13, D-80802 München, Germany. mandl@edupsy.uni-muenchen.de

Heinz Mandl is a full professor of education and educational psychology, at the University of Munich. His research interests are analysis and support of knowledge acquisition and the application of knowledge in schools, universities and organisations/corporations (knowledge transfer); personal and organisational knowledge management; net-based knowledge communication in groups; design, implementation and evaluation of innovative learning environments especially with focus on self-directed and cooperative learning and the integration of new media. Originally trained as a teacher for primary and secondary education Mandl earned his Master degree in psychology in 1971 at the University of Munich, and his Ph.D. degree in 1974 at the same institute. Among his previous positions were a professorship at the University of Tübingen, Director of the German Institute for Distance Education at the University of Tübingen, and Dean of the Faculty for Psychology and Education at the University of Munich. Mandl was the president of the EARLI in 1989-1991.

Tuire Palonen

Centre for Learning Research, FIN-20014 Turku University, Finland. tuire.palonen@utu.fi

Tuire Palonen is a researcher in the Centre for Learning Research in the University of Turku. Her research interests focus on socially shared knowledge, i.e. collective action. She is interested in social network analyses and related methods, which concentrate on relationships among actors working in joint collaboration. She received her MA degree in Sociology in 1987, her Licentiate of Sociology in 1992 and her Ph.D. degree in educational sciences in 2003, all at the University of Turku, Finland.

Stephanie Pieschl

Psychologisches Institut III, Westfälische Wilhelms-Universität Münster, Fliednerstraße 21, D-48149 Münster, Germany. pieschl@psy.uni-muenster.de

Stephanie Pieschl is a researcher at the University of Münster, Germany, Department of Educational Psychology. She received her diploma in Psychology with a thesis about cognitive processes in plant identification in 2002. Since 2003 she is holder of a scholarship in the virtual Ph.D.-program 'Knowledge Acquisition and Knowledge Exchange with New Media'. Currently she is working on her Ph.D. thesis on the influence of epistemological beliefs on meta-cognitive monitoring including regulatory behaviour like help seeking and error management. Her research interests also include the development and evaluation of interactive learning environments.

Katinka J. A. H. Prince
Skillslab, Faculty of Medicine, University Maastricht, PO Box 616, 6200 MD Maastricht, The Netherlands. k.prince@sk.unimaas.nl

Katinka Prince is a general practitioner and works part-time as a skills trainer and researcher at the Skillslab of the Maastricht Medical School. She received her MD degree from University University. Her Ph.D. thesis (expected summer 2004) is in the domain of medical education and concerns the transitions in medical training and the associated problems students are facing, i.e., the transition from the theory-oriented first four years of the undergraduate medical curriculum to clinical training, and the transition from undergraduate medical training to the position of house officer. Her research interests are: learning of students, problem-based learning, and curriculum evaluation.

Eero Ropo
Department of Teacher Education, FIN-33014 University of Tampere, Finland. eero.ropo@uta.fi

Eero Ropo is a full professor of education and vice head at the Department of Teacher Education, University of Tampere, Finland. He made his MA in 1978, licentiate in 1980 and Ph.D. degree in 1984 at the University of Tampere, Finland. He has been a visiting Fulbright scholar at the LRDC, University of Pittsburgh, USA, and a visiting research scholar at the Texas Tech University and Vanderbilt University, USA. Ropo pursues international research interests, specialising in research on teachers and teacher expertise, technology in education and the issues of curriculum theory.

Manon C. P. Ruijters
Twynstra Gudde Management Consultants, PO Box 907, 3800 AX Amersfoort, The Netherlands. mru@tg.nl

Manon Ruijters is working as a senior adviser at Twynstra Gudde Management Consultants in Amersfoort, the Netherlands. Her main field of interest is human resource development (HRD), connecting organisational success and individual growth and well-being. She designs and realizes corporate academies and management development programs, coaches HRD-professionals, maps (group) learning profiles, and realizes learning architecture for complex learning questions. She studied educational sciences, specialising in learning disabilities at Leiden University, where she received her master's degree in 1992. An additional master's degree in learning and development at Tias Business School of Tilburg University was earned in 2000 (cum laude). In her Ph.D. research on 'Language of learning, learning profiles and learning propositions' she connects her interest in science with her working practice.

Mien S. R. Segers

Department of Education, Faculty of Social and Behavioural Sciences, Leiden University, PO Box 9500, 2300 RA Leiden, The Netherlands. segers@fsw.leidenuniv.nl or m.segers@educ.unimaas.nl

Mien Segers is a full professor of educational sciences at the department of Educational Sciences of Leiden University (the Netherlands) and at the department of Educational Development and Research of University Maastricht (The Netherlands). Her major research interests are the evaluation and optimisation of learning in learner-centred learning environments and new modes of assessment within these environments. These research projects take place in school as well as in organisational settings. She has been the coordinator of the Special Interest Group 'Assessment and Evaluation' of EARLI and is currently appointed as the coordinator of the SIG 'Higher Education'. She studied Education at the University of Gent, Belgium (1985) and received her Ph.D. degree from University Maastricht (1993) on a dissertation on quality assurance in higher education.

P. Robert-Jan Simons

IVLOS, Department of Education, Utrecht University, Heidelberglaan 8, 3584 CS Utrecht, The Netherlands. p.r.j.simons@ivlos.uu.nl

P. Robert-Jan Simons is directing a centre of research on ICT in education at Utrecht University as professor of learning and ICT. His main research interest (s) are ICT related learning, professionalisation, learning on the job, communities of practice and computer-supported collaborative learning and working. P. Robert-Jan Simons graduated in psychology (educational and developmental) at the University of Amsterdam in 1973 and received his Ph.D. degree from Tilburg University in 1981. He was the president of the EARLI organisation from 1993 – 1995 and co-organized the 1995 EARLI conference. From 1990 till 2001 Simons was professor of educational psychology at the University of Nijmegen, where he directed the Research Institute for Pedagogy and Education.

Elmar Stahl

Psychologisches Institut III, Westfälische Wilhelms-Universität Münster, Fliednerstraße 21, D-48149 Münster, Germany. stahlel@psy.uni-muenster.de

Elmar Stahl is an assistant professor at the University of Münster, Germany, Department of Educational Psychology. He received his master degree in psychology with a thesis about binocular rivalry (visual perception) in 1995. In 2001 he received his Ph.D. with a thesis about knowledge acquisition and learning processes by writing hypertexts. His current research interests proceeds in this vein. It furthermore includes topics such as development and evaluation of interactive learning environments, help seeking within interactive learning environments and the effects of learner-related factors on learning processes, especially the effects of epistemological beliefs on knowledge acquisition within e-learning scenarios.

Robin Stark

Saarland University, Institute of Education, Working unit 'Personality Development and Education', PO Box 151150, D-66123 Saarbrücken, Germany. r.stark@mx.uni-saarland.de

Robin Stark is a full professor of education at the Saarland University (Germany), unit 'Personality Development and Education'. His research interests are learning with worked-out examples, problem-based learning and teaching, motivational aspects of complex learning, conceptual change, epistemological beliefs, knowledge transfer, and empirical research methods. He received his master degree in psychology from the University of Marburg, with a main focus on pedagogical and clinical psychology. From 1994 to 2003 he held the position of research collaborator and scientific assistant at the University of Munich, Institute of Empirical Pedagogics and Pedagogical Psychology, where he did research projects on example-based learning in various domains. Here he received his Ph.D. degree in 1998, in psychology, philosophy and education. In 2002, he received the 'venia legendi' for psychology and empirical education (habilitation) from the University of Munich.

Josef Strasser

Institute for Education, University of Regensburg, Universitätsstraße 31, D-93040 Regensburg, Germany. josef.strasser@paedagogik.uni-regensburg.de

Josef Strasser is a researcher and PhD student at the department for Research on Learning and Instruction of the University of Regensburg and a trained client-centred counsellor. He is working in the DFG-sponsored project 'Competence acquisition in counselling'. His research interests concern professional learning and experience, communication and counselling, as well as knowledge acquisition and application. After studies in educational science and psychology at the universities of Bamberg and Regensburg, he earned his master degree in education from the University of Regensburg in 1998 (Dipl.-Paed.). He prepares a Ph.D. thesis on the development of expertise in the domain of counselling.

Kim H. P. Szegedi

Faculty of Psychology, University Maastricht, PO Box 616, 6200 MD Maastricht, The Netherlands. k.szegedi@psychology.unimaas.nl

Kim Szegedi is currently employed by the Faculty of Psychology, University Maastricht, The Netherlands, as a staff member for curriculum innovation. Her research interest is in expertise development, during and as a result of working experience, involving complex cognition; she especially focuses the factors that differentiate top professionals from their 'ordinary' colleagues. She earned her master of psychology degree in 2003, University Maastricht, with a thesis on expertise development of management consultants.

Jaana Talvitie

Department of Teacher Education, FIN-20014 University of Turku, Finland. jaana.talvitie@salo.fi

Jaana Talvitie is working as special teacher in the city of Salo. She is a student in educational sciences.

Harm H. Tillema

Department of Education, Faculty of Social and Behavioural Sciences, Leiden University, PO Box 9500, 2300 RA Leiden, The Netherlands. tillema@fsw.leidenuniv.nl

Harm Tillema is a senior lecturer at Leiden University (the Netherlands). He received his Ph.D. in education (1983) at the Utrecht University. He worked as a research coordinator at the Institute of Educational Research of the University of Groningen. He received several grants in the area of development and learning of professionals. Currently he works at the

Department of Education at Leiden University. His main field of interest is professional learning and development, especially in teaching and teacher education. A special field of interest is assessment as a tool for professional learning. In his research, he studied the impact of beliefs and dispositions in student teacher learning as beginning professionals, as well as assessment intervention techniques like portfolio and development centres. In his consultancy work in several organisations he is involved in establishing powerful learning environments, which make use of assessment. He is founding member of the International Association of Teachers & Teaching and one of the editors of Teachers & Teaching. He collaborates with Universities at Haifa, London and Washington in areas of professional learning and assessment. He was a visiting professor at the University of Durham.

Mathieu C. D. P. Weggeman
Faculty of Technology Management, Eindhoven University of Technology, PO Box 513, 5600 MB Eindhoven, The Netherlands.
M.C.D.P.Weggeman@tm.tue.nl

Mathieu Weggeman is a full professor of organisation science and knowledge management at the Department of Technology Management at Eindhoven University of Technology in The Netherlands. He holds a Ph.D. in strategic management from the Tilburg University (The Netherlands). His primary expertise lies in the field of organisational knowledge creation in the early stages of the innovation process, and he is actively engaged in teaching and conducting research in this area. A second area of interest concerns the design of organisations in which professionals are motivated to high performance. As a project leader he conducted several large-scale projects in R&D environments, geared to major structural and cultural change. He is member of the Eindhoven Centre of Innovation Studies (ECIS).

Margaretha W. J. van de Wiel
Faculty of Psychology, Department of Experimental Psychology, University Maastricht, PO Box 616, 6200 MD Maastricht, The Netherlands.
m.vandewiel@psychology.unimaas.nl

Margaretha van de Wiel is an assistant professor of cognitive and educational psychology at the Faculty of Psychology, University Maastricht, where she is responsible for courses on learning processes. Her research interests lie in the relationship between learning and understanding, development of expertise, learning from experience in the professions, and effects of problem-based learning. She has also been working as a consultant on the implementation of problem-based learning in diverse curricula. She graduated in experimental psychology at the University of Nijmegen in 1991 and received her Ph.D.-degree in 1997 at University Maastricht based on her thesis about the development of medical expertise.

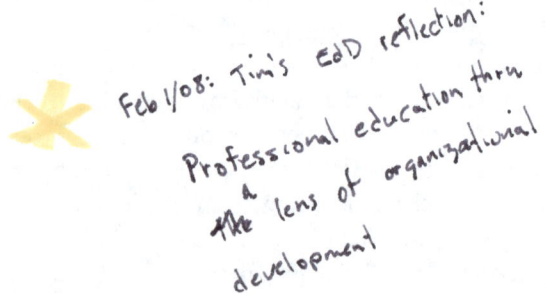

Preface

About the Book Series

The idea for the Book Series "Innovation and Change in Professional Education" (ICPE) was born in 1996. While working on another publication in this area, we noticed that professional educators faced similar problems without even knowing from each other. It was this observation that resulted in examining the possibilities for a new publication platform about professional education with input from different professions. We wanted to develop a publication source that would bring together educators and researchers to exchange ideas and knowledge about theory, research and professional practice. But we were not only striving for a book series informing readers about important themes in the professions. A second goal was to focus on processes of change and innovation. We were heavily involved in innovations going on in our institutions, and were convinced that a better understanding was needed in a wide range of issues critically important to the future of professional education. It was our belief that scholarly publications about innovation processes may support fundamental change in professional education.

ICPE reflects our view that professional education deserves such a publication platform. It aims to approach critical questions of educational innovations, and to examine dynamics of educational change in various professional domains in the context of innovation processes. The books will include contributions from frontline practitioners, leading researchers, or distinguished scholars in professional education, delivering reports of empirical or theoretical research, reviews, interpretations of evaluation studies, or descriptions of innovative approaches. Each volume is organized around one in-depth thematic issue.

About This Book

The main themes of the book are the nature of expertise, the range of ways in which professionals learn, the learning trajectories that characterise professional lives, and the transition from formal learning to workplace learning. It examines in a comprehensive way the nature of professional expertise, and how professional education can gain from insights of research on expertise. The authors address common themes while their chapters treat a wide range of empirical and theoretical work. The present book can serve as a source of reference and new ideas for both educators and researchers who are interested in the field of professional expertise, and its implications for professional education.

Wim H. Gijselaers, Editor-in-Chief,
University Maastricht, The Netherlands

Henny P. A. Boshuizen, Associate Editor,
Open Universiteit Nederland, Heerlen, The Netherlands

LuAnn Wilkerson, Associate Editor,
University of California, Los Angeles, USA

Acknowledgments

We are very grateful that so many experts from so many leading centres in the domain of professional learning and expertise development wanted to join us in our exploration of and quest for a deeper understanding of the gaps and transitions on the way from novice to expert. We highly appreciate their contribution to the book and the discussions we could have with them during the long way from the idea to the finished product.

We would like to give special thanks to Prof. Michael Eraut (University of Sussex, UK), Dr. Jan Vermunt (University Leiden, The Netherlands) and Prof. David Berliner (University of Arizona, USA) for their constructive comments and reviews, which were very helpful and stimulating.

We are grateful to the editorial board of the book series "Innovations and Change in Professional Education" for giving us the opportunity to bring together the research of experts in the field of professional learning.

Johannes Lesser and Birgit Luger, educational-science students of the University of Regensburg, deserve special recognition. They did the final check on inconsistencies, omissions and all the other things that still have to be done after authors and editors think they are done. Henny Dankers (University Maastricht) conscientiously did the layout and final formatting of this book. She was also our liaison with the publisher and was the one who kept us to the deadlines, she herself suffering most when we let it come too close. Our very special thanks go to her.

Heerlen, January 2004

PART 1

INTRODUCTION

Chapter 1

ON THE LONG WAY FROM NOVICE TO EXPERT AND HOW TRAVELLING CHANGES THE TRAVELLER

Henny P. A. Boshuizen[1], Rainer Bromme[2] and Hans Gruber[3]
[1]*Educational Technology Expertise Centre, Open Universiteit Nederland, Heerlen, The Netherlands,* [2]*Psychologisches Institut III, Westfälische Wilhelms-Universität, Münster, Germany,* [3]*Institute for Education, University of Regensburg, Germany*

It sounds like a truism that lifelong learning is necessary in all workplaces, but this idea was not so undisputable only a few decades ago. Imagine a specialist in a hospital who has passed her last examination 20 years ago. Once a day, when discussing a planned treatment for a patient in her team, an advanced medical student suggests a certain procedure he has read of and which is considered by the medical community to be new and successful. The head of the team – the specialist – does not like the new idea. How would she argue? Twenty years ago, in a similar situation, the supervisor might have said that the established procedures are the right ones because they have been used for many years. Nowadays, she would not argue that her procedure was better *because* it was taught for many years, but rather she might argue that the team has collected a lot of experience with the procedure or she might look into empirical evidence on the well-used procedure and the new one and compare them. Nowadays the fact that a certain piece of knowledge or skill *was* once accepted and taught, no longer insures its validity. This scenario reflects a change in how people think and argue about knowledge, at least in modern industrial societies. We do not claim that lifelong learning has become reality in most workplaces. What we do argue is that it is a vision of what it can be and that we must be aware of the conditions, ways and barriers of lifelong learning for experts to maintain their expertise via lifelong learning in the workplace.

This book explores the teaching, training and learning of professionals prior to and during their professional lives. It covers the development of expertise from novice status to high levels, but not for every domain over the whole range, and not for every domain in every respect. Instead, a number of studies have been brought together, each of which highlights salient aspects of expertise development. The main thread of the book is that the development through school or university into professional life is a process of continually transforming the repertoire of knowledge and skills that make up expertise. In the following chapters this transformation will be described as being both a process of individual change (acquisition of knowledge and attitudes), and a process of becoming a member of the culture of a profession. Both are necessary in order to understand expertise development. The use of the concepts *profession, professional knowledge, academic knowledge,* and *expert* is briefly explained in the following paragraphs. These concepts are in the focus of this book.

Professional is an ambiguous term. In some countries and cultures the term is almost identical to vocational or occupational, referring to that stage in life in which work is most prominent. In other places the term is exclusively assigned for the traditional university trained professions such as law, medicine, architecture, etc. In this perspective, professionals are not only highly trained but are also self-responsible. They are not only responsible for the way they practice their profession, but they are also responsible for maintaining their standards as determined by ethics, law, and their peers, and not by employers or experts from other fields. Nowadays there is a strong tendency among different disciplines toward a professional status in the latter sense (e.g., in the field of nursing or teaching). This is true in both those academic professions just discussed and more traditional vocational professions. At the same time a movement in the opposite direction is taking place among traditional professions: Many professionals were confronted with an increasing number of rules and regulations and thus lost their independence; more and more they have to work in (interdisciplinary) teams with other professionals, often employed by a hospital or a company. Hence, in this book we do not make a sharp distinction between professional and vocational groups, but emphasise that these developments require staying up-to-date in order to keep up to changing standards.

Consequently, the concept of *professional knowledge* is understood mainly in contrast to the notion of *academic knowledge.* The relationship between academic knowledge and professional knowledge is important, because the former is transformed into the latter through learning in the workplace. The professional fields covered in this book are medicine, economics, biology, design, and teaching. To become a professional in these fields usually requires extensive formal education ending in an examination. It is necessary to pass an examination in order to obtain a degree, which itself is required as formal legitimatisation for working in the respective professional field (e.g., as a medical doctor). Formal education is usually followed by a more practical second phase, which takes place in institutions typical for the profession, that is clinics for doctors, schools for teachers, law firms for lawyers. Even if professionals will later work outside of these institutions (e.g., many doctors do not work in clinics, many lawyers do not work for a law firm), this second phase serves as opportunity to acquire the more practical skills of the relevant profession and – at least as important – for becoming socialised into the culture of the profession.

The formal training is usually offered by universities or specialised schools of education, of business, etc. These institutions have a more or less strong relationship with domain-related research. The knowledge taught in these institutions is thus called academic knowledge, emphasising that academic knowledge is an important basic source of professional knowledge. But academic knowledge is not identical to professional knowledge. Quite often beginners (e.g., teachers or medical doctors during their first practical year) perceive a gap between the academic knowledge acquired during formal education and the knowledge that is claimed to be "really" relevant by their more experienced colleagues. Experienced practitioners often claim that the knowledge gained during the academic part of professional education should be forgotten because it is often too abstract, not appropriate, etc. Although such claims reflect the important difference between academic and professional knowledge, they are bad advice to newcomers in the field.

The chapters of this book point out the differences between academic knowledge and professional knowledge as well as the close interrelations and linkages between them, aiming at a better understanding of the often-complicated relation between both types of knowledge. Only then can a fruitful view develop about the necessity as well as the limitations of academic knowledge as resource for the development of professional knowledge during practical experience and training.

Experts are often defined as either top performers who excel in a particular field or professionals who achieve at least a moderate degree of success in their occupation. In this book the notion of expert refers to the latter meaning, because modern societies have established formal procedures for selecting and legitimising individuals as professionals. Thus, the concept of expert refers to a social role as well.

Studies defining expertise in the former sense, the notion of top performance, have brought forward valuable insights into the thinking and knowledge-based behaviour of these people. Numerous studies have contributed to the analysis of the perception of problem situations, the organisation of knowledge, and the decision-making processes of experts within different domains. Experts do not just know more than novices, they also have a different way of structuring their domain-specific knowledge. This affects their categorical perception from the outset. Looking at situations from an expert's point of view, determining problems and their causes the way experts do, is exactly the kind of expertise that is applied in many professions to which laypersons do not have access. Accordingly, within the above-mentioned notion of an expert as a professional, knowledge is conceptualised in a broader sense. Attitudes and experience have to be integrated into the concept of knowledge along with explicit declarative and procedural knowledge. Expert knowledge, thus, is a certain (very successful) *perspective* on a particular domain. This is self-evident if more than one profession is involved in problem-solving processes, such as when medical doctors and psychologists try to diagnose and treat psychosomatic diseases. These different professions do not only bring different knowledge to bear in the solution process, but also have different conceptual views of what the problems are that they have to deal with, what the appropriate therapeutic goals might be, etc. Clinical psychologists and medical doctors may well end up with different diagnoses, even if they have to deal with the same patient and start from the same list of symptoms. Not only does this indicate that different diagnoses are possible, different fields of expertise also have different underlying assumptions about the nature of illnesses. Apart from specific information about facts and proven methods of problem solving, professional knowledge includes the world-view that is typical for a certain profession.

Though information processing approaches on expertise have developed important insights into the structure and use of knowledge by experts, the kind of expert that was the object of this research was always the "lonely problem-solver". Social theory approaches, in contrast, emphasise the importance of the social context for becoming an expert. A major difficulty in this kind of research is that the notion of context is difficult to define and, thus, often remains vague. Professional learning is both a process of change within an individual as well as of *enculturation* into a group. Enculturation has to be understood in two senses, namely as a process of change (acquisition of the skills, habits, attitudes of a certain profession) and as a process of becoming accepted and legitimised in a certain context. The notion of enculturation also includes the issue of developing the expert subject's identity, thus the enculturation perspective is necessary to understand how the repertoire of skills and knowledge described in the knowledge approach toward expertise holds together and how it could be adapted to changing contexts. Maintaining a personal identity is of the utmost importance in today's rapidly changing working and social life. In other words, adaptability to continuously changing constraints is a focal element of professional expertise. It is this unstable nature of the environment (i.e., working conditions, task content, and organisational structures) that requires certain stability in the expert's knowledge, skills, and attitudes. The degree of freedom that professionals have in most working contexts when adapting to their environment, has to be taken into account in order to understand that expertise development is more than merely knowledge acquisition.

Different theories on *learning* in the context of expertise development focus different aspects, such as learning as the acquisition and improvement of knowledge and skills, learning as a self-directed and self-organised effort to improve performance, learning as the development of a personal identity including emotion management and self control, and learning as enculturation. Do these different approaches reflect different paradigmatic views on the same issue or do they emphasise different layers of expertise, which all have to be taken into account? The chapters in this book report on evidence supporting the second idea. The diversity of approaches reflects the complex nature of learning to become an expert professional. Of course, the different aspects of professional learning are not equally important for all stages of becoming an expert, but learning occurs during all phases of the development of professional expertise. As mentioned, education begins at school, college or university, and then further develops in practice. These two different contexts are organised in very different ways, and require different learning activities and learning skills. In formal education contexts, explicit knowledge and skills have to be learned, which can be verbalised and demonstrated on demand (in test situations). In working contexts, learning from and through experience as well as reflection on experience and performance becomes more and more important.

The *order of the following chapters* is based upon this course of development. Section 1 focuses on academic education (within rather formal educational contexts), analysing how to *acquire knowledge* to become an *expert*. Section 2 concerns the transition from school to work. It focuses on gaps and transitions when moving from formal educational contexts to working contexts, analysing how to *accumulate experience* to become a *professional*. Section 3 focuses on workplaces and (working) organisations and on inherent learning opportunities within them, analysing how *enculturation* occurs and how it can be fostered on the long way from novice to *expert professional*, a travel that substantially changes the traveller.

PART 2

INITIAL EDUCATION: ACQUIRING KNOWLEDGE TO BECOME AN EXPERT

Chapter 2

THE ROLE OF EXPERIENCE IN PROFESSIONAL TRAINING AND DEVELOPMENT OF PSYCHOLOGICAL COUNSELLORS

Josef Strasser and Hans Gruber
Institute for Education, University of Regensburg, Germany

1. RESEARCH ON TRAINING AND PROFESSIONAL EXPERIENCE IN MENTAL HEALTH PROFESSIONS

Is experience helpful for professional development in such a complex domain like counselling? This question may seem surprising: What else, if not training and experience, will lead to good quality performance? Usually, a major role in professional development is attributed to experience. This holds true, in particular for counselling psychologists, as most clinical training programs are built upon this assumption.

The first part of this chapter presents an overview of research concerning the role of formal training and experience for counselling competence. One major conclusion from this research is that experience does not make a significant difference. In the second part it is shown that this result might be due to theoretical shortcomings. Research on expertise provides a different understanding of counselling competence and its growth through experience. This is illustrated in a study on the development of counsellors' professional knowledge. Finally, practical implications for the formal training of counsellors are explained.

Two lines of research have to be distinguished concerning research about counselling competence. The first focuses on the role of training that is of instruction and special qualification. The second pertains to professional experience and its influence on certain aspects of the profession.

1.1 Training

1.1.1 Training and effectiveness

Two groups of training studies can be differentiated: studies on training and effectiveness, and evaluation studies on clinical training programs. The main interest of research has been in investigating the relation between training and the effects of counselling. Some authors doubt that highly educated professionals in clinical domains are more effective than less educated staff (Dawes, 1994). Durlak (1979) concluded from a meta-analysis on 42 studies that laymen with no or little specific training reached at least the same results as professional helpers. However, such effective lay helpers usually received much support and supervision by professional staff. Professionals show superior performance if the clients' problems increase in complexity (Gunzelmann, Schiepek, & Reinecker, 1987).

1.1.2 Evaluation of clinical training programs

Little reliable evidence exists concerning the influence of specific features of training programs and their instructional design on counsellors' expertise and their action competence. The interest in systematic evaluation of clinical training programs arose only recently, mainly stimulated by discussions about the quality of mental health services. The few existing evaluation studies, are mainly concerned with isolated elements of educational programs, not with programs as a whole. The main focus is on short-term effects. Long-term effects and implementation in "everyday counselling practice" are neglected. One explanation for this is that most training programs are tied to a particular theoretical orientation and therapy modality. Short-term evaluation studies primarily investigate whether the respective theoretical knowledge and treatment techniques have been learned in the correct way. Knowledge application and integration in complex and fuzzy natural situations is rarely focused on (Alberts & Edelstein, 1990).

1.2 Professional experience

1.2.1 General development of counsellors

There is little reliable information concerning professional experience. Some studies describe general pathways of professional development of counsellors and psychologists (Auerbach & Johnson, 1977; Breuer, 1991). These studies show that beginners feel rather unsafe and uncomfortable with their professional role. They have difficulties in applying the theoretical and methodical knowledge they have acquired and thus express feelings of insufficiency. During counselling, beginners are primarily concerned with themselves and therefore pay little attention to the information clients present. They stick to "safe" interventions, which are rather simple and well established. With increasing experience, counsellors are able to supervise their own counselling activities more critically. Evaluation of one's own proceedings include criteria such as functionality and effectiveness instead of methodical exactness. Therefore the theoretical orientation becomes less important, action becomes increasingly eclectic, selecting clinical tools and intervention strategies from different approaches. Such flexibility helps to adapt treatment strategies to individual clients and develop a greater sensitivity to relevant facts, features and issues. Finally, a personal working style emerges that allows comfortable and satisfying working practice.

Stage descriptions provide a first understanding of the development of counsellors, but such global data based on interviews and self-reports neither predict actual performance nor explain the outcome of activities. In order to understand why appropriate or even superior or excellent results are reached, exact criteria must be defined for excellence and expertise of counsellors. This can be part of more detailed studies.

1.2.2 Professional experience and effectiveness

Studies on the effects of psychotherapy are usually concerned with comparing different treatment modalities (e.g., psychoanalytic, cognitive-behavioural), but only rarely deal with the specific skills of individual counsellors. In a review of more than 350 psychotherapy outcome studies, Monchner and Prinz (1991) noticed that therapeutic competence as one possible effective factor had mostly been neglected. The few existing findings are not encouraging. It has been suggested that more experienced counsellors are of a superior quality when confronted with more difficult cases and at the beginning of the counselling process. The advantages of experienced counsellors that could be observed, however, are far more modest than expected (Beutler, Machado, & Neufeld, 1994).

1.2.3 Professional experience and clinical decision-making

Among specific components of counsellors' competence, judgement and decision-making are the most prominent. However, few studies focus on counselling preferring to view clinical judgement from a wider perspective (Caspar, 1995; Garb, 1989).

A number of studies revealed biased or faulty beliefs and attitudes about clients in trained and experienced counsellors. Biases are based on individuals' status as clients, on clients' minority status, on gender characteristics, or on the counsellors' theoretical orientation (Wierzbicki, 1993). Similarly, biases in cognitive processes that counsellors use to arrive at their judgements, were identified, for example confirmatory biases or hindsight biases. These biases eventually decrease the accuracy of a counsellor's clinical judgement.

In general, reviews on the effect of training and experience on the accuracy of clinical judgement found little empirical evidence to support the claim that clinical training and experience actually enhance clinical judgement. Dawes (1994) culminates in the observation that "the empirical data suggest that mental health professionals' accuracy of judgement does not increase with increasing experience" (p. 106).

But why is this so? "If experience within a domain produces expertise in players of chess, restaurant servers, physicists, cabdrivers, and others, why not counsellors and therapists?" (Skovholt, Ronnestad, & Jennings, 1997, p. 362). A closer look at research on expertise reveals some methodological and conceptual shortcomings. These will be reflected upon in the next section.

2. THE CONTRIBUTION OF RESEARCH ON EXPERTISE

Models of expertise and its development "describe cognitive processes as fundamental in expertise and include the more rational/analytical conceptualisations as well as more intuitive components. Perhaps the study of *psychological* expertise (e.g., in the practice of counselling and assessment) should be enriched by several models in order to achieve a more comprehensive and less restrictive view of the processes that experts develop." (Locke & Covell, 1997, p. 243)

The way of thinking about professional expertise has dramatically changed over the years. A few decades ago professional expertise was considered to be based on the amount of specific knowledge a person has accumulated during professional life. Recent approaches stress different dimensions, particularly the development of expertise through experience (Eraut, 1994; Gruber, 1999). Such models try to integrate cognitive aspects and social and cultural dimensions (Billett, 2001). Two seminal results from traditional expertise research play a major role in most recent approaches: the domain-specificity of expertise and the large amount of time needed to acquire expertise.

2.1 Domain-specificity of expertise

In many studies evidence demonstrated that expert performance is domain-specific, and expertise in one area cannot be applied generally to performance outside that specific domain. However, it is still an unresolved question under which conditions two domains are to be considered as completely different or related closely enough so that some components can be transferred (Gruber, 2003).

One cannot assume that an experienced counsellor is superior in all clinical tasks, because counselling might comprise several domains. For example, "drug counselling" or "child guidance" deal with specific problem categories, client difficulties or "disorders". Attempts to define the scope of the domains must carefully examine particular requirements that counsellors meet in their everyday practice. Expertise is apparent when dealing with domain-specific tasks that are difficult and complex. Most studies on counselling expertise did not include tasks of sufficient specificity and difficulty and, thus, failed to uncover the abilities and skills of experienced counsellors. Counselling also consists to a large degree of routine work that can also be successfully managed by novices.

If a computer program is geared low enough, then not just chess masters but chess beginners can match up well ... Differentiation in practitioner ability can be seen at the higher skill levels ... Outcome studies must examine the most complex and difficult cases; for example, severely traumatised clients who find the working alliance very difficult and constantly test and sabotage the therapist. Here we believe major novice-expert differences will be found ... For instance, novice practitioners can bond well with clients who have positive relationship histories. Expertise in this domain is the capacity to bond well with clients who have poor relationship histories. (Skovholt et al., 1997, p. 364f.)

2.2 Time and experience

Acquiring superior domain-specific professional skills requires much time, at least 10 years as suggested by expertise literature (Ericsson & Lehmann, 1996). In many training and practice approaches in the field of counselling, however, the assumption is made that expertise is reached briefly after graduate education. This is reflected in many studies in which the time gap between novice and expert status is too small. Stein and Lambert's (1984) found that the average difference in studies of practitioner expertise was 2.9 years; similar data can be seen in more recent research (Fong, Borders, Ethington, & Pitts, 1997; Ladany, Marotta, & Muse-Burke,

2001). The availability of samples of student counsellors may be a reason for this limitation of the experience continuum.

Correspondingly, descriptive models of counsellor development typically comprise three or four stages, the last of which is completed round about graduation. In contrast, the model by Skovholt et al. (1997) regards counsellor development as a continual process across the professional life span, thus "expertise occurs when the practitioner has evolved to an internalised style after thousands of hours of practice and an average of 15 years of professional experience. At this point, the practitioner has internalised theory and research, found a comfortable working style, developed a method for judging success, and shed elements of the professional role which are incongruent within the self" (Skovholt et al., 1997, p. 364).

2.3 Contemporary conceptions of experience

Practice time is not the sole factor that defines the level of expertise and experience, although most studies on counsellor expertise use this criterion (Lichtenberg, 1997). A number of conceptions of experience are under discussion now, for example Ericssons' conception of deliberate practice (Ericsson, Krampe, & Tesch-Römer, 1993) and Gruber's (1999) notion of experience. Gruber (1999) conceives experience not quantitatively but primarily as subjective relevant learning. Apart from the acquisition and accumulation of declarative knowledge, individuals acquire expertise as they participate in episodes of knowledge application that are personally meaningful to them. Thus, acquisition of expertise usually is embedded in natural situations of great relevance, that are closely related to subjects' knowledge, motivation, and emotions. Similarly, Ericsson et al. (1993) point out the role of deliberate practice, which comprises demanding activities over a long period of time designed to improve performance. Deliberate practice presupposes an active, exploratory attitude, high motivation as well as supportive working conditions that allow continuous training.

The key component of these contemporary concepts of experience is reflection. "Continuous professional reflection consists of a focused inquiry aimed toward attaining a comprehensive understanding of the phenomena encountered in one's professional work." (Skovholt et al., 1997, p. 365)

Experience as active and systematic reflection leads to changes in cognitive structures. This may be the progressive encapsulation of declarative knowledge and the formation of narrative structures such as illness scripts in the domain of medical diagnosing (Boshuizen & Schmidt, 1992). Kolodner's (1983) dynamic memory model describes learning as changes in episodic memory structures through experience. All these models refer to knowledge development and skill acquisition in professional domains that are characterised by rather complex tasks and ill-defined problems.

2.4 Counselling as ill-structured domain

As mentioned above, most studies on clinical decision-making focused on solving well-structured problems. The problems counsellors face in their everyday practice differ from such well-defined tasks. They usually are ill-structured problems. Problem constraints are neither precisely defined, nor is there complete consensus on the correct interventions or even criteria that are applied when evaluating the outcome of a counselling process. Despite the development of manuals based on empirically identified effective factors in counselling, the individual counsellor's approach to clients' problems shows great variety.

When studying differences between experts and novices when approaching ill-structured problems in the social sciences, Voss, Greene, Post, and Penner (1983) found that experts were superior in building a coherent and persuasive explanation (a narrative story). The quality of argumentation, operationalised as connectedness and depth of arguments, increased with experience.

However, it is not easy to benefit from practice alone. It is difficult to initiate reflective learning from experience in ill-structured domains. Thus many counsellors do benefit merely from practical experience. The specific characteristics of the ill-structured domain may account for this deficit:

1. complex and often highly specific cases – similar cases occur often only after a considerable period of time
2. ill-structured tasks that require decisions that have to be made under the pressure of time
3. the plenitude of theoretical and practical approaches
4. components that can successfully be dealt with through routine and thus with little effort
5. lacking or highly selective feedback.

These characteristics often prevent reflection about phenomena of everyday counselling practice and relating them to theories acquired in training programs. Professional activity thus is rarely perceived as occasion for learning and deliberate practice.

2.5 Conclusions for research

Research on counselling can gain by taking up research issues and design features from studies on ill-structured domains. This includes the analysis of domain-specific cognitive aspects:
1. mental representation of problems by experts
2. reasoning processes when dealing with domain-specific problems
3. structure and function of actually applied knowledge
4. content, complexity and development of cognitive structures
5. case-making and argumentation.

From a methodological point of view, studies on counselling should include a number of approaches:
1. post-hoc methods to identify traces of knowledge previously activated (e.g., subjects are asked for explanation of underlying processes after working on a case)
2. on-line methods to tap the knowledge applied during reasoning (e.g., "think aloud protocols" that allow the analysis of contents and propositional aspects)
3. expert-novice contrasts (which implies a "time difference" that is substantial enough for experience to unfold). Measures of "expertise" have to be developed that include advanced credentials, peer-nominations, or intensity and variety of experience. Using more than two groups (not only experts and novices) can help to achieve greater differentiation.

Research on these lines allows the inclusion aspects of the profession that are relevant for the everyday work of the counsellor. (One must keep in mind, however, that cognitive dimensions comprise only one part of expertise in counselling. Others such as interpersonal skills, emotional maturity and personal stability are important as well, but are not discussed in this chapter.) This calls for the use of domain-specific tasks, that are authentic, realistic and contain real life complexity. Methods have to be developed to guarantee this without neglecting general research desiderata such as inter-individual comparability or (quasi-) experimental control.

The development of psychological counsellors' professional knowledge and the role of episodic memory was investigated in a study that aimed to overcome as many of the mentioned shortcomings of existing research as possible.

Only one specific counselling domain was investigated: psychological counselling in educational and child guidance (*domain-specificity*). Content and development of *cognitive structures* are focused on by using *relevant and authentic tasks* of the domain. A *differentiation of levels of expertise* was provided by covering the whole professional span of counsellors, not only graduate students with varying degrees of internship experience.

3. A STUDY ABOUT EXPERIENCE AND THE DEVELOPMENT OF COUNSELLORS' PROFESSIONAL KNOWLEDGE

3.1 Objectives

The main objective of the study was to investigate the role of episodes for the development of counsellors' knowledge in domain-specific problems. The following objectives were set:
1. to investigate changes in the extent of counsellors' knowledge
2. to investigate changes concerning the relevance of (1) basic declarative and (2) experience-based knowledge of counsellors
3. to investigate the role of references to earlier experienced cases for the development of knowledge
4. to investigate how far experience helps counsellors to integrate their own knowledge base further.

3.2 Sample

The subjects were 31 counsellors with different levels of experience, their age ranging from 22 to 60 years ($M = 39.1$ years; $s = 10.9$ years) and experience ranging from six weeks to 33 years ($M = 8.8$ years; $s = 9.6$ years). Three groups were differentiated according to years of professional experience: novices (less than two years), semi-experts (more than two and less than ten years), experts (more than ten years). All participants worked in the domain of educational and child guidance at different counselling centres in southern Germany.

3.3 Procedure

Subjects had to think aloud concerning their knowledge of specific problems relevant to the counselling domain. In a pre-study, professional counsellors not involved in the main study helped to develop the material. From a pool of relevant situations, twenty problem categories were selected according to four criteria:
1. high relevance within the domain
2. substantial variance in the seriousness of the occurring problems

3. reasonable frequency of occurrence in counselling practice
4. possibility to refer to theoretical concepts in the description of the problems.

The resulting domain-specific categories of clients' difficulties ranged from "lack of learning motivation" to "suicidal attempt". Labels of the twenty problems were presented subsequently to subjects on a laptop screen. Subjects were asked to explain the problems and to supply all the relevant knowledge that came to mind. Additionally subjects had to rate their experience with these problems. Participants were tested individually in their workplace. All narratives were audio-recorded. Verbatim protocols were produced.

3.4 Analysis

Subjects' protocols were analysed with respect to quantitative and qualitative aspects of knowledge structures: duration, number of experienced cases referred to, number of episodic statements (both case-related and non-case-related), number of recent cases, number of specific cases, number of experience-based connections. Group differences were tested for significance using analyses of variance and a posteriori Scheffé tests. An alpha of 5% was used throughout.

Duration of sessions provides a suggestion of the amount of available knowledge.

The number of experienced cases the subjects referred to in their problem description is a measure how often subjects referred to (concrete) cases they experienced in their practice in order to explain the problems.

The number of episodic statements assesses how many episodic statements the subjects produced. Statements that were included were those in the past tense using the first person ("I remember ...", "I had a ...", or "I experienced ..."). Episodic statements were divided into case-related statements and non-case-related statements. The first indicate statements in which the subjects recall a case they experienced in their practice, while the latter refers to mentioned episodes that were not based on an actual case.

Number of recent cases and *Number of specific cases*. Two kinds of concrete cases were differentiated. Recent cases are cases the counsellor refers to that are still in progress or have only recently been completed. Specific cases are cases which the counsellor termed as being "particular", "specific", "unusual" or "severe".

The number of experience-based connections assesses how many connections between the single problems subjects can produce. Only those connections are counted that are not based on theoretical reasoning, but are based on the subject's experience.

The Role of Experience

3.5 Hypotheses

The following hypotheses were derived about the protocol variables from theories.

Duration. It was hypothesised that experienced counsellors need more time to solve the task, as their theoretical knowledge gets narratively enriched.

Number of experienced cases. It was hypothesised that semi-experts refer to more concrete cases than experts and novices, as semi-experts are trying apply their theoretical knowledge to their actual experiences.

Number of episodic statements. Analogous to the previous hypothesis it was hypothesised that semi-experts express the largest number of episodic statements.

Number of recent/specific cases. As novices and semi-experts have to struggle to get along with their actual experiences, it was hypothesised that they report recent cases more often, while experts will remember specific cases.

Number of experience-based connections. It was hypothesised that experts, based on their experience, interlink problems more often.

3.6 Results and discussion

Duration. The duration of sessions differed significantly between the groups. It was shortest for novices, both groups of experienced counsellors needed more time.

Number of experienced cases. Although they had some practical experience, the novices rarely referred to cases they had experienced. Semi-experts most often made use of cases they had experienced to explain their knowledge. In the group of experts, the number of mentioned cases they had experienced was smaller that of the semi-expert group.

Number of episodic statements. A similar result was obtained by analysing the amount of episodic statements. Novices significantly differed from semi-experts and experts, expressing less episodic statements. This difference also occurred regarding the number of non-case-related episodic statements.

Number of recent/specific cases. The analysis of variance revealed that semi-experts mainly referred to *recently* experienced cases. They differed significantly from both novices and experts. Counter to expectations, no significant difference was observed between the groups concerning the number of *specific* cases. Figure 1 demonstrates the proportion of specific cases and actual (recently experienced) cases within the three groups. In the expert group the proportion of specific cases differs from the number of recent cases, while there is no difference in the other groups. Thus, specific cases are important for all groups, but whilst for beginners all cases are specific, for experts specific cases are rarely recent ones.

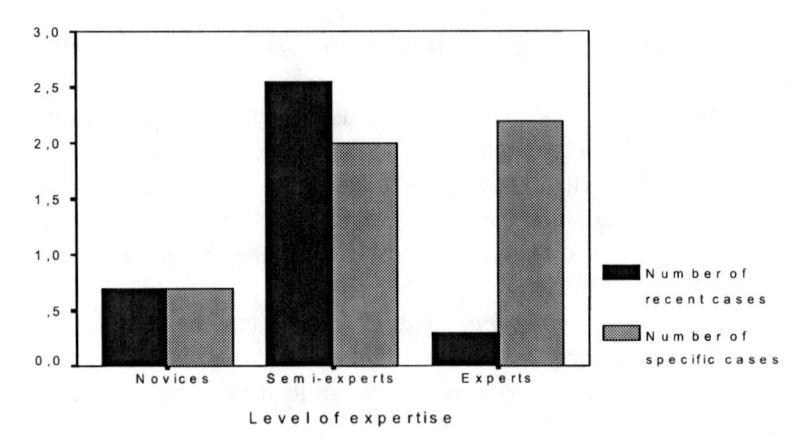

Figure 1. Number of recent cases and of specific cases within the groups

Number of experience-based connections. The largest differences between groups was observed in the connections subjects produced between the different problem categories; all groups significantly differed from each other. Experts provided the most connections, novices the least number of connections.

The results confirm the suggested development of knowledge structures and highlight the progressive narrative enrichment of counsellors' professional knowledge. The proportion of statements in the subjects' verbal protocols differ in the amount of contextual and experiential information depending on the actual experience with real-life cases (Strasser & Gruber, 2003). Thus, the individuals' professional knowledge seems to be highly influenced by "case-based learning". The importance of dealing with a variety of different cases (varying in seriousness, complexity and difficulty) for evolving coherent and applicable knowledge structures, is indicated by the performance of counsellors at intermediate levels of professional experience. Referring to personally meaningful episodes helps them to integrate or re-integrate their declarative knowledge. It still remains to be explained, why semi-experts and experts do not differ more distinctly in the duration of sessions. According to the illness script model, semi-experts are expected to need more time and to produce the largest number of statements, as their knowledge base is not yet coherently structured and they shift between fundamental and experiential knowledge. Clearly, experts produced not only fundamental and case-related statements. Assumptions about the nature of this additional information can be drawn from significant differences in experience-based connections: Increasing experience helps to recognise cross-connections and inter-relations between the different problem categories. The effect of experience on expert counsellors' knowledge thus can be seen in the increasing over-lapping of concepts. This development is probably due to an increase in reflection about one's experiences. The integrated knowledge base allows experienced counsellors to form a meta-perspective view and to reflect extensively upon their work and the different conditions for the respective outcomes.

The results may promote the discussion on the nature and function of counselling experience as they also imply consequences for designing training programs that take into account the need to deal with a variety of real life cases and the importance of narrative reflection.

4. PRACTICAL IMPLICATIONS

When integrating the results of the study and the theoretical analyses, a number of practical implications for the instructional design of counsellor training programs seem plausible. The first two implications can be derived directly from the results of the study. These results underscore the importance of dealing with complex cases during instruction. Consequently, a number of further implications can be drawn.

The necessity of working with complex cases. Subjective relevant experiences with real life cases are usually the starting point for the development of applicable professional knowledge. To close the gap between theoretical and experiential knowledge, trainee counsellors ought to gather practical experience early on in instruction. They should be given opportunities to take responsibility for a wide variety of clients.

The educational importance of difficult cases. The results indicate that expert counsellors' episodic knowledge mainly refers to specific, difficult and severe cases. Such cases stimulate reflective processes. Novices therefore should gradually learn to deal with difficult cases, after having acquired routines for dealing with everyday cases.

The importance of supervision. Ongoing support and supervision by experienced counsellors helps to avoid overstraining counselling novices (Zorga, 2002). Different degrees of supervision can be distinguished: experts serving as model (novices observe experts), experts serving as internal supporters (experts observe novices' counselling activities), and experts serving as external supporters and regular advisors. The experts task can be described as (1) providing informative feedback and (2) story-telling.

(1) Informative feedback. Deliberate practice requires ongoing feedback. In their daily work, counsellors do not automatically receive feedback, but

rather irregular and highly selective feedback. For the development of powerful routines and knowledge structures regular informative feedback has to be provided. A part of counsellors' competence is to be able to decide whether feedback is accurate or biased (Garb, 1989).

(2) Story-telling. Professional counselling does not only rely on available routines and knowledge – motivational and emotional issues are also at stake. In order to take advantage of the subjective experience of older counsellors when coping with "exhausting" counselling processes, informal ways of knowledge sharing, such as story-telling, are important. The study provided some suggestions concerning narrative enrichment of counsellors' knowledge structures. Narrative methods may be a fruitful tool to reflect one's own experiences as well as those of others (colleagues, supervisors etc.) during professional development (Fairbairn, 2002).

The importance of teaching declarative knowledge. Although reflective experience is important during instruction, the acquisition of basic declarative knowledge is central for a number of reasons. A rich conceptual knowledge base is a necessary starting point for the development of routines and also helps to reflect one's own practice. It can therefore be used when dealing with unexpected events and new situations. Declarative knowledge that helps novice counsellors to deal with new counselling situations has to be identified and integrated in training programs.

The importance of teaching problem-solving procedures. Applying declarative knowledge in complex situations requires the availability of highly automatised procedural knowledge and of routines. Routines for diagnosing and interacting with clients have to be systematically integrated in counselling training programs (O'Byrne, Clark, & Malakuti, 1997). Working on real life cases helps to embed routines in a context and prepares counselling novices for deliberate learning from experience.

Learning from experience as explicit learning strategy. Learning from experience does not happen spontaneously. Neither experts nor students spontaneously reflect on their experience in order to enhance their expertise. Wagenaar, Scherpbier, Boshuizen, and Van der Vleuten (in press) investigated health care students' opinions on learning: They reported that during clerkship they mainly learned by doing, but only little through reflection. Authors like Kolb (1984) and Schön (1987) propose an action-reflection-action cycle in order to foster learning from experience. Such systematic ways of reflection, however, need instruction. Learning from experience is only considered worthwhile when it is seen as a learning strategy that must be acquired like other strategies (Boshuizen, 2003).

Training in an adequate context. Expertise develops in social contexts (Billett, 2001; Eteläpelto & Collin, this volume). Thus, varying counselling contexts have to be taken into account in training programs. During training, counsellor novices have to become familiar with relevant contextual factors systematically, with a wide scope of contexts, and with increasing complexity and ambiguity of contexts.

In the present chapter, both theoretical analyses and empirical evidence have contributed to a new perspective on the development of counsellors' expertise. The implementation of practical implications derived from this perspective into training programs looks promising. Pathways have been delineated that foster the elaborate use of one's own experience in counsellors' professional development.

NOTE

The authors gratefully acknowledge the Deutsche Forschungsgemeinschaft (DFG) for a supporting grant.

REFERENCES

Alberts, G. M., & Edelstein, B. A. (1990). Therapist training: A critical review of skill training studies. *Clinical Psychology Review, 10*, 497-511.

Auerbach, A. H., & Johnson, M. (1977). Research on the therapist's level of experience. In A. S. Gurman & A. M. Razin (Eds.), *Effective psychotherapy. A handbook of research* (pp. 84-102). Oxford: Pergamon.

Beutler, L. E., Machado, P. P. P., & Neufeld, S. A. (1994). Therapist variables. In A. E. Bergin & S. L. Garfield (Eds.), *Handbook of psychotherapy and behavior change* (4th ed., pp. 229-269). New York: Wiley.

Billett, S. (2001). Knowing in practice: Re-conceptualising vocational expertise. *Learning and Instruction, 11*, 431-452.

Boshuizen, H. P. A. (2003). Expertise development: How to bridge the gap between school and work. In H. P. A. Boshuizen (Ed.), *Expertise development: The transition between school and work* (pp. 7-38). Heerlen: Open Universiteit Nederland.

Boshuizen, H. P. A., & Schmidt, H. G. (1992). On the role of biomedical knowledge in clinical reasoning by experts, intermediates and novices. *Cognitive Science, 16*, 153-184.

Breuer, F. (1991). *Analyse beraterisch-therapeutischer Tätigkeit. Methoden zur Untersuchung individueller Handlungssysteme klinisch-psychologischer Praktiker.* [Analysis of counselling activity. Investigation of individual action systems of clinical psychologists] Münster: Aschendorff.

Caspar, F. (1995). Information processing in psychotherapy intake interviews. In B. Boothe, R. Hirsig, A. Helminger, B. Meier, & R. Volkart (Eds.), *Perzeption – Evaluation – Interpretation* (pp. 3-10). Bern: Huber.

Dawes, R. R. (1994). *House of cards: Psychology and psychotherapy built on myth.* New York: Free Press.

Durlak, J. A. (1979). Comparative effectiveness of paraprofessionals and professional helpers. *Psychological Bulletin, 86*, 80-92.

Eraut, M. (1994). *Developing professional knowledge and competence.* Washington: Falmer.

Ericsson, K. A., Krampe, R. T., & Tesch-Römer, C. (1993). The role of deliberate practice in the acquisition of expert performance. *Psychological Review, 100*, 363-406.

Ericsson, K. A., & Lehmann, A. C. (1996). Expert and exceptional performance: Evidence of maximal adaptation to task constraints. *Annual Review of Psychology, 47*, 273-305.

Fairbairn, G. J. (2002). Ethics, empathy and storytelling in professional development. *Learning in Health and Social Care, 1*, 22-32.

Fong, M. L., Borders, L. D., Ethington, C. A., & Pitts, J. H. (1997). Becoming a counsellor: A longitudinal study of student cognitive development. *Counsellor Education and Supervision, 37*, 100-114.

Garb, H. N. (1989). Clinical judgement, clinical training and professional experience. *Psychological Bulletin, 105*, 387-396.

Gruber, H. (1999). *Erfahrung als Grundlage kompetenten Handelns.* [Experience as basis for professional competence] Bern: Huber.

Gruber, H. (2003, August). *Changes of expert knowledge during professional learning: Do and should we care about differences within domains or differences between domains?* Paper presented at the expert panel "Professional learning in school and beyond: An expert view on emerging themes", 10th European Conference for Research on Learning and Instruction (EARLI), Padova, Italy.

Gunzelmann, T., Schiepek, G., & Reinecker, H. (1987). Laienhelfer in der psychosozialen Versorgung: Meta-Analysen zur differentiellen Effektivität von Laien und professionellen Helfern. [Lay helpers in mental health care. Meta-analysis on the differential effectiveness of laypersons and professional helpers] *Gruppendynamik, 18*, 361-384.

Kolb, D. A. (1984). *Experiential learning. Experience as the source of learning and development.* Englewood Cliffs: Prentice-Hall.

Kolodner, J. L. (1983). Towards an understanding of the role of experience in the evolution from novice to expert. *International Journal of Man-Machine Studies, 19*, 497-518.

Ladany, N., Marotta, S., & Muse-Burke, J. L. (2001). Counselor experience related to complexity of case conceptualization and supervision preference. *Counselor Education and Supervision, 40*, 203-219.

Lichtenberg, J. W. (1997). Expertise in counselling psychology: A concept in search of support. *Educational Psychology Review, 9*, 221-238.

Locke, T. F., & Covell, A. J. (1997). Characterizing expert psychologist behavior: Implications from selected expertise literature. *Educational Psychology Review, 9*, 239-249.

Monchner, F. J., & Prinz, P. J. (1991). Treatment fidelity in outcome studies. *Clinical Psychology Review, 11*, 247-266.

O'Byrne, K., Clark, R. E., & Malakuti, R. (1997). Expert and novice performance: Implications for clinical training. *Educational Psychology Review, 9*, 321-332.

Schön, D. A. (1987). *Educating the reflective practitioner.* San Francisco: Jossey-Bass.

Skovholt, T. M., Ronnestad, M. H., & Jennings, L. (1997). Searching for expertise in counselling, psychotherapy, and professional psychology. *Educational Psychology Review, 9*, 361-369.

Stein, D. M., & Lambert, M. J. (1984). On the relationship between therapist experience and psychotherapy outcome. *Clinical Psychology Review, 4*, 1-16.

Strasser, J., & Gruber, H. (2003, April). *Counsellors' experience and the development of their professional knowledge.* Paper presented at the 84th Annual Meeting of the American Educational Research Association (AERA), Chicago, USA.

Voss, J. F., Greene, T. R., Post, T. A., & Penner, B. C. (1983). Problem solving skill in the social sciences. In G. H. Bower (Ed.), *The psychology of learning and motivation: Advances in research and theory* (Vol. 17, pp. 165-213). New York: Academic Press.

Wagenaar, A., Scherpbier, A. J. J. A., Boshuizen, H. P. A., & Van der Vleuten, C. P. M. (in press). The importance of active involvement in learning: A qualitative study on learning results and learning processes in different traineeships. *Advances in Health Sciences Education*.

Wierzbicki, M. (1993). *Issues in clinical psychology: Subjective versus objective approaches*. Boston: Allyn & Bacon.

Zorga, S. (2002). Professional supervision as a mean of learning and development of counselors. *International Journal for the Advancement of Counselling, 24*, 261-274.

Chapter 3

THE CASE OF PLANT IDENTIFICATION IN BIOLOGY: WHEN IS A ROSE A ROSE?
Development of expertise as acquisition and use of robust and flexible knowledge

Rainer Bromme, Elmar Stahl, Tobias Bartholomé and Stephanie Pieschl
Psychologisches Institut III, Westfälische Wilhelms-Universität, Münster, Germany

1. THE DEVELOPMENT OF EXPERTISE IN PLANT IDENTIFICATION

Constructivist approaches provide a promising basis for promoting the development of expertise. If such approaches are used as heuristics in planning teaching methods, it should be possible to foster the understanding of relevant concepts within a domain, as well as the application of knowledge to the demands of different contextual cases. Consequently, an acquisition of robust and flexible knowledge, a necessary component of experts' knowledge, can be achieved. On the other hand there are curricular restrictions - like the limited time scheduled for teaching a topic - that often inhibit the integration of constructivist approaches into real curricula. A discrepancy of this kind, between methods that are appropriate to support the development of expertise and, what can actually be offered on university courses, can be found in many disciplines.

In this chapter we present an example of this discrepancy taken from the sub-domain of plant identification in biology. One of the classical tasks of biology is the description and classification of plants within taxonomies of families, genera, species and subspecies. Accordingly, identifying plants constitutes an essential competence of biologists that has been taught at German universities since 1852. Today, knowledge about plant identification is required by a wide range of occupational groups, e.g. biologists, landscape ecologists, geographers, pharmacists, etc. At the same time, there has been a substantial decline of expertise in this domain over the last decades. Most students nowadays develop only rudimentary knowledge about plant identification, and are far from developing an appropriate degree of expertise. Furthermore, the number of professional experts in this domain is already small and decreasing. This paradox between the importance of the knowledge on the one hand and the decrease of expertise on the other hand can be explained by the complexity of the necessary knowledge and increasing limitations of time in the curricula.

As a result botanists are interested in finding new didactic ways to support the development of expertise within this domain. An interactive learning environment on the basis of heuristics derived from constructivist approaches has been developed and integrated into existing courses. The learning environment can be used to support learning within the university courses as well as independent case-based learning beyond the courses. We present this example from the domain of biology to show how a constructivist interactive learning environment can be designed for university courses to combat existing problems and support the development of expertise. One of the most important prerequisites for developing this system was the analysis of botanists' cognitive processes involved in plant identification. We therefore present our approaches for examining these cognitive processes in more detail.

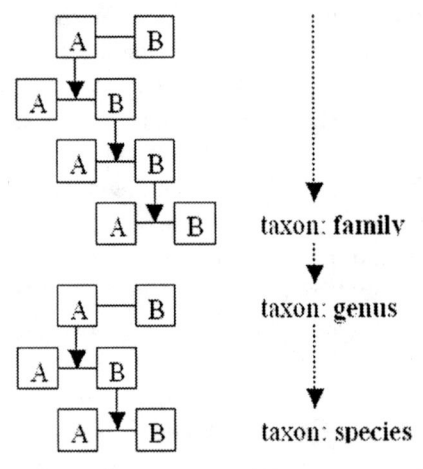

Figure 1. Decision tree with taxa, every A-B combination denotes a decision step

1.1 Learning to identify plants

We begin with a short introduction to the process of plant identification and the necessary knowledge that has to be acquired. This is necessary for an understanding of contemporary problems in teaching botany.

The development of expertise in plant identification is difficult for several reasons. The main problem is the enormous diversity of plants that biologists have to deal with: it is assumed that there are about 500.000 species worldwide (Sitte, Ziegler, Ehrendorfer, & Bresinsky, 1998). In the German flora biologists have to deal with circa 1400 different species. To describe and identify this small range of species they already need 10.000 different features. Additionally to this biodiversity there is broad intra-species variance: depending on their environment the plants within a subspecies can vary significantly in their appearance.

From a psychological perspective it is necessary to acquire dual-coded mental representations concerning these diagnostic plant features. It is not enough to acquire propositional representations of the concepts. To be able to identify these features on a living plant it is necessary to have a mental representation of them. Because of the variability within a species the same features can look very different between subspecies. Therefore botanists not only have to acquire a prototypical mental image of significant features but also a set of mental images including all variations.

Because of this biodiversity and intra-species variability, learning by rote is almost impossible. So-called keys or florae were developed to guide botanists through a systematised process which enables them to identify most species of a country. Common European and American keys include the German Schmeil-Fitschen flora (Senghas & Seybold, 1996) or the flora of North America (Flora of North America Association, 2000). The usage of keys has a long tradition. Schmeil-Fitschen for example was published for the first time in 1903 and is still in use in the 93rd edition.

The main principle of these keys is that they guide biologists through the botanical taxonomy by structured decision trees (Figure 1). Frequently, the process of plant identification comprises at least 20 decision steps and guides the learner through different taxonomical stages. Advanced learners may start at lower taxa if they recognise for example the family or the genus of the plant under consideration.

A fr. egg-conesh., grad. intergradient into an even-dentate beak (1175), mature pointing aslant perpendicular; st. sharp-edged, 3angular, rough at the top; lv. 4-7 mm brd., sharp keeled, rough; 2-3 female spikelets, 2-4 cm lg.; plant 30-80 cm tall, grass-green; perennial; V-VI ditches, watersides, wet meadows, peatbogs, great sedge populations (up to 2000 m); common
 narrow-petalled vesica sedge, C. vesicaria L.
B fr. almost spheroidal, apr. narrowing to lg. beak, teeth straddling (1176), mature stck. o. almost horizontally, female spikelets, 4-7 cm long 78

The basic element of a decision tree is a contrastive description of two sets of plant features,

Figure 2. Example of a decision step (Schmeil-Fitschen, 2000); to point out the alternatives, „A" and „B" have been added. Translation into English

which will be referred to as decision steps (Figure 2). The botanist has to decide whether one or the other set of features applies to the plant in question. To handle the broad variety of plants, each decision step offers a complex description of different features. If a botanist cannot find a specific feature she can search for other listed features. Having made a selection she is guided to the next decision step. This process continues directing the botanist through a sequence of decision steps until she arrives at the final taxon, which in most cases is the species of the plant at hand. Often the key contains a description of the species on the basis of which the learner has to decide whether his/her identification was correct.

Therefore, plant identification with keys can be conceptualised as a process of sequential decision-making. For novices these complex decisions can be interpreted as a problem solving process. At least some decision steps constitute ill-structured problems (because of incomprehensible abbreviations, inconsistent synonyms, undefined quantifiers, overlap of alternatives etc.) in terms of cognition psychology (Knoblich, 2002; Simon, 1999).

It can be concluded that the development of expertise encompasses the acquisition of the declarative and procedural knowledge needed to identify a broad range of plants, the development of skills for handling the botanical keys, as well as skills in the preparation of plants with tweezers and needles to reveal important features of the species. As can be seen in the following paragraphs, some constructivist approaches can be applied to facilitate this development of expertise.

1.2 Development of expertise and situational cognition

For novices it is nearly impossible to learn plant identification without a supervisor, because of the necessity of case-based learning and the required feedback. It can be taken for granted that a professor at the beginning of the 19th century could spend more time with a small number of students, giving customised guidance. He had more time for the whole course and the individual student, and was able to include frequent field trips which were interwoven with short ad hoc theoretical lectures when required. Theoretical principles were directly linked to actual examples. Furthermore, his students had a chance to learn a lot about biodiversity, and the complexity of their country's flora, as well as to gain experience with a broad variety of examples. Therefore these teaching methods were appropriate for fostering the development of expertise.

Although courses in plant identification are still obligatory for students of the relevant subjects, the schedule that is used to teach this knowledge is reduced to a few hours in the whole course of study. Students only have one course in which they practice the professional skill of plant identification with freshly-harvested plant material. About 100 students often attend this course, which makes it hard for the lecturer to cater for the individual student. The theoretical background knowledge is to a large degree separated from the practical work: before such courses start students are asked to learn 50 pages of definitions concerning the different features of the plants. This often results in inert knowledge, i.e. the students are unable to apply their theoretical knowledge to real plants. Therefore the present curricular situation is inappropriate for supporting the development of expertise.

Because of the demands described in the previous section, constructivist approaches based on situational cognition would be a promising way to support the development of expertise in the domain of plant identification. Acquiring robust knowledge about abstract concepts as well as flexible knowledge about specific cases are both essential elements of expertise development in plant classification. Combining abstract and case based knowledge for the sake of flexibility of knowledge us is an important issue within the so called Cognitive Flexibility Theory (Jacobson & Spiro, 1995; Spiro, Feltovich, Jacobson, & Coulson, 1991). The demands placed on students learning plant identification are similar to the demands involved in the development of transfer knowledge that are described within the Cognitive Flexibility Theory (CFT). CFT deals with how knowledge about a complex ("ill-structured") content domain can be acquired in a way that ensures its flexible use. The goal is to stimulate learning transfer and to avoid "inert knowledge", that is, knowledge a learner can reproduce, but fails to apply in new situations (Bereiter & Scardamalia, 1987). According to Jacobson and Spiro (1995) improved learning and transfer of complex knowledge can be fostered by five principles,

1. use of multiple conceptual representations of knowledge;
2. links between abstract concepts and real life examples;
3. early introduction of the domain complexity;
4. accentuation of the interrelated nature of knowledge; and
5. encouragement of knowledge assemblies (this means that the learner should be confronted with learning situations that require him to assemble relevant abstract concepts and case-specific knowledge components to solve the new tasks).

From these principles – used as heuristics for the design of knowledge acquisition in plant identification – it follows that it is necessary to train the identification process with a broad variety of cases so that the learner understands the variability and flexibility of concepts in relation to each other and in differing contexts.

In such a learning scenario the role of the university teachers is similar to the role that an expert should take according to the Cognitive Apprenticeship Approach (Collins, Brown, & Newman, 1989; Seel, Al-Diban, Held, & Hess, 1998). In this approach the expert uses methods such as modelling (students watch the expert to see how he solves the problems), coaching (the expert gives hints and help while they are working on the problems) and scaffolding (the expert helps the students to develop a framework for dealing with problems). On the other hand students are encouraged to learn in co-operation with each other, to discuss and reflect on the topic.

It can be concluded that constructivist approaches would be suited to the demands of knowledge acquisition in the domain of plant identification. To integrate them into existing curricula, appropriate teaching methods have to be considered.

One possibility is to support the learning processes with interactive learning environments that would encourage the students to learn plant identification on their own. Such a learning environment must be able to provide some of the support that is usually given by the university teacher, while also allowing case-based learning. This means that the learning environment should support the learning process in a constructivist sense via extensive help functions, feedback and error analyses.

In a project that was funded by the German Government (BMBF) as part of a program on New Media in Education at University Level the learning environment "Bestimmen-Online" was developed (http://bestimmen-online.uni-muenster.de). The co-operative project involved botanists from five German universities, designers, and computer scientists. (principal investigator for the software development project were M. Hesse and S. Hölzenbein, Biology Department, Münster University). Our research group was in charge of a formative and summative evaluation (Stahl & Bromme, 2002; Stahl, Bromme, Pieschl, Hölzenbein, & Kiffe, in press).

For the development of the learning environment it was essential to identify the cognitive processes of advanced as well as of novice botanists during plant identification. We conducted empirical studies to help us understand how advanced botanists classify plants and which kinds of knowledge and skills are involved. We used the analyses to develop a comprehensive process model of plant identification. The model provided the foundation for planning and designing the help systems and feedback functions that are necessary to support independent, case-based learning processes. Some results of this analysis will be reported in the following section.

2. COGNITIVE PROCESSES IN PLANT IDENTIFICATION

A combination of different methods was used to get an idea of the relevant cognitive processes involved in plant identification. Our preliminary approach was the exploratory observation of university courses. This gave first insights into the different activities involved in identifying plants as well as common problems of novice identifiers.

Additionally, a task analysis was performed. Three psychologists in our team who were laypersons in the domain of botany identified a plant under the supervision of a botanical expert. They verbalised their cognitive processes as well as the demands of the identification process. The statements were put down and transcribed. Whenever the psychologists lacked knowledge or skills necessary to proceed, the expert told them where they could find the information needed or which botanical operation had to be carried out.

To analyse the expert perspective on plant identification in detail, interviews were conducted. Four experienced botanists who lecture about plant identification at German universities, and have also applied their specialised knowledge as authors of botanical keys, were recruited. They were interviewed about cognitive processes and competencies involved in plant identification. Participants at first specified the processes and competencies that they believed to be relevant for plant identification. The contributions were recorded on cards. In a second step, participants clustered and ordered the processes and competencies they had mentioned, employing a mapping technique.

We then examined ten students with an intermediate level of expertise in plant identification to gain more insight into actual cognitive processes during plant identification. They were asked to identify two species with a book key while thinking aloud. We decided to choose skilled students (so called semi-experts) as participants. As we aimed at a model of regular processes in plant identification with a key, it was essential to have participants who already had the ability to demonstrate high performance in plant identification but did not have the high level of automatisation possessed by experts. Experts in botany do not work with keys as a rule because their extended knowledge base allows them to identify the most common plant species in the home flora. Moreover, if they use keys their performance is so accomplished that their identification processes are highly automated. Therefore eliciting these expert processes by means of think aloud techniques would be quite difficult (Ericsson & Simon, 1980; Hinds, Patterson, & Pfeffer, 2001). Thus, semi-experts who still depend on keys and do not display high automatisation in their processes were most appropriate for studying competent plant identification with a key. As an example of our approach we will use the remainder of this section to report on the method and main results of the study.

2.1 Method

Participants. Ten semi-experts (three females, seven males) with an average age of $M = 26.4$ years ($SD = 2.8$) took part. They were advanced students of biology ($n = 4$) or landscape ecology ($n = 6$) with an average of $M = 11.1$ ($SD = 2.3$) semesters. All of them had gathered extended experience in the domain of plant identification. All semi-experts were paid an expense allowance of 10 €.

Plant material. Two living plants differing in their difficulty of identification were selected by an expert botanist. The "easier" species was *Prunella vulgaris* from the family of *Lamiaceae*, the "more difficult" plant belonged to the species *Carex rostrata* from the family of *Cyperaceae*. The difficulty of the plant material was varied in order to study the full range of cognitive and operational processes in semi-experts.

Procedure. Each identification session was carried out individually. The cognitive processes and operations involved in plant identification with a key were elicited by means of the think aloud technique (Alberdi, Sleeman, & Korpi, 2000; Ericsson & Simon, 1980; Eveland & Dunwoody, 2000). At the beginning of a session, semi-experts completed some introductory problem solving tasks to make them familiar with thinking aloud, thus automatising it. Even though there are some hints in the literature that the ability to think aloud may be influenced by verbal fluency (Veenman, Elshout, & Groen, 1993), all of our semi-experts succeeded in thinking aloud fluently. Only one of them sometimes forgot to verbalise but continued when reminded. They were then asked to identify both plants while thinking aloud. The identification trials were recorded on video.

Because semi-experts already have individualised identification strategies that go beyond working with a dichotomous key, the procedure for each plant was divided into two phases. At first, there was a *free identification trial*, where semi-experts were asked to identify a plant in the way they were used to. They were allowed to use any aids available to them, which included different keys and illustrated books. This was to assess the characteristic processes in semi-experts' plant identification. In the following *standardized identification trial*, they had to identify the same plant again, this time using the Schmeil-Fitschen key (Senghas & Seybold, 1996). The semi-experts were instructed to start their standardised identification at the highest taxonomic level. If the combination of the free and the standardised identification exceeded a time limit of 30 min, the trial was interrupted. Therefore, not all semi-experts completed both trials. Each session ended with the completion of a questionnaire assessing demographic variables as well as experience in identifying plants. The reported results are based on the *standardised identification* data and on those parts of the *free identification trials* where semi-experts used the Schmeil-Fitschen flora.

Coding the protocol data. The verbal reports as well as the semi-experts' actions in the process of identification were transcribed from the video recordings, split into units, and categorised using a coding system based on our preliminary work. Each new statement or activity was treated as a new unit. For each unit the cognitive process involved, observable operations (like using magnifying glasses), and perceptual modalities (visual, tactile, olfactory, gustatory) were classified.

Furthermore we assumed that each decision step involves three groups of processes. Biologists have to interact with the key (e.g. reading the decision step), interact with the plant (e.g. searching for the features), and integrate the information into a decision. Therefore each unit was also assigned to one of these three process groups.

In order to assess the reliability of the coding scheme the concordance between two independent raters was determined. A time sample covering 10 % of the time semi-experts spent with the key was taken from the video recordings. Two raters who had been trained with the coding scheme independently categorised semi-experts' statements and operations within the four above-mentioned variables. Concordance for the more content-specific variables (cognitive processes, operations, perceptual modality) was 84 %. For the three groups of processes of plant identification inter-rater reliability was 93 %.

2.2 Results

In this section a model of the cognitive processes involved in plant identification with a dichotomous key is described in detail. This model is based on the preliminary and think aloud analyses.

In order to perform the decision-making process of plant identification successfully, three different groups of processes are required,
1. interacting with the key (key processes),
2. interacting with the plant (plant processes), and
3. integration of information into a decision (integration processes).

The groups of processes for plant identification can appear in flexible order at each decision step. Also smooth transitions between the different process groups were found. Nonetheless, some sequences of process groups were more frequent than others.

The most prevalent succession was the linear one (Table 1): interaction with the key was followed by interaction with the plant, leading to a final decision (integration process).

Table 1. Example of cognitive processes at one decision step; linear succession of process groups

transcript of statements	process group	cognitive process
"They want a herb,	key	reading
or perennial herbs,	key	reading
or plant with woody stem.	key	reading
And this is a herb (takes a close look).	Plant	feature value determined
Then we go to 2."	Integration	decision

Another common strategy was to process the information at one decision step feature by feature. After one feature was decoded from the key, semi-experts tried to identify the feature attributes on the plant.

Table 2. Example of cognitive processes at one decision step; switching between key and plant processes for almost every single feature

transcript of statements	process group	cognitive process
„Even stem	Key	reading
or edgeless and tri-angular?	Key	reading
(tactile sensing)	Plant	inspecting features
Edgeless and tri-angular fits better (tactile sensing).	Plant	feature value determined
2-3 male spicules,	Key	reading
2-5 females,	Key	reading
latter 6-10 mm broad.	Key	reading
Spicule 6-10 mm broad (measuring).	Plant	inspecting feature
Yes, fits too!	Plant	feature value determined
Where was I? 6-10 mm broad, leaves 3-5 mm broad.	Key	reading
That matches, I just measured it, 3 mm really matches better.	Plant	feature value determined
Often rolled.	Key	reading
(takes a close look)	Plant	inspecting features
It's impossible to say that definitely now. It' too dried up (taking a close look).	Plant	knowledge about the stadium of the plant
But often that doesn't play a prominent role.	Plant	knowledge about the usefulness of features
Plant height 30-80 cm,	Key	reading
Grey-green.	Key	reading
(takes a close look)	Plant	inspecting features
Or stem rough at the top.	Key	reading
It's not!	plant	feature value rejected
Yes, then it's Carex rostrata."	integration	decision

Having finished the identification of the first feature they started processing the next feature from the key. Thus, they continually switched between key and plant processes until they had gathered sufficient information. Finally, the different pieces of feature information were integrated into a choice (Table 2, process group column).

Other sequences are conceivable. Often, one of the three process groups is not mentioned throughout a decision step. For example, some attributes from the key are processed and directly afterwards a decision is reached. In this case the plant inspection is not verbalised.

In the subsequent sections, the three process groups are presented in the typical linear sequence of plant identification (Table 1).

Interaction with the key. At each step two options (the alternative feature sets in the key; e. g. option "A" and option "B") are available, each characterised by multiple features (Figure 2). Therefore, the interaction with the key involves comprehension of the decision step. The processes of this group that were relevant for our study are illustrated in Figure 3.

After reading the decision step the information had to be integrated with relevant domain knowledge in order to generate a comprehensive mental model of the decision problem. If the necessary domain knowledge was available it was activated and integrated with the text information. The most relevant knowledge components in the interaction with the key were *representation of technical terms*, *knowledge about abbreviations*, and *taxonomical knowledge*. If semi-experts considered their domain knowledge as insufficient for an adequate representation of the decision step they started to search for information in the key (e.g. *looking up illustrations*, *looking up abbreviations*, *looking up theoretical information*). Having completed their information search they had achieved full comprehension of the decision step.

Interaction with the plant. The main purpose of interaction with the plant is to determine the feature attributes. Starting with a pair of alternative feature attributes from the key, semi-experts interact with the plant in order to select one of the attributes. The processes involved in the interaction with the plant are presented in Figure 4.

The inspection of features of the plant was performed employing several perceptual modalities as well as specific botanical operations and involved all cognitive processes to a considerable degree. Interaction with the plant depended on *visual* perception in the vast majority of cases. In some cases, the *tactile* modality was involved, e.g. when semi-experts felt for the shape of the stem. The *olfactory* and *gustatory* senses were of minor importance in our study due to the plant material. It should be noted that the frequencies of the different modalities of perception found in the study perfectly matched the ranking of importance given in the preliminary expert interviews.

```
                    perception
                         │
                         │      ┌─────────────────┐
                         │      │ reading the     │
                         │      │ decision step   │
                         ▼      │ interpreting text│
                                └─────────────────┘

                 sufficient domain  ◄──────────────────┐
                 knowledge available?                  │
                    ╱        ╲                         │
                   ╱          ╲                        │
                  ▼            ▼                       │
                 yes          no => search for information
         ┌──────────────────┐   ┌──────────────────────┐
         │ representation of │   │ looking up illustrations│
         │ technical terms   │   │ looking up abbreviations│
         │ knowledge about   │   │ looking up theoretical  │
         │ abbreviations     │   │ information             │
         │ taxonomical       │   └──────────────────────┘
         │ knowledge         │              │
         └──────────────────┘               │
                  │        integration of text
                  │        information and
                  │        domain knowledge
                  ▼
         comprehension of the attribute/
         decision step
```

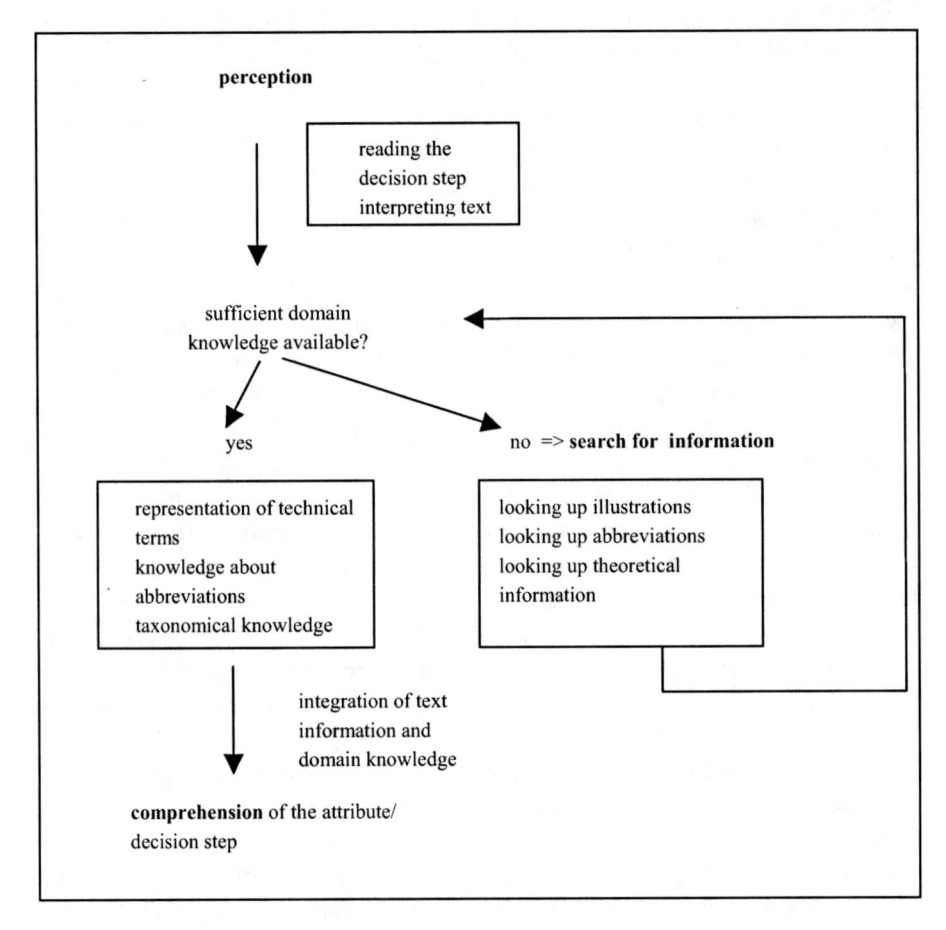

Figure 3. Interaction with the key

The most common botanical operations that were applied in our study to make plant attributes accessible covered *taking a close look*, the use of *magnifying glasses, bending the plant manually, plant dissection with tweezers*, and *manual plant dissection*. The remaining operations listed in Figure 4 were of minor frequency in the study.

The inspection of features necessitated the activation of a large number of knowledge structures. Most often, *anatomical knowledge* was elicited by the think aloud technique. *Representation of technical terms, knowledge about the stage of development of a plant* and *taxonomical knowledge* were quite prevalent during plant inspection, too. Some components of domain knowledge seem to be relevant only during plant inspection (e.g. *knowledge about biological variability; knowledge about the stage of development of the plant; knowledge about the significance of features*), whereas others are

The Case of Plant Identification in Biology 41

relevant in more then one process group. The components of knowledge referred to above apparently guide the process of plant inspection.

inspecting features on the plant

perceptual modalities:
visual
tactile
olfactory
gustatory

domain knowledge:
representation of technical terms
anatomical knowledge
taxonomical knowledge
knowledge about the stage of development of the plant
knowledge about biological variability
knowledge about the significance of attributes
knowledge about the operations

operations:
taking a close look
magnifying glass
ruler/ measuring
manually dissecting the plant
dissecting the plant with tweezers
dissecting the plant with a needle
manually bending the plant
bending the plant with tweezers

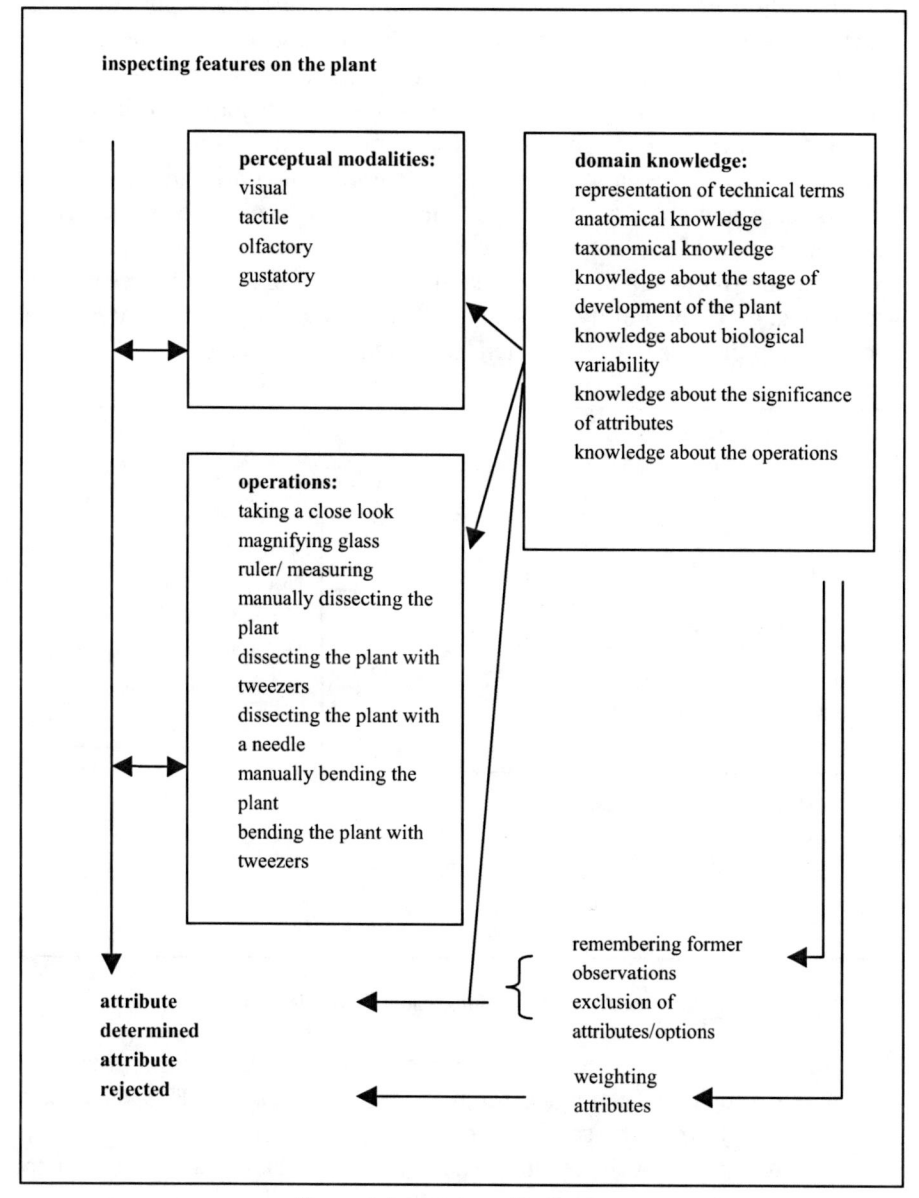

attribute determined
attribute rejected

remembering former observations
exclusion of attributes/options
weighting attributes

Figure 4. Interaction with the plant

After one feature attribute had been provisionally identified on the plant, it was compared with the two alternative feature attributes from the key. If the degree of matching with one of the feature attributes from the key was sufficient, the *feature attribute was confirmed*. If the matching was insufficient the respective *feature attribute was rejected*.

Integration of information into a decision. During these processes the identified feature attributes (see interacting with plant) are integrated into a decision (Figure 5). In the case of a non-weighted integration of features, semi-experts chose the option that possesses the majority of identified feature attributes. The weighting of the different plant features according to importance is a process allowing for the integration of conflicting features as well as for a non-exhaustive analysis limited to the most relevant features. The importance of a plant feature can refer to its discriminative power as well as to the frequency of occurrence of this feature in a specific taxonomic group (e.g. a plant family or genus). Weighting of plant features is a sophisticated process requiring extended botanical knowledge.

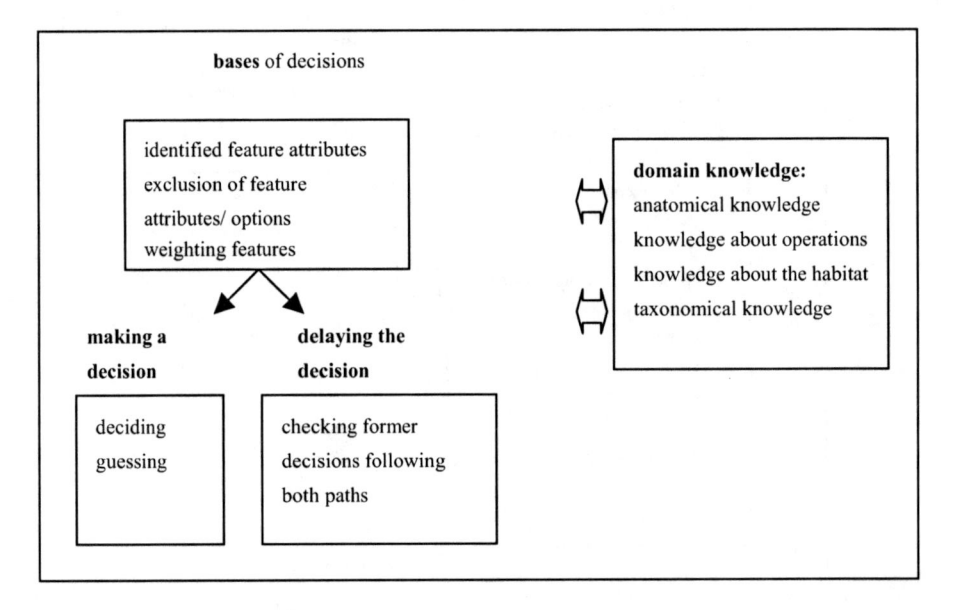

Figure 5. Integrating information into a decision

After finishing the integration process, semi-experts either made a decision or employed strategies for delaying the decision. This happened most frequently when the semi-experts were very uncertain or thought they had already made a mistake. In particular, recapitulation was intended to check if one was still on the right identification track. By following both paths semi-experts broadened their information base, including the feature information required for subsequent decision steps. If both options at a subsequent step were inappropriate, this confirmed that choosing the other path at the previous step was correct.

The Case of Plant Identification in Biology 43

This model incorporates all cognitive and operative processes involved in plant identification. It was an appropriate basis for the development of a learning environment for plant identification and its different kinds of help systems and feedback functions. In the next section the learning environment "Bestimmen-Online" will be briefly illustrated.

3. AN INTERACTIVE LEARNING ENVIRONMENT FOR PLANT IDENTIFICATION

The learning environment can be used in regular courses to support the lecturer as well as foster independent learning at home. Strictly speaking, it allows students to practice the case-based learning without support by an expert, due to the guidance given by help and feedback systems.

The basis of this program is a key that guides the learner through the decision steps (Figure 6).

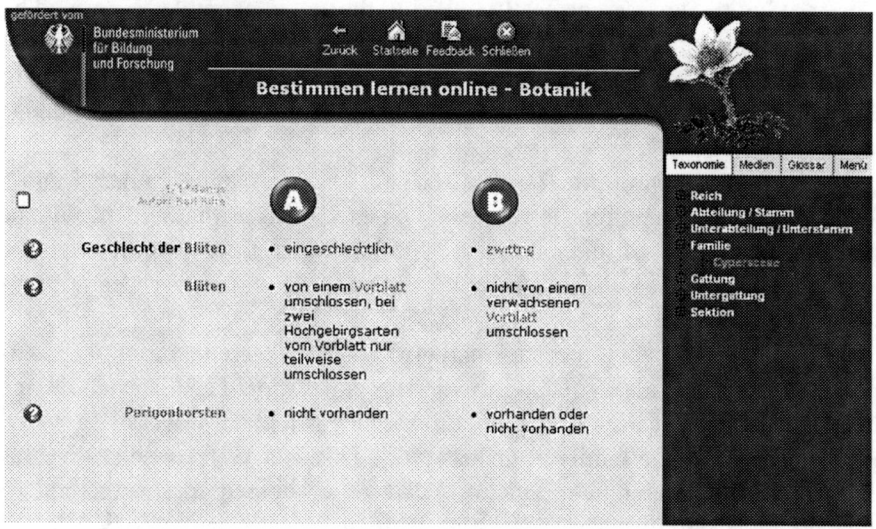

Figure 6. Screenshot of the learning environment. Students are led through a decision tree of a sequence of dichotomous decision steps. At each step they have to decide whether the plant has the features described under point A or under point B

To provide a high level of complexity even at the beginning as suggested by Cognitive Flexibility Theory (CFT), the student works with real plants selected by the teacher of the university course. This teacher has to provide every plant with a code tag (a code number which gives no hint about the plant's name). Typing the code into the computer "tells" the system the correct answer (i.e. which plant was selected) so that it can check results and support error analyses. In contrast to the keys in book-form the decision steps are presented as tables of dichotomous features that the learner has to distinguish.

Some help functions are incorporated into the learning environment that should basically foster the empirically-confirmed cognitive processes and implement some demands of CFT. To support the acquisition of knowledge about concepts a glossary of technical terms is provided. Furthermore, context-sensitive help functions can be accessed that foster dual-coded mental representations which are essential for the plant identification processes described (Figure 4). Each feature is explained via a combination of text and high-quality line drawings (Figure 7). Key concepts in the text are interactively linked to the drawings. For example, if the student points to a term in the text with the mouse, the corresponding area is marked in red in the drawing. These help functions are in line with CFT in two ways: due to the context sensitivity of the help functions, the line drawings are often congruent with the living plant at hand. Therefore, the abstract concepts described in the text can be easily linked to the actual example as claimed by CFT. Furthermore, there is often more than one prototype line drawing per help function. In combination with the help and glossary texts these drawings enable the use of multiple conceptual representations of knowledge as postulated by CFT.

To support the process of integrating all the information gathered into a decision another function is planned. For each feature the student will be able to mark one of the alternatives, allowing a final overview of the decision step as a whole and thereby enhancing the conscious weighting of features.

Additionally, special feedback and error analysis were incorporated, so as to implement the ideas of Cognitive Apprenticeship. Feedback about the results is offered at important points in the identification process (e.g. when students arrive at the family or genus level). This kind of feedback as well as the above mentioned help functions can be compared to the method of coaching in Cognitive Apprenticeship. If the identification is wrong, support is offered with explicit error analysis. These functions are a substitute for the guidance of experts and show the student how to deal with problems. In the language of Cognitive Apprenticeship this could be called scaffolding. Difficult operations, e.g. dissecting an ovary, are demonstrated by short video sequences showing experts modelling these operations.

At the end of the process detailed descriptions of the plants are presented in a combination of text, drawings and photographs, explaining the features of each plant in comparison with others.

The learning environment also includes series of photographs of about 200 different species, allowing the identification process to be trained

The Case of Plant Identification in Biology 45

without real plants. This makes it possible to practice plant identification during the whole year and not only during the limited flowering season.

By means of this range of help functions, independent learning as conceptualised from a constructivist perspective is supported. In order to develop expertise, the learning environment is a meaningful supplement to the existing curriculum.

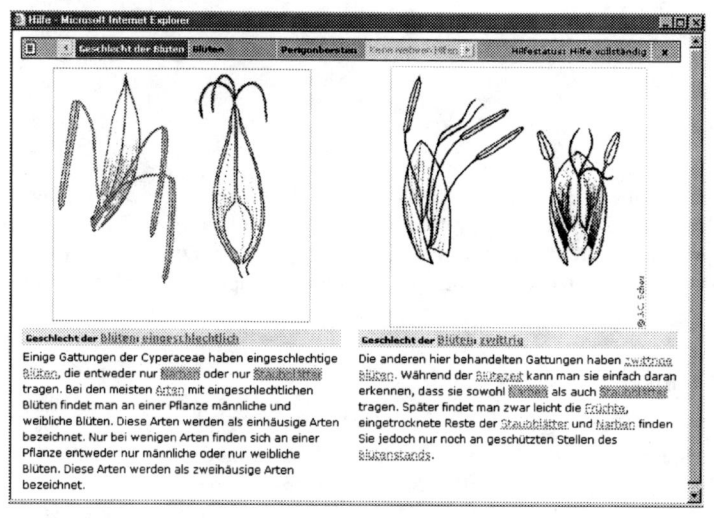

Figure 7. Example of a help window. The features are explained in a combination of text and drawing. Key concepts are interactively linked to the drawings

4. CONCLUSION

In this chapter we illustrated problems and possibilities for the development of expertise within the domain of plant identification. To identify plants novices in botany must acquire a combination of robust but also flexible knowledge from the very beginning. Therefore, constructivist principles as suggested by Cognitive Flexibility Theory and Cognitive Apprenticeship constitute important heuristics for fostering this kind of knowledge acquisition. Because the tight curriculum of university courses does not allow the application of these principles, it needs to be supplemented by new ways of learning. On the basis of an extensive problem analysis as well as a detailed analysis of cognitive and operative processes a learning environment with various help functions especially tailored to the beginners' needs was designed.

The importance of independent learning has always been emphasised in all institutions of professional learning. Nevertheless, support of novices by means of expert guidance is an essential part of the development of expertise. Due to changing demands, e.g. within the curriculum, expert assistance cannot always be guaranteed. Therefore, a need for supplementary guidance arises, e.g. in the form of interactive learning environments or knowledge management systems. This example from the domain of biology shows one possible application. It should provide encouragement for incorporating similar procedures into other domains as well.

NOTE

The research described here was supported in part by the German Ministry of Education and Research (BMBF Program on New Media in Education at University level). Thanks to Dr. S. Hölzenbein, K. Kiffe, and Prof. M. Hesse (Biology Department, University of Münster), who planned and controlled the software development in biology.

REFERENCES

Alberdi, E., Sleeman, D. H., & Korpi, M. (2000). Accommodating surprise in taxonomic tasks: The role of expertise. *Cognitive Science, 24*, 53-91.
Bereiter, C., & Scardamalia, M. (1987). *The psychology of written composition*. Hillsdale: Erlbaum.
Collins, A., Brown, J. S., & Newman, S. E. (1989). Cognitive apprenticeship: Teaching the crafts of reading, writing, and mathematics. In L. B. Resnick (Eds.), *Knowing, learning, and instruction* (pp 453-494). Hillsdale: Erlbaum.
Ericsson, K. A., & Simon, H. A. (1980). Verbal reports as data. *Psychological Review, 87*, 215-251.
Eveland, W. P., & Dunwoody, S. (2000). Examine information processing on the world wide web using think aloud protocols. *Media Psychology, 2*, 219-244.
Flora of North America Association (2000). *Flora of North America*. http://hua.huh.harvard.edu/FNA/index.html (extracted on Oct 15th, 2002).
Hinds, P. J., Patterson, M., & Pfeffer, J. (2001). Bothered by abstraction: The effect of expertise on knowledge transfer and subsequent novice performance. *Journal of Applied Psychology, 86*, 1232-1243.
Jacobson, M. J., & Spiro, R. J. (1995). Hypertext learning environments, cognitive flexibility, and the transfer of complex knowledge: An empirical investigation. *Journal of Educational Computing Research, 12*, 301-333.
Jungermann, H., Pfister, H.-R., & Fischer, K. (1998). *Die Psychologie der Entscheidung: Eine Einführung.* [Psychology of decision making. An Introduction] Heidelberg: Spektrum.
Knoblich, G. (2002). Problemlösen und logisches Schließen. [Problem solving and logical thinking] In J. Müsseler & W. Prinz (Eds.), *Allgemeine Psychologie* (pp. 644-699). Heidelberg: Spektrum.
Seel, N. M., Al-Diban, S., Held, S., & Hess, C. (1998). Didaktisches Design multimedialer Lernumgebungen. Theoretische Positionen, Gestaltungsprinzipien, empirische Befunde.

[Didactical design of multimedia learning environments. Theoretical problems, design principles, and empirical results] In G. Dörr & K. L. Jüngst (Eds.), *Lernen mit Medien. Ergebnisse und Perspektiven zu medial vermittelten Lehr- und Lernprozessen* (pp. 87-119). München: Juventa.

Senghas K., & Seybold, S. (Eds.). (1996). *Schmeil-Fitschen - Flora von Deutschland und angrenzender Länder: Ein Buch zum Bestimmen der wildwachsenden und häufig kultivierten Gefäßpflanzen.* (90th ed.). [Schmeil-Fitschen. Flora of Germany and neighbor countries. A book to identify wild and cultured plants] Wiebelsheim: Quelle und Meyer.

Simon, H. A. (1999). Problem solving. In R. A. Wilson & F. C. Keil (Eds.), *The MIT encyclopedia of the cognitive sciences* (pp. 674-676). Cambridge: MIT Press.

Sitte, P., Ziegler, H., Ehrendorfer, F., & Bresinsky, A. (1998). *Lehrbuch der Botanik für Hochschulen* (34th ed.). [Textbook botany for universities] Stuttgart: Gustav Fischer.

Spiro, R. J., Feltovich, P. J., Jacobson, M. J., & Coulson, R. L. (1991). Cognitive flexibility, constructivism and hypertext: Random access instruction for advanced knowledge acquisition in ill-structured domains. *Educational Technology, 31* (5), 24-33.

Stahl, E., & Bromme, R. (2002). Entwicklung einer Online-Lernumgebung für das Einführungspraktikum "Botanische Bestimmungsübungen". [Development of an online-learning environment for courses in plant identification] In U. Becker & W. Sommer (Eds.), *Learntec 2002. 10. Europäischer Kongress und Fachmesse für Bildungs- und Informationstechnologie. Tagungsband* (pp. 573-579). Karlsruhe: Schrifteneinreihe der Karlsruher Messe- und Kongress GmbH.

Stahl, E., Bromme, R., Pieschl, S., Hölzenbein, S., & Kiffe, K. (in press). Qualitätssicherung bei der Lernsoftware-Entwicklung durch partizipative, formative Evaluation. Das Projektbeispiel "Cyeraceae-Online". [Participative, formative evaluation as a method for quality management during the development of learning software: The case of „Cyeraceae-Online"] *Zeitschrift für Psychologie.*

Veenman, M. V. J., Elshout, J. J., & Groen, M. G. M. (1993). Thinking aloud: Does it affect regulatory processes in learning? *Tijdschrift voor Onderwijsresearch, 18,* 322-330.

Chapter 4

OVERCOMING PROBLEMS OF KNOWLEDGE APPLICATION AND TRANSFER

Development, implementation and evaluation of an example-based instructional approach in the context of vocational school training in business administration

Robin Stark[1], Hans Gruber[2], Ludwig Hinkofer[3] and Heinz Mandl[3]
[1]*Institute of Education, Saarland University, Germany,* [2]*Institute for Education, University of Regensburg, Germany,* [3]*Institute of Educational Psychology, Ludwig-Maximilian-University Munich, Germany*

1. PROBLEMS OF KNOWLEDGE APPLICATION AND TRANSFER

In various domains and instructional contexts learners have considerable difficulties applying their knowledge to new problem situations beyond the instructional context in which they first acquired this knowledge. In a sub-domain of business administration (business management), our research group identified severe problems of knowledge application by confronting university students with a complex computer-based simulation of a company. Advanced students of economics had enormous difficulties using their rich conceptual knowledge base to control the company simulation: They proved to be managers who would have ruined their company in a short time - in spite of being able to reason intelligently about domain-specific matters (Stark, Renkl, Gruber, & Mandl, 1998). Their reasoning was complex, but did not meet the specific constraints of the problem situation at hand. As a matter of fact, it was not flexible enough. Thus, the students' knowledge remained inert. Starting from such a knowledge base which clearly lacks functionality, failures in practice are predictable.

The problem of inert knowledge is by no means limited to instruction at university level which traditionally focuses on systematic teaching of abstract knowledge. It can also be identified at vocational schools. In contrast to instruction on university level, vocational school instruction intends to directly prepare students for practice. Therefore, problems of knowledge application and transfer are even more serious.

For example, students of vocational schools have difficulties applying mathematical formulae needed for compound interest and real interest calculations. Many students do not understand the meaning of the variables and arithmetic connections involved. In many cases they simply learn the formulae by heart and apply them more or less mechanically. The selection of formulae and of specific variables often remains tied to the very surface features of the task - which may be irrelevant for solving the task. Consequently, new surface variations result in low performance even when the deep structure of the task is the same. It has to be mentioned that the known formulae could actually be applied successfully in the habitual mechanical way. However, if the structure of the task is varied - a situation which is very likely to occur on the job - problems of knowledge acquisition as well as negative transfer are predictable.

Similar problems can be diagnosed in another sub-domain of business administration. For instance, students of vocational schools have serious difficulties in applying formal concepts of book-keeping to real business situations mindfully (Salomon & Globerson, 1987). On the basis of domain-specific concepts and principles which are learned by heart, booking entries are often made more or less automatically. Positively speaking, students might thus develop routine expertise, but nevertheless would lack the adaptive expertise (Hatano & Inagaki, 1992) required to cope with new and complex problems in a flexible way.

Studies in the aforementioned sub-domains showed that the problem-solving strategies of vocational students are dysfunctional because they are not flexible enough. The students tend to stick to procedures which proved effective in a specific problem situation without being able to analyse specific constraints and affordances of the problem situation at hand. Thus, they fail to adapt their solution strategy to relevant structural aspects of the situation. Problems of knowledge application and transfer are the consequence.

Vocational school instruction that does not enable students to construct a functional knowledge base that helps them to cope with domain-specific problems in later practice, needs new impulses. Hence, the development, implementation, and evaluation of innovative instructional approaches that foster the acquisition of applicable knowledge thus is both of theoretical and practical relevance. However, multifacet gaps between theory and practice even in disciplines with use-inspired research goals often impair the transfer of relevant scientific knowledge into fields of practice (Stokes, 1997; see also Simons & Ruijters, this volume). (To put it pithy, scientific knowledge about coping with the inert knowledge problem frequently tends to remain inert.)

Obviously, the transfer problem between science (theory) and practice (application) also needs political solutions. Nevertheless, innovative research strategies can contribute to the improvement of instructional practice within the limits of a defined instructional context.

Reflections about the applied research strategy and the instructional intervention strategy are described below. After that, the experimental basis of the instructional approach is reported. Then, consequences are drawn for the implementation of this approach in vocational schools. Finally field studies are described in which this approach was evaluated in practice.

2. RESEARCH STRATEGY: APPLYING AN INTEGRATIVE RESEARCH PARADIGM

The integrative research paradigm used in our studies is inspired by various situated cognition research approaches (e.g., Greeno & The MMAP group, 1998) and in particular by the "design experiment" approach (Brown, 1992) which pragmatically combines controlled laboratory research with applied field research. The abstract goal of our research was to reduce the gaps between theory and practice by explicitly generating scientific knowledge which is functional from a research perspective and a practical perspective. Learning outcomes of students should be improved by conceptualising and implementing innovative learning environments, which are successively improved on the basis of empirical results. In addition, these results have to be replicated and verified in practice in order to clearly determine their functionality.

This approach implies normative consequences on different levels: The level of research methodology and applied methods, the level of theory selection and application, and the level of the concrete organisation of research projects.

2.1 Methodology

Concerning methodology, application oriented basic research has to be systematically combined with controlled field research. It is important that the oscillation between laboratory and field research is not a loose, superficial connection of experimental studies and design experiments, but a systematic and dialectic sequence of studies. In addition, it is important to note that while laboratory studies have to be explicitly conceptualised in terms of their later application of the results in practice, field studies have to be as well controlled as possible, for instance by working with control groups, or by controlling learning prerequisites. The systematic combination of both types of research aims at overcoming the traditional trade-off between internal and external validity.

2.2 Research methods

Application of research methods is guided by a pragmatic, problem-oriented rationale. As a rule, research goals on different levels and the process of successive knowledge construction through sequences of laboratory and field studies require rather broad and pluralistic methodical strategies. For instance, procedures focusing on hypothesis testing and on hypothesis generation have to be combined. This combination results in a combination of quantitative and qualitative research procedures (Renkl, 1999).

2.3 Theory selection and building

Pragmatic pluralism is also inevitable on the level of theory selection and building within the given context. The conceptualisation of innovative learning environments has to be inspired by multiple theories which, as a matter of fact, stem from different research paradigms and traditions. For instance, the design of learning materials can highly profit from situated design principles like narrative format, multiple perspectives etc. (Cognition and Technology Group at Vanderbilt (CTGV), 1992). However, the quality of learning materials can be increased when cognitive concepts like cognitive load etc. are taken into consideration, too (Sweller, Van Merriënboer, & Paas, 1998). In addition, it should be self-evident that the development of learning environments has to be nurtured by motivational concepts (Schiefele, 1996).

2.4 Concrete organisation of research projects

The problem-oriented, instrumental perspective of the integrative research paradigm makes necessary an interdisciplinary project frame. It requires intense co-operation between researchers and experts of the field at hand. It is important to note that expert practitioners should already be involved actively in the planning phases, the experimental phases and, of course, the field phases. Often neglected is the outcome communication and dissemination phase in which the insights of the research project are made available for interested persons in science and practice.

3. INTERVENTION STRATEGY: IMPLEMENTING LEARNING BY WORKED-OUT EXAMPLES

At least as far as initial skill acquisition in well-structured domains is concerned, learning by worked-out examples has proved effective and efficient (VanLehn, 1996). In the context of the studies described here, worked-out examples are sequences of carefully selected problem-solving tasks, which are presented in connection with detailed descriptions of problem-solving steps.

In many textbooks, worked-out examples are often used in a sub-optimal way: For each type of task only one example is provided. Thus, mapping processes and schema induction are almost impossible. In addition, the solution steps presented in textbooks are often fragmentary. This does not only provoke new problems of understanding but often leads to severe knowledge gaps.

In the domains of interest rate calculation and book-keeping on a vocational school level the use of worked-out examples is preferable because the domains are highly structured. Typical problem-solving tasks in these domains can be constructed which can then be solved step by step. Moreover, surface and deep structure information can easily be varied. Last but not least, worked-out examples can be combined easily with additional instructional measures, thus, they can be implemented in various instructional contexts.

4. VARIABLES INFLUENCING THE EFFECTIVENESS OF EXAMPLE-BASED LEARNING

Learning by worked-out examples is not per se more effective than other learning methods (Ward & Sweller, 1990). For instance, when worked-out examples impose a heavy extraneous cognitive load on the working memory (Sweller et al., 1998), they are not superior to traditional problem-solving tasks. Therefore, the presentation format of worked-out examples has to be designed with explicit consideration of cognitive load matters.

Effective examples include clues to attract attention to the underlying conceptual meaning of the task (Catrambone, 1995). One means is the explicit visualisation of relevant sub-goals. Furthermore, effective worked-out examples should be sequenced in a way that makes structural features of the tasks salient, for example by varying only surface task features which do not influence the solution and by keeping constant structural features (Quilici & Mayer, 1996).

The influence of design variables which influence the effectiveness of worked-out examples can be moderated by learner characteristics, especially by their prior knowledge (Kalyuga, Chandler, Tuovinen, & Sweller, 2001). As a thumb rule it may be stated that the more prior knowledge learners have, the less their learning outcomes depend on the quality of examples.

When example-based learning is implemented, not only potential moderator variables but also intervening variables which mediate learning outcomes have to be taken into consideration. The mechanisms by which design effects are mediated can be described in terms of the elaboration behaviour of the learners (Stark, 1999). According to Chi, Bassok, Lewis, Reimann, and Glaser (1989) the quality of elaboration behaviour is related to learning outcomes. From an instructional perspective, it is problematic that the majority of learners seem to elaborate examples in a superficial and passive way when no additional instructional guidance is given (Renkl, 1997). Many learners profit less from example-based learning than they might. Thus, example-based learning can be improved by fostering quality and intensity of example elaboration.

5. EXPERIMENTAL STUDIES TO IMPROVE AN EXAMPLE-BASED INSTRUCTIONAL APPROACH IN THE CONTEXT OF VOCATIONAL SCHOOL TRAINING IN BUSINESS ADMINISTRATION

To avoid the problems of knowledge application and transfer which were identified in our studies about vocational training in business administration, sequences of selected worked-out examples were developed in close co-operation with teachers of vocational schools and training managers from banks. Taking into account theories of situated learning (Collins, Brown, & Newman, 1989; CTGV, 1992, 1997; Spiro, Feltovich, Jacobson, & Coulson, 1991) the worked-out examples were conceptualised in a narrative format. Fictitious clients at the bank had to be advised on questions of investments.

Knowledge Application 55

5.1 Study 1: Effectiveness of a special elaboration training

Study 1 (Renkl, Stark, Gruber, & Mandl, 1998) was carried out in the domain of interest rate calculation. Cognitive effects of a special elaboration training were investigated in an experimental study in which 56 bank trainees participated.

The elaboration training was designed according to principles of the cognitive apprenticeship approach (Collins et al., 1989). The experimenter acted as a model demonstrating deep and metacognitively controlled example elaboration. Additionally, according to the recommendations of Catrambone (1995) the learners were instructed to formulate sub-goals for each solution step. After working on a training example for themselves, the learners received detailed feedback from the experimenter and were allowed to answer questions concerning the elaboration procedure.

By means of this training, example elaboration was fostered in both quantitative and qualitative aspects. With respect to the acquisition of applicable knowledge, the training proved effective, too. In particular, learners with low prior knowledge profited. Thus, the training compensated low prior knowledge. It helped them to focus on solution-relevant example information and to differentiate between deep and surface features. This is an indicator of schema induction and of grasping the meaning of the learning situation.

However, another instructional measure by which structural features of the task at hand should be made more salient had a detrimental effect: Increasing the surface variability of the worked-out examples increased the complexity of mapping processes and of schema induction. When learners had to learn from examples which were dissimilar in context and surface, but which were structurally analogous, they only succeeded after an elaboration training to differentiate between surface and structure. Without that training, the elaboration quality was impaired and resulted in poorer learning (Renkl et al., 1998).

In spite of the elaboration training, a number of students continued to elaborate the examples passively and superficially. Therefore, an activating measure was integrated in the example-based approach. It was investigated in study 2.

5.2 Study 2: Effectiveness of combining worked-out examples with problem-solving tasks

Thirty trainees of a bank participated in study 2. In order to activate learners, example-based learning in the domain of interest rate calculation was systematically combined with learning by problem-solving. Thus we aimed at profiting from the advantages of both learning methods (Stark, Gruber, Renkl, & Mandl, 2000) Difficulties arising from learning solely based on problem-solving can be avoided by providing immediate feedback (Cooper & Sweller, 1987). This can be done rather economically by providing a structurally identical worked-out example after each problem-solving task. Hence, a combination of methods helps to overcome difficulties. By comparing the modelled example solution with the self-generated problem solution in a systematic way, the learners can identify and correct their mistakes. Additionally, the example can be studied selectively to overcome lacking knowledge and problems of understanding which probably occur when the learners are confronted with the problem-solving task (Stark et al., 2000). In the domain of probability calculation, an activating measure had proved effective concerning elaboration quality and acquisition of applicable knowledge (Stark, 1999).

These positive results were replicated by combining worked-out examples with problem-solving tasks in study 2. In contrast to study 1, the effects were not influenced by the learners' prior knowledge. As both the experimental condition and the control condition (worked-out examples only) encompassed a short elaboration training, the influence of the learning condition on example elaboration was smaller than in study 1. However, some aspects of active and deep information processing were fostered by the combination procedure. For instance, the systematic use of an additional instructional text and critical monitoring of the own learning process were improved.

As the prior knowledge level of subjects in studies 1 and 2 was rather low, the cognitive effects achieved with the example-based approach are remarkable and of practical relevance. Nevertheless, this approach still had some shortcomings. If the prior knowledge of the learners is low and problems of understanding are severe, subjects cannot construct an effective knowledge base solely by elaborating worked-out examples. Therefore, the example-based instructional approach has to be enriched by integrating relevant background information. This can be done by implementing additional instructional explanations which enable the learners to follow and understand the solution procedure (Renkl, 2002).

The effectiveness of instructional explanations was investigated in study 3 which was carried out in another sub-domain of business administration, book-keeping (Stark, Gruber, Mandl, & Hinkofer, 2001). In book-keeping, successful problem-solving depends on the flexibility of the learners' knowledge application. Therefore, an additional instructional measure which aimed at systematically confronting the learners with multiple perspectives on book-keeping tasks was conceptualised and applied.

5.3 Study 3: Effectiveness of instructional explanations and multiple perspectives

5.3.1 Conceptualisation

According to the basic role of learner-generated elaboration in the example-based instructional approach, instructional explanations were only used as additional tools. They comprised deeper information on domain-specific concepts, principles and relations as well as their concrete application in the problem situation at hand.

The measure to induce multiple perspectives was predominantly inspired by cognitive flexibility theory (Spiro et al., 1991). In the domain of book-keeping, multiple perspectives can be realised authentically, because business cases in general can be considered from the perspective of all participating business partners. Therefore, learners can be instructed to successively take over the view of each business partner.

As it was planned to implement the instructional approach at vocational schools it was important to take into account motivational aspects, too. Two aspects were focused upon: Self efficacy beliefs and acceptance of the learning method. Both constitute important conditions of persistence in the learning process. In particular, the implementation of longer learning periods at school requires that learners develop positive evaluations of their own learning progress and of the quality of the learning method used. Motivational prerequisites, topic specific self concept and motivational orientation were analysed, which are known to influence learning behaviour and learning outcomes (Schiefele, 1996).

Taken together, study 3 aimed at analysing to what extent learning behaviour and acquisition of applicable knowledge are fostered through instructional explanations and multiple perspectives. In addition, the effects of both instructional measures on self efficacy beliefs and the acceptance of the learning method were investigated.

5.3.2 Method

Fifty-six industrial trainees participated in study 3. They were randomly assigned to four groups of a 2×2-factorial design (factor 1: With vs. without "instructional explanations"; factor 2: With vs. without "multiple perspectives"). All subjects learned individually with pairs of worked-out examples and problem-solving tasks. Additionally, all subjects received a short elaboration training. The learning phase lasted 180 minutes.

Prior knowledge was recorded by a test which consisted of simple business cases to be worked on. Motivational prerequisites, self efficacy, and acceptance of the learning method were recorded by specific rating scales. Acquisition of applicable knowledge was assessed by problem-oriented tasks measuring four aspects: Conceptual knowledge, situational knowledge, action knowledge, procedural knowledge (cf. the taxonomy of knowledge types proposed by De Jong & Ferguson-Hessler, 1996).

5.3.3 Results

The four groups did not differ significantly regarding cognitive and motivational prerequisites. Figure1 shows that learners who received multiple perspectives were more successful in the post test than subjects without multiple perspectives.

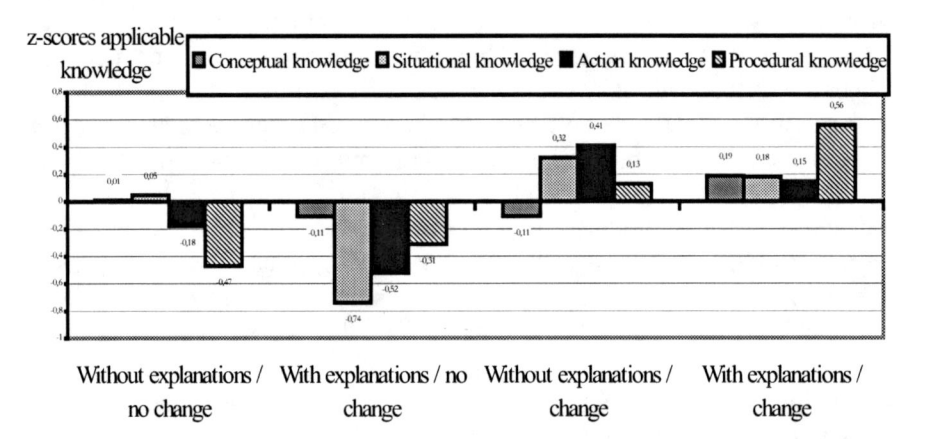

Figure 1. Study 3: Z-scores of four groups (with vs. without "instructional explanations"; with vs. without "multiple perspectives") concerning four aspects of applicable knowledge (conceptual knowledge, situational knowledge, action knowledge, procedural knowledge)

Concerning situational knowledge, action knowledge, and procedural knowledge, the main effect "multiple perspectives" was significant. Large effect sizes resulted for procedural knowledge, medium effect sizes for situational knowledge and action knowledge. The main effect "multiple perspectives" was not significant concerning conceptual knowledge. In neither aspect of applicable knowledge, the main effect "instructional explanations" and the interaction effect reached significance.

Concerning self efficacy beliefs, only small differences between the four groups appeared, none of them being significant. Nevertheless, effects concerning the learners' acceptance of the learning method were observed. Multiple perspectives increased acceptance; however, the main effect "multiple perspectives" narrowly missed the level of statistical significance. Instructional explanations had negative effects on the acceptance. The main effect "instructional explanations" was significant, with a medium effect size.

5.3.4 Discussion

Learners with multiple perspectives were able to apply their knowledge more flexibly to complex tasks than learners who analysed business cases from only one perspective. The degree of mindfulness in the learning and problem solving phase can be increased by confronting learners with the necessity to consider multiple perspectives. However, inducing multiple perspectives did not foster the acquisition of conceptual knowledge. With respect to this aspect of applicable knowledge, a floor effect was identified in all learning conditions which is in contrast to the studies mentioned in which a computer-based simulation of a company was employed. In these studies, learners acquired concepts of business management without learning how to apply them flexibly to changing problem situations. That is, they developed "knowledge that" and lacked "knowledge how". In study 3, however, learners confronted with multiple perspectives obviously learned to make correct booking entries. However, this "knowledge how" was not reliably based on deep conceptual understanding. This difference concerning strengths and weaknesses of resulting knowledge of learners reveals differences in the constraints and affordances of the learning environments provided.

We argue that the relative weakness of the example-based approach concerning conceptual knowledge and the unexpected failure of instructional explanations have the same roots. Observations and brief interviews during and after learning made apparent that the students were primarily concerned with making correct booking entries and not with acquiring new knowledge. This sub-optimal learning behaviour probably reflects the usual requirements of exams and, thus, resulting learning habits. If under certain circumstances such a performance goal (Dweck, 1991) can also be reached by mechanical problem-solving without developing deep understanding of concepts and principles, then it is plausible that a majority of learners uses instructional explanations only casually and superficially.

Such learning behaviour can in the long run be rather dysfunctional. Similar results were obtained in studies in which other learning methods had been implemented. Forthcoming modifications of the example-based approach thus should try to induce more learning-oriented and less performance-oriented attitudes.

Moreover, instructional means should be integrated more thoroughly into the learning material. The presentation format used in study 3 was rather additive. Perhaps it increased extraneous cognitive load so that the presentation format interfered with successful knowledge acquisition and with schema induction.

6. CONCRETE CONSEQUENCES FOR IMPLEMENTING THE EXAMPLE-BASED APPROACH IN PRACTICE

The following conclusions can be drawn for the realisation of example-based learning and teaching in vocational school from studies 1-3.
1. Example-based learning ought to be supported by an adequate elaboration training in order to support active and deep example elaboration and schema induction.
2. An effective activating measure ought to be implemented; the systematic combination of worked-out examples and problem-solving tasks proved to be efficient and effective.
3. Multiple perspectives ought to be realised as authentically as possible; in the domain of book-keeping, learners ought to be instructed to take different perspectives while working on business cases. The use of multiple perspectives might increase complexity and thus ought to be accompanied by additional compensating measures.
4. Instructional explanations ought to be presented in an integrated format in order to reduce extraneous cognitive load; demonstration of competent use of instructional explanations by a model might prove effective.

7. IMPLEMENTATION AND EVALUATION OF EXAMPLE-BASED LEARNING AND TEACHING IN PRACTICE: FIELD STUDIES IN VOCATIONAL SCHOOL

7.1 Adaptation of the example-based approach to vocational school

In close co-operation with headmasters and teachers of vocational schools a time frame to integrate the example-based instructional approach into regular book-keeping lessons was worked out. Two 90 minute lessons were planned. The outline of an evaluation study was designed.

Worked-out examples and problem-solving tasks as well as the instructional measures were adapted to the specific constraints and affordances of vocational school lessons. The result was a complex model of example-based learning and teaching. The most central components were worked-out examples and problem-solving tasks which resembled those employed in study 3. In addition, incomplete examples were developed. A kind of fading procedure (Renkl, Atkinson, Maier, & Stanley, in press) was integrated into the model. A short training phase on how to work on business cases and how to make use of instructional explanations competently was also built into the lessons.

In contrast to study 3, instructional explanations were completely integrated into the basic example format. The solution of each business case was elaborated and additional background information was given.

By implementing reciprocal teaching (Palincsar & Brown, 1984), the instructional measures of elaboration training and of multiple perspectives were realised in an authentic way. Teams of two students each entered the reciprocal teaching procedure.

The vocational school teacher was trained to function as a moderator of example-based and problem-oriented learning processes. Being a model in the sense of the cognitive apprenticeship approach (Collins et al., 1989), the teacher had to demonstrate effective example elaboration and systematic use of instructional explanations.

7.2 Concrete realisation of the example-based lessons

7.2.1 Worked-out examples and problem-solving tasks

In both lessons, three business cases were given. The first business case of the first lesson was presented as a completely worked-out example which had to be worked through after the teacher modelled problem-solving in front of the class. The second one was an incomplete example which had to be completed by the students. The third business case was a problem-solving task which had to be solved by the students on their own. In the second lesson one incomplete example and two problem-solving tasks were presented.

Each business case was combined with presentation of relevant background information and authentic accounting vouchers. A complete example consisted of a description of the problem situation followed by four problem-solving steps. The first step involved the extraction of relevant information from the problem situation and the respective voucher. In the second step the accounting records were formulated. In the third step the records were transferred to the general ledger account. The final step provided the rationale for the solutions of steps 2 and 3. Additional background information was given in the last step, too. Thus, step 4 replaced the instructional explanations procedure used in study3.

Incomplete examples had the same structure as complete ones, with the exception of the fourth solution step: This step had to be completed by the students on their own. Each learner had to work individually on his or her business case. Afterwards, the learners received the correct solution of the fourth step from the teacher. The learners had to compare their own solution with the model solution. Then, the model solutions had to be explained to the other team member, sitting beside him or her. In order to avoid boring redundancy, each team member worked on a business case which slightly differed from the business case of their colleague.

When problem-solving tasks were presented, all solution steps had to be generated individually by the learners. Each team member first had to solve his or her business case from a different perspective. Then, the model solution was presented and had to be explained by each team member to the other.

7.2.2 Modelling and reciprocal teaching procedures

Working on the first business case was modelled by the teacher in front of the class. Hereby she systematically employed principles of cognitive apprenticeship. The solution steps of the first business case were then used by the students in the first worked-out example. They were instructed to reconstruct both the solution steps and the elaboration of the teacher.

On the basis of the first worked-out example, the teacher also explained and demonstrated principles of reciprocal teaching. This procedure was called "explanation method" in the class. It replaced the individual elaboration procedure used in study 3. In dyad teams, one team member took over the role of the teacher and either explained a solution step (in the case of incomplete examples) or the complete solution of a business case (in the case of problem-solving tasks) to the other member of the dyad. Afterwards team roles were changed.

In the case of problem-solving tasks, each "teacher" had to explain the solution of the business case from a different perspective. Thus, both instructional measures (elaboration, multiple perspectives) were integrated into the reciprocal teaching procedure. In the course of both lessons, the teachers' involvement faded out successively. The teacher was instructed to intervene only when interaction problems arose which the dyads could not overcome autonomously.

8. STUDY 4: EVALUATION OF THE EFFECTIVENESS OF EXAMPLE-BASED LESSONS IN VOCATIONAL SCHOOL

In order to evaluate the example-based learning and teaching model, effects of the example-based lessons on applicable knowledge were compared with effects of "traditional" lessons. In addition, we wanted to identify strengths and weaknesses of the example-based lessons arising from the perspectives of learners and of the implementing teacher.

8.1 Traditional book-keeping lessons at vocational school

Of course it is an oversimplification to describe "the" traditional book-keeping lesson at vocational school. Even within certain countries (here: Germany), a large variety of lessons occurs. However, some characteristics of traditional lessons can be observed in many vocational classrooms. Teachers in most cases are didactic leaders who try to control learning processes by explaining contents to learners in front of the class. In such teacher centred instruction the schoolbook is of great importance. It contains instructional texts and example tasks which are solved by the teacher at the board. Often the schoolbook also contains a few problems for which solutions are provided as well. Such schoolbook examples, however, must not be confused with worked-out examples. In our example-based lessons, the solution steps and the elicited learning processes are elaborated in much more detail. Furthermore, selection and sequence of examples are explicitly theory-based.

8.2 Method

Study 4 was carried out at a vocational school in Bavaria. In the experimental class ($n = 20$), two example-based lessons on book-keeping (90 minutes each) were implemented. A control class ($n = 16$) was taught the same subject matter traditionally. The teacher of the control class was not acquainted with the example-based approach.

Before the first lesson started, in both classes biographical aspects, subjective prior knowledge and motivational prerequisites were assessed. After one week the next lesson was carried out.

Two weeks after the second lesson the post test was administered. It was a short version of the test used in study 3. Three aspects of applicable knowledge were analysed: Conceptual knowledge, situational knowledge, procedural knowledge. In the same week learners of the experimental class were asked open questions concerning strengths and weaknesses of the example-based lessons. The teacher of this class was interviewed on her personal experiences with these lessons.

8.3 Results

Students of both classes did not differ significantly in biographical aspects, subjective prior knowledge, and motivational learning prerequisites. As Figure 2 shows, students of the experimental class achieved higher scores in all aspects of applicable knowledge. All differences between the two classes were significant and substantial. In contrast to study 3, no floor effects were observed in conceptual knowledge. Thus, the students of the experimental class not only outperformed those of the control class with respect to the accounting records they had to generate, they also acquired more knowledge of concepts, facts and principles, and they were more successful in analysing problem situations concerning solution-relevant information.

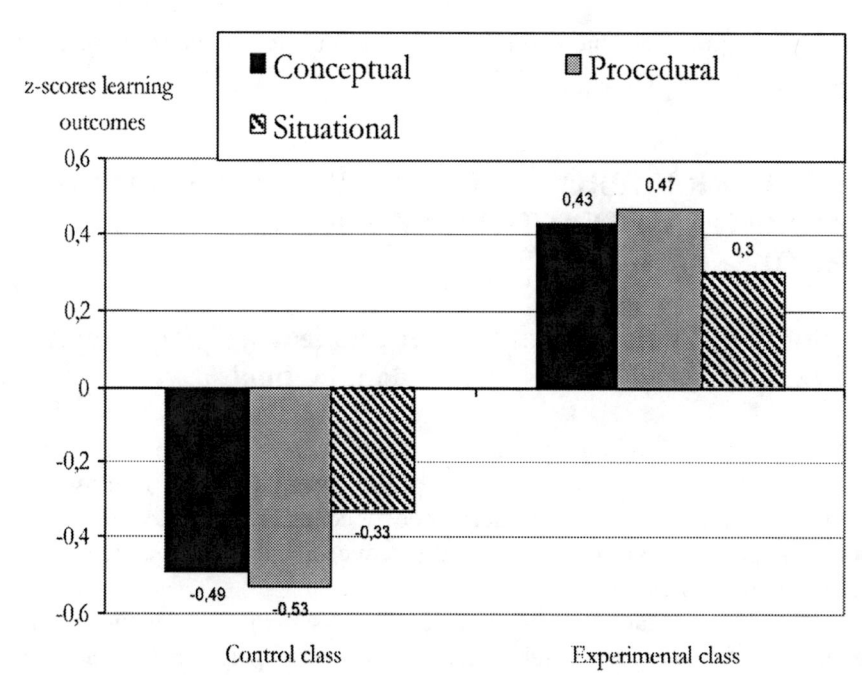

Figure 2. Study 4: Z-scores of experimental class and control class concerning three aspects of applicable knowledge (conceptual knowledge, situational knowledge, procedural knowledge)

Both learners and teacher gave positive evaluations of the example-based lessons. Most positive judgements of the learners concerned (1) the learning material and its helpfulness in understanding the matter, (2) the efficiency of the example lessons, (3) the highly motivating nature of the co-operative explanation method, and (4) the perceived independence from both the schoolbook and the teacher.

Most negative learner comments addressed the richness of the learning material and related orientation problems. Many learners felt that the provided time-on-task for co-operative work on the examples and problem-solving tasks was too short. The explanation method was regarded as cognitively demanding. Another problem arose from an obvious lack of discipline. Some learners mentioned that there was too much noise in the classroom.

The teacher felt that some learners would have profited more from the example-based lessons if provided with more teacher support. She also formulated the hypothesis that the method would have been even more effective if both learners and teacher had been prepared and trained in a more systematic way how to use the alternative kind of teaching and learning.

These critiques were the basis for on-going improvements of the method and its implementation.

9. FURTHER IMPROVEMENT OF EXAMPLE-BASED LEARNING AND TEACHING AT VOCATIONAL SCHOOL

9.1 Study 5: Evaluation of teacher and learner preparation for example-based lessons in vocational school

Based on the encouraging results of study 4, a revised version of the example-based learning and teaching approach was developed in close co-operation with the same vocational school teacher (Hinkofer, 2003). The amount of printed learning material was reduced and the structure of the worked-out examples improved.

In addition, a detailed script was developed which pre-structured both example-based lessons to a high degree. In this script, elements of the new approach were combined with more traditional elements, increasing the teacher-centring of the approach in the first lesson. The sequence of both lessons was simulated and practised with the teacher. A short training procedure for learners in how to use the co-operative components of the approach was developed.

The effectiveness of the revised example-based lessons was investigated in study 5, which also was realised at a vocational school in Bavaria. The procedure was similar to that of study 4. The main results of the former study were replicated (Hinkofer, 2003): Learners of the experimental class who underwent the example-based instruction clearly outperformed their traditionally instructed colleagues with respect to conceptual knowledge, situational knowledge, and procedural knowledge.

9.2 General discussion

Starting from problems of knowledge application and transfer, which can be observed in the context of vocational school training in business administration, an example-based instructional approach was conceptualised and further developed on an empirical basis. The conceptualisation of the described studies was guided by an integrative research paradigm.

In the sub-domain of interest rate calculation, it was shown that example-based learning was more effective when it was enriched with an elaboration training and systematically combined with problem-solving tasks. These insights were transferred to and tested within another sub-domain (bookkeeping), which is also part of the vocational school curriculum. The main goal of study 3 was testing the effectiveness of two additional instructional measures: Instructional explanations and multiple perspectives. At least the latter one fostered substantially the acquisition of applicable knowledge. In contrast to studies from other research groups, instructional explanations did not increase the effectiveness of the example-based approach.

The predominant testing culture at vocational schools and the resulting performance orientation of the learners were used to explain the difficulties. Additionally, cognitive overload problems might have been caused by the presentation format, which was rather additive. As a consequence, the example-based approach was modified. Its ecological validity was tested in two design experiments (studies 4 and 5). The example-based learning and teaching model was implemented successfully at vocational schools. Thus, the results from studies 1-3 did not only serve scientific progress, they also constituted a functional basis for developing example-based lessons by which knowledge acquisition can be fostered in practice. Consequently, the abstract goal of the applied integrative research paradigm was achieved: The often bemoaned and even more often ignored gaps between theory and practice were reduced.

9.3 Recommendations for further improvements of example-based lessons

By implementing example-based lessons, domain-specific applicable knowledge was increased substantially in a short time span. The acceptance of this kind of lessons was high, both on the side of the learners and the teacher. However, in study 4 the learners and the teacher also diagnosed a number of shortcomings, which provided valuable information to further improve the example-based approach. In study 5 some of these shortcomings were no longer apparant. Nevertheless, orientation problems of the learners resulting from a rather old-fashioned paper-based presentation mode were not yet resolved. Especially when a large amount of authentic learning material is provided, example-based lessons clearly profit from the employment of modern computer technology. Renkl (2002) implemented learning by worked-out examples in the domain of probability calculation using a computer-based learning environment. Electronic media can be used to realise effectively adaptive forms of learner support.

Beyond employment of technology, additional training measures for the learners are indicated, especially when co-operative learning sequences are implemented. The short training sequences, which were realised in study 5, were still not sufficient. The method of reciprocal teaching requires a systematic training procedure for learners and teachers. The training for teachers is rather demanding, since new strategies of interacting with the learners have to be developed, but also changes of habits and of epistemological beliefs about successful teaching and learning.

9.4 Guidelines for the implementation of innovative research strategies and instructional approaches

Following the integrative research paradigm, the whole project frame was organised on an interdisciplinary basis - psychologists and educationalists worked together with experts of business administration as well as with vocational school teachers and other experts from practice. Therefore, the context for implementing the example-based approach in vocational schools was exceptionally good. It became clear that the degree of practitioners' integration in development and design processes is directly related with the degree of responsibility they take over. Taking this characteristic of the integrative research paradigm seriously is at least as complex and demanding as the whole research enterprise itself. As problems have to be reconstructed from multiple perspectives and each side is often trapped in its own language games, common solution strategies have to be negotiated deliberately. In order to overcome communication problems and language barriers which often impede fruitful discourse between researchers and practitioners, the co-operation between theory and practice should be organised in the form of learning communities. Summarising the experience of the authors of the Jasper implementation project (CTGV, 1997), it can be stated that one-shot trainings do not work!

NOTE

The authors gratefully acknowledge the Deutsche Forschungsgemeinschaft (DFG) for a supporting grant.

REFERENCES

Brown, A. L. (1992). Transforming schools into communities of thinking and learning about serious matters. *American Psychologist, 4*, 399-413.
Catrambone, R. (1995). Aiding sub-goal learning: Effects on transfer. *Journal of Educational Psychology, 87*, 5-17.
Chi, M. T. H., Bassok, M., Lewis, M. W., Reimann, P., & Glaser, R. (1989). Self-explanations: How students study and use examples in learning to solve problems. *Cognitive Science, 13*, 145-182.

Cognition and Technology Group at Vanderbilt (1992). The Jasper series as an example of anchored instruction: Theory, program description, and assessment data. *Educational Psychologist, 27,* 291-315.

Cognition and Technology Group at Vanderbilt (1997). *The Jasper project: Lessons in curriculum, instruction, assessment, and professional development.* Mahwah: Erlbaum.

Collins, A., Brown, J. S., & Newman, S. E. (1989). Cognitive apprenticeship: Teaching the crafts of reading, writing, and mathematics. In L. B. Resnick (ed.), *Knowing, learning, and instruction* (pp. 453-494). Hillsdale: Erlbaum.

Cooper, G., & Sweller, J. (1987). Effects of schema acquisition and rule automation on mathematical problem-solving transfer. *Journal of Educational Psychology, 77,* 347-362.

De Jong, T., & Ferguson-Hessler, M. G. M. (1996). Types and qualities of knowledge. *Educational Psychologist, 31,* 105-113.

Dweck, C. S. (1991). Self-theories and goals: Their role in motivation, personality, and development. In R. A. Dienstbier (ed.), *Nebraska Symposium on Motivation* (pp. 199-235). Lincoln: University of Nebraska Press.

Greeno, J. G., & The Middle School Mathematics Through Applications Project Group (1998). The situativity of knowing, learning and research. *American Psychologist, 53,* 5-26.

Hatano, G., & Inagaki, K. (1992). De-situating cognition through the construction of conceptual knowledge. In P. Light & G. Butterworth (Eds.), *Context and cognition: Ways of learning and knowing* (pp. 115-133). Hillsdale: Erlbaum.

Hinkofer, L. (2003). *Konzeption und Erprobung von Unterrichtssequenzen an der kaufmännischen Berufsschule auf der Basis eines beispielbasierten Instruktionsansatzes.* [Conception and evaluation of lesson sequences at vocational school of business administration on the basis of an example-based instructional approach] Unpubl. doctoral diss., Ludwig-Maximilians-Universität München, Germany.

Kalyuga, S., Chandler, P., Tuovinen, J., & Sweller, J. (2001). When problem solving is superior to studying worked examples. *Journal of Educational Psychology, 93,* 579-588.

Palincsar, A. S., & Brown, A. L. (1984). Reciprocal teaching of comprehension-fostering and comprehension-monitoring activities. *Cognition and Instruction, 1,* 117-175.

Quilici, J. L., & Mayer, R. E. (1996). Role of examples in how students learn to categorise statistics word problems. *Journal of Educational Psychology, 88,* 144-161.

Renkl, A. (1997). Learning from worked-out examples: A study on individual differences. *Cognitive Science, 21,* 1-29.

Renkl, A. (1999). Jenseits von $p<.05$: Ein Plädoyer für Qualitatives. [Beyond $p<.05$. Pleading for qualitative analyses] *Unterrichtswissenschaft, 27,* 310-322.

Renkl, A. (2002). Worked-out examples: Instructional explanations support learning by self-explanations. *Learning and Instruction, 5,* 529-556.

Renkl, A., Atkinson, R. K., Maier, U. H., & Stanley, R. (in press). From example study to problem solving: Smooth transitions help learning. *Journal of Experimental Education.*

Renkl, A., Stark, R., Gruber, H., & Mandl, H. (1998). Learning from worked-out examples: The effects of example variability and elicited self-explanations. *Contemporary Educational Psychology, 23,* 90-108.

Salomon, G., & Globerson, T. (1987). Skill may be not be enough: The role of mindfulness in learning and transfer. *International Journal of Educational Research, 11,* 623-637.

Schiefele, U. (1996). *Motivation und Lernen mit Texten.* [Motivation and learning with texts] Göttingen: Hogrefe.

Spiro, R. J., Feltovich, P. J., Jacobson, M. J., & Coulson, R. L. (1991). Cognitive flexibility, constructivism, and hypertext: Random access instruction for advanced knowledge acquisition in ill-structured domains. *Educational Technology, 31* (5), 24-33.

Stark, R. (1999). *Lernen mit Lösungsbeispielen. Einfluß unvollständiger Lösungsbeispiele auf Beispielelaboration, Lernerfolg und Motivation.* [Learning with worked-out examples. The influence of incomplete worked-out examples on example elaboration, learning success, and motivation] Göttingen: Hogrefe.

Stark, R., Gruber, H., Mandl, H., & Hinkofer, L. (2001). Wege zur Optimierung eines beispielbasierten Instruktionsansatzes: Der Einfluss multipler Perspektiven und instruktionaler Erklärungen auf den Erwerb von Handlungskompetenz. [Improving an example-based instructional approach: The impact of multiple perspectives and instructional explanations on the acquisition of action competence] *Unterrichtswissenschaft, 29,* 26-40.

Stark, R., Gruber, H., Renkl, A., & Mandl, H. (2000). Instruktionale Effekte einer kombinierten Lernmethode: Zahlt sich die Kombination von Lösungsbeispielen und Problemlöseaufgaben aus? [Instructional effects of a combined learning method. Does the combination of worked-out examples and problem-solving tasks pay off?] *Zeitschrift für Pädagogische Psychologie, 14,* 205-217.

Stark, R., Mandl, H., Gruber, H., & Renkl, A. (1998). Indeed, sometimes knowledge does not help: A replication study. *Instructional Science, 26,* 391-407.

Stokes, D. E. (1997). *Pasteur's quadrant. Basic science and technological innovation.* Washington: Brookings.

Sweller, J., Van Merriënboer, J. J. G., & Paas, F. G. W. C. (1998). Cognitive architecture and instructional design. *Educational Psychology Review, 10,* 251-296.

Van Lehn, K. (1996). Cognitive skill acquisition. *Annual Review of Psychology, 47,* 513-539.

Ward, M., & Sweller, J. (1990). Structuring effective worked examples. *Cognition and Instruction, 7,* 1-39.

PART 3

GAPS AND TRANSITIONS: ACCUMULATING EXPERIENCE TO BECOME A PROFESSIONAL

Chapter 5

DOES PRACTICE MAKE PERFECT?
A slow and discontinuous process

Henny P. A. Boshuizen
Educational Technology Expertise Centre, Open Universiteit Nederland, Heerlen, The Netherlands

1. FROM NOVICE TO EXPERT

Before someone becomes an expert in a field, many years of theoretical education and practical training have passed. How much education and how many years of training depends on the field. For example, musicians (especially expert performers) have already spent about 10,000 hours practising by the age of 20 (Ericsson, 1996). In Western societies, a substantial part of these teaching and learning processes have been formalised. The content that has to be mastered is prescribed and checked by national examinations. The mix of formal education and practical experience is agreed upon by the different schools. Examinations are supervised by external reviewers, and after graduation professionals are required to stay up-to-date, if not by governmental bodies, then by their own professional organisation that controls accreditation and offers post-academic courses, organises evidence-based standardisation procedures, etc. Amidst this interplay of forces and interests, students are being trained up to a certain level of mastery, a level that is supposed sufficient to be able to work under supervision, and to enable them to develop further to become a real master. This chapter explores how students build up knowledge and skill and the competences up to this level.

Let me start with the following claim, which is not very surprising given the amount of supporting evidence and the length of time this evidence has been around. The claim is that, in medicine at least but probably in the many other diagnostic professions, differences between experts and novices cannot be explained by differences in reasoning skill (Elstein, Shulman, & Sprafka, 1978; see Bédard, 1989, for a good example in the domain of accountancy). Everyone, novice and expert alike, generates hypotheses in diagnostic reasoning and tests these hypotheses by gathering distinguishing information that either confirms or denies them. Despite the overwhelming evidence it is important to bear this in mind, since many educators in medicine see students' problems in clinical reasoning as a lack of general skill, as a lack of proper training in this area, or as a competence that students have not yet mastered completely. Contrary to this view, I claim that building up domain knowledge, in combination with learning the required skills, is the key (Boshuizen & Schmidt, 1992; Schmidt & Boshuizen, 1992; Schmidt, Boshuizen, & Norman 1992). In this sense, the process of acquiring medical expertise does not differ from that of acquiring expertise in other, non-diagnostic domains (e.g., in chess: De Groot, 1965; engineering: Ackermann & Barbichon, 1963; statistics: Allwood & Montgomery, 1981; mathematics: Bloom & Broder, 1950; physics: Chi, Feltovich, & Glaser, 1981). The novice-to-expert learning process in medicine can be taken as a prototype in order to derive hypotheses for other domains.

Medical knowledge consists of thousands of concepts, principles, rules, skills, procedures and patterns that are not learned for their own sake, but with the aim of diagnosing and treating sick people (Box 1). It is therefore necessary for this knowledge to be organised in a way that it can be verified, easily activated in relevant contexts, and easily applied in reasoning, and that it is complete in the sense that it concerns the prevention, diagnosis, treatment, and management aspects of patient care. There are two learning processes that guarantee that this goal is reached. One of these consists of the following steps: knowledge accretion, validation and integration, a process that takes much more

Box 1.
Medicine is a special domain when it comes to knowledge integration. By its nature and by tradition it can be characterised as a reductionistic science. Biomedical research on growth processes and development, (patho)-physiology, (patho)-anatomy, biochemistry, or biophysics, at the level of organs and (sub)-cellular level, about genetics, the influence of bacteria, viruses, toxins, etcetera, is done to understand disease processes and to develop new treatment. Insights into these processes are also used in patient care, if knowledge of specific diseases does not provide a clue about what might cause a patient's complaints. What seems apparently contradictory is the claim that a patient should not be reduced to the affected organ or system. For example, doctors and nurses should not talk about the proverbial "decompensated pregnant diabetes in room 12"; instead they she should treat her as a person having a disease that not only affects her health, but also her daily life, family, spouse and (future) children as well. This holistic approach requires knowledge of other disciplines than the reductionist use of the biomedical sciences. Again this knowledge must be used in an integrative manner.

time than teachers might expect. The integration and integrated use of knowledge from different domains, subject matters and disciplines (e.g., biochemistry, pathophysiology or microanatomy integrated with the clinical sciences) are particularly tricky and may take a lot of time (Boshuizen & Van de Wiel, 1998; Groothuis, Boshuizen, & Talmon, 1998). This kind of learning takes place mostly in the first years of training, when the student's clinical reasoning process is characterised by lines of reasoning consisting of chains of small steps commonly based on detailed, biomedical concepts, sometimes supported by notes and sketches. These kinds of exercises result in a well-integrated, validated knowledge network.

Once the student has acquired these well-integrated networks, he or she can make direct lines of reasoning between different concepts. The more often these direct lines are activated, the more the concepts they include cluster together and the more a student is able to make direct links between the first and last concepts of such a line and skip the intermediate ones. This is the second learning process we have discerned. This process was termed "knowledge encapsulation". This concept includes the clustering aspect of the process and accounts for the automation involved (Boshuizen & Schmidt, 1992; Schmidt & Boshuizen, 1993; Van de Wiel, 1997). As a result of this encapsulation process, the level of granularity in clinical reasoning protocols increases and students no longer need such supporting tools as sketches that they are often seen to make when analysing a case. A new type of clinical or semi-clinical concept appears in the protocols, providing a powerful reasoning tool. Examples are micro-embolism, aorta-insufficiency, forward failure, megaloblastic anaemia, or extra-hepatic icterus.

The third learning process is illness-script formation. Scripts are based on experience. They are knowledge structures that describe stereotyped sequences of action (Schank & Abelson, 1977). The archetype of a script in memory research literature is the restaurant script, which describes the procedure of eating in a restaurant, the roles of the different participants and their actions, the objects involved, etcetera. Scripts also indicate where variations are allowed and what is really necessary. The restaurant script requires that food is served and that the guests pay for it. Scripts can form families with a common structure but with different combinations of variables, such as 3-star restaurant, cafeteria, fast-food restaurant, Chinese take-away, or sushi bar. Likewise, illness scripts describe the process of contracting a disease: the conditions or constraints under which a disease occurs (the Enabling Conditions), the pathophysiological process that takes place (the Fault, represented in encapsulated form), and the signs and symptoms caused by a specific disease (the Consequences). Illness scripts also include the course a disease may take and the kind of action required to cure it. Physicians have scripts similar to restaurant scripts for all the disease and patient types they commonly see in their practice (also see Feltovich & Barrows, 1984, who introduced this theoretical notion).

In these learning processes complex learning and competence development go hand in hand. Therefore we see a big difference between clinical reasoning based on networks of concepts and clinical reasoning based on illness scripts. Network-based reasoning is done step-by-step. In the case of encapsulated networks, these may be big steps, but they are still taken one at a time. Illness scripts, on the other hand, are activated as a whole. This means that once an illness script has been activated, the other elements of the script are also activated, immediately and automatically. People whose knowledge is organised in illness scripts therefore have an advantage over those who have only semantic networks at their disposal. A physician who solves a problem activates one or a few illness scripts. Information provided by the patient is matched to the illness script elements (Enabling Conditions and Consequences). Furthermore, illness scripts generate expectations about other signs and symptoms the patient might have. Hence, activated illness scripts provide a list of phenomena to look for when taking the patient's history and during physical examination. In the course of this process a script may become further instantiated, i.e. expected values are substituted by real findings. On the other hand, when findings do not match a script become deactivated. The fully instantiated script yields a diagnosis or a differential diagnosis when only a few competing scripts remain active. For the sake of completeness we must add a fourth learning process. Diagnosing and treating patients leaves traces in the memory. These traces can be used later and function as a shortcut to activate relevant knowledge (case-based reasoning, Kolodner, 1993). These changes in the organisation of knowledge bring about changes not only in the appearance of clinical reasoning but also in the amount of control required and, hence, in the demands made on cognitive capacity (Table 1). The latter two aspects are directly related to the number of mistakes that are made in the problem-solving process and with learning efficiency (Sweller, Van Merriënboer, & Paas, 1998).

Table 1. Knowledge structure, learning and cognitive demand in problem solving at subsequent stage of expertise development, derived from Boshuizen and Schmidt (2000)

Expertise level	Knowledge structure	Learning	Problem solving	Control required in clinical reasoning	Demand on cognitive capacity
Novice	Networks (incomplete and loosely linked)	Knowledge accretion, integration and validation	Long chains of detailed reasoning steps through networks A	Active monitoring of each reasoning step	High
Interme-diate	Networks (tightly linked and integrated) C	Encapsulation C	Reasoning through encapsulated network; abbreviated B	Active monitoring of each reasoning step	Medium
Expert	Illness scripts	Illness script formation	Illness script activation and instantiation D	Monitoring of the level of script in-stantiation	Low
	Memory traces	Instantiated scripts	Automatic reminding	Check relevance	Low

From: Clinical reasoning in the health professions, by Higgs and Jones (Eds.). Adapted and reprinted by permission of Elsevier Ltd.

2. NETWORK-BASED REASONING: AN ANNOTATED PROTOCOL

To give you the reader an idea about the problems faced by a student who has to reason through a knowledge network, let me demonstrate a protocol of a case on severe anaemia (presented in Box 2).

Our student was in his 5th year, which is classified as a low intermediate level of expertise. At this level students are immersed in practice as part of their clinical rotations, which start after the 4th year. One may expect reasoning through encapsulated, abbreviated networks, and active monitoring of the problem-solving process (Table 1).

The think-aloud protocol this student produced revealed several remarkable things. Among these are a lack of or insufficient knowledge, a large number of uncertainties, several errors and trials to correct these errors, and revisions and re-evaluations of earlier hypotheses or conclusions. All this can be seen as proof of self-monitoring. Furthermore we see little encapsulated reasoning. Instead, several detailed auxiliary lines of reasoning

---

Box 2 (derived from Boshuizen & Schmidt, 1995)
The bold numbers in brackets refer to remarks in the think-aloud protocol presented later in the text.

The patient is a 65 year old man. He is married and has three children. One girl, 15 years old, still lives with her parents. He is a former entrepreneur and breeds dogs as a hobby. Thirty-five years ago he had a stomach resection because of recurring gastric ulcers; no relapses since then (1). Has had a pharyngitis, 6 to 8 weeks ago, which had healed quickly with a course of penicillin. He does not smoke, but drinks 2-3 glasses of wine per day. Present complaint is that he has become tired and forgetful in the last six months. He feels washed-out and his throat has remained sensitive (2).
Appetite not too good. No nausea or vomiting; micturation no special findings; defecation sometimes a bit mushy. He often has a burning feeling in both feet and lower legs (3).
Physical examination, inspection, patient makes a fatigued, but not very sick impression. His nutritional status is reasonable. Pulse rate 100/min. regular (4). Tension 130/75 mm Hg. Temperature normal. No dyspnoea, oedema or cyanosis. Skin pale-yellowish (5). No spider naevi nor erythema palmare (6). Eyes: pale conjunctivae, normal sclerae. Mouth some discoloration due to recent pharyngitis, smooth tongue surface (7). Thorax: lungs percussion and auscultation no specific findings; heart: strong systolic ejection murmur (3/6) over the aortic area (8). Abdomen: operation scar in the middle of the upper abdomen, liver and spleen not palpable (9). Rectal investigation no findings. Haemocult. negative. Neurological investigation no findings. Laboratory: Hb 4.0 mmol/l. MCV 120, MCH 43, MCHC 32. Reticulocytes 0,5% Leukocytes 4.0, Thrombocytes 110,000 (10). Blood smear: erythrocytes poikilocytosis and macro-ovalocytosis, leukocytes normal differentiation, hyper segmentation of the granulocytes (11). Urine: no findings. Serum: creatinin normal; indirect bilirubin increased (2x) (12); direct normal. SGOT/SGPT normal. LDH increased (3x). Haptoglobin decreased (13). Coombs test direct and indirect negative. Schilling test: decreased absorption (2%) (14).

---

appear. At point (1) in the case, he thinks that this patient may be very susceptible to stress. At point (2) he wonders why the inflamed throat does not heal. Is it a malignancy somewhere due to the stomach resection, resulting in a low resistance and a simple inflammation now? At point (3) he thinks of neuropathy and secret drinking, while at (4) he thinks the patient might be nervous or have an infection. At (5) he thinks of liver pathology, while at (6) he is a little bit reassured about the amount of drinking ("*You should drink a lot to get that.*"). At point (7) he starts reasoning about the smooth tongue surface and the pale conjunctivae.

These remind him of iron deficiency leading to an anaemia; and he recapitulates the causal line of reasoning he is building up: *"The man drinks too much, hence poor feeding pattern, hence iron deficiency and hence burning feet."* The systolic murmur at (8) is dismissed as having no relation at all with the complaint; while at point (9) he concludes again that the effects of alcohol are not so bad (yet). The laboratory findings at (10) make him specify his anaemia hypothesis *"An anaemia, megaloblastic anaemia, hyperchromous",* but due to lack of knowledge he is a little bit confused about the cause and tests some findings against a new hypothesis:

> Then you would think of a *deficit of folic acid*; erm *reticulocytes low*, that is strange, then there would be a sort of *bone marrow process* going on; *thrombocytes* are rather low and few *reticulocytes* and if I would think of *megaloblastic anaemia* then the *reticulocytes* should be rather high, so that is strange. [HB: The student thinks that these findings cannot go together, which is not the case.]

At (11) he thinks that blood cell maturation may be slow, while at (12) he concludes that there is an increased breakdown of blood cells, which is correct. Then at (13) we find some explicit detailed reasoning, again based on incomplete knowledge about direct and indirect bilirubin:

> Low *haptoglobin* means that there is a breakdown of *blood cells* and that increased level of *indirect bilirubin* does indicate that as well, <pause> but *direct bilirubin* is normal, so <pause>.

However, suddenly this train of thought is interrupted and the systolic murmur is reinterpreted, which is a nice example of monitoring his own reasoning process:

> No!, I'm still thinking of that *systolic murmur*, that he might have a *valve problem* and that's why, that this causes an *anaemia*, but then you would expect a *monochromous, normocytic anaemia*. Erm, ... so there is an increased breakdown of *blood cells*, that is clear, but I don't see why the *indirect bilirubin* is increased while the *direct [bilirubin]* is normal.

And again he comes to a dead end, due to imperfect knowledge. At (14) he remembers that the Schilling test is meant for vitamin B12 absorption and concludes that there will be a shortage and he grasps at this straw. His diagnosis at that point is Vitamin B12 deficiency causing anaemia.

We see a student who tries to combine information, but is often not very successful. There are many loose ends and items that are not explained in the light of the final diagnosis. Yet, when asked to explain his diagnosis afterward, he seems to realise some of these mistakes or inconsistencies:

Yes I think of vitamin B12, yes, vitamin B12 deficiency; then you develop an anaemia, hyperchromous, megaloblastic, and then in hindsight I also think that that's why those granulocytes are hypersegmented, and if he had such a severe anaemia of 4 then I see his systolic murmur has a relation to that and erm his drinking, I relate that to this vitamin B12 deficiency, also because of that burning feeling in his feet and his lower legs, erm let me see <pause> Now I also see that his indirect bilirubin is increased, that there is an increased breakdown of blood cells but that the liver can still excrete that, so that the bilirubin can stay normal, so no disturbed liver functions, not yet. Erm <pause>. Yes that he looks so pale-yellowish will have the same cause. Let me see, the Schilling test indicates a deficiency of vitamin B12. Oh wait a minute, <pause> oh wait, that could be because of his stomach resection and that's why he does not have any intrinsic factor any more and cannot take up vitamin B12 in the distal ileum and that's why he will develop that anaemia.

What we see happening here is that this student tries to knot together the loose ends of his think-aloud protocol. The centrepiece of his solution remains the same, vitamin B12 deficiency, but he re-evaluates the cause. Further contemplation on the Schilling test suggests to him that it is not due to secret drinking (which he has suspected, but has no evidence for) but lack of intrinsic factor, due to an old stomach resection. This sudden insight seems to sufficiently solve the problem. Indeed, the student has come quite far applying his knowledge. In terms of quality, the process was a very effortful process with a lot of dead ends; the student was aware of mistakes and inconsistencies; his conclusion is 85 % right, but the student is no longer in doubt. In terms of learning: the knowledge base has been thoroughly explored and all kinds of links have been activated. If the student wants to get more out of it, the process can also yield numerous starting points for reflection and self-directed learning, but the protocol itself does not give us clues that the student intends to do that.

3. (DIS)CONTINUITY OF THE DEVELOPMENT

The description of expertise development so far may suggest that the processes described are continuous and uninterrupted. This indeed has long been hypothesised. Research shows, however, that these processes are less smooth than theory predicts, and based on the above protocol the reader might suspect what kind of problems such a student might run into when s/he suddenly has to work with real patients in real time. In the following paragraphs I first go into more detail regarding the cognitive changes taking place in the process from novice to expert. Based on that I try to find out more about disturbances that may occur. Then I treat the question of what underlies these irregularities and investigate gaps. This treatment is based on an analysis of research findings. Finally we investigate the implications for education.

3.1 A review of studies on knowledge integration and encapsulation

The theory of expertise development suggests that up to the intermediate level predominantly knowledge accretion, validation and encapsulation appear in the student's problem solving. These processes would lead to
1. an initial increase followed by a decrease in the number of biomedical concepts used in clinical reasoning, and also after some time to
2. abbreviations in the reasoning paths. Furthermore, due to the ongoing integration of biomedical and clinical knowledge it would also lead to
3. a better theoretical, biomedical underpinning of the clinical concepts that are often used by experienced physicians in their communication about patients (Table 1).

Working our way backwards through these predictions and the empirical evidence accumulated, we see that prediction C was confirmed in research by Van de Wiel, Boshuizen, Schmidt, and Schaper (1999). They investigated the biomedical grounding of frequently used (higher-order) clinical concepts. Using a knowledge production task they asked subjects with different levels of experience to explain what was meant by that concept, e.g. by uremic complaints, portal hypertension or ascites. Subjects were 4th year medical students who had almost completed the preclinical period, 5th year students after completion of the three-month internal medicine clerkship, and experienced internists. Van de Wiel et al. could show that the amount of biomedical knowledge subsumed by these concepts gradually increased over the years.

More support for the encapsulation hypothesis can be found in results of Boshuizen and Schmidt (1992), who used a knowledge application context. They asked medical students and experts to diagnose a case while thinking aloud. Subjects were 2nd year, 4th year, and 5th year medical students and experienced family physicians. Boshuizen and Schmidt found that the reasoning paths of medical experts were abbreviated indeed, while especially 4th year medical students used more detailed reasoning steps (prediction B).

Schmidt and Boshuizen (1993) investigated the application of biomedical knowledge by asking subjects of different levels of expertise to explain the process that had caused the medical problem described in a clinical case.

Subjects were health sciences students (lay people regarding the domain), 2nd year, 4th year (prediction A), and 6th year medical students, and experienced internists (prediction B). As expected, the number of detailed, biomedical concepts applied in the explanations showed an inverted U-shaped relation with expertise level: The number of biomedical concepts applied by the students increased with increasing expertise levels (A), while experienced physicians used fewer and less detailed biomedical concepts to explain the case (B). This finding suggests an initial increase in biomedical knowledge in the earlier stages of development, followed by a process of knowledge encapsulation under clinical concepts. Custers and colleagues (Custers, 1995; Custers, Boshuizen, & Schmidt, 1999) found similar results. They asked advanced students and experts to describe 20 diseases. Subjects were 4th year and 6th year medical students, interns in training as family physicians and experienced family physicians. Again the more experienced the subjects were, the fewer biomedical concepts they used (prediction B).

So what we see in these studies is a *decrease of use* of biomedical knowledge in clinical reasoning and case explanations, *combined with a continuous increase* in the amount of biomedical knowledge that is *integrated* in the higher order, encapsulating clinical concepts. Apart from integration and encapsulation processes, the data also showed illness script formation and application. For example, Schmidt and Boshuizen (1993) varied the case presentation time. One third of the subjects had a mere 30 seconds to scan the case, while another third was allowed 1 minute 15 seconds. The reading time of the third group was 3 minutes 30 seconds. Subjects of different expertise levels were differently affected by this manipulation. First, the extent of the explanations of the experienced physicians and health sciences students was hardly affected by processing time available, while the more time the medical students (2nd, 4th and 6th year students) had to work on the case, the more extensive their explanations. This finding was in line with the assumption that due to illness script formation expert knowledge can be activated as a whole (represented as "D" in Table 1), while students' knowledge must be activated step-by-step in an active, conscious process.

So far the research described seems to support the hypotheses proposed. However, a couple of research outcomes raise doubts. Custers' design was more complicated than described so far. Actually the study was meant to investigate illness script development. Half of the subjects were asked to describe the clinical picture, while the other subjects were asked to describe prototypical patients having that disease. The reason for these two different questions was that Custers wanted to investigate if subjects describing prototypes would volunteer more information about the kind of patients afflicted by that specific disease than subjects describing clinical pictures.

Especially experienced physicians who had seen more patients during their professional careers would "benefit" more from the prototype instruction. Remarkably, again the subjects of intermediate levels of expertise were largely affected by the different instructions. When they were asked to describe a prototypical patient, their descriptions included far more experiential knowledge than when asked to describe the clinical picture. Again experts and relative novices were hardly affected by the different instructions. Their protocols did not show these discrepancies. These findings suggest that persons at the intermediate levels of expertise do not use one integrated knowledge base; instead students rather switch between bodies of knowledge. Depending on the trigger stimulus they receive, they seem to activate different bodies of knowledge. Novices do not switch, probably because they do not have multiple knowledge bases; experts do not switch because their biomedical, clinical and experiential knowledge is highly integrated and is hence accessible by a multitude of stimuli ("D" in Table 1).

In the theory of expertise development described so far, these kinds of irregularities cannot be accounted for. Another indication that the integration of knowledge bases is not as gradual as expected is given by the results found by Boshuizen and Schmidt as early as 1992. In fact, it was the very first think-aloud study we did, but for a long time we neglected this outcome. Subjects were 2nd year, 4th year, and 5th year medical students and experienced family physicians. The results of this study suggest that 5th year medical students (shortly after they have entered the clinical clerkships) use hardly any biomedical knowledge in think-aloud, clinical reasoning tasks, while the 4th year students do a lot. This finding could be interpreted as an adaptation to their clinical environment where long detailed lines of reasoning are not encouraged. However, the biomedical knowledge applied in the explanations of the case the subjects provided afterwards did *not* show a corresponding dip. Therefore, this discrepancy might again indicate that students at this stage switch knowledge bases depending on the perceived task demands or trigger stimuli.

So although there is strong evidence in favour of a continuous process of knowledge integration followed by knowledge encapsulation and illness script formation, other findings suggest a *discontinuity* in the development. The outcomes also suggest that this observed discontinuity is *triggered by the start of the clinical clerkships.* However, firm conclusions cannot be drawn based on these studies, because most experiments reported here employed groups that were quite far apart in levels of expertise. Usually differences between these groups are at least two years. An exception is the Boshuizen and Schmidt 1992 study, in which 2nd year, 4th year, 5th year students and family physicians participated. However, in this study the number of subjects was rather small (five per expertise level). Hence a new experiment was designed that will be presented here in a bit more detail. It was meant to investigate the process of biomedical knowledge application using larger groups of subjects with expertise levels that are less far apart, hence enabling a more detailed analysis of the developmental path (Boshuizen, 1994).

3.2 A large-scale think-aloud study on biomedical and clinical reasoning

A large-scale think-aloud study using both follow-up and cross-sectional data was conducted. The participants we recruited for this study were 4th- and 5th year medical students who analysed four cases; two cases were presented at the end of their 4th and 5th year respectively, the other two cases were presented one year later. Indeed, most students participated twice; only one 4th year student could not be contacted, while two 5th year students were not available for the second session one year later. Hence data of 30 4th year, 53 5th year and 22 6th year medical students could be collected. Furthermore, a reference group of a sample of 16 experienced physicians was included. Due to equipment failure and time available per session several subjects did not generate the four protocols that could be expected. In this way 184 (!) analysable protocols were collected: 59 produced by 4th year students, 66 by 5th years, 42 by 6th years and 17 by medical specialists.

The following measures were derived from the protocols. The quality of the reasoning process is reflected in the quality of the outcome, i.e. the diagnosis. Expertise development should also be associated with a decrease of the length of the think-aloud protocol. Furthermore, a decrease in the application of biomedical concepts can be expected, as well as a decrease of a specific kind of biomedical reasoning, the use of auxiliary reasoning where first the normal situation is recalled and, based on that, a case finding is interpreted. Examples can be found in the protocol analysis given before. Due to the considerable number of missing values, data were analysed as if it were a cross-sectional design. Apart from ANOVA, group differences were tested with a Bonferoni-Dunn test at the 5 % level.

Does Practice Make Perfect?

What we found was the following. First of all the accuracy of the diagnosis increased with expertise level. As is shown in Figure 1, experts had better diagnoses than 6th year students who had better diagnoses than 5th year students and so on. Yet the differences between the 4th and the 5th year students and the 6th year students and specialists were not significant. This increase is expected, but the fact that one year of clinical experience did not add significantly to it was not. Even more telling about disruptive processes taking place in the first practical year were the findings on the reasoning process that resulted in this diagnosis.

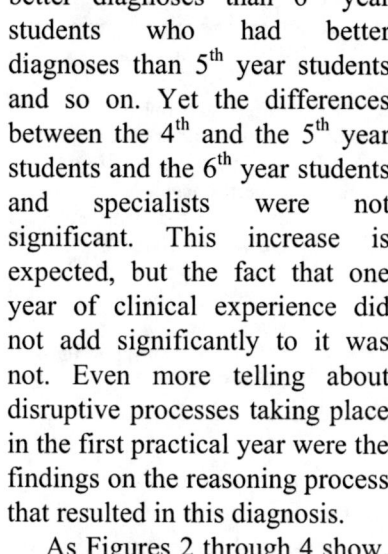

Figure 1. Diagnostic accuracy of subjects of four expertise levels (4th, 5th and 6th year students and medical specialists). All group differences are significant, except the difference between 4th and 5th year students, and between 6th year students and specialists.
($F(3,241) = 10.87$, $p < .001$, $MSe = 1.43$)

As Figures 2 through 4 show, again especially the difference between the 4th year students and the other groups is striking: the 4th year students generated the longest protocols, used most biomedical concepts and generated most auxiliary lines of reasoning, followed by a steep decline; on all measures the 5th year students showed fewest elaborations.

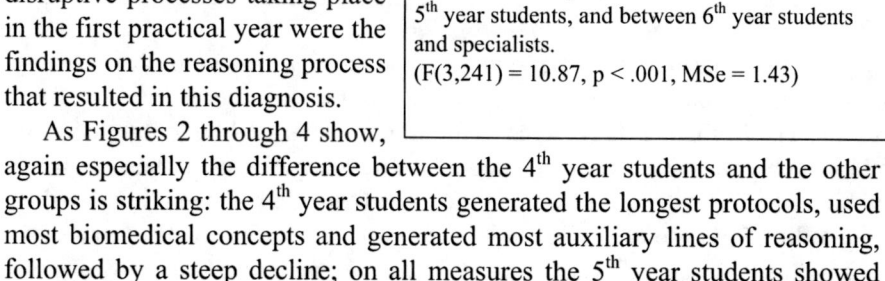

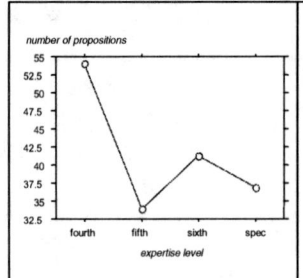

Figure 2. Number of knowledge application propositions generated by subjects of four expertise levels (4th, 5th, and 6th year students and medical specialists). Differences between 4th and 5th year students are significant. ($F(3,186) = 4.74$, $p < .01$, MSe= 957.74)

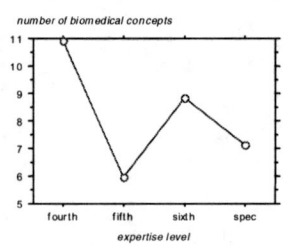

Figure 3. Number of biomedical concepts used by subjects of four expertise levels (4th, 5th, and 6th year students and medical specialists). Differences between 4th and 5th year students are significant. ($F(3,182) = 5.48$, $p < .01$, MSe = 48.94)

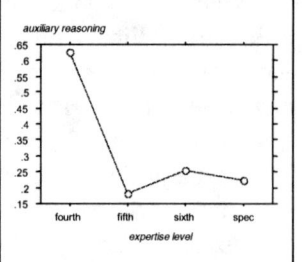

Figure 4. Number of auxiliary lines of reasoning used by subjects of four expertise levels (4th, 5th, and 6th year students and medical specialists). Differences between 4th and 5th year students are significant. ($F(3,182) = 3.73$, $p < .05$, MSe = .63)

Before declaring that this outcome indicates a crisis in the learning process, it is wise first to have a look at less painful interpretations of the results. The following three come to mind: incidental finding, output editing, and switching between not-yet-integrated knowledge bases. Given the large number of subjects and the fact that the same outcome has been found earlier with a different case and with subjects of partly different levels of expertise (but with the 4th and 5th year students we have employed here as well), we must conclude that it is a consistent finding. The explanation of output editing has been brought forward by critics of earlier studies (e.g., Boshuizen & Schmidt, 1992). The critics proposed that the finding that 5th year students, for whom the role of a clerk or intern is still quite new (it was their second or third rotation), would use significantly fewer biomedical concepts to adjust themselves to the norms of the clinic (the faster and shorter an answer is, the better) and hence would suppress long detailed lines of reasoning. Our objection at that time to this 'output editing explanation' of the finding could only be that the protocols were obtained in a situation very different from the daily clinical work and that a think-aloud instruction rather encourages verbosity than brevity. It can now be extended with the observation that it is a consistent finding and that the protocols of the 6th year students tend to be more extensive than those produced when they were in their 5th year. Moreover, there is no ground for assuming that the 6th year students have less reason to suppress detailed reasoning; on the contrary, they might have even better adapted to the clinical situation.

Given the sharp decrease in biomedical concepts applied in clinical reasoning, the hypothesis of knowledge encapsulation as a continuous process due to knowledge application in (practical) clinical cases probably cannot be sustained. A third alternative explanation for the finding could be that students at this level of expertise development switch between knowledge bases that only later become integrated. The idea is that lay people, novices and experts would use one integrated knowledge base, while 5th and 6th year students switch between biomedical and practical knowledge, depending on the task, as in the Custers et al. (1999) study. Indeed, overall the application of auxiliary, biomedical lines of reasoning indeed decreases after the 4th year: 5th year students and more experienced subjects hardly ever use this kind of reasoning. However, if 5th- (and 6th-)year students switched knowledge bases and applied clinical knowledge in diagnostic tasks, then not only the number, but also the proportion of biomedical concepts in their think-aloud protocols should sharply diminish. This is not the case: The mean proportion of biomedical concepts in these protocols does not vary very much over the groups and is about 15 % ($F < 1$). However, the standard deviations are largest for the 5th and 6th year students. This suggests that some 5th and 6th year students proceed to apply biomedical knowledge (like the 5th year student whose protocol is used in this article to demonstrate network-based reasoning), while others do not. However, the outcome that 5th year students on average produce the shortest protocols does not fit very well with the idea that they use one of two knowledge bases that are still in the process of reconstruction.

So, is there a crisis in learning and development? What is happening with the 5th year students, who after a few rotations find themselves in a situation where their diagnoses are not better than those given by 4th year students, and their post-hoc explanations are not better either, although these become less detailed and more coherent (Boshuizen, 1994), and who use fewer biomedical concepts and auxiliary lines of reasoning in their clinical reasoning, while a year later they seem to have partly overcome these effects? At least they say they feel lots of stress and are required to develop new study skills. Both factors could account for this delay (see Prince & Boshuizen, this volume). The phenomenon also reminds us of processes in child development, in which a child may move from one stage of skill mastery to a next, but before the next level is reached goes through a period during which performance is lower than before and after. Examples can be found in the domain of language development: a two- or three-year-old who learns the past tense and past particle of irregular verbs. At first the child may say "broke", later followed by "breaked", finally ending as "broke". In this transition period they are figuring out new rules and when/how they apply. A process like this may be based on complete reorganization of the knowledge base, but also on fine-tuning of the knowledge to the conditions under which they apply in (clinical) everyday life (Klahr, 1995). Our own data are not suitable to test such a hypothesis. However, the research outcomes of Scherpbier (1997) may corroborate this hypothesis. Scherpbier's subjects were 2nd to 6th year students from the same medical school as used in the study presented here. They completed a knowledge-about-skills test. This is a paper-and-pencil test that investigates students' knowledge about the conditions for application of specific diagnostic and therapeutic procedures and about the clinical implications of the outcomes. Scherpbier expected an increase in performance on this test, which is routinely found in practical skills tests in this population. Indeed, he found such an increase in test performance, except for the 5th year students. In the first year of practical clerkships knowledge on skills had not significantly improved, while a naive expectation would be that this experience would instead boost the growth of this kind of knowledge. Evidently this is not the case. Learning about application conditions might be more difficult than one would expect; it is not simply an automatic fine-tuning process, but a process that might require restructuring as well.

4. EDUCATIONAL IMPLICATIONS

Regardless of the reason for the cognitive discontinuity observed, it is a phenomenon that should alert clinical and preclinical teachers. If students, during this phase of their training, are not well able to activate relevant knowledge, then the educational practices in the clinical and preclinical periods should be scrutinised. Probably the sharp contrast between these two stages in their training, even in the problem-based curriculum of the University Maastricht (paper cases and simulated patients vs. real patients; ample time vs. time pressure; peer group setting vs. hierarchical setting; student-centred vs. patient-centred; no responsibility for patients at all vs. some responsibility; etc.), might be the cause for a knowledge structure that does not fit the requirements of the tasks in the clerkships and non-matching learning skills. A more gradual change, with more practical patient-centred experiences in the preclinical phase and more problem-based tutorials in the clinical phase might help students to bridge this gap.

4.1 Knowledge structure

The knowledge structure students build up is the result of the cognitive action they perform on this knowledge. The processes of knowledge validation and integration, encapsulation and illness script formation only take place when students do tasks that afford these processes *and* when they do them is such a way that this specific learning effect is elicited. For example, a paper patient case may be supposed to induce the analysis and combination of case data, hypothesis generation and testing, comparing the plausibility of possible diagnoses, and, based on that evaluation and other criteria, decide what action should be taken. Yet, this will only lead to an illness script-like structure when the students indeed take all these steps. However, if they take a shortcut by identifying the unique feature of a specific diagnosis (which is often available in designed paper cases, but hardly ever in real practice), and reason back from this diagnosis, then a knowledge structure develops that does not fit the requirements in practice, as was apparent in Prince's study (Prince, Van de Wiel, Scherpbier, Van der Vleuten, & Boshuizen, 2000).

Many authors emphasise the importance of whole task training that requires authentic tasks; authentic in task appearance and authentic in cognitive processing. To make things easier for the student and hence more instructive, a great variety of learning tasks has been developed, ranging from worked-out examples to the traditional practice assignments. Other formats are completion tasks that invite the learner to fill in the blanks or to complete the story; and annotated worked-out examples that show the learner the strategic choices and knowledge and skill application. Remarkably, these different kinds of formats are hardly used in university and college, which is a pity, as different learning tasks have different effects on cognitive load, and hence on learning efficiency and outcome (Sweller et al., 1998). And as we have seen earlier in this chapter, level of expertise is inversely related to the demands on cognitive capacity of a specific task. Hence we should be careful with plunging students right into real cases. This should best be preceded by other formats, provided that these induce authentic cognitive processes. From this perspective the claim by De Vries Robbé, Stuyt, and Van der Meer (1995) can be interpreted, who strongly advocate that students learn a systematic decision-making method, not for the sake of the method as such, but because seeing cases worked out this way and doing it themselves would lead to knowledge that is better organised.

4.2 Learning skills

Practical experience as a learning resource is thought to support several learning goals: learning to work and working procedures, competence building, fine-tuning of skills and scripts, connecting knowledge to application conditions, and, depending on the quality of the knowledge base, restructuring or encapsulation. Learning in and from practice requires teaching and learning skills and beliefs about learning that are not fostered in formal education. Applying knowledge in a practical setting has some automatic learning effects on links and structure. However, practical learning is more than that. Learning from and through experience is a far more self-directed and active process, and has some in-built contradictions, which makes it difficult. First, learning from practice takes place in an environment that is not built for learning. The environment requires performance: patients should be treated, cars repaired, meals served, cows milked, aircraft flown to their destination. There is always a tension between requirements for learning and performance, especially for students who enter such a situation with a known lack of knowledge. Furthermore, in order to learn from practice students should be aware of their own learning goals, search for and use opportunities and monitor the status of their learning, and they have to do this in an environment that is only partly under their control.

Some of the learning goals can best be reached through implicit learning. Script enrichment and fine-tuning of skills are probably examples, as is link strengthening. What is unclear is what the optimal conditions are for implicit learning that happens as a by-product of action or experience (Hayes & Broadbent, 1988).

The very nature of experiential learning makes it hard for learners or even teachers or coaches to plan. The only possibility can be to offer or seek out opportunities. All an individual can do otherwise is to try to make the best of it. This, however, requires students to at least understand what their experiences entail and what it is that they have come across. Better students, or better experiential learners, know in advance what they might see and experience in an upcoming situation. Without an interpretation frame and without preparation, students may completely overlook essential aspects of an episode they observe.

> For example, a student told us that he had been sitting in with a counsellor who had told him that his plan was to tell a client that it was about time to pick up the thread of her life again and get a job. The student had been rather sceptical about this plan and was very surprised that it worked out the way the expert had told him it would. Without knowing this plan in advance, the student might not have even seen that something remarkable, at least by his own standards, had taken place before his eyes. Now he was aware that he had witnessed something very instructive, and afterward he was able to identify the critical elements that had contributed to this positive outcome.

Having an interpretation frame (developed by the student him- or herself or passed on by an expert) and planning and preparing for experiences contributes to learning results. The question is whether students and teacher do this routinely as a strategy for learning from experience. Probably not.

A strategy that is especially supposed to be effective for competence building is the action-reflection-action cycle that we find in many different forms in the work of such authors as Boud, Keogh, and Walker (1988), Kolb (1984), Korthagen (1992, 1999), and Schön (1987). These authors assume that reflecting on experiences plays a critical role in learning. Reflection should lead to plans for new actions in which novel approaches and ways of dealing with problems can be tested. Again, the question is whether students do this. But again, the answer is probably not, as a study undertaken by Wagenaar and colleagues shows (Wagenaar, Scherpbier, Boshuizen, & Van der Vleuten, 2003). Students (again medical and health sciences students during their clerkships) reported that they learned mainly by doing, which is an implicit way of learning, and a little bit by observing or from preparation and reflection. No student reported full cycles of action-reflection-action. Korthagen (1999) found similar results, i.e. that novice teachers display little continuity in their reflection-based learning process. This means that novice teachers may well come to conclusions about the good and less optimal aspects of their behaviour and problem solutions, but they then fail to draw conclusions on how these could be improved, never draw up concrete action plans for future situations or, if they do, do not implement these concrete plans. Korthagen also investigated barriers to reflection in beginning teachers, who evidently hold beliefs about learning that reflect the passive 'hand over' view of learning that still prevails in formal education. From these analyses it may be concluded that experiential learning requires different study and teaching skills that need explicit attention and should be included in the design of such learning arrangements.

To conclude this topic, it is valuable to realise that features of the workplace itself also add to this. The first feature relates to the learning strategy of preparation and trying out new action. The better one can predict and control situations, the easier it is to use this strategy. However, in many domains an experience does not consist of discrete episodes. An experience can be hard to prepare for in the way the student did who witnessed a client being helped back on her feet again. For newcomers in particular, many real-life tasks can be quite unpredictable. It is hard for them to see when and in combination with which other competencies a specific competence should be applied. In such situations deliberate action is the exception, not the rule. Teaching is a good example. Teachers have to apply multiple competencies simultaneously, depending on the emerging situation; for example they have to teach the subject matter, monitor the students' understanding of it, monitor and evaluate student behaviour and subsequently act on it, take the person of the student into consideration, and all this in real time. Eraut

(2003) calls this a situation in which 'routines are punctuated by rapid decisions'. Learning in these situations will require whole-task approaches to make sure that the student learns the rhythm of the situation and the conditions under which things can happen. Situations may be simplified (e.g., schools should not give the most difficult groups to newcomers), support and scaffolding may be offered, but the tasks cannot be reduced nor can the rapid decisions be practised and prepared for in isolation. Training isolated subtasks is only relevant for tasks that can be routinised independently (Van Merriënboer, 1997).

4.3 A slow and discontinuous process?

In a final remark I want to readdress the issue that expertise development is a slow and discontinuous process. In this chapter I have presented a theory that gives the impression that expertise development is a continuous process and empirical findings that show that this is not (always) the case. The effects of some of the causes for that discontinuity can be largely alleviated with educational measures that address learning skills, redesign of experiential learning (including teacher skills) and the use of authentic learning tasks with adequate cognitive load given the level of expertise of the student.

For many students practical experience is what makes them tick, even though they dread the stress. Keeping them in school too long will lead to loss of motivation, learning for exams instead of learning for competence, all other kinds of dysfunctional study behaviour and a knowledge base that does not match practical requirements. So another trick is to design learning in such a way that practical experience is introduced into the curriculum as early as possible. However, the workplace does not give free and full access to newcomers. In Wenger's (1998) terms, legitimate peripheral participation may be allowed, but the entrance ticket must be paid by doing chores and being of use (Fessey, 2000). Students are very well aware of this situation.

Regarding the slowness of development, I am not sure how much this can be speeded up. Earlier in this chapter I presented evidence that integration of basic science knowledge seems to take much longer than teachers expect. These complex learning processes have to be integrated in competence building as a whole. However, it is very hard to reach these goals through authentic cases, even if these cases lend themselves perfectly to that (Van de Wiel, Boshuizen & Schmidt, 1998). Many students seem to prefer to elaborate on the professional perspective of the case over the scientific and analytic; taking both perspectives will definitely lead to increased cognitive demands. Therefore, timing and interleaving complex learning and competence learning deserves our full attention. The domain of complex learning has been neglected recently in educational research but definitely needs our renewed attention.

NOTE

The author gratefully acknowledges the NAE / Spencer Foundation for a supporting grant.

REFERENCES

Ackermann, W., & Barbichon, G. (1963). Conduites intellectuelles et activité technique. *Bulletin CERP, 12*, 1-16.

Allwood, C. M., & Montgomery, H. (1981). Knowledge and technique in statistical problem solving. *European Journal of Science Education, 3*, 431-450.

Bédard, J. (1989). Expertise in auditing: Myth or reality? *Accounting, Organizations and Society, 14*, 113-131.

Bloom, B. S., & Broder, L. J. (1950). *Problem solving processes of college students.* Chicago: University of Chicago Press.

Boshuizen, H. P. A. (1994). Cognitive effects of practical experience in high and low achieving medical students. *Learning and Instruction, 4*, 313-329.

Boshuizen, H. P. A., & Schmidt, H. G. (1992). On the role of biomedical knowledge in clinical reasoning by experts, intermediates and novices. *Cognitive Science, 16,* 153-184.

Boshuizen, H. P. A., & Schmidt, H. G. (1995). De ontwikkeling van medische expertise; implicaties voor het practisch en theoretisch medisch onderwijs. In J. C. M. Metz, A. J. J. A. Scherpbier, & C. P. M. Van der Vleuten (Eds.), *Medisch onderwijs in de praktijk* [Medical education in practice] (pp. 25-39). Assen: Van Gorcum.

Boshuizen, H. P. A., & Schmidt, H. G (2000). The development of clinical reasoning expertise. Implications for teaching. In J. Higgs & M. Jones (Eds.), *Clinical reasoning in the health professions* (2nd, completely rev. ed., pp. 15-22). Oxford: Butterworth-Heinemann.

Boshuizen, H. P. A., & Van de Wiel, M. W. J. (1998). Multiple representations in medicine; How students struggle with it. In M. W. Van Someren, P. Reimann, H. P. A. Boshuizen, & T. De Jong (Eds.), *Learning with multiple representations* (pp. 237-262).Amsterdam: Elsevier.

Boud, D., Keogh, R., & Walker, D. (1988). Promoting reflection in learning: A model. In D. Boud, R. Keogh, & D. Walker (Eds.), *Reflection: Turning experiences into learning* (pp. 18-40). London: Kogan Page.

Chi, M. T. H., Feltovich, P. J., & Glaser, R. (1981). Categorization and representation of physics problems by experts and novices. *Cognitive Science, 5*, 121-152.

Custers, E. J. F. M. (1995). *The development and function of illness scripts; Studies on the structure of medical diagnostic knowledge.* Maastricht: UPM.

Custers, E. J. F. M., Boshuizen, H. P. A., & Schmidt, H. G. (1999). The role of illness scripts in the development of medical expertise: results from an interview study. *Cognition and Instruction, 16*, 367-398.

De Groot, A. D. (1965). *Thought and choice in chess.* The Hague: Mouton.

De Vries Robbé, P. F., Stuyt, P. M. J., & Van der Meer, J. W. M. (1995). Onderwijs in methodisch denken in de praktische geneeskunde. In J. C. M. Metz, A. J. J. A. Scherpbier, & C. P. M. Van der Vleuten (Eds.), *Medisch onderwijs in de praktijk* [Medical education in practice] (pp. 58-68). Assen: Van Gorcum.

Elstein, A. S., Shulman, L. S., & Sprafka, S. A. (1978). *Medical problem solving: An analysis of clinical reasoning.* Cambridge: Harvard University Press.

Eraut, M. (2003). Transition of knowledge between education and the workplace. In H. P. A. Boshuizen (Ed.), *Expertise development: The transition between school and work* (pp. 55-73). Heerlen: Open Universiteit Nederland.

Ericsson, K. A. (1996). The acquisition of expert performance: An introduction to some of the issues. In K. A. Ericsson (Ed.), *The road to excellence: The acquisition of expert performance in the arts, and sciences, sports and games* (pp. 1-50). Mahwah: Erlbaum.

Feltovich, P. J., & Barrows, H. S. (1984). Issues of generality in medical problem solving. In H. G. Schmidt & M. L. De Volder (Eds.), *Tutorials in problem-based learning. A new direction in teaching the health professions* (pp. 128-142). Assen: Van Gorcum.

Fessey, C. (2000). Capturing expertise in the development of practice: Methodology and approaches. *Learning in Health and Social Care, 1* (1), 47-58.

Groothuis, S., Boshuizen, H. P. A., & Talmon, J. L. (1998). Is endocrinology as easy as they say? An analysis of the conceptual difficulties of the domain. *Teaching and Learning in Medicine, 10,* 207-217.

Hayes, N., & Broadbent, D. (1988). Two modes of learning for interactive tasks. *Cognition, 23,* 80-108.

Klahr, D. (1995). Computational models of cognitive development: The state of the art. In T. J. Simon & G. S. Halford (Eds.), *Developing cognitive competence: New approaches to process modeling.* (pp. 355-375). Hillsdale: Erlbaum.

Kolb, D. A. (1984). *Experiential learning: Experience as a source of learning and development.* Englewood Cliffs: Prentice Hall.

Kolodner, J. (1993). *Case-based reasoning.* San Francisco: Morgan Kaufman.

Korthagen, F. (1992). Reflectie en professionele ontwikkeling van leraren. [Reflection and professional development of teachers] *Pedagogische Studiën, 69,* 112-123.

Korthagen, F. (1999). Linking reflection and technical competence: the logbook as an instrument in teacher education. *European Journal of Teacher Education, 22,* 191-207.

Prince, K. J. A. H., Van de Wiel, M. W. J., Scherpbier, A. J. J. A., Van der Vleuten, C. P. M., & Boshuizen, H. P. A. (2000). A qualitative analysis of the transition from theory to practice in undergraduate training in a PBL-medical school. *Advances in Health Sciences, 5,* 105-116.

Schank, R. C., & Abelson, R. P. (1977). *Scripts, plans, goals and understanding.* Hillsdale: Erlbaum.

Scherpbier, A. J. J. A. (1997). *De kwaliteit van vaardigheidsonderwijs gemeten.* [The quality of skills teaching investigated] Maastricht: UPM.

Schmidt, H. G., & Boshuizen, H. P. A. (1992). Encapsulation of biomedical knowledge. In D. A. Evans & V. L. Patel (Eds.), *Advanced models of cognition for medical training and practice* (pp. 265-281). New York: Springer.

Schmidt, H. G., & Boshuizen, H. P. A. (1993). On the origin of intermediate effects in clinical case recall. *Memory and Cognition, 21,* 338-351.

Schmidt, H. G., Boshuizen, H. P. A., & Norman, G. R. (1992). Reflections on the nature of expertise in medicine. In E. Keravnou (Ed.), *Deep models for medical knowledge engineering* (pp. 231-248). Amsterdam: Elsevier.

Schön, D. A. (1987*). Educating the reflective practitioner.* San Francisco: Jossey-Bass.

Sweller, J., Van Merriënboer, J. J. G., & Paas, F. (1998). Cognitive architecture and instructional design. *Educational Review, 10,* 251-295.
Van de Wiel, M. W. J. (1997). *Knowledge encapsulation: Studies on the development of medical expertise.* Maastricht: Universiteit Maastricht.
Van de Wiel, M. W. J., Boshuizen, H. P. A., Schmidt, H. G., & Schaper, N. C. (1999). The explanation of clinical concepts by expert physicians, clerks, and advanced students. *Teaching and Learning in Medicine, 11,* 153-163.
Van de Wiel, M. W. J., Boshuizen, H. P. A., & Schmidt, H. G. (1998). A failure to replicate the intermediate effect in clinical case recall. *Academic Medicine, 73,* 894-900.
Van Merriënboer, J. J. G. (1997). *Training complex cognitive skills.* Englewood Cliffs: Educational Technology.
Wagenaar, A., Scherpbier, A. J. J. A., Boshuizen, H. P. A., & Van der Vleuten, C. P. M. (2003). The importance of active involvement in learning: A qualitative study on learning results and learning processes in different traineeships. *Advances in Health Sciences Education, 8,* 201-212.
Wenger, E. (1998). *Communities of practice; Learning meaning, and identity.* Cambridge: Cambridge University Press.

Chapter 6

FOSTERING MANAGERIAL PROBLEM-SOLVING
From cognitive research to instructional design to expertise

Jos A. R. Arts, Wim H. Gijselaers and Mien S. R. Segers
Faculty of Economics and Business Administration, Department of Educational Development and Educational Research, University Maastricht, The Netherlands

1. MANAGEMENT EDUCATION AND PROBLEM-SOLVING SKILLS

Management education is expected to produce graduates who have the knowledge and skills needed to function effectively in the workplace. However, management programs have long been criticised for their failure to prepare graduates adequately for dealing with daily business reality. Many critics of management education argue that graduates are not prepared to respond to work situations in ways for which employers are calling (Bigelow, 2001). A recurring criticism of graduates in management concerns their problem-solving abilities (Boyatzis, Cowen, & Kolb, 1995; Business-Higher Education Forum, 1999). In this article, we explore how managerial problem-solving abilities develop over time. We examine how cognitive performance varies from managerial novices (students) to those in the work place with high levels of expertise. Finally we provide an example of a learning environment in which the aim is to foster the solving of ill-structured managerial problems. The instructional design of this learning environment draws on outcomes from the current and previous studies of the expertise required for problem-solving.

Today, problem-solving abilities are expressed as core skills and competencies in management curricula. Management education is considered indispensable in contributing to the acquisition of such skills and competencies. Yet management education has been regularly criticized on the grounds that graduates are not equipped with appropriate problem-solving skills. In other words, they are too alienated from the managerial workplace (Business-Higher Education Forum, 1999). A weakness perceived by employers is that business schools currently focus more on problem analysis than on problem finding, creating novel approaches to problem solution and risk taking (Porter & McKibbin, 1988).

Those who employ management graduates do not complain of a lack of specialized knowledge, rather they criticize their ability to face today's problems and to acquire new knowledge (Gijselaers, 2000). Given their selection criteria, employers seem to prefer graduates with generic skills. A possible reason for this is that current information and knowledge has a short lifecycle and accumulates more rapidly than ever (Boshuizen, 2003; Gijselaers, 2000). Whatever the reason for this mismatch between the qualities of graduates and the expectations of the business world, schools of management should not fall into the trap of neglecting the role of knowledge in their curricula. As many authors argue, generic problem-solving abilities can only be acquired through the use (application) of content knowledge (Bowden & Marton, 1998; Bransford & Schwartz, 1999). In this context, Bransford and Schwartz (1999, p. 94) warn that "A potential danger of the preparation for future learning perspective is that it could lead to claims such as 'I'm teaching for future learning, so I don't worry about mastery of content.'" Therefore, we take the view that problem-solving skills can only be acquired and developed in the context of applying content knowledge.

During the 1990s business schools made increasing efforts to address criticisms of management education by, for example placing greater emphasis on skills acquisition and designing multidisciplinary courses intended to foster integration between disciplines in developing the managerial skills of students. Despite these efforts, the Business-Higher Education Forum's 1997 report, "Spanning the Chasm", noted that changes were still needed to facilitate the transition from high school university campus-to-the workplace, and to encourage closer links between the academic and corporate sectors. Similarly, a survey of employers by ACNielsen (2000) concluded that graduates are deficient in various skills and have a lack of understanding of business practice. Overall, there is still little evidence that undergraduate programs have responded sufficiently to these criticisms (Bigelow, 2001).

Despite all the attempts at reform, many business schools still face the problem of bridging the gap between educational and professional practice. This creates a challenge for management education as it seeks to provide a better fit with the demands of the workplace. In order to optimise management curricula (content) and instruction (form) it is important to get a better understanding of how management education can equip students with the knowledge and skills, that contribute to effective managerial problem-solving, and of how these connect to the needs of the managerial workplace. Approaches to optimising education in this respect have often been driven by demands from the workplace about what is required from graduates and not on a sound, factual analysis of differences between new graduates and experts in performing relevant tasks. Therefore, in studying managerial problem-solving an important question is: What are the cognitive performance differences between managerial novices and experts?

The novice-expert approach that we use in this article typically focuses on assessing expert behaviour in terms of outstanding performers. In the novice-expert research paradigm, expert behaviour is compared with that of managerial novices (students) in order to develop an improved understanding of students' problem-solving behaviour.

2. THE MANAGERIAL PROBLEM-SOLVING CONTEXT

The experimental studies highlighted in this article were conducted in the managerial domain (in the field of marketing and organization). As such, the managerial domain serves as the broad context of study. The most obvious object of study in the managerial domain is an organization (e.g. a firm). Within an organization we can consider (1) the role and functioning of *humans as objects* and (2) the managerial *problems* that are encountered.

Below we will illustrate that the characteristics of these managerial problems can influence the problem-solving. Next we will investigate how the expertise (in quantity and quality) of the problem solver influences problem-solving.

2.1 Characteristics of managerial problems related to problem-solving

Unlike problems that can be solved with procedures, business problems have some distinctive features that are considered below.

2.1.1 Ill-structuredness

Management represents a domain where most problems are ill-structured and there are few consistent solutions (Lash, 1988). For many managerial problems the information sifted in seeking to solve them is often incomplete and ambiguous and may prove to be redundant. Alongside the distinction between ill-structured and well-structured problems is that between formal and practical problems (Wickelgren, 1974). Examples of formal problems are those of a 'to-prove' nature, which are found in quantitative areas such as mathematics and physics, where knowledge is relatively well structured (Lash, 1988). Practical or ill-structured problems are different from well-defined formal problems as there are no specific ways (algorithms) to solve them (Wickelgren, 1974). These ill-structured problems can have a number of causes and often have more than one possible solution. There is no such thing as the answer to a managerial problem (Baets & Van der Linden, 2000). For instance, there can be a number of different reasons why company X has lost turnover or market share. In providing data and other evidence one can argue that a certain cause is the most likely reason for this business problem but, depending on one's the point of view, other causes can also be suggested. In general, the range of all the outcome possibilities for ill-structured, practical problems (generally referred to as problem space) is wider than for formal problems. Moreover, when the level of agreement about possible solution paths for a problem is low, the problem space is large. A typical feature of ill-structured problems is that the multiplicity of possible diagnoses and solution paths can lead to a large number of problem searches (Simon, 1973; Wickelgren, 1974). This illustrates the point that solving managerial problems can be a complex process.

Mintzberg (1973) has argued that a lot of management schools are more effective in training students to handle structured than unstructured problems. Mintzberg further contends that students are too often trained in the making of choices, rather than problem-solving, since they are provided with a package of data, issues and problems, rather than having to derive or find these for themselves. Managerial problem-solving, however, is characterized by ambiguity, which means that very little information and analysis is given to the manager, and almost none of this is structured (Mintzberg, 1973). The ability to cope with fragmentation and unpredictability is in fact the major requirement for managers (Mintzberg, 1980; Peters, 1988). Real world problems do not come in well-scripted, "canned", 10-page cases from Harvard. Instead, they are messy, with incomplete and sometimes inaccurate data (Revans, 1980). A feature of managerial problems - related to ill-structuredness - is that in practice the symptoms are not always clearly visible on the surface. In business practice it is up to the manager to *determine* whether or not a situation can be considered a problem. Symptoms of managerial problems are not always presented explicitly, as is regularly the case in medical practice. And the interpretation of indicators is dependent on the context. For example, a business result of 4 % might be very good in one context, like supermarkets, but a disaster in other fields, such as flight security. Therefore, a first step in managerial problem-solving is to identify problems and to decide on the basis of the available data whether or not a problem exists and, if it does, the nature of the problem.

2.1.2 Multi-disciplinarity

A second important feature of managerial problems is that many are of a multi-disciplinary nature (De Leeuw, 1996). Given that the managerial sciences have originated from a variety of disciplines, such as economics, sociology and psychology (Clegg & Ross-Smith, 2003), this should not be unexpected. Thus, a business problem can be related to psychology (consumer behaviour), to organisational structures, or to quantitative economics. As a result, an interdisciplinary approach to solving problems is required (De Leeuw, 1996). Applying one discipline may only lead to a partial solution. Because of the multidisciplinary approach required for tackling many business problems, it may be unclear which particular area of expertise is required to arrive at acceptable solutions (O'Rourke, 1998).

2.1.3 Complexity

From the previous section it can be concluded that real managerial problems are complex because they require multiple viewpoints and have multiple solution paths. Mintzberg indeed has argued that managerial problems are often extremely complex (Mintzberg, 1973). Since professional *team* settings offer the possibility of sharing multiple viewpoints and ideas, it can be argued that such teams are most likely basis for effectively solving authentic business problems. Besides, today business problems are too complex and too large to be solved by individuals working alone.

2.2 Conclusion

We have illustrated that characteristics of business problems (ill-structuredness, multi-disciplinarity and complexity) can influence the process of managerial decision-making. An implication is that managerial education should be based on further awareness and understanding of the cognitive processes that are involved in information processing and decision-making in a management setting. Better understanding of these processes can improve the role of managerial education in providing the right knowledge and skills for students. For the remainder of the paper we will use the term *expertise* for the appropriate use of managerial knowledge and demonstration of cognitive skills.

3. STUDYING MANAGERIAL PROBLEM SOLVING.

In the 1990s considerable emphasis was placed on the cognitive aspects of managerial reasoning in resolving complex managerial problems (Walsh, 1995). Isenberg (1986) was one of the first to investigate managerial problem solving by using a cognitive approach. In comparing management students and experienced managers, Isenberg showed that managers were less reflective than students in how they went about performing the case analysis. One would have expected that experienced managers would be more reflective, but other research has also shown that, in fact, novices are more expressive in a field with which they are unfamiliar (Boshuizen, 2003). Isenberg's other findings were that managers commenced action planning sooner than students and that managers reasoned from information rather than merely categorized it (Isenberg, 1986). Lash (1988) and Van Fossen and Miller (1994) also found substantial differences between experienced managers and management students in the knowledge structures underlying managerial performance. Similar studies have been conducted in traditional and more established domains, such as medicine (Patel & Groen, 1991; Schmidt, Norman, & Boshuizen, 1990) and physics (Chi, Glaser, & Farr, 1988). In the management domain, few studies have examined the development of the problem solving expertise of novices and experts. In particular, there is a shortage of studies involving a large number of research subjects.

The study reported here investigated managerial problem-solving performance. It focuses, in particular, on investigating the quality of the reasoning process of persons with different levels of expertise in the managerial arena.

3.1 A fine-grained study on managerial problem-solving abilities

As indicated in the previous section, limited information exists on managerial reasoning processes. Above all, previous research has generally been carried out with relatively few research subjects and a limited number of levels of expertise. In order to gain further understanding of problem-solving performance of students, of graduates who had recently entered the workplace, and of experts in the managerial field, Arts, Gijselaers, and Boshuizen (2000) undertook a study of managerial problem-solving. In total 115 subjects participated, representing nine different levels of expertise ranging from younger novices to older experts with over 25 years of work experience in business administration. Subjects analysed and solved realistic, ill-structured and representative managerial tasks, as discussed above.

The materials consisted of two case studies on organizational development. These cases contained neither interpretations nor analysis; we presented the case information merely as a set of data and events, not adapted for educational use. The cases contained both case-relevant and case-irrelevant cues. Irrelevant cues did not contain false information; their only purpose was to distinguish experts from non-experts more effectively (Boshuizen, 1989).

The subjects' task was to select relevant information, define problems, analyse the ill-structured situations and solve problems, which were realistic tasks in professional situations. The cases were intended to represent a realistic problem situation in the format of a business story. Both cases began with a section in which the leading character is introduced and the context in which he or she is working, followed by a set of factual information.

Arts et al. (2000) examined the development of problem-solving abilities. In so doing, they focused on problem diagnosis and the production of problem solutions as the main activities in the process of managerial problem-solving. In addition, the time factor was included in relation to problem-solving.

3.1.1 Accuracy of case-diagnosis in problem solving.

Diagnostic accuracy covers identifying, defining and explaining case problems, in terms of sources and causes, followed by explaining and classifying the phenomena encountered. Classical studies in the medical domain have demonstrated that diagnostic ability develops in practitioners in a linear, monotonic way (Elstein, Shulman, & Sprafka, 1978; Patel & Groen, 1991). In other words, experts generally make more appropriate and more complete diagnoses than novices (Boshuizen, 1989).

In measuring diagnostic ability, we considered both inaccurate and accurate diagnoses that all subjects produced in tackling the two case studies. We defined diagnostic accuracy as the ability to identify and explain correctly a case problem in terms of sources and causes. We scored accuracy by giving 2 points for a fully accurate diagnosis, 1 point for a partially accurate diagnosis, and 0 points for an inaccurate diagnosis.

In describing the data in Figures 1 through 3, reference is made to three general phases: (1) the training phase, (2) the transition from university to the workplace phase, and (3) reaching the managerial competence phase.

Figure 1 depicts the number of inaccurate (incorrect) and accurate diagnoses that the subjects produced.

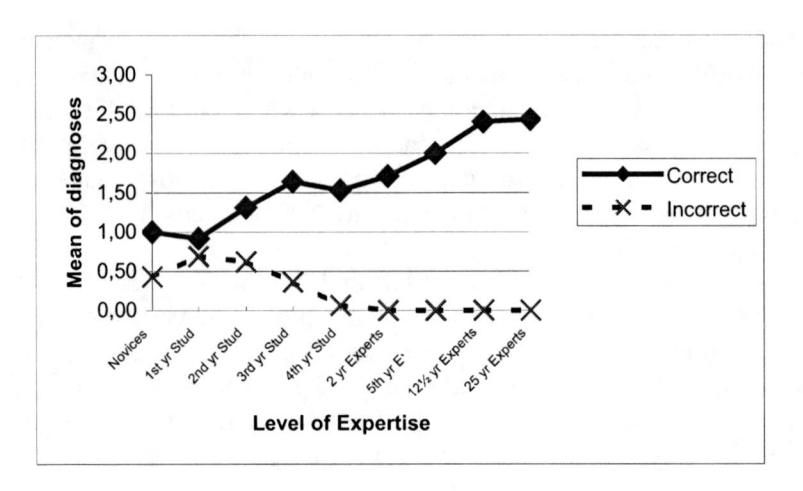

Figure -1. The development of accurate and inaccurate diagnoses

Incorrect diagnoses. Figure 1 shows that only the student groups made *incorrect* diagnoses while the experts produced no incorrect diagnoses at all. We found that the relation between expertise level and making incorrect diagnosis was negatively linear [$F(8,93) = 3.29$; $MSe = 0.25$, $p < .01$], (negative measure of association $R = -.28$).

During training, the number of incorrect diagnoses increases and a maximum is reached in the first year of the curriculum. In the second phase the number of incorrect diagnoses diminishes as students reach higher levels and, after a few years of work experience, incorrect diagnoses are no longer made.

Correct diagnoses. With respect to the number of *correct* diagnoses, we found significant differences between the groups [$F(8,91) = 2.22$; $MSe = 1.12$, $p < .05$]. The production of accurate diagnoses showed a positive and linear relation with level of expertise [$F(8,82) = 11.20$; $MSe = 13.18$, $p < .01$]. In the first phase of Figure 1, diagnostic ability initially grows rapidly and develops during a long period until graduation level. In the second phase (the transition to workplace) diagnostic ability seems to decline at first but is then activated again. At the third and final phase, diagnostic power reaches its maximum and the number of correct diagnoses does not grow any further. The results of this analysis confirm those of expertise research in other content domains, indicating that diagnostic performance shows a linear relation with level of expertise.

3.1.2 Accuracy of solutions provided during solving case problems

We defined solution accuracy as the ability to provide correct case solutions in terms of guidance or further action that the company should take. Traditionally, literature on expertise has focused on the process of problem diagnosis and not on the production of problem solutions (Eraut, 1994). While problem diagnosis involves analytic activities, the provision of solutions is more a deductive activity. Therefore, rather different models of expertise can appear when the activity of producing problem solutions is reviewed (Eraut, 1994). Research in the social sciences has demonstrated that experts have more power in providing accurate (correct) problem solutions than novices (Voss, Tyler, & Yengo, 1983). In studying experts' problem-solving behaviour in the social sciences, Voss et al. (1983) found that experts provided one (coherent) solution while novices tended to produce multiple and disparate solutions.

Arts et al. (2000) examined the ability to produce accurate case solutions by studying the whole set of problem solutions generated by participants in tackling the two case studies. Case solution accuracy was scored as follows: A full correct solution received 2 points; partially correct case solutions received 1 point; and an inaccurate solution received 0 points.

Total number of provided case solutions. As a quantitative indicator of cognitive output, the total number of solutions was obtained. For the total number of solutions found, a significant effect of level of expertise was found $[F(8,105) = 15.76, MSe = 9.60, p < .001]$. This implies significant differences between the different levels of expertise. This effect could be further specified as a significant quadratic component ($p < .001$). This implied that the relation between expertise level and the number of solutions provided is characterized as an inverted U-curve. Besides this a significant linear component was found ($p < .001$), see Figure 2.

Figure 2 (2a and 2b): The total number of provided case solutions and weighted scores for the quality of case solutions.

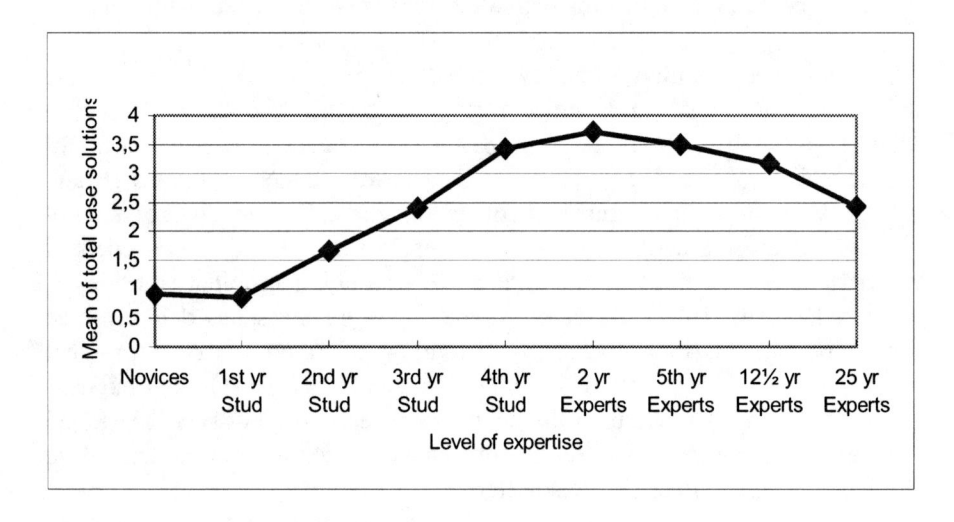

Figure 2a. Mean number of total provided case solutions as a function of expertise level

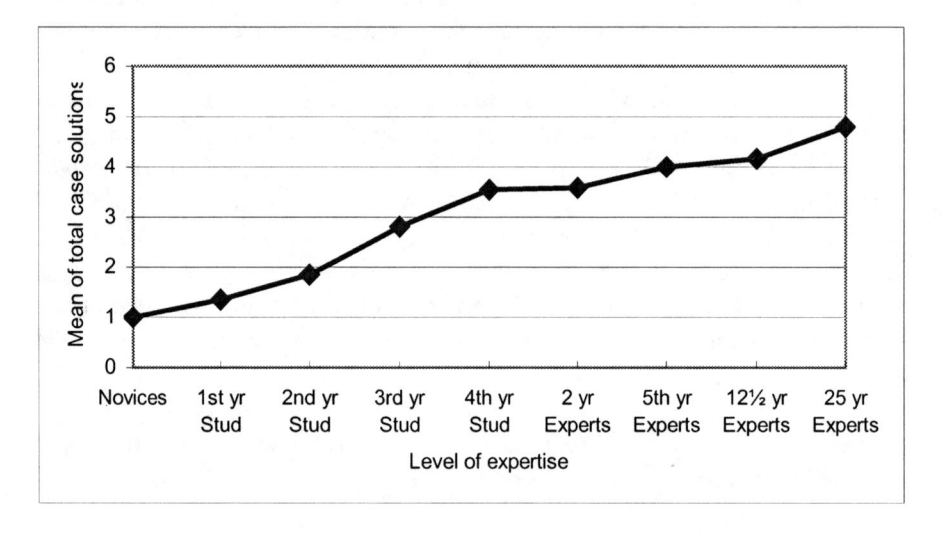

Figure 2b. Weighted scores for the quality of case solutions

The first phase shows a steady growth in the number of solutions produced during the whole period of training. Just after graduation an intermediate effect occurs: The number of produced solutions is already high at graduate level and reaches a maximum two years after graduation. The third phase shows a decrease. It seems that the more professional experience subjects acquire, the more the absolute number of solutions produced decreases. Interestingly the number of solutions produced after 25 years of experience in professional practice equals the low level of fourth year students.

Total quality score of the case solutions. A weighted score for the quality of case solutions was calculated: A fully accurate case solution: 2 points, a partially accurate solution: 1 point, incorrect solutions: 0 points. It was found that in general individuals provided more than a single case solution. In addition, the analyses showed a linear positive relation between level of expertise and the quality of the solution. A significant effect was found between the nine measured levels of expertise [$F(8,91) = 7.73$, $MSe = 16.91$, $p < .001$]. Figure 2 suggests that - as expected - experts may be distinguished from novices by the quality of their case solutions and not the quantity of these solutions.

Finally, the production of correct solutions, partially correct solutions, and incorrect solutions were analysed separately. Significant differences were found at the level of expertise for (1) the mean number of correct solutions [$F(8,91) = 5.51$, $MSe = 2.96$, $p < .001$], (2) the mean number of partially correct solutions [$F(8,91) = 6.92$, $MSe = 4.63$, $p < .001$], and (3) for the mean number of incorrect solutions [$F(8,91) = 2.56$, $MSe = 2.94$, $p < .05$]. Figure 3 shows that, after an initial increase in the number of incorrect solutions produced, from the level of 1st year students a sharp decline in incorrect solutions occurs. From the level of 2 years of work experience, no incorrect solutions occur anymore.

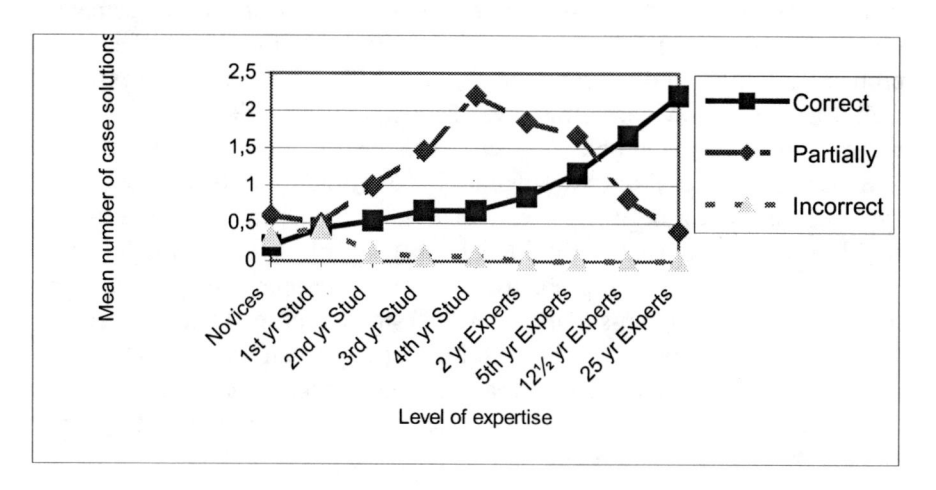

Figure 3. The development of correct, partially correct, and incorrect case solutions

Arts et al. (2000) found that the mean number of partially correct solutions continuously grows and reaches a maximum at the level of intermediate students, just before graduation. Meanwhile, the number of correct solutions increases slowly, but never reaches a peak. In the second phase, after graduation, the mean number of correct solutions starts to increase rapidly. Apparently, once individuals have entered professional practice, the number of correct solutions they generate grows rapidly while at the same time the number of partially correct solutions decreases sharply! It seems that after graduation a trade-off occurs between the number of correct and partially correct solutions, as their development is strongly opposite. Finally, after a long period, that is about 10 years of professional practice, a phase of competence is reached. This implies that the average expert has acquired the ability to perform excellently. At this level of expertise, the mean number of correct solutions exceeds the number of partially correct solutions. The researchers concluded that the results seem to indicate that it takes about 10 years of training (university education plus experience in the workplace) before individuals produce more correct solutions than partially correct solutions.

3.1.3 Time used during problem-solving

Based on this research, Arts, Gijselaers, and Boshuizen (in prep.) continued their studies and examined how the time used during the process of problem-solving influences the provision of diagnoses. Previous research on time and problem- solving (Boshuizen, 1989; Elstein et al., 1978) showed that experts often used less time to provide a correct diagnosis, as compared to novices (students). These authors suggested that the speed of experts' problem-solving could probably be explained by the experts' possession of well-organized knowledge structures. The experts' knowledge base - that is adapted to practical problems - enables experts to retrieve rapidly the necessary (and relevant) knowledge to solve problems. Arts et al. (in prep.) hypothesized that a negative linear relation of time with level of expertise could be expected. That is the higher the level of expertise, the less time would be used for solving problems. Arts et al. (in prep.) indeed found that time used for problem-solving showed significant differences between managerial novices and experts. The highest expert groups used about half the time that third and fourth year students needed for diagnosing and solving case problems. Experts used even less time than novices to process and reason upon case information.

3.2 Conclusion and discussion

In general, the studies by Arts et al. (2000) show ineffective problem-solving behaviour of students at intermediate level and recently graduated students. Intermediate students provided many case solutions but their diagnoses and solutions were either of a moderate quality or not yet correct. Moreover, they used almost twice as much time as experts. It was found that the measure *"provision of case solutions"* showed that *intermediate* students generate many solutions by comparison with experts. Results suggest that a transition seems to occur from a high level of output in quantitative terms at intermediate level (providing many, but moderate solutions) to the provision of fewer but qualitatively better solutions at the higher expertise levels.

Researchers, such as Boshuizen and Schmidt (1992) and Patel and Groen (1991), hypothesized that intermediate students process a great deal of case information in an elaborate way. As students cannot filter out irrelevant information, they perform many inappropriate problem searches and also make mistakes when reasoning. Students process much (irrelevant) information and consequently are less effective in reasoning. This ineffective problem-solving behaviour can also explain why in the present research (novice) students provided most *incorrect diagnoses* and *incorrect solutions*. Apparently, intermediate students experience difficulties in selecting appropriate information and in using their knowledge effectively. As a consequence it is likely that intermediates performed many irrelevant searches leading to many irrelevant (and incorrect) problem solutions. The studies by Arts et al. (in prep.) seem to confirm this hypothesis. Analysis of *time* used during problem solving showed that intermediate students used almost twice as much time as experts. This finding can be explained by reference to the idea that experts work very effectively. Experts are, due to their experience, more capable of distinguishing between relevant and irrelevant information (Arts et al., 2000). As a consequence their 'problem space' is smaller from the start and therefore experts can concentrate their efforts on fewer solution paths. Thus, they produce relatively few solutions and need relatively little time to do so.

The studies by Arts et al. (2000) seem to suggest the following conclusions. First, the quality of managerial expertise (in terms of problem-solving competencies) develops in a linear way, while cognitive output in quantitative terms shows an inverted U-curve effect. This result, with its distinction between a qualitative and a quantitative approach, is a refinement on previous studies of expertise. Second, the findings on diagnostic accuracy showed that this ability is linearly related to the level of expertise. An important implication of this finding is that models of diagnostic ability of other subject domains also seem to apply to the domain of managerial sciences. Taken together, our research suggests that three cognitive phases may be identified with respect to the development of expertise in the managerial sciences:
1. The first phase is characterised by a numerical increase in the production of diagnoses and solutions during reasoning.

2. A second phase (that generally occurs after graduation) is characterized by consolidation and 'confusion'. It seems that once graduates enter practice, they have to re-think their problem-solving behaviour and in the process perform many irrelevant reasoning searches.
3. The third phase, which we entitle 'toward qualitative (competent) performance', is characterised by a transition from business schools to practice that is not a smooth, linear path but a series of (small) shocks, trade-offs and increases and decreases in cognitive outputs.

3.3 Implications for managerial education

Previous research (Patel, Arocha, & Kaufman, 1999) has shown that many novice (student) problem solvers demonstrate ineffective problem solving behaviour. Novice problem solvers "jump" into a problem and rapidly search for a diagnosis or solution. Afterwards they select and sort out (ir)relevant problem data (backward reasoning). Patel et al. (1999) argue that PBL curricula in particular tend to stimulate backwards reasoning by rapidly focusing on hypotheses. By contrast, successful and more experienced problem-solvers study problem data first, thereby limiting their problem space and subsequently generate a small number of hypotheses. These outcomes suggest that explicit attention should be paid to training students in expert-like problem solving behaviour. Second, confronting students with authentic (ill-structured) cases might stimulate expert-like problem solving behaviour, such as studying problem–data and forwards reasoning. The research by Arts and his co-workers further demonstrated that only after about ten years work experience does excellent performance emerge in terms of very accurate diagnosing and problem-solving. Expert abilities seem to be preceded by a long period characterized by processing too much (irrelevant) information, and hence performing many inappropriate problem searches. A time span of more than 10 years to develop effective and accurate problem-solving seems to be rather a long preparation period for business practice. This is because it is quite common in the management workplace for graduates to be in responsible jobs, requiring well-developed problem-solving skills, only 5 years after graduation.

As a consequence, attempts to reduce this theory-to-practice-gap by making changes in instructional methods seem to be worthwhile. Based on our studies we suggest that research effort should be directed at examining whether the embedding of practical "workplace" contexts into educational settings fosters the development of managerial problem-solving skills. The principal question is whether instruction should and can be grounded in real practice examples, in order to foster the usability of knowledge in new situations (Christensen, 1987). The next section contains a review of examples of recent research conducted at University Maastricht illustrating the idea of building authentic problem-solving environments.

4. BEST PRACTICE EXAMPLE: AN AUTHENTIC, TECHNOLOGY-RICH AND PROBLEM-BASED LEARNING ENVIRONMENT

In the previous sections we have shown that managerial experts differ from novices with respect to their reasoning and problem-solving abilities. In this section we describe how we redesigned a 'regular' PBL course in order to enhance the quality of reasoning. We refined an initial PBL design on (1) the instructional implications of the presented research, of (2) expertise research in general and (3) research within PBL curricula. In addition, we used advice from those teaching on the course in the academic year 1999-2000. The study that we describe here examined the effects of an authentic, computer-supported and problem-based course on the level of expertise of undergraduate students (Arts, Gijselaers, & Segers, 2002).

The original design of PBL in the Maastricht School of Economics and Business Administration is based on an approach initially developed by Barrows and Tamblyn (1980). This can be characterized in terms of three instructional dimensions: The task, the social and the procedural (Arts et al., 2002; Barrows & Tamblyn 1980; Williams, 1992). What follows is a short description of regular PBL based on these dimensions.

Task dimension. Students receive a set of problems as a starting point for their learning activities. In general each is a short, linear, written case that describes the problem and provides relevant contextual information about the company. The problem refers to one or more aspects of international marketing. The problems are all formulated in the context of one company, in this case a brewery.

Social dimension. Students meet in groups of 14 students. There are two meetings per week. Outside the meetings, students mainly work on the problems as individuals. Teachers perform a tutoring role. They facilitate group meetings by monitoring the group process and by helping the students identify the knowledge needed to explain and resolve the problem. A student chairperson hosts the discussion and a student secretary prepares the minutes of the meeting and distributes them to all the group members by e-mail. The tutor assigns and monitors these student-roles.

Procedural dimension. The learning process starts with a preliminary analysis of the problem (the pre-discussion and brainstorming phase), based on students' prior knowledge. For any unexplained issues, the group formulates learning goals. Students need to investigate these issues during individual self-study time. At the following meeting(s) students report on what they have learned (report phase). This completes the PBL learning cycle. Next, students start to analyse a new problem, again following the same procedure. Arts et al. (2002) used this regular PBL design as a control setting for their research.

4.1 Refined PBL design

An elaborate description of the refined PBL design is given in Arts et al. (2002). The present description outlines the most important elements of the design.

4.1.1 The task dimension

Mandl, Gräsel, and Fischer (2000) argue that the limited information in the traditional PBL problem description probably encourages students to develop a superficial representation of the problem which allows them to focus on one instead of multiple hypotheses (De Grave, Boshuizen, & Schmidt, 1996). According to Patel et al. (1999), poor hypothesis formulation leads to diagnoses of poor quality. A rich case environment can avoid the danger of students pinning themselves down to one hypothesis (Mandl et. al., 2000). An additional argument, brought forward by Patel et al. (1999) is that acquiring knowledge in a traditional PBL-context stimulates "backwards thinking" (starting with hypotheses). This deviates from successful problem-solving by experts in the real environment, which is characterised by forward reasoning. Based on these research outcomes we concluded that the new design should confront students with more authentic learning contexts with problem descriptions containing a rich set of data, in order to stimulate forward reasoning.

Therefore, for the acquisition and application of knowledge, we used authentic, information rich materials. These consisted of (1) problem descriptions as well as (2) a variety of accompanying company materials (these two components together will be referred to as "case information"). Together, these elements provided a broader context for brainstorming on problems than the regular initial PBL-setting.

The case materials consisted of actual data from a large international company (L'Oreal). They included non-interpreted parts of annual reports and internal management presentations. The materials did not include interpretations and were not adapted for educational use. They were intended to enable students to simulate the real-life process of identifying and analysing problems and reaching conclusions from ill-structured data. The students were prompted to reason from raw, un-interpreted data to general conclusions. By this means, it was intended to enhance (1) inductive, forward reasoning and (2) the ability to divide data into critical and non-critical case material. Besides giving students more problem information, we also offered them richer information, by enabling them to access several information sources. The ill-structured and rich authentic company materials were offered in a non-linear multimedia format (Arts et al., 2002). In the original PBL-setting, the information relating to company cases was presented in a linear way. A multimedia hypertext format allowed us to simulate features of professional problems that become apparent only as the situation unfolds (Lawrence, 1998). By clicking on buttons, students could obtain the necessary case information.

Nowadays in business practice, most information is in an electronic format, available from the intranet or Internet, which make use of a variety of media such as databases, presentations, commercials, etc. This was another reason why, in the refined PBL-setting, authentic company material was offered in a multimedia format. The Internet was also used to compare the main company with another company. Every week, students had to relate the problem facing the main company under study with a similar problem facing another company. For instance, globalisation issues concerning the main company L'Oreal were related to those affecting a different company, such as McDonalds. This comparison was intended to stimulate multiple views on business concepts and to transfer knowledge acquired from one specific case to another. Above all, the use of Internet (a non-static, dynamic environment) provided students with up-to-date information on the companies that were investigated.

4.1.2 The social dimension

For the social dimension, we adjusted the size of the tutorial groups in the regular PBL design (about 14 persons). According to Lohman and Finkelstein (2000) research suggests that very small student groups can yield more substantial learning outcomes than medium sized or large groups. According to Kagan (1989), the ideal number of group members is four, as a higher number of group members can lead to the greater possibility of non-participation and "group production losses".

In the redesigned PBL, the brainstorming phase started with preparation by students individually. This was followed by team meetings, each consisting of about four students, for carrying out the pre-analysis of problems, thereby simulating teamwork in business. To increase the team's depth of problem analysis and the quality of decisions, interaction between the team-members was facilitated and supported by electronic discussion tools such as discussion lists (Pinsonneault & Kraemer, 1989). The student teams performed the problem analysis independently from their tutor. They could send questions to the tutor by e-mail. The tutor acted as a facilitator of the learning process and, to a lesser extent, a source of learning. This approach can result in the production of a wide variety of ideas, perspectives and problem explanations, which is important in initial problem analysis (Ge & Land, 2002). In the report phase three to four small groups were combined into one medium-sized tutorial group of about 14 members, coached by a faculty tutor. These groups only met once a week.

Overall, the refined PBL design allowed students to gain more control over aspects of their learning process, such as pace, place and formulation of learning goals, than in the regular format.

4.1.3 The procedural dimension

In the regular PBL design, company information is made available *after* the students have brainstormed on the small problem description. In the redesign however, both the problem description and the authentic accompanying information from companies were offered to students at the same time. On the basis of this rich environment, the students performed an individual brainstorm and reported this to their small team. In both the refined and the initial setting, students discussed two PBL-problems per week. In the refined PBL setting, however, students were not restricted in the amount of time they devoted to problem-analysis, since they worked independently from their tutor. In the regular design, a meeting was restricted to two hours, supervised by a tutor.

At the end of the brainstorm/problem-analysis phase, the small student teams were asked to schematise their analysis of the business case study on a specific template. This form required the students to focus thoroughly on the problem analysis (not on solutions), to categorize data, symptoms and possible problem explanations. The template was a scaffolding strategy to support students' cognitive and meta-cognitive problem-solving skills. Students were encouraged to state multiple explanations (hypothesis) for problems and to make explicit their arguments in explaining problem causes.

Finally, students were urged to bring so-called "issues for discussion" to the group. These "discussion points" were meant to go beyond comprehension and to bring specific knowledge and skills to a more general, de-contextualised level. They helped students to become aware of the reasoning they were applying as they learned. In that sense, the discussion points stimulated transfer between different problem contexts (Kolodner, Gray, & Fasse, 2003).

The assessment of the curriculum must be congruent with cognitive learning goals. As we aimed to improve the quality of reasoning in the refined instructional design this also implied assessing "higher order learning goals" associated with the quality of reasoning. Secondly, we confronted and trained students in a more authentic learning environment. Consequently we also assessed the cognitive merits of the renewed instructional design within realistic business problem contexts. Such realistic problems had the characteristics of managerial problems (ill-structuredness, multi-disciplinarity) as described above.

4.2 Research outcomes

The feasibility of the redesign was tested in a second year course on International Marketing with 75 students participating in the original PBL setting and in the experimental (refined) setting. There were two separate groups studying the International Marketing in parallel but being exposed to the two different forms of PBL (the experimental group followed the refined PBL-format and the control group followed the regular PBL-format. We assumed that, given the coherent set of changes in the task, social and procedural dimensions of the PBL design, the students who took part in the refined PBL setting would outperform the students in the original PBL setting in various respects. We expected a more advanced level of (1) inductive reasoning, (2) diagnostic ability and (3) problem-solving. The tasks of the research subjects were to select relevant problem information, define problems, analyse the ill-structured situations and solve problems. These are realistic tasks in professional situations. The case that we used represented a realistic problem situation in the format of a business story together with authentic company data from L'Oreal.

The results of the experimental group on *reasoning directionality* indicated that the experimental students produced more inductions (indicators of forward reasoning) during problem-solving (Arts et al., 2002). This result is interesting since current research indicates that PBL-curricula stimulate the development of backward reasoning as opposed to forward reasoning skills (see Prince & Boshuizen, this volume). The explicit focus of the refined design on inductive reasoning might explain this result.

In addition, the experimental group outperformed the control group on the *quality of the diagnoses and solutions* presented. By contrast, no differences were found in the number of case diagnoses and the number of case solutions provided. The finding that students in the refined PBL setting produced higher quality diagnoses and problem solutions, with no differences being found in the number of diagnoses and solutions, was very encouraging since this was our aim. These results indicate that the refined

PBL design achieved the goals of improved diagnoses and problem solutions which enhanced the quality of the problem-solving.

Another principal question is whether the adapted instructional setting fosters the usability of knowledge in new situations. In a study, Arts et al. (2002) have addressed this knowledge transfer issue. In a quasi-experimental comparative design, second year students completed a case study at the end of a marketing course. Both the company and the problems were *new* for the students. The scores on this knowledge application test indicated that the redesigned PBL-format contributed significantly to improved transfer of knowledge (Arts et al., 2002).

4.3 Implications for instruction

Our studies on the effects of redesigning PBL show that it has the potential to improve the problem-solving performance of learners. Elements that can strengthen learning are what Albanese (2000) refers to as the active ingredients of constructivist settings.

A first important element in our adapted instructional environment was working with small teams of four students. These have the characteristics of cooperative and professional teams. The small team setting was used for brainstorming on the initial analysis of a problem. Next, a thorough analysis and solution(s) of the problem (the post-discussion) was performed in groups of 14 students. Secondly, we used a variety of cases with case information consisting of problem descriptions together with raw ("authentic"), critical and less critical company data. Thirdly on the procedural side, we used a template to (1) guide the steps for students to take in the initial analysis of the problem, (2) structure the feedback from the tutor and (3) foster the discussion of issues addressed by the students. The positive results from this study confirm the idea that meta-cognitive or strategic knowledge (such as that typically fostered by the problem-solving template) can be useful in solving ill-structured problems and can compensate for a lack of content knowledge (Ge & Land, 2002).

Our study appears to have identified several dimensions in the instructional design of PBL that seem to be effective in promoting student learning and the use of the PBL materials to prepare them for professional practice. Social interactions in a student group, characteristics of the task and the problem procedure followed by students are viewed as critical to the success of the entire process.

Overall, the research results indicate that the *combination* of all these changes in the design facilitated the acquisition by students of the more advanced level of expert knowledge and skills in problem-solving for which we aimed. This result may encourage educators to use elements of the redesigned PBL-format thereby further improving their educational settings.

REFERENCES

ACNielsen. (2000). *Employer satisfaction with graduate skills. Evaluations and investigations programme.* Canberra: Higher Education Division Department of Education, Training and Youth Affairs.

Albanese, M. (2000). Problem-based learning: Why curricula are likely to show little effect on knowledge and clinical skills. *Medical Education, 34,* 729-738.

Arts, J. A. R., Gijselaers, W. H., & Boshuizen, H. P. A. (2000, April). *Expertise development in managerial sciences: The use of knowledge types in problem-solving.* Paper presented at the Annual Meeting of the American Educational Research Association, New Orleans (ERIC document reproduction service ED 440276).

Arts, J. A. R., Gijselaers, W. H., & Boshuizen, H. P. A. (in prep.). *Understanding developments in learning of professional abilities from a cognitive approach. Transitions from school to workplace.*

Arts, J. A. R., Gijselaers, W. H., & Segers, M. S. R. (2002). Cognitive effects of an authentic computer-supported problem-based learning environment. *Instructional Science, 30,* 465-495.

Baets, W., & Van der Linden, G. (2000). *The hybrid business school: Developing knowledge management through management learning.* Amsterdam: Prentice Hall.

Barrows, H. S., & Tamblyn, R. M. (1980). *Problem based learning: An approach to medical education.* New York: Springer.

Bigelow, J. D. (2001). *Preparing undergraduates for organizational situations: A frames/problem-based approach.* Unpublished paper, Boise State University.

Boshuizen, H. P. A. (1989). *The development of medical expertise: A cognitive-psychological approach.* Haarlem: Thesis Publishers.

Boshuizen, H. P. A. (2003). How to bridge the gap between school and work. In H. P. A. Boshuizen (Ed.), *Expertise development: The transition between school and work.* (pp. 9-38) Heerlen: Open Universiteit Nederland.

Boshuizen, H. P. A., & Schmidt, H. G. (1992). The role of biomedical knowledge in clinical reasoning by experts, intermediates and novices. *Cognitive Science, 16,* 153-184.

Bowden, J., & Marton, F. (1998). *The university of learning. Beyond quality and competence in higher education.* London: Kogan Page.

Boyatzis, R. E., Cowen, S. S., & Kolb, D. A. (1995). *Innovation in professional education: Steps on a journey from teaching to learning.* San Francisco: Jossey-Bass.

Bransford, J. D., & Schwartz, D. L. (1999). *Rethinking transfer: A simple proposal with multiple implications.* Review of Research in Education, 24, 61-100.

Business-Higher Education Forum. (1997). *Spanning the chasm: Corporate and academic cooperation to improve work-force preparation.* (http://www.acenet.edu/bookstore/).

Business-Higher Education Forum. (1999). *Spanning the chasm: A blueprint for action.* Washington: Business-Higher Education Forum.

Chi, M. T. H., Glaser, R., & Farr, M. J. (Eds). (1988). *The nature of expertise.* London: Erlbaum.

Christensen, C. R. (1987). Teaching and the case method. Boston: Harvard Business School.

Clegg, S. R., & Ross-Smith, A. (2003). Revising the boundaries: Management education and learning in a postpositivist world. *Academy of Management Learning and Education, 2*, 85-98.
De Grave, W. S., Boshuizen, H. P. A., & Schmidt, H. G. (1996). Problem based learning: Cognitive and metacognitive processes during problem analysis. *Instructional Science, 24*, 321-341.
De Leeuw, A. C. J. (1996). *Bedrijfskundige methodologie, management van onderzoek.* [Methodology of business administration, management of research] Assen: Van Gorcum.
Elstein, A. S., Shulman, L. S., & Sprafka, S. A. (1978). *Medical problem-solving; An analysis of clinical reasoning.* Cambridge: Harvard University Press.
Eraut, M. (1994). *Developing professional knowledge and competence.* London: Falmer.
Ge, X. & Land, S. M. (2002, April). *The effects of question prompts and peer interactions in scaffolding students' problem-solving processes on an ill-structured task.* Paper presented at the Annual Meeting of the American Psychological Association, New Orleans.
Gijselaers, W. H. (2000). *Studeren voor nieuwe geleerden: Over de kunst van het organiseren.* [Studying for new learners: On the art of organizing] Maastricht: Universiteit Maastricht.
Isenberg, D. J. (1986). Thinking and managing: A verbal protocol analysis of managerial problem-solving. *Academy of Management Journal, 4*, 775-788.
Kagan, S. (1989). Cooperative learning. San Juan Capistrano: Resources for Teachers.
Kolodner, J. L., Gray, J. T., & Fasse, B. B. (2003). Promoting transfer through case-based reasoning: Rituals and practices in Learning by DesignTM classrooms. Cognitive Science Quarterly, 3, 183-222.
Lash, F. B. (1988, April). Problem solving and the development of *expertise in management.* Paper presented at the Annual Meeting of the American Psychological Association. Atlanta.
Lawrence, J. A. (1988). Expertise on the bench: Modeling magistrates' judicial decision-making. In M. T. H. Chi, R. Glaser, & M. J. Farr (Eds.), *The nature of expertise* (pp. 229-259). Hillsdale: Erlbaum.
Lohman, M. C., & Finkelstein, M. (2000). Designing groups in problem-based learning to promote problem-solving skill and self-directedness. *Instructional Science, 28*, 291-307.
Mandl, H., Gräsel, C., & Fischer, F. (2000). Problem oriented learning: Facilitating the use of domain-specific and control strategies through modelling by an expert. In W. J. Perrig & A. Grob (Eds.), *Control of human behaviour, mental processes and consciousness* (pp. 165-182). Mahwah: Erlbaum.
Mintzberg, H. (1973). *The nature of managerial work.* New York: Harper & Row.
Mintzberg, H. (1980). *Managerial effectiveness.* New York: McGraw-Hill.
O'Rourke, B. K. (1998). Roles of economics in business and management education. In G. M. Milter, J. E. Stinson, & W. H. Gijselaers (Eds.), *Educational innovation in economics and business* (pp. 51-63). Dordrecht: Kluwer.
Patel, V. L., Arocha, J. F., & Kaufman, D. R. (1999). Expertise and tacit knowledge in medicine. In R. Sternberg & J. Horvath (Eds.), *Tacit knowledge in professional practise. Researcher and practitioner perspectives* (pp. 75-99). Mahwah: Erlbaum.
Patel, V. L., & Groen, G. J. (1991). The general and specific nature of medical expertise: A critical look. In K. A. Ericsson & J. Smith (Eds.), *Toward a general theory of expertise: Prospects and limits* (pp. 93-125). Cambridge: Cambridge University Press.
Peters, T. (1988). *Thriving on chaos.* London: Macmillan.
Porter, L., & McKibbin, L. (1988). *Management education and development: Drift or thrust into the 21st century?* New York: McGraw-Hill.

Pinsonneault, A., & Kraemer, K. I. (1989). The impact of technological support on groups: An assessment of the empirical results. *Decisions Support Systems, 5*, 197-216.

Revans, R. (1980). *Action learning.* London: Blond & Briggs.

Schmidt, H. G., Norman, G. R., & Boshuizen, H. P. A. (1990). A cognitive perspective on medical expertise: Theory and implications. *Academic Medicine, 65*, 611-621.

Simon, H. A. (1973). The structure of ill structured problems. *Artificial Intelligence, 4* , 181-201.

Van Fossen, P. J., & Miller, S. L. (1994, April). *The nature and constructs of relative expertise in economic problem-solving.* Paper presented at the Annual Meeting of the American Educational Research Association, New Orleans.

Voss, J. F., Tyler, S. W., & Yengo, L. A. (1983). Individual differences in the solving of social science problems. In: R. F. Dillon & R. R. Schmeck (Eds.), *Individual differences in cognition* (Vol. 1, pp. 205-232). New York: Academic. Press

Walsh, J. P. (1995). Managerial and organizational cognition: Notes from a trip down memory lane. *Organization Science, 6*, 280-321.

Wickelgren, W. A. (1974). *How to solve problems: Elements of a theory of problems and problem solving.* San Francisco: Freeman.

Williams, S. M. (1992). Putting case-based instruction into context: Examples from legal and medical education. *Journal of the Learning Sciences, 2*, 367-427.

Chapter 7

FROM THEORY TO PRACTICE IN MEDICAL EDUCATION
Effect on knowledge application, clinical reasoning and learning

Katinka J. A. H. Prince[1] and Henny P. A. Boshuizen[2]
[1]*Faculty of Medicine, Skillslab, University Maastricht, The Netherlands,* [2]*Educational Technology Expertise Centre, Open Universiteit Nederland, Heerlen, The Netherlands*

1. TRANSITIONS: WHAT CHANGES?

In medical schools students are trained to become medical doctors. The development from medical student to medical expert is a process that extends over many years. Medical curricula last four to six years and are often divided into a pre-clinical phase of two to four years and a clinical phase of two years, the latter generally consisting of clerkship rotations in hospital and community settings. In the pre-clinical phase the emphasis is on the acquisition of basic science knowledge and students' learning is mainly focused on understanding and explaining relevant phenomena. This results in the formation of a validated and closely connected knowledge base (Boshuizen & Schmidt, 2000). In the clerkships students assist junior and senior medical staff. They clerk patients, assist in theatre, et cetera. During this period the emphasis shifts towards the application of knowledge and skills in problem solving, extension of domain-specific knowledge and the acquisition of practical knowledge. Students learn to think and act like clinicians and learn to apply in patient care the abstract knowledge acquired in earlier years. However, they do not have full responsibility for patient care. Full responsibility is postponed until after graduation, when medical doctors usually work as house officers/trainees in a hospital or in family practice. In postgraduate training application of knowledge and skills is emphasised and training is focused on one of the specialties.

Research has revealed that the two major transitions in the medical education continuum, namely the transition from pre-clinical to clinical training and the transition from undergraduate to postgraduate training, are problematic for most students. Boshuizen (this volume) describes a discontinuity in the development of expertise, which was probably caused by the start of clinical clerkships. Stress as well as a change in required study skills may account for this delay in students' development. Galton, Morrison, and Pell (2000) showed that failure of students to adapt to new learning environments and teaching approaches resulted in a remarkable hiatus in academic progress in about 40 % of the students who transferred during their school career. The transition from being a predominantly pre-clinical science student to being an apprentice doctor was found to be the most frequently described stressful transition in a study by Radcliffe and Lester (2003). Research by Prince, Van de Wiel, Scherpbier, Van der Vleuten, and Boshuizen (2000) showed that students had difficulty bridging the gap between the theoretical and clinical phase of the curriculum. In addition to professional socialisation processes, the application of theoretical knowledge in clinical practice posed problems for students.

The transition after graduation was also found to be accompanied by perceived inadequacy of knowledge for practice and uncertainties regarding the ability to handle responsibility (Prince, Van de Wiel, Van der Vleuten, Boshuizen, & Scherpbier, under editorial review). At present, there is not much evidence on the transition itself, but ample research has been done on junior doctors' experiences and the preparedness of recent graduates for the role of junior doctor. Outcomes indicated that workload was high and that there was little formal education. Junior doctors were found to have difficulty prioritising, lack experience in organisational skills and require additional training in practical procedures (Bogg, Gibbs, & Bundred, 2001; Calman & Donaldson, 1991; Gillard, Dent, Aarons, Smyth-Pigott, & Nichols, 1993; Roche, Sanson Fischer, & Cockburn, 1997). Jones, McArdle, and O'Neill (2002) demonstrated that graduates from innovative courses felt better prepared for the role of house officer than did graduates from traditional courses. However, other studies have shown that PBL graduates also experienced difficulties with respect to responsibilities, workload, contact with other health care workers and teamwork (Prince et al., under editorial review).

There is a considerable gap between the study of learning in psychology and the various complex forms of learning in higher education, including medical education. In this chapter we will explore educational theories and an implementation of these theories (problem-based learning, PBL). Although PBL is supposed to help students bridging the gap between theory and practice, the transitions are still problematic for most students from PBL medical schools. We will consider research findings concerning these transitions in the light of theories from the fields of education and cognitive psychology. We will propose ways to ease these transitions and illustrate our conceptions with illustrations from a concrete medical school.

2. EDUCATIONAL APPROACHES TO NARROW THE THEORY-PRACTICE GAP

Several educational theories have proposed a framework that can narrow the theory-practice gap. The most radical one is the situated learning theory (Lave & Wenger, 1991). It questions the principle of separating learning from practice. Situated learning theory departs from the situation in which and for which students are learning. Novices or apprentices are allowed peripheral participation, but are always participating in real practice. Others have translated this assumption of situated learning theory into solutions that can be managed within school bounds. In these solutions authentic problems and authentic environments play a crucial role (e.g. Jasper Woodbury Problem Solving Series; Cognition and Technology Group at Vanderbilt, 1994). They developed interactive video environments that present students with challenging authentic problems that require them to understand and apply important mathematical concepts. Students who work with the series have shown gains in mathematical problem solving, communication abilities, planning skills and attitudes toward mathematics (Bransford, Brown, & Cocking, 1999). The idea behind problem-based learning is very similar, that is, to present students with challenging authentic problems derived from real practice. Remarkably, PBL theorists base the defence for the choice of this kind of problems as a starting point for learning on a rather different paradigm (Schmidt, 1983, 1993). These publications take a cognitive psychological perspective, emphasising ease of learning and the quality and practical applicability of the resulting knowledge base. In this view activation of prior knowledge and elaboration, active knowledge construction, and the importance of context play a crucial role. Authentic problems serve as a vehicle to both activate prior knowledge and to provide relevant contexts. Finally, competence-based education bridges the gap between theory and practice by using authentic problems as a means for whole-task practice of complex skills (Van Merriënboer, 1997). In Van Merriënboer's view these training programmes should be carefully designed by building up complexity of the task and by interleaving skills training with prerequisite and supportive information. The success of the approach is a result of a cautious decomposition of the skill in its constituent components that form the basis for the training and cognitive congruence between the skill as trained and the skill as it has to be performed in real life. This suggests that an authentic task or situation will only have the desired effect when it tempts or forces the students into cognitive behaviour that is similar to what is expected of professionals. If it allows students to take shortcuts, the learning effect will be sub-optimal, if not counterproductive. Of the three approaches described only PBL has been implemented as a principle for curriculum construction in medical education.

3. PROBLEM-BASED LEARNING IN MEDICINE

Problem-based learning (PBL) is an educational method that can be regarded as an alternative to the traditional, discipline-based, approach to medical education. In a problem-based medical school, students acquire knowledge by working through (clinical) "problems" in small groups facilitated by a tutor. These problems usually consist of descriptions of sets of observable phenomena or events that need explanation. By discussing a problem, students activate and elaborate on their existing knowledge and identify what they already know and what they still need to learn to solve the problem and explain its critical features. This analysis results in learning issues that are pursued in self-study. In a following session, students discuss what they have found in the literature and use this knowledge to come to a deeper understanding of the problem and how it can be dealt with (Barrows & Tamblyn, 1980).

PBL is supposed to enhance acquisition, retention, and use of knowledge by activating prior knowledge and by elaboration (Norman & Schmidt, 1992). The initial discussion of a problem in the tutorial group stimulates the activation and elaboration of prior knowledge, which, in turn, facilitates the processing, comprehension, and recall of the information. Moreover, by relating new knowledge to existing knowledge, deeper meaning is increased and this enables the learner to reconstruct knowledge if, in the course of time, it is forgotten.

Because in PBL basic science is integrated with clinical science in the simulated clinical problems that serve as the starting points for student learning, PBL is thought to narrow the gap between basic and applied or clinical science (Norman & Schmidt, 1992). Basic science knowledge can be defined as the knowledge that contributes to the understanding of the functioning and dysfunctioning of the human body, like anatomy, physiology and biochemistry. Surgery and pathology are examples of clinical sciences. In traditional medical curricula basic and clinical science are taught separately.

> Box 1: Maastricht Medical School.
> *Dutch undergraduate medical education lasts six years. Students enter medical school after six years of secondary education. Graduates are entitled to register as a licensed medical doctor. Postgraduate GP training lasts three years and training in most of the other specialties lasts about six years. Many doctors take non-training posts in a hospital before entering specialty training.*
>
> *Maastricht Medical School offers a problem-based curriculum in the four preclinical years of the curriculum. Years 1 and 2 focus on basic science and the focus shifts to clinical science in years 3 and 4. Years 5 and 6 consist of clerkship rotations in hospital departments and general practice. Students are responsible for their own learning. In the first four years there are six-week block courses devoted to specific themes. Students meet twice weekly in small groups with a tutor to work on 'problems'. The problems in the first two years deal with the normal functioning human body and consist of a description of a set of phenomena in need of an explanation. In years 3 and 4 the focus is on abnormal functioning and most of the "problems" are patient cases. The cases are intended to prompt students' thinking and studying concerning differential diagnosis, additional investigations, patho-physiology, prognosis, management, therapy, and course of the disease. About half of the cases consist of descriptions of a history, physical examination, and laboratory results. The other cases present a brief description of a patient and students have to gather more information by questioning the tutor. Besides providing information in free-inquiry cases, the tutor critically follows the group discussion, only intervening to stimulate students' thinking and co-operation. Most tutors are members of the multidisciplinary team that designed the block in question and experts in the domain under study. In addition to the two weekly group sessions, students attend one or two lectures per week. In the four pre-clinical years the Skillslab offers a longitudinal skills training programme. The programme consists of procedural and laboratory skills as well as controlled and systematic training in communication skills, including consultations with simulated patients in which students play the role of the doctor. The assessment programme comprises four progress tests every year, end-of-block tests and annual OSCEs to test clinical skills.*

According to Barrows, another goal of PBL is to foster clinical reasoning or problem-solving skills in students (Barrows & Tamblyn, 1980). Barrows assumed that through continuous exposure to real-life problems with solution strategies modelled by their tutor, students would acquire the craft of evaluating a patient problem, deciding what is wrong, and making decisions about appropriate actions to treat or manage the problem.

Furthermore, since PBL stimulates active learning, it is also expected to provide students with lifelong learning skills. Consequently, one would expect PBL students to be better prepared for clinical practice than students in a traditional curriculum.

4. TRANSITIONS: THE EFFECTS

Although PBL is supposed to prepare students for practice, the transitions from being a pre-clinical student to being an apprentice in practice and from being a clerk to being a junior doctor cause problems for students, also for students from PBL medical schools. The problems are closely related to the way medical education is structured. Training in the first four years takes place in an artificial environment and it is not until the clerkships that students enter a real practice environment. Although pre-clinical training is supposed to prepare students for practice, the problems arise partially as a result of the disparity between the demands of pre-clinical training and the demands and expectations students encounter upon entering clinical practice. The empirical findings reviewed in this section have been mainly collected by a research group at University Maastricht, with prime investigators Prince, Van de Wiel and Wagenaar.

The problems students experience when entering the clinical phase of the curriculum arise partly from professional socialisation processes. Students perceive a dramatic difference between the theoretical and clinical phase of the curriculum and feel insecure because they do not know what is expected of them (Prince et al., 2000). Problems related to professional socialisation concern the long working hours and the time and energy students have to expend in adapting to their new environment. Radcliffe and Lester described changes in learning environment, teaching styles and expectations as particular causes of stress (Radcliffe & Lester, 2003). Moss and McManus' study of students at the beginning of clinical training found that students perceived relationships with senior staff to be anxiety-inducing (Moss & McManus, 1992).

Students also find it difficult to apply theoretical knowledge in clinical practice. In a study by Radcliffe and Lester (2003), students described feeling useless, unable to contribute to patient care, because they had insufficient knowledge or skills to take an active role. In the study by Prince et al. (2000) clerks mentioned difficulties in applying the knowledge acquired in the pre-clinical years to real patient problems. They also perceived deficiencies in basic science knowledge, particularly in anatomy and pharmacology. Boshuizen (this volume) found that 5th year medical students, halfway the clerkship period, experienced a kind of "crisis" in their learning process. They performed less well on a diagnostic task compared with 4th year and 6th year students. They did not come up with better diagnoses and used less biomedical and clinical knowledge compared with 4th and 6th year students. These results suggest that the application in practice of knowledge acquired in the theoretical phase of the curriculum is problematic.

In addition, clerks discovered that their knowledge was structured the wrong way around (Prince et al., 2000). They had learned to reason from theory to practice, that is, starting from a diagnosis or disease, they could list the corresponding symptoms. For example, they knew that myocardial infarction is often accompanied by chest pain, nausea, and fatigue. However, in the clerkships they discovered that they lacked memory retrieval pathways that connected information about symptoms to relevant diagnostic knowledge. Their retrieval pathways were one-way streets leading from diagnosis to symptoms only. These results are in line with findings by Van de Wiel, Boshuizen, Schmidt, and Schaper (1999), who showed that students in the pre-clinical phase did not reason from symptoms (for example chest pain) to disease (myocardial infarction), but from disease (myocardial infarction) to its manifestations (chest pain). Another problem seems to be that students are not used to considering a problem with a view to generating a differential diagnosis. They have been given the impression in the pre-clinical phase that for every clinical problem there is one single "solution" in the shape of a diagnosis that explains all symptoms. In clinical practice, patient problems are often not so clear-cut and several diagnoses may seem possible. The final diagnosis and all possible alternatives are called "differential diagnosis". After formulating the differential diagnosis, a doctor may order additional investigations to arrive at the most likely diagnosis, while at the same time initiating treatment. These steps are unknown to students when they move from the pre-clinical to the clinical phase.

Many students indicate that how they study and their motivation for doing so change in the clinical phase. One of the reasons why students experience the transition from pre-clinical to clinical phase as particularly stressful is that they feel they are no longer "studying merely in order to pass an examination, but for the future health of their patients".

In conclusion, transitions in medical education are accompanied by many problems with respect to knowledge application, integration, clinical reasoning and learning. These will be discussed in the following sections.

4.1 Acquisition, retention and use of knowledge

To help students retrieve information and put it into practice, teachers should enhance the meaning of information, adapt the learning context to the application context, help students process information in a way that resembles real practice, and have students practise with different tasks in different situations. PBL is supposed to enhance acquisition, retention, and use of knowledge by activation of prior knowledge (Norman & Schmidt, 1992) and the use of problems as context for students' learning. Nevertheless, medical students from a PBL school were found to experience difficulties in applying knowledge acquired in the theoretical part of the curriculum in clinical practice settings (Prince et al., 2000; Van de Wiel, Schaper, Scherpbier, Van der Vleuten, & Boshuizen, 1999). Apparently, students knowledge was appropriate for passing tests, but not for application in real practice situations. There are several possible explanations for this phenomenon.

Firstly, new knowledge may not have been connected with prior knowledge. This may be attributable to insufficient elaboration of knowledge in the tutorial groups, where students may have failed to perceive elaboration as a useful learning strategy, because they did not see any immediate benefits. If students do not elaborate in the tutorial groups, PBL will fail to fully realise its purported advantage of providing better understanding, processing and retrieval of knowledge.

Secondly, it is well-known that assessment drives learning (Van der Vleuten, 1996). As long as success in exams depends on recall of isolated facts, students' learning is unlikely to be directed at the gaps in their knowledge discovered by discussing a case in the tutorial group. Instead they will concentrate on the requirements of the end-of-block test, namely facts related to the block theme. This emphasises the importance of a good match between intended learning outcomes and assessment. In the end, studying for short term success on a test will be ineffective vis-à-vis the final learning objectives of medical education, unless the test reflects the relationship between what is assessed and the requirements of professional practice.

Another flaw in medical education, which can be attributed to the assessment system in many medical schools, is that transfer of knowledge, that is application of knowledge to slightly different problems, is hardly ever tested. Transfer of knowledge from one problem to another is difficult for novices, because their limited domain-specific knowledge makes it difficult for them to detect similarities that go beyond the surface features of a problem. As a result, any change in surface features will impede transfer, since the novice cannot recognise similarity between problems at a deeper, structural level. Transfer can be facilitated when educators have students practise with different examples of similar problems (Eva, Neville, & Norman, 1998).

Not only the number, but also the types of examples influence transfer. In medical education most topics are repeated throughout the curriculum, but students hardly ever practise with different examples of one problem. The common type of instruction in medical school, and many other learning environments, is the use of what can be termed "blocked instruction" or "blocked practice" (Hatala, Norman, & Brooks, 2003). This means that students are presented with a specific concept, which they have to master. The concept is explained and then demonstrated in typical problems or examples, which are presented in "blocks". The students are assumed to use the prototypical problems to expand and deepen their understanding of the concept. The next step should be to present students with slightly less typical examples of the problem. This exposure to multiple examples is the foundation of deliberate practice, personalised supervised training on a specific topic using repetition and enhancement, which is deemed critical for the development of expertise (Ericsson & Charness, 1994). The use of slightly different examples is not very common in medical education. Another critical step that is missing in the learning process is having students learn how to discriminate between a diagnosis and other differentials, once they have established a basic understanding of a concept. This discrimination can be taught by having students contrast (patients with) different diagnoses and allow them to become aware of the similarities and differences between these patients. Although the initial steps of presenting typical and less typical cases are still important, "mixed" (i.e. contrastive) practice is vital to train students to discriminate between diagnoses and highlight the differences between diseases. The theory that underpins the effectiveness of mixed practice is that decision making is facilitated by the consideration of discriminating versus supportive features. In the field of medical education very few studies have addressed the effectiveness of "contrastive" or "mixed" versus "blocked" learning (Hatala et al., 2003). The use of examples is discussed in the chapter by Stark and collegues in this book (Stark, Gruber, Hinkofer, & Mandl, this volume).

Practising is also effective in learning to identify situations in which a particular problem-solving routine is likely to be useful. Often concept learning is supplemented by practice in applying the concept to a set of problems. These problems are often arranged in such a way that the concept always applies one way or another. Thus, students gain experience in explaining how a concept applies to various cases, but not in determining whether a concept is appropriate for a particular problem. In their work as doctors students will be confronted with real patient problems, which may represent any of a huge array of concepts from which they will have to select the one that is relevant to the case. Therefore, medical education should offer students ample opportunity to practise selecting the appropriate concept for a problem, so that they will obtain a knowledge base that enables them to do so in day-to-day practice. Students also need to learn why other concepts are not appropriate. Students must be challenged to retrieve and use information repeatedly and in circumstances where they might not have predicted that it would be applicable. Only through repeated testing in this manner will students be able to retrieve or activate specific information in the appropriate situation.

4.2 Integration of basic and clinical sciences

In the medical domain basic science knowledge must be integrated with clinical knowledge, and both have to be transferred to clinical practice. Basic science seems quite abstract in the eyes of many medical students, whereas clinical medicine is much more concrete. For example, not many students will ever "see" a hormonal regulation cycle, while a patient with diabetes is a common phenomenon. The challenge for medical schools is to strike the right balance between presenting information in applied contexts (i.e. illustrated by a clinical problem) and allowing students to derive the appropriate abstractions and generalisations to further develop their models of conceptual, that is basic science, understanding (Patel & Kaufman, 1995).

PBL explicitly presents basic science knowledge in the context of clinical problems. Therefore, PBL is assumed to enhance integration of basic science knowledge and clinical knowledge, thereby providing excellent preparation for diagnostic performance by students (Norman & Schmidt, 1992). However, students from PBL schools have repeatedly expressed the opinion that basic science knowledge is important, but that they feel insufficiently prepared for practice in this respect (Prince et al., 2000; Woodward & Ferrier, 1983). Anatomy and pharmacology in particular are mentioned as topics to which more attention should be devoted in the curriculum. (Prince et al., 2000; Van Mameren, Leiner, Wanders, & Van der Vleuten, 1997).

Research into the perceived and actual level of undergraduate students' basic science comprehension, in this case anatomy knowledge (Prince et al., 2003), showed that perceived insufficiency is common among students of the eight Dutch medical schools, regardless of the type of curriculum. Students of the Maastricht PBL school experienced similar problems and obtained similar results on an anatomy test compared with the students from the other, more traditional, schools. A possible explanation is that in the pre-clinical phase students only manage to establish few and weak links between biomedical knowledge and diseases (although PBL offers students somewhat more opportunity than traditional, non-integrated medical schools). Apparently, these links are insufficient to enable application of biomedical knowledge in clinical practice, where the problems students encounter are more complex and vague than in the pre-clinical phase. Moreover, students say that they study underlying disease mechanisms between tutorial group sessions, but almost never elaborate on these mechanisms in the tutorial meetings. Van de Wiel, Schaper et al. (1999) showed that in the tutorial group only the results of students' literature study were reported and discussed. Hardly ever did students attempt to apply biomedical knowledge to the case or explain the patient problem in terms of underlying mechanisms or management consequences.

4.3 Reasoning

Maastricht students reported that they discovered that their knowledge was structured "the other way around", when they started the clinical phase of their studies. One student literally said: "It struck me that we have learned everything the other way around compared to what you see in practice. We do not see a patient with a heart attack, we see a patient with certain symptoms and we have to find out what it is." (Prince et al., 2000) Apparently, students have difficulty reasoning from symptoms to diagnosis. Before we address this problem, we will first consider the literature on clinical reasoning.

Clinical reasoning has often been conceptualised as a categorisation task – once the physician has categorised the patient's problem into a class of diseases, the problem is considered solved (Custers, Regehr, & Norman, 1996). However, in contrast with the categorisation tasks examined in laboratory studies, real life medical diagnosis categorisations are pervaded by ambiguity in the presence and identification of features and a large number of possible alternatives that often do not form clearly separable options (Brooks, LeBlanc, & Norman, 2000).

It is well-known that clinical reasoning is not a skill that can be taught and learned separately, without explicit reference to the way knowledge is structured. Instead, clinical reasoning seems closely related to the structure and organisation of knowledge in memory. Information from a case activates information or concepts or examples within the cognitive network, which in turn activate other relevant information or concepts, and so on. Thus, very rapidly the full weight of the elaborate, organised memory structure can be brought to bear on the new case. Relevant information is immediately available and the implications of that information follow rapidly. This provides the expert physician with certain assumptions and hypotheses that, in turn, guide further inquiry until a solution is formed. From this conceptualisation of expertise it follows that acquiring information in isolation leads to inert knowledge and is unhelpful. Only when information is integrated into the individual's network will it be available and functional for future purposes. Moreover, it is inappropriate to try to teach clinical reasoning skills independently of clinical content. The two are intertwined for the expert physician and must be integrated during the development of expertise.

Maastricht students have indicated that they had not "learned" to reason from symptoms to diagnoses (Prince et al., 2000). In the literature this problem has been described in terms of forward and backward reasoning (Patel & Groen, 1986). Forward reasoning is defined as reasoning from symptoms via explanations of these symptoms to diagnoses (e.g. this patient has intermittent pain in the upper abdomen; that is where the gallbladder is located; the pain is intermittent, that means it could be caused by gallstones), while backward reasoning refers to the retrieval of symptoms on the basis of a certain diagnosis (gallstones cause pain in the upper abdomen). Eva, Brooks and Norman (2002) have shown that the use of these reasoning strategies is not associated with degree of experience. Medical students as well as medical doctors use both ways of reasoning, depending on the difficulty of the problem. Maastricht students have indicated that during their pre-clinical studies they mostly used backward reasoning. In the tutorial groups they reasoned from diagnosis to symptoms to solve mostly prototypical cases with very obvious clues to direct them to the correct diagnosis (Prince et al., 2000). Although the cases were realistic, students said they generally identified the right diagnosis within minutes and did not take the trouble to develop appropriate learning objectives. Students reported a tendency in most tutorial groups to tackle the problem presented to the group by looking up a diagnosis and the related symptoms. During their pre-clinical studies they did not see different examples of the same disease, or examples with less clear-cut diagnoses. Neither were they presented with highly complex cases, which forced them to use forward reasoning that is from symptoms to diagnosis. In the clinical phase, they suddenly found themselves confronted with patients with complaints and symptoms that were less distinct and they were frustrated by their inability to make an immediate diagnosis. It appeared that students had acquired knowledge around diagnoses. Activation of a diagnosis activated all related knowledge. To activate this knowledge network, students needed one typical cue (for example chest pain for a myocardial infarction). However, the patients they saw after the transition to clinical practice presented with less typical symptoms. Because students have not practised integrating different symptoms to arrive at a diagnosis (chest pain may also indicate stomach problems; dyspnoea in combination with nausea and paleness may also be suggestive of myocardial infarction, even without evident chest pain), they feel inadequate to deal with patient problems. They discover that they have to change the direction of their reasoning and as a result experience stress and feelings of uncertainty.

In conclusion, students have acquired knowledge mostly around diagnoses, which enables them to reason backwards, but therefore they need an obvious clue. In practice they do not see the possible diagnoses right away, and therefore they need to reason forward, but they are not used to do so.

4.4 Learning

A training programme is supposed to prepare the students not only for work, but also for learning while working. Developments in medicine can move very rapidly. Knowledge may have a very short life cycle and the increase in knowledge, even within a rather narrow field, may be daunting. In order to provide patients with optimal care, physicians must keep up to date and master the information overload. Therefore, students and physicians have to become lifelong learners. Physicians, who were exposed to self-directed learning as students, tend to be better at keeping up to date with the latest developments than their colleagues with no experience with self-directed learning. Thus, it appears preferable for students to be active learners rather than passive recipients of information.

The differences between learning in formal education, like the first years of the undergraduate curriculum, and experiential learning in the workplace are significant. During the first years of undergraduate medical training, students learn mainly from textbooks, lectures, et cetera. Formal learning is emphasised; the learning goals and activities are specified and subject matter is well defined. Junior doctors and undergraduate clerks participate in health care, where they carry out their appointed tasks. During this phase of their training students and graduates alike are supposed to be learning in action, and the emphasis is on informal learning (Bolhuis & Simons, 1999).

Informal learning occurs spontaneously, even when no special attention is being paid to it. On the job learning has some characteristics that make it a strong process. Firstly, informal learning is implicit and implicit knowledge and skills are elements of expertise. Secondly, informal learning is directly connected with performing actions. Learning occurs concurrently with the application of what is being learned. Learning and learning outcomes can be said to be entwined. Thirdly, repetition influences learning. Once students have experienced a situation in which they had to take action and that situation occurs again, they will be able to make quicker judgments and take immediate action without going through the same mental process as they did the first time. A final advantage is that learning in practice is related to the development of a professional identity: Becoming a doctor (Bolhuis & Simons, 1999).

Despite these clear advantages of informal learning, many students believe that learning takes place only when they are explicitly being taught something or study from books. They do not see learning as something that can occur during the daily routine of clinical work (Wagenaar, Scherpbier, Boshuizen, & Van der Vleuten, 2003). Both students and graduates fail to perceive informal, spontaneous learning as real learning or recognise that learning in this way is possible. Junior doctors indicated that there were only few formal learning activities, like lectures, courses and continuing medical education courses for specialists (Prince et al., under editorial review). They appeared to be unaware of their informal learning, learning by experience and social interaction. And they are right in saying that their learning in practice is not as effective as it should be, but for different reasons than the ones they cited. Most clinical clerks spend their days observing house officers, registrars and consultants at work, mostly without taking an active part in what is going on. One might say that even in the midst of clinical practice, students are not really engaging in experiential learning. They may watch events, but they have no idea of the problem at hand or why it is being addressed in a particular manner. Obviously, this is not the optimal learning situation.

Not much research has addressed how clinical clerks learn. Processes involved in learning in practice are difficult to study, because practice settings are unstructured and complex, and learning processes often occur spontaneously. From the literature it appears that reflection and supervision influence the learning process. According to Schön (1987) reflection is helpful for students to generalise their experiences to new situations. An interview study by Wagenaar et al. (2003) showed that medical students hardly ever explicitly mentioned that they reflected on their experiences as clerks.

The teacher/supervisor also influences the learning process. A facilitating rather than a didactic approach appears to score the best effects. Students can influence their learning by active participation in clinical work. Wagenaar et al. (2003) showed that students failed to make optimal use of the learning opportunities in practice. However, it is unclear what caused this. Students may have been discouraged by teachers/doctors, who sometimes perceive students' questions and actions as interruptions that interfere with their daily routine. In addition, students may entertain misperceptions, like the idea that some things can only be learned from books. It is very likely that they are not familiar with the concept of learning while working. However, students may have some justification for their perception that books are the main source of useful knowledge. The final objective of clerkship still seems to be to pass the exam at the end, which generally depends on having mastered theoretical knowledge. That is precisely what students work at, acquiring masses of facts from textbooks instead of practical knowledge from clinical experience.

5. PRACTICAL IMPLICATIONS

In this chapter we have identified several factors that make theory to practice transition difficult for medical students. All these factors are part of the educational arrangement offered to the students, hanging together in a very subtle way. The balance can be disturbed by numerous effects, ranging from a change in the examination system to normal wear and tear of the authentic problems that once were very successful in initiating student learning, but whose solution became known to later generations of students and hence no longer stimulate their learning.

Medical education has at least three inbuilt dilemmas that prevent that straightforward conclusions can be drawn from our findings. The first dilemma has to do with the necessity to learn basic, biomedical sciences. Most medical curricula spend about equal time to clinical and biomedical knowledge in the first four years. Without biomedical knowledge clinical knowledge will remain an unrelated bundle of facts; without biomedical knowledge students will not be able to judge the importance of future developments. Yet, authentic situations derived from physicians' day-to-day work do not emphasise the application of this kind of knowledge, let alone that these situations force students to learn basic sciences. It is even worse; even teachers appeared to neglect the necessity of learning basic sciences in these situations. The second dilemma relates to the level of authenticity of the tasks presented to the students. Should authenticity be traded for simplicity or transparency to make sure that the whole-tasks presented to students have the level of complexity they can deal with? And what kind of reductions can be used to reach that level? The apparent disadvantage of the paper cases widely used in PBL curricula is that they allow shortcuts in clinical reasoning, resulting in reasoning "the other way round", as the students said. Rich video cases might not have this problem, but are much harder to make. It seems that cognitive similarity between simulation and real task performance might be more important than situational authenticity. The third dilemma relates to knowledge vs. skills acquisition and is strongly related to the first dilemma. A curriculum that puts knowledge first, even a curriculum that has been constructed to facilitate knowledge applicability in real contexts, runs the risk that this knowledge will not be connected to professional skills and strategies (e.g., the lack of differential diagnosis skill mentioned earlier in this chapter). On the other hand, a medical curriculum that puts competence first will soon run into trouble with planning the knowledge parts. All solutions suggested so far in the literature - the spiral curriculum, or the integrated skills curriculum – struggle with an optimisation problem, because too many elements should be integrated and different objectives ask for contradictory actions. For example, the necessity of using multiple examples of similar problems to promote transfer (suggested earlier in this chapter) is very time consuming and if not done in an unobtrusive way may evoke unwanted student behaviour.

Probably the most important lesson to be learnt from this analysis is that a medical curriculum is inherently overloaded and hence requires choices that are conscious of unwanted side-effects. As a consequence it is not possible to conclude this chapter with a strategy for curriculum design. Instead the yield of the analyses so far are no more than a list of do-s and don't-s, such as: Use methods that stimulate active learning, activation of prior knowledge and elaboration on new knowledge. Prevent that students build up an unconnected knowledge base, by emphasising the explanatory power of basic sciences. Use multiple and varied examples. Use an assessment system that requires knowledge application in authentic situations instead of knowledge reproduction. Introduce more practical experience in the pre-clinical phase and more theory learning in the clinical phase. Early practice can enrich abstract concepts. Once students (or graduates) are participating in practice, they need sufficient time to reflect on their learning. Informal learning should be made more explicit. Explicit learning and critical reflection on implicit habits and opinions are necessary for junior doctors' professional development. A more balanced structure of the curriculum with a gradual increase in responsibilities for students, more complex tasks, and gradual withdrawal of guidance by supervisors should optimise the training of competent medical doctors.

A final word about transition: The transition from theory to practice, from school to work, is never a smooth process and often disrupts learning. Adapting to a new environment causes stress in students. How far stress can be reduced largely depends on the domain involved. Many professional disciplines – such as medicine, nursing, air traffic control, teaching or police work - are inherently stressful; the workplace has its own dynamics, errors may have dramatic and fatal consequences, the environment may be noisy, the public offensive, and, for medicine and nursing in particular, pain and death are an integral part of professional life. Supervisors should try to reduce the stress for students by showing respect, by emphasising that it is a learning environment and by reassuring students that they will not be put into situations that overstretch their skills and responsibilities.

NOTE

The authors gratefully acknowledge the Van Walree Fund for a supporting grant.

REFERENCES

Barrows, H. S., & Tamblyn, R. M. (1980). *Problem-based learning: An approach to medical education*. New York: Springer.

Bogg, J., Gibbs, T., & Bundred, P. (2001). Training, job demands and mental health of pre-registration house officers. *Medical Education, 35*, 590-595.

Bolhuis, A. M., & Simons, P. R.-J. (1999). *Leren en werken (series: Opleiden en leren)*. [Learning and working; series: Education and learning] Deventer. Kluwer.

Boshuizen, H. P. A., & Schmidt, H. G. (2000). The development of clinical reasoning expertise; Implications for teaching. In J. Higgs & M. Jones (Eds.), *Clinical reasoning in the health professions* (2nd, completely rev. ed., pp. 15-22). Oxford: Butterworth-Heinemann.

Bransford, J. D., Brown, A. L., & Cocking, R. R. (Eds.). (1999). *How people learn: Brain, mind, experience, and school*. Washington: National Academy Press.

Brooks L. R., LeBlanc V. R., & Norman, G. R. (2000). On the difficulty of noticing obvious features in patient appearance. *Psychological Science, 11*, 112-117.

Calman, K. C., & Donaldson, M. (1991). The pre-registration house officer year: A critical incident study. *Medical Education, 25*, 51-59.

Cognition and Technology Group at Vanderbilt (1994). From visual word problems to learning communities: Changing conceptions of cognitive research. In K. Mc Gilly (Ed.), *Classroom lessons: Integrating cognitive theory and classroom practice* (pp. 157-200). Cambridge: MIT Press.

Custers, E. J. F. M., Regehr, G., & Norman, G. R. (1996). Mental representations of medical diagnostics knowledge. A review. *Academic Medicine, 71*, 55-61.

Ericsson, K. A, & Charness, N. (1994). Expert performance, its structure and acquisition. *American Psychologist, 49*, 725-747.

Eva, K. W., Brooks, L. R., & Norman, G. R. (2002). Forward reasoning as a hallmark of expertise in medicine: Logical, psychological, phenomenological inconsistencies. In S. P. Shohov (Ed.), *Advances in psychological research* (vol. 8, pp. 41-69). New York: Nova Science.

Eva, K. W., Neville, A. J., & Norman, G. R. (1998). Exploring the etiology of content specificity: Factors influencing analogic transfer and problem solving. *Academic Medicine, 73*, 1-5.

Galton, M., Morrison, L., & Pell, T. (2000). Transfer and transition in English schools: Reviewing the evidence. *International Journal of Educational Research, 33*, 341-363.

Gillard, J. H., Dent, T. H., Aarons, E. J., Smyth-Pigott, P. J., & Nichols, M. W. (1993). Pre-registration house officers in eight English regions: Survey of quality of training. *British Medical Journal, 307*, 1180-1184.

Hatala, R., Norman, G. R., & Brooks, L. R. (2003). Practice makes perfect: The critical role of mixed practice in the acquisition of ECG interpretation skills. *Advances in Health Sciences Education, 8*, 17-26.

Jones, A., McArdle, P. J., & O'Neill, P. (2002). Perceptions of how well graduates are prepared for the role of pre-registration house-officer: A comparison of outcomes from a traditional and an integrated PBL curriculum. *Medical Education, 36*, 16-25.

Lave, J., & Wenger, E. (1991). *Situated learning: Legitimate peripheral participation*. Cambridge: Cambridge University Press.

Moss, F., & McManus, I. (1992). The anxieties of new clinical students. *Medical Education, 26*, 17-20.

Norman, G. R., & Schmidt, H. G. (1992). The psychological basis of problem-based learning: A review of the evidence. *Academic Medicine, 67*, 557-565.
Patel, V. L., & Groen, G. J. (1986). Knowledge-based solution strategies in medical reasoning. *Cognitive Science, 10*, 91-116.
Patel, V. L., & Kaufman, D. R. (1995). Clinical reasoning and biomedical knowledge: Implications for teaching. In J. Higgs & M. Jones (Eds.), *Clinical reasoning in the health professions* (pp. 117-128). Oxford: Butterworth-Heinemann.
Prince, K. J. A. H., Van de Wiel, M. W. J., Scherpbier, A. J. J. A., Van der Vleuten, C. P. M., & Boshuizen, H. P. A. (2000). A qualitative analysis of the transition from theory to practice in undergraduate training in a PBL-medical school. *Advances in Health Sciences Education, 5*, 105-116.
Prince, K. J. A. H., Van de Wiel, M. W. J., Van der Vleuten, C. P. M., Boshuizen, H. P. A., & Scherpbier, A. J. J. A. (under editorial review). *Junior doctors' opinions about the transition from the learning environment of medical school to the working environment of daily practice*. Submitted.
Prince, K. J. A. H., Van Mameren, H., Hylkema, N., Drukker, J., Scherpbier, A. J. J. A., & Van der Vleuten, C. P. M. (2003). Does problem-based learning lead to deficiencies in basic science knowledge? An empirical case on anatomy. *Medical Education, 37*, 15-21.
Radcliffe, C., & Lester, H. (2003). Perceived stress during undergraduate medical training: A qualitative study. *Medical Education, 37*, 32-38.
Roche, A. M., Sanson Fischer, R. W., & Cockburn, J. (1997) Training experiences immediately after medical school. *Medical Education, 31*, 9-16.
Schmidt, H. G. (1983). Problem-based learning: Rationale and description. *Medical Education, 17*, 11-16.
Schmidt, H. G. (1993). Foundations of problem-based learning: Some explanatory notes. *Medical Education, 27*, 422-432.
Schön, D. A. (1987). *The reflective practitioner. How professionals think in action*. New York: Basic.
Van der Vleuten, C. P. M. (1996). The assessment of professional competence: Developments, research and practical implications. *Advances in Health Sciences Education, 1*, 41-67.
Van de Wiel, M. W. J., Schaper, N. C., Scherpbier, A. J. J. A., Van der Vleuten, C. P. M., & Boshuizen, H. P. A (1999). Students' experiences with real patient tutorials in a problem-based curriculum. *Teaching and Learning in Medicine, 11*, 12-20.
Van de Wiel, M. W. J., Boshuizen, H. P. A., Schmidt, H. G., & Schaper, N. C. (1999). The explanation of clinical concepts by expert physicians, clerks and advanced students. *Teaching and Learning in Medicine, 11*, 153-163.
Van Mameren, H., Leiner, T., Wanders, A., & Van der Vleuten, C. P. M. (1997). Anatomie/embryologieonderwijs aan de Universiteit Maastricht: Het oordeel van studenten geneeskunde. [Anatomy/embryology teaching at the University of Maastricht: Medical students'opinions] *Bulletin Medisch Onderwijs, 16*, 91-100.
Van Merriënboer, J. J. G. (1997). *Training complex cognitive skills*. Englewood Cliffs: Educational Technology.
Wagenaar, A., Scherpbier, A. J. J. A., Boshuizen, H. P. A., & Van der Vleuten, C. P. M. (2003). The importance of active involvement in learning: A qualitative study on learning results and learning processes in different traineeships. *Advances in Health Sciences Education, 8*, 201-212.

Woodward, C. A., & Ferrier, B. M. (1983). The content of the medical curriculum at McMaster University: Graduates' evaluation of their preparation for postgraduate training. *Medical Education, 17*, 54-60.

Chapter 8

EMBEDDING AND IMMERSION AS KEY STRATEGIES IN LEARNING TO TEACH

Harm H. Tillema
Department of Education, Leiden University, The Netherlands

1. RETHINKING LEARNING TO TEACH

From the literature on teacher learning, it is by no means clear what prompts a meaningful transition from student teachers' initial - and often implicit - beliefs on teaching to a professional oriented framework for teaching. To foster conceptual change in professional learning, especially in prospective teachers, it may be necessary to challenge long held approaches to "learning to teach" and rethink the professional preparation in teacher education. Reflection-oriented learning has been put forward as well as plentiful practice teaching as ways to actively involve student teachers in changing and (re)constructing their knowledge base for teaching and to align it with validated knowledge on teaching. In this study, the dynamic interchange between reflection on action and immersion into practice teaching is related to the process of belief change, in a setting in which student teachers are engaged in self-directed teaching. Our findings challenge some of the held assumptions by indicating that reflection after practice may be a more professionally fruitful way of a lasting belief change than reflectively preparing student teachers before they enter their practice teaching. This study points to the dangers of reflection on beliefs which is not grounded in the student teacher's own teaching experience.

2. STUDENT TEACHER LEARNING FOR THE PROFESSION

Every field of scholarly inquiry and study has its typical problems that are persistently investigated over many years. These characteristic problems may alter in name or label, depending on the perspectives and conceptual understandings developed over time, but remain in their diversity of appearances a matter of recurrent intense debate and deliberate thinking. The field of student teacher learning has its own persistent problem (Hamilton, 1998) frequently labelled as: "How does validated knowledge or 'theory' contribute to a knowledge base for practice?"; or conversely: "How does knowledge generated in practice contribute to professionally shared theory?", which at the current level of understanding now could better be framed as: "How does reflection/or conversely action contribute to action/or conversely reflection?" (Gore & Zeichner, 1991; Hofer & Pintrich, 2001; Loughran & Northfield, 1996; Shulman, 1996; Van Manen, 1995). Since the "reflective turn" (Mayer-Smith & Mitchell, 1997; Richardson, 1997) in student teacher learning, the current thinking clearly has shifted towards a reflective approach to practice. It is being advocated that student teachers' learning and their construction of a professional identity is in effect building upon and influenced by their own teaching conceptions and "practice theories" (Campbell & Kane, 1998; Loughran, 1996; Richardson, 1997).

3. DEALING WITH BELIEFS AND DISPOSITIONS

In coming to terms with the position of initial and pre-existent conceptions, strategies in student teacher learning predominantly have encouraged the development of a personal teaching approach (Calderhead & Shorrock, 1997; Oosterheert, 2001; Wideen & Grimmett, 1995). However, dealing with the personal beliefs and practice theories (Hofer & Pintrich, 2001) may contrast with an interest in fostering a validated knowledge base and a legitimate understanding of practice (Lave & Wenger, 1997), thus constituting a persistent dilemma in student teacher learning and professional education of teachers (Wideen, Mayer-Smith, & Moon, 1998). However, it may be helpful, as we propose in the following, to reframe this problem and shift perspectives (Dole & Sinatra, 1998).

As we contend, two different approaches or solutions typically have been put forward to maintain the relation between theory and practice in student teacher learning and professional development of teachers (Figure 1), characterized by the main interventions chosen to link existing (student) teacher beliefs with new, often belief challenging knowledge.

Changing beliefs in learning to teach	
By EMBEDDING	By IMMERSION
(theory first)	(practice first)
Reflection ▶ Practice	Practice ▶ Reflection
leading to knowledge 'incrementation"	leading to knowledge "confrontation"
(focus on building explicit and valid knowledge)	(focus on gradual growth of personal knowledge)

Figure 1. Two distinct approaches in learning to teach

The first approach in linking (student) teacher beliefs with a (validated) knowledge base on teaching (Campbell & Kane, 1998; Feiman-Nemser, 1990; Fenstermacher, 1994; Fessler, 1995; Richardson, 1996) may be labelled an *embedding orientation*. Embedding is interpreted as: Using lay theories or (student) teachers' initial beliefs as a starting point for explicating the implicit know-how contained in them while at the same time gradually insert and link new prevalent and adjacent knowledge on teaching to the knowledge base of the student (Bennett & Carre, 1993; Holt-Reynolds, 1992); thus preparing and scaffolding teacher learning with "adequate", reflective conceptions before engaging in the immediacy and pressures of classroom teaching. An embedding orientation favours in essence an "incremental" process of belief change and gradual building of a professional knowledge (Dole & Sinatra, 1998; Tillema, 1995).

The second approach, which may be labelled an *immersion orientation*, however, seeks to challenge teachers beliefs as well as tries to encapsulate or bind them by using the preconditions set by practice (Hargreaves, 1994). This approach intends to balance pre-existing personal theories with direct learning experiences in practice to arrive at a felt need to reconcile conflicting beliefs in a coherent personal knowledge base. It is assumed this confrontational process of belief change might result in reconstruction of existing beliefs and (re)building of a reflective knowledge base on practice (Edwards & Collison, 1996; Winitzky & Kauchak, 1997).

4. STRATEGIES IN LEARNING TO TEACH

Recognising the dilemmas both orientations face in dealing with building professional knowledge, it is important to clarify under what conditions actual change in conceptions and beliefs occurs (Hofer & Pintrich, 2001) that aligns with a validated knowledge base on teaching. This is a particular problem in the context of learning to teach. Interventions by teacher educators to introduce student teachers to new professional knowledge repeatedly point to the existing conceptional frameworks as being apparently changed – at least on a short term – but in effect remaining inert (Tillema, 1995). These outcomes may support the notion of the stability of conceptions. Other studies, however, show (Richardson, 1996; Zuzowsky, 1995) change may occur, although not always in a unidirectional or intended way (Hamilton, 1998). In these cases, practice teaching seems to be the strongest factor in changing beliefs (Zuzowsky, 1995). The occurrence of change in beliefs may, therefore, well be attributed to the way in which the student teacher's beliefs are challenged. An incremental or embedding approach (Tillema, 1995) in which reflection and conceptual deliberation are used first, to open up and "ground" existing beliefs may have ultimately the effect of stabilizing practice experiences, and even a knowledge-generating effect (Oosterheert, 2001). Whereas a confrontational or immersion approach, in which the student teacher is confronted with new and different insights may either lead to an inevitable and quick adaptation to the demands of practice or, in reaction, a protective "shield" being drawn around the existing beliefs (Buchman & Floden, 1992; Lundeberg, Levin, & Harrington, 1999).

In this study, we were interested in gauging whether student teachers change their initial beliefs as a result of reflective inquiry prior to immersion in practice or, alternatively, as a result of their immersion into practice teaching whether these situations gave way to reflective and deliberate change of their beliefs.

5. INTERVENTION

To study the effects of belief change according to either an immersion or an embedding approach, two groups of student teachers were compared with regard to learning a communal topic, i.e., learning to teach self-directed methods in their practice teaching (Areglado, Bradley, & Lane, 1996). This teaching approach was thought to be appropriate for eliciting outspoken beliefs in student teachers (Kremer Hayon & Tillema, 1999) and therefore suitable for studying belief change as a result of either immersion or embedding.

With respect to introducing self directed teaching methods, so called study teams were used as a differential treatment or intervention in the regular training program of student teachers (Tillema, 1997; Hamilton, 1998; Joyce, Murphy, Showers, & Murphy, 1989). The study team method, which in itself is a self directed teaching method, offers the opportunity to support an inquiry-oriented study activity, using practice assignments which eventually will provide concrete teaching solutions in planning and executing actual teaching situations. A study team consists of a group of student teachers as learners who, after having received a concrete teaching problem or case (Lundeberg et al., 1999) decide upon their targets for study by engaging in a process of debate and inquiry aimed at constructing a concrete solution for the problem to be enacted in practice teaching situations. A study team organizes its own learning through studying an issue from different perspectives and by sharing existing knowledge and beliefs whilst working cooperatively towards a common solution.

5.1 Constituting elements of the study team approach

5.1.1 Conceptual exchange and reflective dialogue

As is apparent in the work of Engeström (1994) as well as others, discourse and debate are major routes for explicating tacit knowledge and implicit beliefs. Exchange, dialogue and conversation lie at the heart of self-generating knowledge (Wallace & Louden, 1994). Professional beliefs must be opened for debate and exchange in order to become of relevance for professional action. This occurs when it can be shared with others. Exchange and dialogue are therefore central features in the study team approach. Engeström (1994) studying the process of exchange (among engineers, operators, teachers) showed that unfolding ideas in a discourse allows for multiple perspectives and value-added solutions that not only contribute to a better and mutual understanding, but also to the productive generation of new knowledge.

5.1.2 Self-directedness in learning

A second principle that contributes to learning in study teams is self-regulation (Zimmerman & Schunk, 2001). Essentially, self-regulation is about a process by which one directs and controls learning to attain personal goals in learning, thereby using learning strategies as well as metacognitive monitoring in developing knowledge. This dynamic view not only gives the learner freedom to learn, but also a greater degree of responsibility for accomplishing one's goals. It requires active involvement in learning and setting personal standards that can be reached. Knowledge construction is seen as a tool or a vehicle not as an objective for study and inquiry of relevant problems, i.e., studying issues are at the core of building a professional's knowledge base. In this respect, the (beginning) professional becomes a manager of his or her own learning. This learning need not necessarily be equated with individual, isolated learning per se; it also implies learning to operate in teams and cooperate with others.

5.1.3 Collaboration in teams

Wallace and Louden (1994) described some of the dynamics of collaboration that occur in team learning. They describe a picture of the "deeply personal nature" involvement in successful collaboration. They base their analysis on the personal qualities and characteristics of knowledge, and on the central place of biography and experience in the professionals' work lives that brings forward practical knowledge. Collaboration is taken to include "a relationship that involves 'receptivity of the other', one that pays careful attention to the other's voice".

In their description of collaboration, Baldwin and Austin (1995) have identified six dynamics of team based collaboration: A degree of jointness (distinctive roles vs. shared responsibility), definition of roles and responsibilities (explicit definition vs. none), flexibility of roles (rigid vs. flexible), similarity of standards and expectations (uniform vs. different), proximity of partners (same location vs. distant), and depth of relationship (personal and professional vs. work relation mainly). This description of collaboration indicates at least some of the complexities that occur in. team based learning.

5.2 The study team steps

The study team method is regarded as a method to elicit existing beliefs (See step 1-3 below), to reflect and challenge these beliefs (step 4-7), and to link reflection to action (step 8-10). Study teams have been adopted as an approach in collaborative professional learning (Hamilton, 1998). The notion of study teams has been laid out in 10 successive steps.

Mission and goal. Study teams work towards a concrete and tangible product with regard to practice teaching and learning in classrooms.

Step 1: Task or problem definition. Determination and boundaries of the problem situation. This step is to explore and collect background materials with regard to a problematic teaching situation (in this study with respect to the employing the strategy of self directed learning in classrooms). To offer a clear focus for activity, a study team has to decide upon a practical outcome to be achieved (e.g. a lesson plan, a lesson assignment, or pupil materials).

Step 2: Exploration of beliefs. Identification and discussion of the study team's prior experiences and beliefs with respect to the selected problem. This step is to explicate each one's implicit conceptions and tacit knowledge and to examine their coherence and fruitfulness as a possible contribution to the proposed outcome.

Step 3: Reflection on beliefs. Analysis of strengths and weaknesses in each other's ideas about solving the problem. This step stresses the function of a study team in validating existing beliefs, as well as the need for an inquiry into these beliefs and the co-construction of new knowledge.

Step 4: Searching for solutions. Brainstorm about possible, provisory but nonetheless tangible solutions. This step's objective is to formulate specific and clear questions for further study in order to collect missing information or to resolve discrepancies from earlier discussions.

Step 5: Going through selected (or offered) materials. Exploring relevant information and solutions. In this step the study team searches for external information that would answer the questions posed and/or evaluate the materials provided to them in order to decide about further inquiry needs. This step offers the teacher educator an opportunity to insert relevant validated, i.e., professional knowledge to the student teachers.

Step 6: Inquiry and research. Inquiry, study and "recherché" into existing uncertainties and exploring the feasibility of offered solutions. In this step the study team enters into a research-oriented process of collecting and analysing external information (written or provided by experts) that could solve the problem.

Step 7: Producing solutions. Working out solutions in a tangible format. This step is aimed at producing a fruitful and concrete teaching product as a solution to the identified problem, e.g. in the format of sheets, charts, materials, checklists and so forth.

Step 8: Forum presentation. Discussion and presentation of solutions to others. This step is used to scrutinize and assess the feasibility of solutions and discuss the acceptance of solutions found by requesting feedback from others, i.e., peers. This can take the form of an exhibition, a presentation or a poster session.

Step 9: Redefinition of solutions. Determination of the final solution and delivering a product or outcome based on the evaluations from the previous step. This step is to finalise the critique and handle the received feedback and alterations needed.

Step 10: Process evaluation and learning outcomes. Establishing the study team's learning results interpreted as beliefs changed. In this step the study team evaluates the working process as well as goes back to the initial discussions on their beliefs in step 2 and 3.

6 METHOD

Thirty-four student teachers from two teacher training colleges participated in a seminar on teaching self-directed learning methods to pupils in primary schools. The seminar was divided into three separate periods.
1. A three-month embedding period, during which the student teachers were acquainted with the principles of self-directed learning.
2. A three-month immersion period during which the student teachers were supervised whilst teaching in primary schools in accordance with self-directed teaching methods.
3. A follow-up period of practice teaching lasting for three months during which the student teachers were further observed and interviewed. One group of 21 student teachers entered the embedding period first. Another group of 13 student teachers, entered the immersion period first. Each group was assessed during the follow-up period by their mentor teacher.

Each study team in the seminar consisted of about seven student teachers; a total of five teams was formed, three in the embedding mode and two in the immersion mode. Two seminar tutors (one for each mode) supervised the progress of the study teams during the three-month reflective period, and coached the student teachers in solving problems while working in the study teams.

6.1 Vignette instrument

A vignette instrument was used to test actual student teachers' beliefs with respect to self directed learning and teaching according to this method. Two cases (Lundeberg et al., 1999) were offered to student teachers involving a typical professional teaching problem related to self-directed learning. The student teachers were asked to write their comments on each in order to (1) provide arguments with respect to the analysis of the problem, (2) outline the course of action which they would prefer in order to solve the problem, and (3) justify that action with argumentative justifications.

The vignette test was administered on each of four assessment occasions: At pre-test, after period one with either the immersion or embedding approach, after period two with conversing approaches, and after the follow-up period. In order to score the argumentative texts produced, the instrument described by Winitzky (1992) was utilised, which provides a determination of the level of reflection and argumentation in the student's writing. Scoring with this instrument was carried out with respect to
1. the number of arguments given (this is to establish the extensiveness of knowledge and to indicate the elaborateness of reflections), and

2. the level or degree of reflective thinking found in the arguments given, in order to establish the reflectivity of beliefs, i.e., to establish the degree of reflective reasoning (on a scale from 0-10) as apparent in the student teachers' comments by classifying the statements.

6.2 Belief test

To measure belief change as a result of the intervention, a teaching-beliefs questionnaire was constructed to measure student teachers' beliefs about self-directed learning, with forced-choice responses based upon 20 opposing statements. This questionnaire based on a study by Tillema (1994) was completed with items from Areglado et al. (1996) in the following categories on a five-point contrast scale:
1. ways of content delivery (5 items); e.g. "Pupils learn best by self determining the way they handle an assignment."
2. pupil interaction (5 items); e.g. "It is important not to steer conversations among pupils."
3. teaching methods (5 items); e.g. "My role as a teacher is best described as scaffolding what pupils learn."
4. assessment of pupil's learning growth (5 items); e.g. "In grading it is important to diagnose pupil's weaknesses and strengths."

A reliability score, using Cronbach's alpha, for the 20 items was found to be .86.

7 RESULTS

With respect to overall belief change related to self-directed teaching, based on the belief questionnaire during the subsequent intervention periods, the findings are presented below in Table 1.

Table 1. Means on a 4-point scale under the two interventions as measured by the belief test

	Embedding intervention	Immersion intervention
Pretest	3.24	3.36
after Period 1	3.74	2.76
after Period 2	2.79	3.12
after Follow up	3.21	3.34

The belief-test data make clear that student teachers' remain having a positive attitude toward self-directed learning throughout the whole intervention period (well above the scale median of 2.50). No differences were found between groups prior to the intervention i.e., at the pre-test). However, for the post-test measurement, also no significant differences between the immersion and embedding groups were found, with $F(1,32) = 3.34$; $p < .10$. A within-subject F test taking into account the change in beliefs between the different belief-test intervals, i.e., reversal of intervention periods in the two groups, showed a small effect, with $F(3,102) = 2.91$; $p < .05$. The interaction effect between group and period was found to be statistically significant, with $F(3,102) = 2.80$; $p < .05$, which was localised (Tukey test) as a significant difference between the two groups at the end of period one - i.e., a difference was found between the embedding group and the immersion group during their first acquaintance with the principles of self-directed teaching. No change between groups was found after period two, i.e., after having completed both the study team activity and the practice teaching.

This is taken to imply that student teachers' beliefs differ as an outcome of the intervention during the study team period, but not as a result of the practice period. It has to be noted that the change was found in relation to the previously-held beliefs of the student teachers.

With respect to the number of arguments and levels of reflective reasoning of student teachers as an indicator of their beliefs under the two interventions, the main findings are presented in Table 2.

Table 2. Means of the number of arguments and level of reasoning in the vignette test of teaching beliefs

	No. of Arguments		Level of Reasoning	
	Embedding condition	Immersion condition	Embedding condition	Immersion condition
Pretest	5.75	6.19	4.25	4.05
After Period 1	9.05	6.98	5.61	4.56
After Period 2	8.51	8.63	5.53	5.99
After Follow up	8.03	8.18	5.51	5.72

As to the vignette test, a general and significant increase in the number of arguments was found after period 1 for the embedding group and after period 2 for the immersion group, hence an increase in the elaborateness of the reasoning of student teachers after the study team intervention was noted. The means found for the successive intervals also show an overall increase in the level of reflection after the study team activity, indicating more sophistication in the student teachers' arguments as a result of deliberate inquiry.

The F-test for level of reasoning in reflection on the vignette test, showed no overall significant difference. The period of intervention (with $F(3,102) = 1.38$) was not significant either. This is taken to imply that the level of reflective reasoning by the student teachers was not affected by the intervention period. The data on the number of arguments only showed a small effect on the (difference between) period of intervention with $F(3,102) = 2.78; p < .05$, but no effect was found for the intervention itself (i.e., being either embedding or immersion).

8 DISCUSSION

This study was intended to clarify how to foster beginning professional learning, especially how student teachers' learning is affected by different strategies to promote change in conceptions on teaching. It was hypothesized that a student teacher's beliefs play a diverse role in knowledge acquisition and preparation for a professional practice. The way in which these beliefs are dealt with in teacher learning i.e., in programs on learning to teach may differentially affect the student teacher's belief change. In an immersion strategy, beliefs are dealt with in a 'local', i.e., contextual and implicit way, letting practice experiences have a decisive and confrontational effect upon the student teacher's rebuilding and personal construction of a professional knowledge base. In an embedding approach, these beliefs are dealt with more explicitly from the viewpoint of validated knowledge to construct, in a gradual sense, a reflective professional knowledge base as a platform and stronghold to interpret and enact (future) practice situations.

It was assumed that a reflection-first, i.e. embedding intervention scaffolds positive beliefs towards, in this case, self-directed learning which then may be put to the test in practice teaching. Perhaps, initially, these constructed beliefs will be found to fall short of their expected worth because of the conditions set in practice, but subsequently, evoke reflective evaluations in order to maintain or change beliefs. On the other hand, when a practice-oriented immersion approach precedes explicit and intentional learning about, in this case, a beliefs evoking teaching method like self directed learning, initial and more or less implicit beliefs of student teachers may become experientially scrutinized, which eventually lead to a situation in which the student teacher recognizes a personally felt need to reconcile and change these beliefs in a constructive way.

The results of this study showed no belief change of student teachers on the combined effect of both conditions as measured over the whole intervention period. Looking at the respective means for periods in both interventions, it looks like immersion and embedding compensate for each other's effect. However, on a more detailed level - i.e., when the changes during intervention period intervals are taken into account - beliefs do change. This finding could be summarized as follows: The practice period has a conservative or reducing effect upon initial positively-held beliefs with regard to self-directed learning; the reflective period while working in study teams has led to an increase in positive beliefs as compared to the pre-test. As might be expected, the reflective, study team period showed a positive effect on the number of arguments. Student teachers gave more elaborated deliberations with respect to justifying their beliefs, and this holds, although to a lesser degree, with regard to the level of reasoning. This result is the case irrespective of the order in which the intervention was delivered, i.e., either practice first or reflection first. Contrary to what might be expected, no strong relationship was found with regard to the overall direction of the belief change as a result of the interventions after a retention period; what remains is that beliefs become better verbalised, which may be taken for a greater explicitness of the student teachers' beliefs as a result of the interventions.

According to these findings, reflection-oriented strategies to promote belief change can be considered fruitful in offering or imposing meaningful structures for the personal construction of a knowledge base by the student teacher (Feiman-Nemser, 1990; Fenstermacher, 1994; Hofer & Pintrich, 2001) The meaningfulness of reflection, however, depends not just upon explicating the beliefs which implicitly exist. Also the primacy and directness of practice adds to the reconstruction of beliefs by establishing or demanding a conceptual congruence between held beliefs. As a result of this congruence (Tillema, 1994) between experiencing practical demands and existing beliefs, they become embedded in a professional knowledge base and can be 'worked' upon accordingly (Calderhead & Shorrock, 1997). One could even assert that the greater the correspondence between practice experiences and beliefs, the easier it is to accept and build a coherent knowledge base for teaching and - conversely - that the more tenuous the correspondence is, the more relevant and supportive reflection can be.

A reflection-first strategy could make pre-existing beliefs more positively evaluated, and - when critically assessed in practice - leaving student teachers in a position to solve the incongruities between what has been learned or studied and what has been experienced. Reflection, for instance in study teams, may change the beliefs of student teachers by 'opening up' their existing belief structures, but without immersion into practice these beliefs remain less stable and vulnerable. This dual process of practice immersion and reflective embedding offers strong opportunities for promoting belief change in student teachers. The position on belief change advocated here is one of a mutual accommodation of reflection and immersion, positioning beliefs as interpretative frameworks (DiSessa, 1993) which can provide meaning following practice. As this study shows, student teachers are ready to refine and adapt their beliefs. Teacher education programs have a powerful position and possibilities in selecting and framing relevant interventions in learning to teach.

In this respect the method of study teams is of interest. The features of this approach to learning resemble what Shuell (1990) earlier called 'active meaningful learning', denoting a constructive, cumulative and goal-directed learning process (Claxton, 1995). This method of study teams, not only requires a special orientation towards the conceptual beliefs and (prior) work experiences of the (beginning professional) learner, but also requires a work oriented context and communication between learners to evoke relevant knowledge (Engeström, 1994). This is necessary in order for them to adopt solutions that can be tested and scrutinized while studying and developing a personal and practical knowledge base.

Principles in the design of interventions to stimulate this type of learning include:

1. conceptual dialogue and exchange among peers (Spiro, 1990) in which reflection and dialogue between collaborating learners are taken as the starting point for exploring new concepts or strategies;
2. collaborative learning in teams (Katzenbach & Smith, 1993; Wallace & Louden, 1994) using team based work and cooperation as platforms for generating new knowledge; and
3. self regulated learning and inquiry in which study and discovery into the analysis and design of work and practice is being used to become more knowledgeable about one's own environment (Tillema, 1997).

These principles proved to be important constituting elements of learning for the profession.

REFERENCES

Areglado, R. J., Bradley, R. C., & Lane, P. S. (1996). *Learning for life. Creating classrooms for self-directed learning.* Thousand Oaks: Corwin.
Baldwin, R. G., & Austin, A. E. (1995). Toward greater understanding of faculty research collaboration. *The Review of Higher Education, 19* (2), 45-70.
Bennett, N., & Carre, C. (1993). *Learning to teach.* London: Routledge.
Buchman, M., & Floden, R. E. (1992). Coherence: The rebel angel. *Educational Researcher, 21* (9) 4-9.
Calderhead, J., & Shorrock, S. B. (1997). *Understanding teacher education.* London: Falmer.
Campbell, A., & Kane, I. (1998). *School-based teacher education. Telling tales from a fictional primary school.* London: Fulton.
Claxton, G. (Ed.). (1996). *Liberating the learner.* New York: Routledge.
DiSessa, A. (1993). Towards an epistemology of physics. *Cognition and Instruction, 10,* 105-225.
Dole, J., & Sinatra, G. (1998). Reconceptualizing change in the cognitive construction of knowledge. *Educational Psychologist, 33,* 109-128.
Edwards, A., & Collison, J. (1996). *Mentoring and developing practice in primary schools.* Buckingham: Open University Press.
Engeström, Y. (1994). Teachers as collaborative thinkers. In I. Carlgren (Ed.), *Teachers' minds and actions* (pp. 45-56). London: Falmer.
Feiman-Nemser, S. (1990). Teacher preparation. Structural and conceptual alternatives. In W. Houston (Ed.), *Handbook of research on teacher education* (pp. 212-234). New York: MacMillan.
Fenstermacher, G. D. (1994). The knower and the known. The nature of knowledge in research on teaching. *Review of Research in Education, 20,* 3-56.
Fessler, R. (1995). Teacher education as a career-long process. In R. Hoz & M. Silberstein (Eds.), *Partnerships of schools and institutions of higher education in teacher development* (pp. 263-280). Jerusalem: MOFET.
Gore, J. M., & Zeichner, K. M. (1991). Action research and reflective teaching in pre-service teacher education. *Teaching and Teacher Education, 7,* 119-136.
Hamilton, M. L. (1998). *Reconceptualizing teaching practice. Self study in teacher education.* London: Falmer.

Hargreaves, A. (1994). *Changing teachers, changing times. Teachers' work and culture in the postmodern age.* London: Cassell.
Hofer, B. K., & Pintrich, P. R. (2001). *Personal epistomology. A psychology of beliefs about knowledge.* Mahwah: Erlbaum.
Holt-Reynolds, D. (1992). Personal history-based beliefs as relevant prior knowledge in coursework. *American Educational Research Journal, 29,* 325-349.
Joyce, B. R., Murphy, C., Showers, B., & Murphy, J. (1989). School renewal as cultural change. *Educational Leadership, 47* (3), 70-77.
Katzenbach, J. R., & Smith, D. G. (1993). *The wisdom of teams. Creating the high performance organization.* Boston: Harvard Business School Press.
Kremer Hayon, L., & Tillema, H. H. (1999). Self-regulated learning in the context of teacher education. *Teaching and Teacher Education, 15,* 507-522.
Lave, J., & Wenger, E. (1997). *Situated learning. Legitimate peripheral participation.* Cambridge Cambridge University Press.
Loughran, J. (1996). *Developing reflective practice. Learning about teaching and learning through modelling.* London: Falmer.
Loughran, J., & Northfield, J. (1996). *Opening the classroom door. Teacher, researcher, learner.* London: Falmer.
Lundeberg, M. A., Levin, B., & Harrington, H. (1999). *Who learns what from cases and how?* Mahwah: Erlbaum.
Mayer-Smith, J. A., & Mitchell, I. J. (1997). Teaching about constructivism. Using approaches informed by constructivism. In V. Richardson (Ed.), *Constructivist teacher education. Building a world of new understandings* (pp. 129-153). London: Falmer.
Oosterheert, I. (2001). *How student teachers learn. A psychological perspective on knowledge construction.* PhD Thesis, University of Groningen: The Netherlands.
Richardson, V. (1996). The role of attitudes and beliefs in learning to teach. In J. Sikula (Ed.), *Handbook of research on teaching* (pp. 102-119). New York: MacMillan.
Richardson, V. (Ed.). (1997). *Constructivist teacher education. Building a world of new understandings.* London: Falmer.
Shuell, T. J. (1990). Phases of meaningful learning. *Review of Educational Research, 60,* 531-547.
Shulman, L. (1996). Just in case. Reflections on learning from experience. In J. Colbert, P. Desberg, & K. Trimble (Eds.), *The case for education. Contemporary approaches using case methods* (pp. 197-217). Boston: Allyn & Bacon.
Spiro, R. J. (1990). Cognitive flexibility and hypertext. In: D. Nix & R. J. Spiro (Eds.), *Exploring ideas in high technology* (pp. 56-81) Hillsdale: Erlbaum.
Tillema, H. H. (1994). Training and professional expertise. Bridging the gap between new information and pre-existing beliefs of teachers. *Teaching and Teacher Education, 10,* 601-615.
Tillema, H. H. (1995). Integrating knowledge and beliefs. Promoting the relevance of educational knowledge for student teachers. In R. Hoz & M. Silberstein (Eds.), *Partnerships of schools and institutions of higher education in teacher development* (pp. 9-24). Jerusalem: MOFET.
Tillema, H. H. (1997). Reflective dialogue in teams. A vehicle to support belief change in student teachers. *European Journal of Teacher Education, 20,* 283-296.
Van Manen, M. (1995). On the epistemology of reflective practice. *Teachers & Teaching, Theory and Practice, 1,* 33-50.
Wallace, J., & Louden, W. (1994). Collaboration and the growth of teachers' knowledge. *Qualitative Studies in Education, 7,* 323-334.

Wideen, M., & Grimmett, P. (1995). *Changing times in teacher education*. London: Falmer.
Wideen, M., Mayer-Smith, J., & Moon, B. (1998). A critical analysis of the research on learning to teach. *Review of Educational Research, 68,* 130-178.
Winitzky, N. (1992). Structure and process in thinking about classroom management. An explorative study of prospective teachers. *Teaching and Teacher Education, 8,* 1-14.
Winitzky, N., & Kauchak, D. (1997). Constructivism in teacher education. Applying cognitive theory to teacher learning. In V. Richardson (Ed.), *Constructivist teacher education. Building a world of new understandings* (pp. 59-84). London: Falmer.
Zimmerman, B. J., & Schunk, D. H. (2001). *Self-regulated learning and academic achievement. Theoretical perspectives*. Mahwah: Erlbaum.
Zuzowsky, R. (1995). Professional development of student teachers during pre-service training. A follow-up study. In R. Hoz & M. Silberstein (Eds.), *Partnerships of schools and institutions of higher education in teacher development* (pp. 39-62). Jerusalem: MOFET.

PART 4

WORKPLACE AND ORGANISATION: ENCULTURATION TO BECOME AN EXPERT PROFESSIONAL

Chapter 9

TEACHING EXPERTISE
Empirical findings on expert teachers and teacher development

Eero Ropo
Department of Teacher Education, University of Tampere, Finland

1. RESEARCH ON THE NATURE OF EXPERTISE

Research on teacher expertise can be advocated from at least two frameworks. The first is the concern and dissatisfaction with the schools and quality of school education. Policy makers, particularly in the United States, have often complained about the quality of teacher education and called for changes in the training and certification of teachers (e.g. The Holmes Group, 1986; U.S. Department of Education, 2002). These statements have often been criticized by educational researchers, who argue that much of the criticism is politically motivated and is not supported by the research evidence (Berliner & Biddle, 1995; Darling-Hammond & Youngs, 2002). From this point of view it is important to understand, for instance, what kind of knowledge successful teachers have and how teacher education can promote the acquisition of this knowledge.

Another motive is the theoretical interest in the phenomenon of expertise. It is important to understand expertise to be able to promote its development in the work environments and further education.

In the following I will focus on the latter point of view. I start by reviewing empirical studies on expertise and particularly teacher expertise and summarize the results into a few propositions. My second purpose is to review research theorizing the phenomenon of teacher expertise. I will also discuss the future research on teacher expertise.

Although the focus of this chapter is in expertise it is important to notice that there are several other approaches to studying teacher knowledge (Munby, Russell, & Martin, 2001). For instance, Shulman (1986) described experienced teachers' knowledge base by dividing it into several content categories and forms of knowing. That knowledge is represented in the mental structures of one's knowledge base. Bromme and Tillema (1995) refer to the activity-oriented knowledge of practitioners as professional knowledge. This knowledge includes representations of theoretical rules and statements but also images, metaphors, and attitudes for successful practice. They also include teachers' beliefs and orientations into the professional knowledge base.

Different approaches to studying professional knowledge are needed for many reasons. One of those is that the domain areas differ. For instance, the most recent research on expertise has suggested that expertise between domain areas may differ in such amounts that even the research paradigms are hard to transfer from one area to another (Boshuizen, Schmidt, Custers, & Van de Wiel, 1995; Bromme & Tillema, 1995).

Studies on expertise have made an important contribution to our thinking about professional knowledge and skills. The beginning of research on the nature of expertise can be traced to the 1960s, when De Groot (1966), among others, studied the playing skills of chess masters and their information processing during a game. Those studies proved that chess masters did not function as predicted, but rather used a high level of intuition. Computer programs developed at the time, although designed to emulate the way people played chess, functioned quite differently. De Groot's studies (1978) showed that world class chess players accessed the best moves during their initial perception of the game board situation rather than searching for possible moves and analysing their consequences for the situation. It was later estimated that master level chess players have at least 100,000 different game situations in store and these can be recalled rapidly and intuitively in the game situation (Chase & Simon, 1973). According to these researchers the development of expertise requires more than ten years of experience and full-time practice.

Since the late 1960s and early 1970s, the nature of expertise has been studied in many professional fields. In addition to chess players, for example, physicists, radiologists, computer programmers (Chi, Glaser, & Farr, 1988) and social scientists (Voss, Greene, Post, & Penner, 1983) have been studied. The first studies were conducted in the domain areas that can be called knowledge-rich; rich referring, for instance, to well defined and developed theories in the domain area. According to these studies, novice physicists, for instance, who possessed the necessary knowledge to solve a physics problem, tried to solve it backwards from the question, whereas expert physicists retrieved a solution plan the other way round, as part of the normal comprehension process. Chi, Feltovich, and Glaser (1981) showed that the physics experts had more knowledge than the novices and that it was better organized in their memory. The experts could therefore represent the problems in terms of relevant physics theories, whereas the novices' representations were mainly based on salient surface features of the problems.

On the basis of the above studies and many others, it is possible to draw at least two conclusions on how research has approached expertise (Ericsson & Smith, 1991). First, research efforts have been focused on observing outstanding performance in relatively standardized conditions. In these studies, expertise has usually been defined as the ability to successfully execute problem-solving tasks related to one's professional field.

The second conclusion is that the theoretical concern of the studies has been with the analyses and descriptions of cognitive processes related to expert performance. One of the results of this approach has been the development of methods not only for measuring but also for eliciting expert knowledge and describing its structure and organization in specific domain areas (Cooke, 1994; Hoffman, 1992, 1995). In many cases the processes studied are the same as those described in the theories of skill acquisition (Anderson, 1983, 1993).

The efforts of the first two decades in finding out the "secrets" of expertise have led to fairly clear conclusions on the nature of experts' knowledge bases. Experts seem to possess better-organized and more specific knowledge structures that they can access almost intuitively in the problem situations. Nevertheless, it is not clear what the mechanisms of the development of this knowledge are and how they are related, for instance, to the amount and quality of experience or the innate characteristics of a person. Typically experts show superior performance in the domain areas in which there are well-developed theories that support reasoning, such as medicine, physics, chess, bridge and so on (Ericsson & Lehmann, 1996). In the earlier expertise studies performance and the structure and content of one's knowledge base are shown to be closely related.

Experience has also been linked to expertise in several studies. For instance, Leprohan and Patel (1995) found that the number of years of experience correlates positively with nurses' performance in screening emergency calls for medical help. The amount of auditors' experience was found to relate poorly to the accuracy of their performance in the study by Bonner and Pennington (1991). Similar results were obtained in the studies by Rosson (1985) and Doane, Pellegrino, and Klatzky (1990). All these studies have shown that experts do not always demonstrate superior performance in the activities representing their domain area tasks. Sometimes the reason seems to be in the nature of expertise, which is highly specialized and restricted to a narrow domain area.

2. THE NATURE OF TEACHER EXPERTISE

In contrast to the domain areas described above, in which the problems given to subjects are often specific and isolated from the social or cultural context, teaching is very different. The effectiveness of individual performance can be relatively easily described in such domain areas as physics or chess, but the phenomenon seems to be different in the school classroom. Instead of being good at a specific and well-defined problem, expert teachers have to be performers in the problems situated in socially and culturally complex contexts.

The first problem is to find the expert teachers for the studies. One of the criteria that have been used is student learning in academic subjects. Expert teachers are those whose students perform well in the achievement tests. For instance, Leinhardt has used teachers' long-term success in their profession as a criterion for expertise, measuring success by the students' results in academic achievement tests (Leinhardt & Greeno, 1986).

However, there are problems in this kind of criterion because we do not know enough about the functions teachers have in student learning and in their test results. Teachers are supposed to make a difference in student learning, but this relation is not simple. Teaching as a domain field can be described as a knowledge-lean domain area because of the complexity of the instructional context and the lack of comprehensive theories explaining it. The theories of teaching and instruction are vague and the school context is too complex to be described with only those theories. This all makes it difficult to explain how a teacher's expertise influences student achievement or to assume that the students whose achievements are excellent must have expert teachers.

However, teachers have important roles in organizing studying, directing the conversation and affecting the students' lives in many other ways in schools. Therefore, we may say that teacher expertise in such partly intuitive and artistic, partly learned interventions, can be assumed to make a difference in student learning (Gage, 1978).

If we adopt such a conception of the nature of teacher expertise, the perspective on teacher knowledge and performance becomes very complicated. Artistic and intuitive decisions may be based on knowledge, but their origins may be more in the situation. It is, therefore, important to approach teacher expertise from a more contextual point of view than in some other fields. One example of this kind of theorizing is the stage model first proposed by Dreyfus and Dreyfus (1986).

According to this the development of expertise proceeds in five stages: Novice, advanced beginner, competent performer, proficient performer, and expert (Dreyfus & Dreyfus, 1986). Berliner (1988) has described a novice, advanced beginner and a competent performer as rational and the proficient performer as intuitive in decision-making, for instance, in a problem situation. Berliner (1988) describes experts as irrational. Experts possess intuition with which they can create an overall representation of a situation. Their actions are flexible and fit the situation at hand. Experts seem to know what to do without necessarily being able to describe to an outsider the grounds for their action or how their thinking proceeds. Thinking seems to be rational in the sense that there is logic behind it. However, the rules of decision-making are hidden and intuitive, or tacit if we want, even for an expert himself/herself. A person is an expert because he or she seems to understand the requirements of the situation better and is able to fit his/her own decision, actions and interaction into the context.

A popular research strategy in describing expertise in domain fields similar to teaching has been to identify typical differences between the experts and novices. Those studies have produced a list of factors or characteristics that seem to differentiate expert teachers from novices. I summarize those results in the following six propositions.

2.1 Expertise develops in only a narrow field of knowledge and the knowledge base is tightly bound to a context

Expertise can only emerge after long experience. It has been estimated that chess masters have spent between 10,000 and 20,000 hours at the game, expert radiologists during their active career have studied about 100,000 X-rays and expert teachers have taught at least 10,000 contact hours, prior to which they have spent at least 15,000 hours in the classrooms as students (Berliner, 1990). Thus it does not seem possible for an individual to obtain thorough knowledge in many different areas. Expertise cannot be particularly wide-ranging, either.

Berliner (1990) describes the situation-specific nature of knowledge in a study in which a group of expert and novice teachers as well as beginners were asked to teach a 30-minute unit to high-school students. The subjects were given half-an-hour to plan the contents of the unit, after which they taught the lesson. The lesson was videotaped and afterwards, while watching the video, the subjects were asked to describe what they had been thinking in the original situation. To the surprise of the researchers, the expert teachers were very emotional about the situation. None of the experts liked the task they had been given, though they seemed to possess the skills to handle the situation more effectively than the beginners or novices. One of the expert subjects dropped out of the study, one began to cry while watching the lesson, and all the rest expressed hostility towards the researchers. The reason for their hostility seemed to be that the experts did not feel they did well in a situation where they had been removed from their own class and from familiar situations. While they had been given 30 minutes to prepare, some wanted three hours or even a whole week to prepare the lesson. In addition, they were unhappy about not personally knowing the students in the class.

The studies on the nature of teacher knowledge show that teachers seem to develop situation-specific action patterns for classroom instruction. This may indicate that they have a related, situation specific knowledge base, too. I take two examples from the research findings. The first deals with teachers' questioning during the lessons and the second teachers' methods of scaffolding student learning.

Questioning has been studied extensively in the past. For instance, Evertson, Emmer, and Brophy (1980) have found that more successful teachers ask more questions. Their average number of questions during a successful mathematics period was 24 whereas less successful teachers asked only 8.5 questions per period on average. In a related study Ropo (1990a) found that experienced mathematics teachers asked 32.6 questions and less experienced student teachers 17.1 questions per period on average. For experienced teachers of English as a second language the average number of questions was 32.2 and for less experienced novice teachers 24.3 questions per period (Ropo, 1991). The number of questions seems to be systematically greater for experienced teachers in typical face-to-face instruction.

Scaffolding student learning is a metaphor derived from building construction (Wood, Bruner, & Ross, 1976). Scaffolds provide support, they extend the range of a worker and they allow the worker to accomplish tasks not otherwise possible. Palincsar and Brown (1984) applied this concept in their study of reciprocal teaching. The extent to which children need scaffolding seems to vary. Teachers also differ in the extent to which they provide scaffolds for their students. Ropo found that experienced mathematics teachers applied 8.2 scaffolds per period whereas novice teachers had only 4.3 scaffolds per period on average. There was also a qualitative difference between the scaffolds provided. Experienced math teachers divided the original questions into more simple partial questions more often than novices, if a student could not answer the question correctly. Experienced teachers also applied more a strategy in which a student was given a series of sub questions or specific questions that aimed at leading his/her thinking to the ideas or thoughts needed to answer the original question correctly (Ropo, 1990a).

Experienced teachers of English applied 6.9 scaffolds per period and novices 5.7 on average. This difference is not as large as that found in mathematics teaching. However, it is similar to mathematics teachers. One

Teaching Expertise 165

qualitative difference between the scaffolds of experienced and inexperienced teachers was found in the use of examples. Experienced teachers gave examples 2.5 times per period whereas novices did not use this at all (Ropo, 1991). The samples in the above studies were small and the results cannot be generalized in a larger population. However, they indicate that expert teachers also differ from novice teachers in their teaching behaviour.

2.2 Experts have automatic ways of reacting to frequently recurring situations

Expertise studies have focused on describing the development of cognitive skills, particularly, subjects' automatic patterns or responses in specific task situations. Glaser (1987), for instance, notes that the quick and automatic comprehension of written text typical of skilful readers frees some of their working memory capacity for processing other aspects of the situation. This same phenomenon is well known in the area of motor skills. Processing capacity increases because the verbal mediation in the performance of a task disappears and the procedure becomes more and more automated and rapid (Anderson, 1985).

In teaching, the automatisation of instructional actions allows teachers to direct their attention elsewhere, thus enabling them to better manage the teaching period as a whole. One example of the automatisation of teachers' skills can be found in Leinhardt and Greeno's study (1986) in which they compared the ways experts and novices started a mathematics lesson in elementary school. The results showed that on average an expert teacher took about a third less time to start a lesson than a novice. Second, during the start of a lesson an expert was able to observe the activity of the students, find out who had done their homework, and assess who would need help later during the lesson. Third, as a result of the automatic routines that both they and their students had learned, experts maintained a fluid control of their classes.

In the same study novices' lessons could be described nearly the opposite. Novices were not in full control of the progress of the lessons. They had difficulties in getting the students to be attentive and in ascertaining who had done their homework. The questions novices asked about homework were not as clear as those of the experts, and this led the novices to judge the difficulty of the homework assignments incorrectly (Leinhardt & Greeno, 1986).

An interesting example assumed to be related to the level of automaticity was found in the language usage of experienced and novice history teachers. In a study of Finnish teachers of history it was found that experienced teachers did not use their native accent during the lessons but used the standard, written language expressions and accent while novices having the same background did not switch their language to standard usage during the history lessons. Both groups used their native accent during the interviews (Ropo, 1992). This result may be interpreted to show that the automaticity of the lesson routines allowed the experienced teachers to monitor their language while novices had to direct most of their information processing capacity to controlling the flow of instruction.

2.3 Compared to novices, experts are more sensitive to individual students in class situations and the characteristics of task situations

In the study of problem solving it has been found that experts are more able than novices to take into account the specific characteristics of a given context and the limitations inherent in a specific problem (Chi, Glaser, & Rees, 1982; Glaser, 1987). Housner and Griffey (1985) studied this issue by comparing experienced and novice physical education teachers. The subjects of the study were given the task of planning and implementing a relatively short teaching unit. In the planning stage, teachers in both groups asked similar numbers of questions concerning areas such as numbers of students, their age and gender distribution. However, the experts asked more questions than the novices about the abilities, experience and background of the students as well as about the features of the space and equipment available. Five of the eight experienced teachers even wanted to see the space they were to teach in before they started planning, while none of the novices asked to do so. Later when they were doing the teaching, the experienced teachers adapted their teaching according to the situation more than the novices, thereby deviating from their initial plans.

Another interesting difference between expert and novice teachers has been found in the teachers' knowledge of their students. For instance, Carter, Sabers, Cushing, Pinnegar, and Berliner (1987) compared expert, novice and postulant teachers' processing and use of information about their students in a simulation of taking over a class. Postulant teachers were people working in business or industry and having an interest in teaching. However, they had no formal teacher education. The study showed that expert teachers seemed to have deeper knowledge of the students and classroom problems than novices or postulants. Experts made richer analyses of the students' earlier experiences than the other groups. They also seemed to rely more on their own information gathering about the students than the two other groups (Carter et al., 1987).

In a related study I compared experienced (at least 10 years of experience) and novice (2-3 years of experience) elementary school teachers' knowledge of their own students (Ropo, 1990b). The teachers were asked to describe four randomly selected students from their class. The results showed that overall experienced teachers gave longer descriptions than novices. Experienced teachers' average protocols were 559 words per student compared to the novices' 414 word descriptions per student. Typically both groups described almost 30 different characteristics per student. Qualitative analyses showed that experienced teachers seemed to know more than novices about the past or current family events of their students. They also made more connections between the student's family background and his/her school behaviour or problems. Experienced teachers had more explanations for the origins or reasons for students' performance in different school subjects. However, the novices seemed to know more about the students' hobbies outside school than the experienced teachers. The experienced teachers discussed only the school-related hobbies whereas the novices listed at least three other hobbies for each student. There were also differences in the time span of describing students' performance or difficulties in the school. The time span was longer for experienced teachers who seemed to use the past as the basis for predicting the future success of the students at school.

The conclusion of the study was that both teacher groups seemed to acquire knowledge of their students. This acquisition seemed to follow two principles. The first principle may be stated as "Collect and store information relevant in helping students to learn and adapt to life in school". The second principle was "Orient to individuality and individual features". The results indicated that experienced teachers seemed to be more advanced in applying those principles than novices (Ropo, 1990b).

2.4 Expert teachers are faster and more accurate in their observations than novices

This characteristic has been observed in studies of chess masters and experienced radiologists. The representations that experts make of the situation may not be judged as correct or incorrect. Even experts differ in their explanations or subjective theories of a specific situation. Rapid recognition and interpretation of situations is based on the quantity and quality of knowledge stored in one's memory. Another prerequisite for fast interpretation is that knowledge structures are organized in a way that enables rapid recognition without the need for extended processing. Rapid recognition of situations is useful, since it reduces the processing needed in various situations, thereby freeing an individual's processing capacity for measures required by the situation.

It has been found that expert teachers are typically quicker than novices at recognizing specific task situations and interpreting them. In instructional conversations experienced teachers typically follow the students' learning more carefully than novices and make focused efforts to correct misunderstandings with specific scaffolds (Ropo, 1990a, 1991). Experienced teachers also have more accurate plans for lessons and they even seem to be better at following the flow of time during a typical 50-minute period (Ropo, 1992).

2.5 Experts take longer to represent a problem to themselves, but they end up with a better representation of it

Results obtained by analysing problem-solving processes of physicists and social scientists have shown that experts spend more time forming a representation of a problem than novices (Chi et al., 1981; Voss et al., 1983). Hanninen (1983) observed similar differences in problem-solving between expert and novice teachers. In his study subjects were presented with a problem concerning the teaching of gifted students. Hanninen measured the time it took for the subjects to start writing the solution. The novices spent an average of 2.6 minutes whereas experienced expert teachers of gifted students took an average of 9.8 minutes before they began to write out their solutions. Experienced teachers of normal students took an average of 3 minutes to do the same task (Berliner, 1990). From these results we can deduce that a person's level of experience correlates with the amount of time it takes him/her to represent and solve a problem. The more an individual knows, the better s/he is able to take into account the complexity of a situation in his/her representation of the problem. With physicists and social scientists this was manifested through incorporating theory into problem-solving (Chi et al., 1981; Voss et al., 1983). With expert teachers solutions related to situations in classrooms included more lengthy and thorough analyses of situational factors or more substantial and more logical arguments for the solutions selected.

2.6 Compared to novices expert teachers' knowledge is wider concerning the levels of abstraction and more hierarchically organized

Differences have been found in the ways experts and novices organize their knowledge. These results suggest that experts are able to organize their knowledge into more hierarchical levels than novices. In a study by Chi et al. (1981), for example, expert physicists represented a problem involving an inclined plane by including the basic laws of physics, which the novices (beginner physics students) did not mention at all in their representations of the problem. Voss et al. (1983) found similar differences of hierarchical representation in the ways social scientists formulated and solved problems.

In my own studies experienced teachers were found to categorize the instructional goals differently from novice student teachers. Experienced teachers grouped the objectives hierarchically making a difference between the school levels (e.g. elementary and middle school), grade levels (e.g. grade levels 7, 8 and 9), and the generality of the goals and objectives. For instance, one expert expressed her overall goal for mathematics education that she wants to show students how beautiful mathematics is. Expert teachers also divided the overall goal into more specific goals for each grade level. They also seemed to have individual goals and teaching objectives for particular students in their classes. Novices typically described their instructional goals at the level of individual lessons without having the same kind of hierarchies of objectives (Ropo, 1987).

3. A PROTOTYPE VIEW OF TEACHER EXPERTISE

The above propositions and the studies behind them indicate that expert and novice teachers' groups differ a lot. The studies have also shown that in addition to the differences between the groups there is variance within the groups (Ropo, 1990a, 1991). Experts are not similar in every respect and do not constitute a typical category in the traditional sense of the concept. However, experts seem to be similar in many respects. This kind of research evidence raises a question on the nature of expertise. Can it be described and defined by the above type of propositions based on the lists of differences or do we need different types of theories of expertise?

We have already described the so-called Dreyfus and Dreyfus (1986) model in theorizing the nature of expertise and its development. Sternberg and Horvath (1995) have also addressed the question of the nature of expertise and proposed a model that they call a prototype view. The purpose of this model is to explain the within group variance among experts. The prototype view serves as middle ground between a definitional and ad hoc description of teacher expertise. With the definitional description authors refer to conceptions in which expertise is defined restrictively in terms of certain characteristics (e.g. reflective practice, or the teacher as a researcher). The ad hoc fashion refers to the lists of characteristics differentiating experts and novices (Sternberg & Horvath, 1995).

In the prototypical view the main idea is to postulate a central or "prototypical" category member that serves as a summary representation of the category (Rosch, 1978; Sternberg & Horvath, 1995). According to this view members of a category may resemble the prototype member to differing extents in different features. If this were true, then two members of a category would not necessarily be similar in a given respect, even if they belong to a category because of overall similarity in other respects. The second aspect of the prototype view is the differential weighting of features in the computation of overall similarity to the prototype (Sternberg & Horvath, 1995). The third characteristic of the model is that the features making up the category may be correlated, which means that they may occur together in a category member at a level greater than chance.

Sternberg and Horvath (1995) use their model to sketch an outline of features important for a prototype expert teacher. They use the same literature base we have referred to in this article to identify the features that differentiate experts from novices. The first feature Sternberg and Horvath (1995) choose is knowledge. Experts bring more knowledge to problem situations and as a result solve them more effectively. The second feature is efficiency of problem-solving. Experts are faster and more efficient in their problem-solving than novices. The third feature is insight. This has been included in the prototype model because experts seem to be more likely to arrive at novel and appropriate solutions to problems within their domains than novices.

One implication of the prototype view is that it seems to respect the naturally fuzzy nature of expertise found in empirical studies. Experts are different from each other, although they are at the same time similar. One teacher may have wide knowledge of subject matter, another a lot of pedagogical knowledge on teaching of a subject matter, and a third is insightful about students. All may be categorized as expert teachers. Sternberg and Horvath (1995) argue that the prototype view broadens the picture of teacher expertise without making every experienced teacher an expert.

Another implication the authors mention for the model is that it makes it possible to describe an expert with a smaller set of features than other theorizations offer. Bereiter and Scardamalia (1993) give an example of this by saying that an expert can be defined as one who works on the leading edge of his or her knowledge and skill. This means that a real expert complicates even simple problems to the edge whereas a nonexpert seeks to reduce the problem to fit available methods into it (Sternberg & Horvath, 1995).

The last implication of the model refers to the perception of expertise in the social context. If we define teacher expertise as a broad and rather fuzzy prototype then this may enlarge the view people have about an expert teacher. In particular policy makers who may have a restricted picture of teacher expertise may find that the prototype model broadens their own view significantly. This may have implications for ways of evaluating teachers or for the recruitment and training of teachers.

Overall, Sternberg and Horvath have formulated an interesting proposition that helps in understanding the nature of teacher expertise. It is related to the earlier Dreyfus model in the fuzziness of the category of expert teacher. However, Sternberg and Horvath take more detailed account of the later empirical research than the Dreyfus model.

4. DEVELOPING EXPERTISE IN NATURAL CONTEXTS

So far we have reviewed research focusing on the typical characteristics of expert teachers and the nature of the concept. We have found that there are experts and novices who differ from each other in many crucial ways. In addition to knowing this, it is also important to understand the processes of acquiring expertise.

The literature on the acquisition of expertise can be divided into at least three rather separate perspectives. First, the acquisition of expertise may be viewed from the standpoint of individual giftedness, intelligence, or exceptional abilities that develop through experience or interaction between heredity and experience with the environment. The second perspective is the so-called cognitive view that emphasizes the role of acquired knowledge (both declarative and procedural) in the process of developing expertise. The third framework in the current literature deals with the social theory of learning in which the acquisition of knowledge and expertise is typically seen as a kind of side effect of gaining membership of a social network.

The last two frameworks both emphasize the role of experience in the process of acquiring expertise. We may argue that one of the key issues in understanding the acquisition of expertise is to understand better the functions experience has in the process. Studies addressing expert performance in open and ill-defined tasks have shown that the nature of subjects' experience explains the performance better than the amount or length of experience (Sonnentag, 1995; Waltz, Elam, & Curtis, 1993). Bereiter and Scardamalia (1993) have suggested that the central determinant of high-level expertise is the subject's ability to surpass his or her previous level of knowledge and competence. Consequently, we may ask if the experts are those who have had qualitatively exceptional experiences or if their experiences and individual characteristics, such as giftedness, have interacted in an appropriate manner resulting in the development of expertise. I will discuss this notion in the following.

4.1 Expertise and giftedness

The concept of expertise has started to attract growing attention among researchers of intelligence and giftedness. For instance, Sternberg (2001) has made a proposition in his recent article that relates expertise and giftedness in an interesting way. He asks if giftedness could be seen as developing expertise. Sternberg's argument is that by the concept of developing expertise we can integrate two theories of giftedness –static and dynamic. The static conception states that intelligence is a relatively stable entity. Although certain kinds of intelligence areas may increase or decrease with age, rank orders remain fairly stable over time (Sternberg, 2001). An alternative, dynamic, view is that giftedness is to be found within a zone of proximal development. This means that it is an ability 'to advance from abilities that are ready to be developed to those that are developed' (Sternberg, 2001, p. 159).

From the expertise research point of view we may turn Sternberg's idea the other way round and ask if expertise could be conceptualised as developing giftedness. If so, the abilities and giftedness underlying expertise would be seen as developing from novice level to full blown expertise. Expertise develops because of "the ongoing process of the acquisition and consolidation of a set of skills needed for a high level of mastery in one or more domains of life performance" (Sternberg, 2001, p. 160).

Sternberg's idea of the close relation between abilities and expertise is an interesting one. Although the existence of this kind of relation has not been denied, the discrepancy between the two research traditions has been a paradigmatic one. Typically expertise researchers have emphasized the role of knowledge in the acquisition of expertise and left such concepts as abilities and gifts to researchers interested in the nature of intelligence. Theorizing on giftedness and intelligence has most often emphasized the static view of human performance in which the more or less inherited abilities have been seen to be in the main role.

However, it is possible also to view expert performance from the perspective of exceptional skills and abilities. Particularly, if our goal is to find out why some individuals develop into experts and others do not, it may be fruitful to analyse the individual characteristics interacting with the environmental factors. Sternberg's idea of seeing giftedness as developing expertise may narrow the gap between the research on expertise and on intelligence. Experts may have had skills and abilities that have 'reacted' well to the practice in a constructive environment. If the research on intelligence and giftedness adopts Sternberg's idea, this may lead to advances in the research on expertise as well.

4.2 Expertise and knowledge

The cognitive approach to expertise research has dominated the field since its beginning. It hypothesizes that exceptional performance is due to well organized knowledge that experts can access rapidly in a problem situation. Empirical evidence supports this view. How this knowledge is acquired is an important question. Cognitive research has typically looked for explanations for exceptional performance either in the information processing skills or in the contents of an expert's knowledge base. The cognitive view typically assumes the existence of knowledge structures in memory.

In the current research on learning the so-called situative, sociohistoric, or social view has gained popularity (Greeno, Collins, & Resnick, 1996). This view emphasizes the notion that learning is inherently a social process. Learning is a way of becoming a member of and participant in the culture and social networks and acquisition of expertise is part of that process (Lave & Wenger, 1991; Wenger, 1998). Therefore, expertise is not as much as the cognitive view assumes, an individual characteristic of one's knowledge structures, but an outcome of being a member of the social and communicational networks of individuals and groups. Expertise from this point of view is a kind of side effect of acquiring membership of and legitimate rights in a social network. This perspective views knowledge differently from cognitive framework. Knowledge is not a static schematic structure, stored in one's head, but rather a way of relating and participating in the immediate social networks around oneself (Agnew, Ford, & Hayes, 1997; Brown & Duguid, 1994; Wenger, 1998).

The concept that is widely applied among social theorists of learning is identity. Identity has had at least two different meanings in the studies. First, it has been applied to refer to the membership aspect of the social network. It is assumed that in the process of becoming a group member a person's growing identity as a legitimate member having more expertise and power supports the acquisition of knowledge. Second, a person's identity as an active and responsible learner is also assumed to support the acquisition of knowledge (Greeno et al., 1996).

It is assumed that identity processes and knowledge construction are related, although we are only at the beginning of empirical research on this issue. There is, however, interesting literature on the issue that can direct future studies. For sociologists identity is a concept related to one's relation to the historical, cultural and social environment. In the changing world an individual identity is "a reflexive project" that is under continuous change and development (Giddens, 1991). Although sociologists have typically discussed the development of identity and self in a broad context such as the global post-modern society, there is also literature that may offer more concrete frameworks for empirical studies on the relations of identity and expertise. For instance, Van Langenhove and Harré (1999) have proposed the so-called positioning theory, which argues that the human self develops by taking positions in specific contexts. A position is related to a concept of role and it is conversational in nature. A person takes a position and changes it as the conversation develops (Van Langenhove & Harré, 1999) From this perspective expertise might develop if a person makes deliberate decisions of taking a developing expert's position in a specific situation. For instance, a child might take a position on becoming a mathematician at school. This position will lead to personal identity and the acquisition of mathematical knowledge if it persists long enough. However, situational positioning can only persist if the environment supports the positioning. The will and motivation to surpass one's level of earlier performance may be supposed to come from the processes related to the construction of personal identity (Bereiter & Scardamalia, 1993). At the moment we have very little empirical research on this issue. The existing empirical research suggests that contextual factors are important in developing expertise and that it may have different roles at different stages of acquisition process (Eteläpelto & Collin, 2001, this volume; Schmidt & Boshuizen, 1993).

5. CONCLUSIONS

In this final section I discuss a few conclusions emerging from the past theorizing on teacher expertise. First, I argue that teacher expertise is an important research area that should be studied in the future, too. Although empirical research on teaching expertise has decreased during the last decade these studies have important implications in understanding the development of excellence. Being a pedagogical expert is at the same time similar and different from expertise in other domain fields. Pedagogical expertise can be regarded as a domain area having its own specialties in the same sense as engineering or medicine. Expert teachers have knowledge, skills, and social networks that are typical for them alone. The core of school teachers' expertise, for instance, is in a person's performance in a classroom with a group of students teaching a specific and complex mixture of values, knowledge, and skills.

Teachers as experts are professionals whose work is accomplished in a social situation in which they are typically alone with their students. The concept of an expert teacher and expertise in teaching is relevant for the current political discussion on the quality of education or teacher education. It is therefore necessary that we continue research on the nature and development of teaching expertise.

Teachers as experts are professionals whose work is accomplished in a social situation in which they are typically alone with their students. The concept of an expert teacher and expertise in teaching is relevant for the current political discussion on the quality of education or teacher education. For instance, the recent results of the OECD organised PISA studies on comparing student performance in the OECD countries has shown that good teaching makes a difference in the students' performance in the school (PISA, 2000). It is therefore necessary that we continue research on the nature and development of teaching expertise.

The second conclusion of the research on teacher expertise (or pedagogical expertise if you like) is that it is necessary to study expertise in authentic contexts. Educational practice benefits most of the studies describing the characteristics of expert teachers in relation to the social context of their authentic work or duties. Studies on expertise in other fields indicate that expertise develops as long as the individuals are exposed to situations in which they have to overcome the restrictions of their earlier knowledge. The work context has, consequently, a major role in directing or affecting the person's development in expertise. This notion is not only important for our conceptions of teacher expertise but our conceptions of teachers' work and working conditions. We need to ask if the changes taking place in the work and its context support the continuous development of teacher expertise.

Let me refer to a related discussion in the area of school education. According to Apple and Jungk (1990), many factors indicate that the nature of teachers' work has in the last decades taken a turn for the worse from the viewpoint of professional development. According to him, teachers' work has become more one-sided and less rich, teachers' abilities to manage their work as a whole have declined, and the intensity and quantity of work has increased. This has resulted in increased stress among the teachers. At the same time there are developments that emphasize the accountability of teachers' work in terms of only simple measurements of student learning.

The last implication deals with the nature of theorizing behind the empirical studies on teacher expertise. It seems fruitful to adopt a multidisciplinary framework in the research on expertise. Our discussion has already shown that many of the novel ideas in the current research are multidisciplinary, coming from various directions, such as sociology, philosophy, psychology as well as education. In the future research we have a lot of new ideas to explore. For instance, autobiographical theory and the processes related, studied in literature, philosophy, psychology, and sociology has not yet influenced on the analyses of expertise and professional development.

REFERENCES

Agnew, N. M., Ford, K. M., & Hayes, P. J. (1997). Expertise in context: Personally constructed, socially selected, and reality relevant? In P. Feltovich, K. M. Ford, & R. R. Hoffman (Eds.), *Expertise in context: human and machine* (pp. 219-244). Menlo Park: MIT Press.
Anderson, J. R. (1983). *The architecture of cognition.* Cambridge: Harvard University Press.
Anderson, J. R. (1985). *Cognitive psychology and its implications.* New York: Freeman.
Anderson, J. R. (1993). Problem solving and learning. *American Psychologist, 48,* 35-44.
Apple, M. W., & Jungk, S. (1990). "You don't have to be a teacher to teach this unit." Teaching, technology, and gender in the classroom. *American Educational Research Journal, 27,* 227-251.
Bereiter, C., & Scardamalia, M. (1993). *Surpassing ourselves – An inquiry into the nature and implications of expertise.* Chicago: Open Court.
Berliner, D. C. (1988). Implications of studies of expertise in pedagogy for teacher education and evaluation. In *New directions for teacher assessment.* Proceedings of the 1988 ETS Invitational Conference.
Berliner, D. C. (1990, September). *Characteristics of experts in the pedagogical domain.* Paper presented at the International Symposium "Research on Effective and Responsible Teaching". University of Fribourg, Fribourg, Switzerland.
Berliner, D. C., & Biddle, B. J. (1995). *The manufactured crisis.* Reading: Addison-Wesley.
Bonner, S. E., & Pennington, N. (1991). Cognitive processes and knowledge as determinants of auditor expertise. *Journal of Accounting Literature, 10,* 1-50.
Boshuizen, H. P. A., Schmidt, H. G., Custers, E. J. F. M., & Van de Wiel, M. W. J. (1995). Knowledge development and restructuring in the domain of medicine: The role of theory and practice. *Learning and Instruction, 5,* 269-289.
Bromme, R., & Tillema, H. (1995). Fusing experience and theory. *Learning and Instruction, 5,* 261-267.
Brown, J. D., & Duguid, P. (1994). Patrolling the border: A reply. *Human – Computer Interaction, 9,* 137-143.
Carter, K., Sabers, D., Cushing, K., Pinnegar, S., & Berliner, D. C. (1987). Processing and using information about students: A study of expert, novice, and postulant teachers. *Teaching & Teacher Education, 3,* 147-157.
Chase, W. G., & Simon, H. A. (1973). The mind's eye in chess. In W. G. Chase (Ed.), *Visual information processing* (pp. 215-281). New York: Academic Press.
Chi, M. T. H., Feltovich, P. J., & Glaser, R. (1981). Categorization and representation of physics problems by experts and novices. *Cognitive Science, 5,* 121-152.
Chi, M. T. H., Glaser, R., & Farr, M. J. (Eds.). (1988). *The nature of expertise.* Hillsdale: Erlbaum.
Chi, M. T. H., Glaser, R., & Rees, E. (1982). Expertise in problem solving. In R. Sternberg (Ed.), *Advances in the psychology of human intelligence* (pp. 1-75). Hillsdale: Erlbaum.
Cooke, N. J. (1994). Varieties of knowledge elicitation techniques. *International Journal of Human – Computer Studies, 41,* 801-849.

Darling-Hammond, L., & Youngs, P. (2002). Defining "highly qualified teachers". What does "scientifically-based research" actually tell us? *Education Researcher, 31* (9), 13-25.
De Groot, A. D. (1966). Perception and memory versus thought: Some old ideas and recent findings. In B. Kleinmuntz (Ed.), *Problem solving: Research, method and theory* (pp. 19-50). New York: Wiley.
De Groot, A. D. (1978). *Thought and choice in chess*. The Hague: Mouton.
Doane, S. M., Pellegrino, J. W., & Klatzky, R. L. (1990) Expertise in a computer operating system: Conceptualization and performance. *Human – Computer Interaction 5,* 267-304.
Dreyfus, H., & Dreyfus, S. (1986) *Mind over machine*. Oxford: Blackwell.
Ericsson, K. A, & Lehmann, A. C. (1996). Expert and exceptional performance: Evidence of maximal adaptation to task constraints. *Annual Review of Psychology, 47,* 273-305.
Ericsson K. A, & Smith, J. (1991). Prospects and limits of the empirical study of expertise: An introduction. In K. A. Ericsson & J. Smith (Eds.), *Toward a general theory of expertise: Prospects and limits* (pp. 1-38). Cambridge: Cambridge University Press.
Eteläpelto, A., & Collin, K. (2001, August/September). From individual cognition to communities of practice: Theoretical underpinnings in analysing professional learning and expertise. Paper presented at the 9th Biennial Conference of the European Association for Research on Learning and Instruction (EARLI), Fribourg, Switzerland.
Evertson, L., Emmer, E., & Brophy, J. (1980). Predictors of effective teaching in junior high mathematics classrooms. *Journal for Research in Mathematics Education, 11,* 167-178.
Gage, N. L. (1978). *The scientific basis of the art of teaching*. New York: Teachers College Press.
Giddens, A. (1991). *Modernity and self-identity: Self and society in the late modern age.* Stanford: Stanford University Press.
Glaser, R. (1987). Thoughts on expertise. In C. Schooler & W. Schaie (Eds.), *Cognitive functioning and social structure over the life course* (pp. 81-94). Norwood: Ablex.
Greeno, J. G, Collins, A. M., & Resnick, L. B. (1996). Cognition and learning. In D. C. Berliner & R. C. Calfee (Eds.), *Handbook of educational psychology* (pp. 15-46). New York: MacMillan.
Hanninen, G. (1983). *Do experts exist in gifted education?* Unpublished manuscript, University of Arizona, College of Education.
Hoffman, R. R. (Ed.). (1992). *The psychology of expertise. Cognitive research and empirical AI*. New York: Springer.
Hoffman, R. R. (1995). Eliciting knowledge from experts: A methodological analysis. *Organizational Behavior and Human Decision Processes, 62,* 129-158.
Housner, L. D., & Griffey, D. C. (1985). Teacher cognition: Differences in planning and interactive decision making between experienced and inexperienced teachers. *Research Quarterly for Exercise and Sport, 56,* 44-53.
Lave, J., & Wenger, E. (1991). *Situated learning: Legitimate peripheral participation.* Cambridge: Cambridge University Press.
Leinhardt, G. (1988). Situated knowledge and expertise in teaching. In J. Calderhead (Ed.), *Teachers' professional learning*L (pp. 146-168). London: Falmer.
Leinhardt, G., & Greeno, J. G. (1986). The cognitive skill of teaching. *Journal of Educational Psychology, 78,* 75–95.
Leprohan, J., & Patel, V. L. (1995). Decision making strategies for telephone triage in emergency medical services. *Journal of Medical Decision Making 15,* 240-253.
Munby, H., Russell, T., & Martin, A. K. (2001). Teachers' knowledge of how it develops. In V. Richardson (Ed.), *Handbook of research on teaching* (pp. 877-904). Washington: AERA.

Palincsar, A. S., & Brown, A. L. (1984). Reciprocal teaching of comprehension-fostering and comprehension-monitoring activities. *Cognition and Instruction 1*, 117-175.

PISA (2000). *The OECD programme for international student assessment*. Retrieved: Nov 24th, 2003, from http://www.pisa.oecd.org/index.htm.

Ropo, E. (1987, April). *Teachers' conceptions of teaching and teaching behavior: Some differences between expert and novice teachers*. Paper presented at the Annual Meeting of the American Educational Research Association, Washington.

Ropo, E. (1990a). Teachers' questions: Some differences between experienced and novice teachers. In H. Mandl, E. De Corte, S. N. Bennett, & H. F. Friedrich (Eds.), *Learning and instruction. European research in an international context* (pp. 113-128). Oxford: Pergamon.

Ropo, E. (1990b, September). *What teachers know about their students: Some differences between experienced and novice elementary school teachers*. Paper presented at the Conference of Effective and Responsible Teaching, Fribourg, Switzerland.

Ropo, E. (1991). Expert and novice English teaching: Differences in the lessons of experienced and novice English teachers. In M. Carretero, M. Pope, P. R.-J. Simons, & J. I. Pozo (Eds.), *Learning and instruction. European research in an international context* (pp. 539-560), Oxford: Pergamon.

Ropo, E. (1992, June). *Expert and novice history teaching: Eight differences between experienced and beginning history teachers*. Paper presented at the First European Conference of Educational Research, Enschede, The Netherlands.

Rosch, E. (1978). Principles of categorization. In E. Rosch & B. Lloyd (Eds.), *Cognition and categorization* (pp. 27-48). Hillsdale: Erlbaum.

Rosson, M. B. (1985). The role of experience in editing. *Proceedings of INTERACT 84 IFIP Conference on Human – Computer Interaction* (pp. 45-50). New York: Elsevier.

Schmidt, H. G., & Boshuizen, H. P. A. (1993). On acquiring expertise in medicine. *Educational Psychology Review, 5*, 205-221.

Shulman, L. S. (1986). Those who understand: Knowledge growth in teaching. *Educational Researcher, 15* (2), 4-14.

Sonnentag, S. (1995). Excellent software professionals: Experience, work activities, and perceptions by peers. *Behavior and Information Technology, 14*, 589-599.

Sternberg, R. J. (2001). Giftedness as developing expertise: A theory of the interface between high abilities and achieved excellence. *High Ability Studies, 12*, 159-179.

Sternberg, R. J., & Horvath, J. A. (1995). A prototype view of expert teaching. *Educational Researcher, 24* (6), 9-17.

The Holmes Group (1986). *Tomorrow's teachers: A report of the Holmes Group*. East Lansing: The Holmes Group.

U.S. Department of Education (2002). *Meeting the highly qualified teachers challenge: The Secretary's annual report on teacher quality*. Washington: U.S. Department of Education, Office of Postsecondary Education, Office of Policy, Planning, and Innovation.

Van Langenhove, L., & Harré, R. (1999). Introducing positioning theory. In R. Harré & L. Van Langenhove (Eds.), *Positioning theory: Moral contexts of intentional action* (pp. 14-31). Oxford: Blackwell.

Voss, J. F., Greene, T. R., Post, T. A., & Penner, B. C. (1983). Problem-solving skill in the social sciences. In G. H. Bower (Ed.), *The psychology of learning and motivation: Advances in research theory* (pp. 165-213). New York: Academic Press.

Waltz, D., Elam, J., & Curtis, B. (1993). Inside a software design team. *Communication of the ACM, 36*, 63-77.

Wenger, E. (1998). *Communities of practice: Learning, meaning and identity.* Cambridge University Press.
Wood, D. J., Bruner, J. S., & Ross, G. (1976). The role of tutoring in problem solving, *Journal of Child Psychology and Psychiatry, 17,* 89-100.

Chapter 10

PROFESSIONAL LEARNING: DELIBERATE ATTEMPTS AT DEVELOPING EXPERTISE

Margaretha W. J. van de Wiel[1], Kim H. P. Szegedi[2] and Mathieu C. D. P. Weggeman[3]
[1]*Faculty of Psychology, Department of Experimental Psychology, University Maastricht, The Netherlands, [2]Faculty of Psychology, University Maastricht, The Netherlands, [3]Department of Technology Management, Eindhoven University of Technology, The Netherlands*

1. DELIBERATE LEARNING IN THE PROFESSIONS

The development of expertise has been investigated in a great variety of domains encompassing music and arts, sports, games, sciences, general academic skills such as reading and writing, and a range of professions (Chi, Glaser, & Farr, 1988; Ericsson, 1996; Ericsson & Lehmann, 1996; Ericsson & Smith, 1991). Although there is general agreement that expert levels of performance can only be reached by an extended period of practice in which a highly specialised body of knowledge is acquired, the focus of research and the definitions of expertise used differ between domains. In music and sports, as well as in some games such as chess, people devote their lives to excel. Being an expert in these domains means that performance is recognised as outstanding in national and international competitions. It is a common belief that only talented people can attain these high levels of performance. Research on the development of expertise has challenged this belief, and has therefore focused on the phases that are passed through and the activities that are undertaken in becoming an expert (Bloom, 1985; Charness, Krampe, & Mayr, 1996; Ericsson, 1996; Ericsson, Krampe, & Tesch-Römer, 1993; Howe, 1999). The evidence indeed suggests that it is not talent but hard work, a stimulating environment and motivation that determine who will excel. Mere practice is not enough; it is more important that practice is carefully designed so that weaknesses in performance are overcome and level of performance improves. Ericsson et al. (1993) termed these activities *deliberate practice*.

In most professional situations, however, people have work to do and cannot spend their time predominantly on improving their performance. Moreover, those who not only work to make a living but also pursue a career or develop themselves, need to allocate a great deal of their working time to accomplishing job-related tasks. As a further contrast to the domains of music, sports and chess, in most professions it is difficult to define standards for excellent performance: Products are diverse and complex and usually not subject to formal evaluations by other colleagues. Expertise research in professional domains such as medicine, computer programming, auditing, architectural design and management and organisational science (Adelson, 1984; Davies, 1993; Ettenson, Shanteau, & Krogstad, 1987; Rambow & Bromme, 1995; Schmidt, Norman, & Boshuizen, 1990; Van de Wiel, Boshuizen, & Schmidt, 2000; Walsh, 1995), therefore, focused on experience rather than eminence. Emphasis is on the knowledge and reasoning processes that are applied by groups with different levels of professional training and experience when they perform representative tasks in their domain. Expertise is here typically defined as having several years of relevant work experience, and expertise is confined to tasks that are performed on a regular basis. A general finding in this research is that experts represent problems on a more abstract or deeper level allowing them to perform routine tasks fast and adequately. The detailed analyses of the differences between problem representations and problem-solving procedures of experts and novices mainly aimed to contribute to theory building. In some cases, e.g. in medicine (Boshuizen & Schmidt, 2000), outcomes were also used as input for the development of formal educational programmes. Learning is usually described as a process of knowledge change through study and experience. So the restructuring and tuning of knowledge to the tasks performed is central to this research and not the activities that are undertaken to learn from these experiences. In studies of software design, Sonnentag (1995, 1998) indeed differentiated length of experience from excellent performance by job performance and peer-nomination measures, showing that it was not the years of experience but the nature of activities employed during work that distinguished between excellent and average performers.

The question to be explored in this chapter is which deliberate practice activities experienced professionals apply to enhance their expertise and to learn from their experiences. This question is particularly pertinent because of the rapid advancements in knowledge and technologies in most professional domains. Professionals need to keep up and to react to the dynamics of the field to maintain high-quality performance and, thus, need to become effective life-long learners.

In order to establish a framework for research on deliberate learning in the professions, we will first examine the theory of deliberate practice by Ericsson et al. (1993). Secondly, we will investigate how the concept of deliberate practice relates to the concepts of self-regulated learning and goal-orientation as applied in studies in educational psychology. These studies have shown that students who actively self-regulate their learning reach higher levels of academic performance. Thirdly, we will examine the literature on professional learning, experiential learning, reflective learning, adult learning and expertise development for main commonalities and differences in how professionals learn from their experiences. Finally, we will present an interview study in which the framework is applied to the professional domain of strategy and organisational consultancy. We distinguished top professionals from experienced professionals based on a published ranking (Quote Professionals 2002-2003). In addition, we distinguished professionals working in a short half-life domain from professionals in a long half-life domain, assuming that professionals who work in a short half-life-domain, where knowledge gets out of date fast, need to apply more deliberate activities to develop their competence than professionals working in a long half-life domain.

2. DELIBERATE PRACTICE

The learning of individuals who perform at an international level in domains such as music, sports and arts has been shown to follow three phases (Bloom, 1985; Ericsson et al., 1993). In the early phase, learning and teaching in the domain is predominantly playful. Students, though, already practise on a regular basis and show rapid progress. This progress is in itself rewarding but also leads to recognition by others. In the middle phase, students practise intensively guided by more expert teachers in the field. These teachers demand great perfection and effort and set clear long- and short-term goals. Students are highly motivated to learn. In the later phase, students have committed themselves fully to excel in their domain. They study with master teachers who help them to analyse their own performance and that of other outstanding individuals in detail, to overcome particular difficulties and to perfect their style. An ultimate phase was added by Ericsson et al. (1993) for individuals who develop eminence: These individuals go beyond the available knowledge and make a unique contribution to their domain. Whereas stimulation and support from parents and teachers is very important in the early phase, motivation to improve one's performance dominates in the later phases. The practice activities that are carried out in these phases are highly structured and especially designed to accomplish this goal. For this reason, these activities are called deliberate practice by Ericsson et al. (1993).

Deliberate practice is further characterised as practice that requires effort, full attention and concentration, is repetitive in nature, and is not inherently enjoyable (Ericsson et al., 1993). Exercise is regularly, but balanced in such a way that exhaustion is avoided. Individualised supervision by trainers and coaches helps to attend to critical aspects of performance and to focus on knowledge of results so that effective self-monitoring during practice is enhanced. Trainers and coaches also provide informative feedback and try to find new methods and strategies to improve training and performance.

Research on deliberate practice tries to find relationships between the amount and nature of practice activities in the past and present and the level of expertise obtained. The general rule is that at least 10 years of practice are required to become an expert (Ericsson, 1996; Ericsson et al., 1993). Questionnaires, interviews and diaries are used to discern how much time is spent on relevant practice activities in a domain. In music and chess accumulated and current amount of practice alone has been found to be the major determinant of expert performance (Charness et al., 1996; Ericsson et al., 1993). Estimates of duration of practice alone in a recent typical week were found to be higher than duration recorded in diaries but this was a consistent finding in all expertise groups (Ericsson et al., 1993). In sports it was also found that time spent on deliberate practice is higher for top-level athletes (Starkes, 2000). That deliberate practice makes a difference is clear, but major questions that remain are the specific nature and structure of relevant practice activities and how (future) elite performers motivate themselves to engage in the long arduous hours of practice.

In work settings, research on the influence of deliberate practice on job-competence was done in teachers (Dunn & Shriner, 1999) and insurance agents (Sonnentag & Kleine, 2000). In both studies lists of relevant practice activities were gathered and reflected upon by professionals in interviews. In teaching, preparation of materials, planning of activities, evaluations of students' performance and behaviour and discussions with colleagues could be considered deliberate practice activities when they were carried out mindfully and effortfully. The major goal of teachers, however, was to improve instruction and to help students rather than to improve self-competence. In the study with insurance agents, an activity was categorised as deliberate practice when it was carried out at least once a week and with the goal of competence improvement. Activities that were performed as deliberate practice by at least 10 % of the participants were mental simulation, asking for feedback, preparation, consulting colleagues and concluding and assessing afterwards. Regression analyses showed that the number of cases handled and the current time spent on deliberate practice activities predicted professional performance. Years of experience as such, as well as cumulative amount of deliberate practice, did not contribute. Professional performance of insurance agents was rated by their supervisors on "meeting the sales goals" and "acquisition of new clients". Through clearly disentangling years of experience from the nature and amount of effort devoted to the job, Sonnentag and Kleine were able to corroborate earlier findings (Sonnentag, 1995, 1998) that the length of experience does not influence excellent performance as characterised by peer nomination procedures, but that the nature and the amount of work accomplished does.

In a similar vein as in deliberate practice research, we will see in the next section that research on self-regulated learning can discern successful from poor academic students by the type of learning activities that these students undertake and the type of motivation that drives them.

3. GOAL-ORIENTATIONS AND SELF-REGULATED LEARNING

Research in educational psychology has shown that students who have a mastery orientation in learning believe that effort influences study outcome (Ames, 1992; Pintrich, 2000). Their goal in learning is to increase their competence by developing skills and building understanding. These students explain success as a result of effort and failure as a lack of knowledge and use of the right strategies. They will search for effective strategies in the study tasks they are confronted with and self-regulate their learning. Mastery goals in learning are contrasted with performance goals. Students with performance goals find it important to prove their competence, to be recognised by others, and to outperform others in competitive settings. They feel their competence is best proven when they succeed without effort and help-seeking. They might also be negatively motivated to avoid failure or to avoid looking incompetent, for example by not choosing challenging tasks. Failure evokes negative feelings and makes the learner doubt about her/his ability. Especially students with avoidance-performance goals were found not to regulate their learning well. But also students with an approach-performance goal might use learning strategies that are too superficial to meet performance requirements. So to be an effective and high-quality learner in the long term one needs to have a mastery orientation and to be a good self-regulated learner.

Research on self-regulated learning tries to delineate systematic patterns in learning that are associated with effective competence building and performance improvement (Boekaerts, 1997; Zimmerman, 1998, 2000). It is directed not only at cognitive aspects of learning but also at motivational and behavioural aspects, as well as on the context in which learning takes place (Boekaerts, 1997; Ertmer & Newby, 1996; Pintrich, 2000). A common and often-cited definition of self-regulation is that of Zimmerman (2000, p.14): "Self-generated thoughts, feelings and actions that are planned and cyclically adapted to the attainment of personal goals." Self-regulation is not considered as a trait, ability, or stage of competence, but as a process that might be applied in certain situations but not in others. This may depend on experience and prior knowledge in a domain, as well as on self-beliefs and affective reactions.

In process models of self-regulated learning, at least three phases are distinguished, roughly summarised as planning, monitoring and evaluation (Pintrich, 2000). These phases are remarkably similar to the steps described in the problem-solving cycle (Sternberg, 1999). The similarity is not a coincidence since self-regulation is applied when one tries to learn from goal-directed performance. In the planning or forethought phase, goals are set, perceptions and knowledge of the task, the context and the self in relation to the task are activated, and strategies are planned. During task performance, subsequent actions and results are monitored to check whether one is on the right track or needs to adjust goals, plans and the implementation of strategies. After task performance, the outcome and process are evaluated and reflected upon in relation to the goals set, the effectiveness of the strategies applied and the feelings that are evoked as a result of the causal attributions made. The phases in task performance and self-regulation do not necessarily follow a time-ordered sequence, but rather dynamically interrelate as information from phases may feed into each other. The knowledge and insights gathered on the task, the context and the self are incorporated in the body of prior domain and metacognitive knowledge, both on a cognitive and personal affective level. This change of prior knowledge is learning. Ertmer and Newby (1996) emphasise that reflection mediates the interaction between prior knowledge and task performance and is crucial in learning from experience.

As self-regulated learning is considered a skill that may be developed in certain domains, it is important to see in what way naive learners differ from expert learners, and how the skill may be developed. Based on his social cognitive model of self-regulation, Zimmerman (1998) describes the characteristics of good self-regulated learners. Besides having a mastery orientation, an intrinsic interest in the task and a high self-efficacy, i.e. the belief that one has the capability to learn or perform at a certain level, good self-regulated learners know how to set their goals so they can adequately monitor and evaluate their learning efforts. Their goals are specific, challenging but achievable, and hierarchically organised so that the path to the long-term goal is clear. Their self-evaluations tend to be favourable because they compare their last attempts with a self-referenced standard. This leads to an adaptive pattern of attributions associated with positive feelings feeding their self-efficacy, mastery orientation and intrinsic interest. Through these positive self-fulfilling cycles motivation is sustained during practice as well as for working on future progress. Naive learners, in contrast, set too non-specific distal goals, do not really monitor their behaviour, and tend to evaluate the outcomes rather negatively because they compare themselves with others. This leads to a demotivating cycle with destructive attributions decreasing their self-efficacy and interest. In addition, good self-regulated learners are very focused during performance and concentrate their attention fully on the task. They further help themselves to effectively implement strategies by verbalising what they are doing and why and by imaging situations and examples. When their learning attempts were less successful than expected, they search for effective strategies and make systematic variations in their approach.

This social cognitive model of Zimmerman makes clear how motivation during deliberate practice may be sustained. In other models of self-regulated learning, more emphasis is given to the dependency of adaptive self-regulated learning skills on the development of domain knowledge. In the following we will discuss the development of self-regulated learning skills in relation to the context and the domain of learning.

The learning of self-regulated learning skills may be considered, on the one hand, as similar to the learning of other skills, and as part of the learning of other skills on the other (Alexander, 1995; Boekaerts 1997; Ertmer & Newby, 1996; Kanfer & Ackerman, 1989; Winne, 1995a, 1995b). Self-regulated learning can best be described as a cognitive skill as it involves substantial knowledge of how to approach a learning task, and so theories of cognitive skill acquisition might apply to the learning of these self-regulatory skills. In addition, self-regulated learning skills develop hand in hand with domain knowledge and skills, and so contribute to the further advancement of domain learning. Theories of cognitive skill acquisition generally describe the course of skill acquisition as a gradual transition from a deliberate cognitive activity requiring attention resources when knowledge is applied to a task, to a more rapid, automated activity without conscious control (Anderson, 1999; Anderson & Lebiere, 1998; Van Lehn, 1996). Although controlled processes, such as monitoring and reflection, seem to be inherent to self-regulated learning, several authors argue that self-regulation might become an automatic habit (Boekaerts, 1997; Winne, 1995a, 1995b). For example, when learners gain experience with a certain task, they will automatically represent the task at an appropriate level and select the most suitable strategies to tackle it. This example clearly illustrates that the selection of strategies as a self-regulatory skill is fully integrated in task representation and domain knowledge. However, for beginners in a domain, self-regulation may put such a high demand on cognitive resources that it may interfere with skill acquisition. In these cases, external control exerted by supervisors may scaffold the learning process initially, whereas self-regulation and self-directed practice may be stimulated in later phases of learning.

These two contexts of learning, the social context and the self-directed experiences, form the two essential sources for learning self-regulated learning skills. Significant others such as teachers, parents or peers can influence student self-regulated learning skills not only by direct instruction and feedback (Bielaczyc, Pirolli, & Brown, 1995; Boekaerts, 1997; Winne, 1995a, 1995b), but also in a more implicit way by modelling behaviour. In the tradition of social learning theory, Zimmerman (2000) describes four levels that are passed through in developing a regulatory skill. At the observational level, learners can induce from watching a model's task performance the relevant elements of the skill, as well as the associated self-regulatory aspects such as goal orientations, performance standards and persistence. At the emulation level, learners can generally apply the skills and self-regulatory processes to a task but need guidance to correct and improve their performance. At the self-controlled level, learners shift to intensive self-directed practice in which they focus on monitoring their performance based on an internal representational standard. At the final self-regulated level, performers have mastered the skill itself and focus their attention to optimally adjust the outcomes to their goals in specific conditions. Also in this model, it is evident that the acquisition of self-regulatory skills is very much interwoven with the acquisition of domain knowledge and skills and may be automated to a certain extent. In playing tennis, for example, the act of serving can be fully automatic needing no conscious process control, so attention can be focused on placing the ball on the right spot.

It might be clear that there are obvious correspondences between theories of self-regulation and the theory of deliberate practice. First, they both describe how the development of knowledge and skills may be fostered to obtain high-level performance. Second, they both stress the important role that parents, teachers and coaches have in creating a socially supportive environment that triggers and stimulates their pupil's development and enhances their focused effort in self-directed practice. Third, there is considerable overlap in the kind of activities that are discerned as self-regulatory and deliberate practice, such as preparation, planning, strategy selection, monitoring of performance, reflection on performance and help-seeking, as well as the conscious control that these activities generally need. Fourth, both in theories on self-regulation and the theory of deliberate practice the representation of the task in various conditions and the representation of the desired level of performance are considered crucial, as well as the representation of performance by significant others, such as in analysing a race of a competitor skater or previous chess-games by grandmasters. Fifth, both theories emphasise the role of motivation and especially goal-orientation in attaining high-level performance. A mastery goal or wanting to improve one's competence is required. Research and theories in educational psychology, however, provide better specified models for the complex interactions between learning activities and motivation than the theory of deliberate practice, and may contribute to this theory in explaining long-term and high-quality involvement in learning. A final comment we would like to make here is that not only mastery goals but also performance goals may add to success. To become an expert it is not only important to master the task, but also to be recognised by others as being able to do so. Therefore, one needs to commit oneself to the standards in a domain and to participate in competitions or to become well-known all over the world. For example, being a great scientist is not of much use to the domain without publishing, teaching and/or presenting. Some strategic behaviour is necessary when one wants to be acknowledged as a top-performer. See also the example of the golfer Moe Norman who could hit the ball like no one else, but did not gain the reputation he could have (Starkes, Deakin, Allard, Hodges, & Hayes, 1996).

Since we are particularly interested in learning in the professions, in the next section we review literature describing how professionals learn from their experience. Although the focus of this literature is clearly different from the focus of research on deliberate practice and the research on self-regulated learning, there are important common themes in these different approaches that will be outlined.

4. LEARNING FROM PROFESSIONAL EXPERIENCE

There is a vast literature from very different traditions, such as professional learning in higher education, expertise development, experiential learning and adult learning that sheds a light on how professionals may learn from their experiences. A key-concept in many of these writings is reflection (Boud, Cohen, & Walker, 1993; Boud & Garrick, 1999; Boud, Keogh, & Walker, 1985; Eraut, 2000; Mezirow, 1990; Simons & Ruijters, this volume; Warner Weil & McGill, 1989). Although the terminology used, the definitions provided and the context from which ideas originated differ, there is a common recognition of basic processes. Commonly learning from experience is regarded as a deliberate process mediated by reflection as a reaction to an unexpected situation or initiated by the intention to learn. The reflective process results in new knowledge and understanding of one's beliefs, actions and feelings so it may lead to higher personal and professional effectiveness in the future. Experiences do not just occur to people, but they are part of it and so contribute to the experience themselves. Experiences may especially be created or chosen to learn from both by people themselves as well as by others. The active self-directed aspect of learning is emphasised in adult learning theory (Merriam & Caffarella, 1991; Smith & Pourchot, 1998). The process of learning from experiences is in general described as starting with the identification of a problem that one wants to solve. Additionally, one seeks information to better understand the conditions under which the problem occurred. These conditions may include actions, feelings and implicit assumptions underlying the experience. Based on the insights required one plans to approach a situation differently in the future and again reflects on the outcomes when the plan is executed. Kolb (1984) summarises this process as a cycle of concrete experience, reflective evaluation, abstract conceptualisation and active experimentation. He compares this cyclic behaviour with problem-solving and the empirical cycle of inquiry and research.

Like the theory of deliberate practice and theories of self-regulated learning, experiential learning theories similarly focus on goal-directed and problem-solving behaviour. However, whereas the first two theories emphasise goal-directed performance that may be improved through processes of deliberate practice and self-regulated learning, the experiential and reflective learning literature also emphasises that deliberate learning may be triggered by surprising or conflicting situations that are regarded as a problem for one's functioning or development. Further correspondence between the theories concerns the environmentally supported and self-directed nature of learning: Reflective learning is held to be enhanced by formal education, the supervision of mentors and coaches and ways that help to structure experiences, as well as by the learner's own intentions (Rogers, 2001). Finally, all three types of theories focus on the deliberate aspect of learning from experience. Learning is thus defined as a change in knowledge and skills that leads to improved performance.

This focus on deliberate learning contrasts with the incidental learning from task performance and experience that it is emphasised in research on the development of professional expertise. The latter can be based on theories of cognitive skill acquisition in which repeated practice is a prerequisite for developing skills. When tasks are frequently performed, the knowledge underlying task performance becomes so organised that problem representations are quickly formed and relevant procedures are immediately activated. This results in adequate and fast or rather automatic behaviour. The learning mechanisms underlying this process adapt the knowledge structure to the statistical structure of the environment by adjusting activation and association strengths of knowledge elements to the frequency of past use (Anderson, 1996; Anderson & Lebiere, 1998). For example, in medicine, physicians automatically adapt their knowledge structures to the patients they have encountered in their practice and are so formed by their individual and specific experiences. This knowledge guides medical diagnosis and treatment of subsequent patient encounters (Schmidt et al., 1990; Van de Wiel et al., 2000). Because, in routine tasks, experts immediately activate relevant knowledge for performance, they do not consciously represent all underlying knowledge during performance and so may not be able to verbalise it. Some authors, therefore, conclude that experienced performance relies on a great body of tacit knowledge (Sternberg & Horvath, 1999), or even argue that making this knowledge explicit may help reflection and further development (Schön, 1983, 1987). This last suggestion may indeed be useful when professionals routinely choose from a well-known repertoire of analyses and tools to handle a problem in their domain without making a thorough analysis and having deep underlying knowledge. This phenomenon is known in organisational science as *pigeon holing* and undermines expertise development and learning from experience by too strong adaptation to using familiar routines (Perrow, 1970; Simon, 1977).

To conclude, it is clear that effective and high-level professional performance, as well as its development requires both automatic and controlled processes. Automatic behaviour may dominate in routine tasks, but as Ericsson (1998) convincingly argues cognitive control is necessary to perform at expert level and to surpass routine automatic behaviour.

5. THE PRESENT STUDY

In the present study we focus on the deliberate processes that add to the development of expertise in the professional domain of strategy and organisational consultancy. We chose this domain because of the availability of a publication in which the most expert professionals in the Netherlands were listed based on a peer and customer nomination procedure (Quote Professionals 2002-2003). In this way we were able to distinguish between professional expertise and professional experience. Research on expertise in management and organisational science, so far, has been very disparate in focus (Walsh, 1995), addressing issues of representation, development and use of knowledge structures at the individual, group, organisation and industry level. In this research, the knowledge structures that have evolved from experience have often been regarded not only as enabling strategic decision making, but especially as biasing decision making because of oversimplification of the complex, ill-structured problems in the domain. Although some studies describe the influence of different work experiences and personality variables on the nature and development of knowledge structures, none of the studies cited by Walsh investigated expertise development from a deliberate practice or self-regulated learning perspective, as we do in the present study.

The main question to be answered in our study was whether recognised top professionals apply more deliberate practice or self-regulated learning activities than professionals with comparable levels of experience. A second question being investigated was whether professionals working in a short half-life knowledge domain would apply more deliberate practice or self-regulated learning activities than professionals working in a long half-life knowledge domain. The half-life time of knowledge is the time in which only half of the original knowledge can still be meaningfully applied, because the rest of the knowledge has already been out-dated (Weggeman & Berends, 1999). To answer these questions we conducted interviews with four types of professionals in which we asked whether the professional applied activities that could be considered deliberate practice or self-regulated learning activities based on the literature reviewed, and for what reason they did.

6. METHOD

6.1 Participants

Participants were 23 strategy and organisational consultants who were assigned to one of four groups based on a 2×2 design of level of expertise (top professionals vs. experienced professionals) and half-life of domain (short vs. long half-life domain).

The participants comprised 17 males and 6 females with an average age of 48.6 years, ranging from 32 to 64. The top professionals were selected using a list of expert professional strategy and organisational consultants published in Quote Professionals 2002-2003. This list was created by asking colleagues and customers to identify who they found an expert professional within their work domain. Criteria that were given to guide the answers were: Someone who has the best knowledge or experience, someone who is

Deliberate Attempts at Developing Expertise 193

actively involved in domain development, and someone who gives the customer the feeling to be involved. The top professionals that volunteered to participate were asked to name a colleague from the same organisation who had just as many years of experience as her/himself, but had not reached the top. This was done to control for factors that could have an influence on the development of expertise, such as experience and work environment. The response rate was 11 out of 16 for the top professionals and 12 out of 16 for the experienced professionals. Unfortunately, two participants could not be included in our sample, because of recording problems.

The differentiation between consultants working in a short half-life and long half-life knowledge domain was based on the advice of an expert in the consultancy domain defining management consultancy as a short half-life domain, and boardroom consultancy as a long half-life domain.

6.2 Instrument

A semi-structured interview was constructed to get insight into the factors that could contribute to the development of expertise. The interview consisted of 16 questions that could be summarised in four categories: general time investment, work-related activities, updating activities and long-term professional goal. All questions were as open as possible and were followed by clarification questions when necessary.

General time-investment was covered in questions 1-4 asking for age, work experience, working hours, and travel time. For the last item the participants were also asked what they did during travelling.

In questions 5-12, the participants were questioned about activities that they employed in their daily work. The activities asked about were based on deliberate practice and self-regulated learning activities as described in the theory of deliberate practice and theories of self-regulated learning. The work-related activities concerned preparation, making a proposal, making adjustments to the proposal, asking help from a colleague, asking help from an expert, evaluation, and using a new strategy. The terminology was adjusted to the work of strategy and organisational consultants. Participants were not only asked whether they performed a certain activity and what it entailed, but also with what goal and how often they did it. This procedure was similar to that used by Sonnentag and Kleine (2000).

Updating activities performed by the participants were charted in questions 13-15. An agenda method was used to get to know whether participants joined a conference or course in their domain, and read professional or scientific literature. Participants were also asked how often they performed these activities and with what goal. In addition, they were asked whether they contributed to the innovation within their domain, by for example publishing an article or book or by doing research. Finally, they were asked which activities they thought were the most important to keep on developing themselves as a professional and to increase their competence. In question 16, participants were questioned whether they had a long-term professional goal they wanted to achieve.

6.3 Procedure

Participants were informed when they were recruited as well as in the introduction of the interview that the aim of the study was to chart the personal knowledge development activities of consultants. Before the interview was taken participants reasoned through two cases in the consultancy domain that were not analysed for this study. The meetings took on average one hour. The interviews were recorded and transcribed.

6.4 Analysis

Initially, the study was designed to be a 2×2 between-subject design (top versus experienced professionals and long versus short half-life domain). The dependent variables were categorised under the labels of general time investment, work-related activities, updating activities, and long-term professional goal. These will be described in more detail below. Because sample size was relatively small we measured differences between the top professionals and the experienced professionals and between short half-life domain and long half-life domain professionals separately using the independent samples t-test, the Mann-Whitney U-test (for variables without a normal distribution) and the Fisher's Exact test (for dichotomously scored variables with expected cell counts < 5) applying a significance level of .05. In addition, the data were qualitatively analysed. All data were blindly scored.

General time investment was measured by the dependent variables age, work experience, working hours and travel time. The identified work-related activities (preparation, making a proposal, making adjustments to the proposal, asking help from a colleague, asking help from an expert, evaluating and using a new strategy) were quantified in three ways: number of participants that performed an activity, time spent on or frequency of performing the activity, and number of participants having a mastery, performance or professional goal when performing the activity. Based on the educational psychological literature (Ames, 1992; Pintrich 2000), a mastery goal was scored when a participant expressed the personal urge to learn and develop, and a performance goal was scored when the main goal of a

Deliberate Attempts at Developing Expertise 195

participant was to become the best (i.e. better than others) within the profession or to avoid failure. A professional goal was scored when a participant indicated that an activity was performed because it was part of the profession, necessary to obtain a good result, or expected by the customer. Similar to the procedure used by Sonnentag and Kleine (2000) and in line with the theory of deliberate practice, an activity was only scored as a deliberate practice activity when performed with a mastery goal in mind.

Updating activities were classified as attending a conference, following a course, reading the newspaper, reading professional literature, reading scientific literature, and taking part in innovation. The dependent variables measured were the number of participants that performed an activity, the total time spent on updating activities, and the goal with which they are performed. In addition, the activities that were mentioned by participants as most important to develop themselves were categorised. The number of participants mentioning each category was counted. The dependent variable long-term professional goal was qualitatively analysed.

7. RESULTS

7.1 General time investment

Analyses showed that top professionals were older than experienced professionals and put in more working hours (see Table 1 for an overview of the data). The difference in years of work experience was not significant but should be described as a trend. Together this means that the top professionals had more work-related experiences. The professionals in the long half-life domain were older and had more work experience than those in the short half-life domain. Travel time was similar for all professionals, as well as the type of activities performed during travelling. Activities most commonly mentioned were listening to informative programmes on the radio, calling colleagues and customers, reading, discussions with colleagues when travelling together, and mental preparation.

Table 1. Overview of the means, standard deviations and outcomes of the t-test regarding the general time investment variables for top professionals vs. experienced professionals, and for professionals working in a short vs. long half-life domain

	Top professionals n = 11		Experienced professionals n = 10		Test results	Short half-life domain n = 11		Long half-life domain n = 10		Test results
	M	SD	M	SD		M	SD	M	SD	
Age	53.1	9.2	44.6	7.9	$t(19) =$ 2.26, $p < .05$	42.8	7.7	55.9	5.8	$t(19) =$ -4.37, $p < .01$
Years of work experience	23.8	8.7	16.5	8.2	$t(19) =$ 1.98, $p < .10$	14.6	5.6	26.7	7.8	$t(19) =$ -4.13, $p < .01$
Working hours per week	59.2	8.0	49.1	7.9	$t(19) =$ 2.91, $p < .01$	55.0	9.7	53.7	9.3	$t(19) =$ 0.31, n.s.
Travel time - hours per week	11.9	5.8	10.6	3.1	$t(19) =$ 0.63, n.s.	12.0	3.7	10.5	5.6	$t(19) =$ 0.73, n.s.

7.2 Work-related activities

For none of the work-related activities was there a significant difference between the participant groups in the number of participants that performed the activity. Nor were there significant differences in the number of participants that had a mastery, performance or professional goal in mind. Most participants prepared their visit to a customer, made a proposal, made adjustments to the proposal, asked help from a colleague and evaluated the consultancy afterwards. For the activities preparation and making a proposal, almost all participants had a professional goal and no other goals. For the activities asking help from colleagues and evaluating participants had not only professional goals, but also mastery goals. Preventing pigeon holing was frequently mentioned as a reason. Evaluations were made with the customer, with colleagues and alone with the intention to verify whether the customer was satisfied, to learn from the effort put in the assignment and/or to enhance personal development. New strategies mentioned by the participants were very diverse and mostly used to tackle specific situations. Because an activity is classified as a deliberate practice activity when it is performed with a mastery goal, 21 % of the performed work-related activities could be considered deliberate practice (22 out of 105).

Deliberate Attempts at Developing Expertise 197

Furthermore, the amount of time spent on work-related activities or the frequency of their performance was not significantly different between groups, except that professionals in the short half-life domain more frequently asked their colleagues for help than professionals in the long half-life domain. The activities adjusting a proposal, asking help from a colleague (colleagues were considered experts) and evaluating were performed in a large part of the assignments by most professionals, and this tended to be even larger in top professionals. Top professionals tended to prepare more often than experienced professionals and to write more extensive proposals. The kind of preparation activities were similar. Generally, participants prepared themselves by searching for information about the organisation on the internet, by reading documents received from the customer, by consulting colleagues, and by mentally preparing.

7.3 Updating and developmental activities

Top professionals spent more time on updating activities than experienced professionals, whereas professionals in the short half-life domain spent less time on such activities than those in the long half-life domain.

Although the number of participants that performed the updating activities did not significantly differ between groups, there was one clear exception (Table 2): Top professionals more often reported reading scientific literature. Updating activities displayed by most professionals were reading professional literature and taking part in innovation. The innovative activities participants were involved in mainly concerned publishing books or articles and lecturing, teaching or coaching students or colleagues. Apart from coaching colleagues and incidentally giving lectures, only 6 top professionals and 2 experienced professionals were involved in teaching students and post-graduates on a regular basis. These teaching activities contributed considerably to the time spent on updating activities. Half of the experienced professionals admitted not spending a lot of time on performing updating activities except for reading newspapers and/or professional magazines to keep themselves informed about the latest developments within their profession. Only 6 participants spontaneously indicated a mastery goal for performing updating activities, whereas 12 participants indicated a professional goal (Table 3).

Table 2. Means (proportion of participants), standard deviations, and outcomes (p-values) of the Fisher's Exact test for the number of participants that performed an updating activity for top professionals vs. experienced professionals, and for professionals working in a short vs. long half-life domain

	Top professionals n = 11		Experienced professionals n = 10			Short half-life domain n = 11		Long half-life domain n = 10		
	M	SD	M	SD	p	M	SD	M	SD	p
Reading the newspaper	0.18	0.40	0.40	0.52	0.36	0.18	0.40	0.40	0.52	0.36
Reading professional literature	0.91	0.30	0.90	0.32	1.00	0.91	0.30	0.90	0.32	1.00
Reading scientific literature	0.55	0.52	0.10	0.32	0.06	0.45	0.52	0.20	0.42	0.36
Attending a conference	0.45	0.52	0.40	0.52	1.00	0.36	0.50	0.50	0.53	0.67
Following a course	0.18	0.40	0.20	0.42	1.00	0.18	0.40	0.20	0.42	1.00
Taking part in innovation	1.00	0.00	1.00	0.00	-	1.00	0.00	1.00	0.00	-
Research and development	0.27	0.47	0.30	0.48	1.00	0.36	0.50	0.20	0.42	0.64
Publishing books or articles	0.82	0.40	0.70	0.48	0.64	0.82	0.40	0.70	0.48	0.64
Lecturing, teaching, coaching	0.91	0.30	0.60	0.51	0.15	0.64	0.50	0.90	0.32	0.31

Table 3. Means (proportion of participants), standard deviations, and outcomes (p-values) of the Fisher's Exact test for the number of participants that had a specific goal in mind in performing updating activities for top professionals vs. experienced professionals, and for professionals working in a short vs. long half-life domain

	Top professionals n = 11		Experienced professionals n = 10			Short half-life domain n = 11		Long half-life domain n = 10		
	M	SD	M	SD	p	M	SD	M	SD	p
Mastery goal	0.36	0.50	0.20	0.42	0.64	0.27	0.47	0.30	0.48	1.00
Performance goal	0.18	0.40	0.10	0.32	1.00	0.18	0.40	0.10	0.32	1.00
Professional goal	0.55	0.52	0.60	0.52	1.00	0.64	0.50	0.50	0.53	0.67

Activities reported to be most important for professional development are summarised in Table 4. Talking with colleagues was mentioned by the majority of participants and reflection by almost half of them.

Table 4. Means (proportion of participants), standard deviations, and outcomes (p-values) of the Fisher's Exact test for the number of participants that mentioned activities they found most important for professional development, for top professionals vs. experienced professionals, and for professionals working in a short vs. long half-life domain

	Top professionals n = 11		Experienced professionals n = 10			Short half-life domain n = 11		Long half-life domain n = 10		
	M	SD	M	SD	p	M	SD	M	SD	p
Reading the newspaper	0.09	0.30	0.20	0.42	0.59	0.09	0.30	0.20	0.42	0.59
Reading professional literature	0.36	0.50	0.10	0.32	0.31	0.36	0.50	0.10	0.32	0.31
Lecturing, teaching, coaching	0.27	0.47	0.20	0.42	1.00	0.18	0.40	0.30	0.48	0.64
Research and development	0.27	0.47	0.10	0.32	0.59	0.27	0.47	0.10	0.32	0.59
Publishing books and articles	0.27	0.47	0.30	0.48	1.00	0.36	0.50	0.20	0.42	0.64
Consultancy practice	0.27	0.47	0.11	0.33	0.59	0.27	0.47	0.11	0.33	0.59
Talking with colleagues	0.73	0.47	0.70	0.48	1.00	0.82	0.40	0.60	0.52	0.36
Talking with customers	0.36	0.50	0.30	0.48	1.00	0.45	0.52	0.20	0.42	0.36
Reflection	0.55	0.52	0.40	0.51	0.67	0.45	0.52	0.50	0.53	1.00

7.4 Long-term professional goal

From the top professionals, 9 out of 11 had a professional goal they wanted to achieve in the future, whereas only 4 out of 10 experienced professionals did. No remarkable differences were found between the professionals in the short (6 out of 11) and long half-life domain (7 out of 10). The type of goals was quite diverse, such as exploring a new domain, starting a new business and to be recognised as an expert within their domain.

7.5 Organisation of work

The interviews indicated that some organisations implemented work procedures that promoted deliberate practice activities. Several consultants reported that they always worked on large multidisciplinary assignments in teams of professionals with different levels of experience. Asking help from colleagues was therefore seen as a way of working. Also evaluation practices were more structurally implemented in these organisations, for example by having a consultant who was not a member of the team conduct an evaluation with the customer, as well as by personal and peer evaluations by members of the team. In some organisations doing research and publishing was also policy, so the professionals working in these organisations spent more time on these activities.

8. DISCUSSION

The present study showed that in the domain of strategy and organisational consultancy professionals do use deliberate activities to improve their work performance. These activities were both performed when working on an assignment and when keeping up-to-date.

However, most activities were performed because they were seen as part of the job and necessary to deliver good work to the customer. The work-related activities, asking colleagues for advice and evaluating assignments, were most frequently carried out with the intention to learn and were therefore the activities most often designated as deliberate practice. Moreover, talking with colleagues and reflection were most often mentioned as the activities most important for professional development and competence building. The activities of consulting knowledgeable others, evaluation, and reflection are indeed highly valued in theories of deliberate practice (Ericsson et al., 1993) and self-regulated learning (Pintrich, 2000; Zimmerman, 2000) and seem more apt than other work-related activities to result in learning, as also indicated by other deliberate practice studies in a working context (Dunn & Shriner, 1999; Sonnentag & Kleine, 2000). Most updating activities were performed because they were seen as inherent to the job, since professionals tended to indicate that they had a professional goal rather than a mastery goal. However, when directly asked for the activities they found most important to develop themselves and to improve their competence, most professionals mentioned a few including reading professional magazines. Presumably, most participants saw professional development as part of their job.

Although, in general, the type of activities performed by the participant groups were quite similar, there were some clear differences between the groups. Top professionals had more work-related experiences than experienced professionals, partly because they were older but also because they put in more working hours. So, their cumulative amount of practice was higher. In addition, they spent twice as much time on updating activities. These findings are in line with the theory of deliberate practice. To keep up-to-date, more top professionals read scientific literature and were involved in teaching on a regular basis. They also tended to prepare a visit to a customer more often and made a more extended proposal. This is in agreement with expertise research and theories of self-regulated learning, because experts are known to orient themselves better on a problem before they begin.

Professionals in a short half-life domain were younger and had less work experience than professionals in a long half-life domain. This finding is not surprising, since new and rapidly developing domains are more accessible for younger, recently graduated people than the established domains. The short half-life domain professionals asked their colleagues for advice more often, but remarkably spent less time on updating activities. In contrast to the other findings, this last finding is not in accordance with our expectation that one needs more time to keep up-to-date when one works in a short half-life domain, where knowledge gets out of date fast. It could be that in the short half-life domain of management consultancy it is more common practice to invest in working together than in individual acquisition of knowledge. Time investment, however, could not be compared, because we asked for the frequency of assignments in which a colleague was consulted.

Besides the fact that professionals simply have work to do and are not able to focus all their time on improving their performance, there may be additional reasons for the small differences between participant groups. The sample was small, because we worked with a highly limited group of top professionals. This group, however, was representative considered the response rate. Further, we relied on the ranking published in Quote Professionals 2002-2003 and did not cross-validate this measure. If possible, this should be done in future research. Similar, in distinguishing between a short half-life and long half-life domain we followed the advice of an expert consultant. In future research, criteria should be formulated that can be tested. Furthermore, the assignments consultants worked on varied in complexity, and were carried out individually or in teams, so it might have been difficult for the participants to estimate how much time they generally spent on work-related activities. However, no bias is expected across the different groups. In future research, a thorough analysis of the tasks and assignments of professionals and the use of timekeeping methods may ensure more precise time estimations. Finally, differences may be small because all participants were highly experienced professionals who had been working in their domain for an average of 20 years.

In this study it became clear that professionals spent more time on deliberate practice and self-regulated learning activities when the organisation structurally implemented procedures that promoted co-operation between professionals in multidisciplinary teams, evaluation and research. The practices in these organisations show that the environment, in line with the theories of deliberate practice, self-regulated learning and reflective learning, is an important contributor to learning by stimulating reflection on and exchange of knowledge and experience. So, when organisations value the development of their professionals to improve individual and hence organisational competence, they are advised to create a working environment that is also a deliberate learning environment. Deliberate, because, as clearly expressed by some professionals, learning also automatically occurs while working. Only by deliberately recognising issues for and advances in learning can individuals and organisations establish a climate for continuous development (Simons & Ruijters, this volume). The organisation, therefore, should set standards for both the working habits that may promote learning and the goals for competence improvement. This may be partly realised by modelling of behaviour and goals by more expert colleagues when professionals work together in teams (Zimmerman, 2000). Professionals may also be motivated to further improve when they experience satisfaction and success in their work (Ames, 1992; Pintrich, 2000; Simons & Ruijters, this volume; Zimmerman, 2000), so it would be advisable to create situations in which these experiences are encountered.

Future research on deliberate learning in the professions can best pinpoint those activities that discriminated between top professionals and experienced professionals or were most often performed with a mastery or developmental goal in mind, such as preparation, consulting with colleagues, evaluation, reflection, scientific reading, and teaching in the expertise domain. The first four activities are prominent in theories and studies of deliberate practice and self-regulated learning, whereas the last two activities may contribute to reflection and knowledge building that, in these theories, as well as in theories of experiential and reflective learning, are also inherent to competence building. The deliberate activities of planning and mental simulation that were discerned in theories and studies of deliberate practice and self-regulated learning, were not clearly distinguished in this study and subsumed under the activity of preparation. Those activities might be better disentangled in follow-up studies. The same is true for evaluating and reflecting on task performance afterwards and monitoring during task performance. The relevance of this difference, however, depends on the level of automaticity with which a task can be performed. In relatively complex and long-lasting tasks monitoring can also be deliberate and contribute to the final outcome, whereas in skilled and routine performance monitoring will be rather automatic and might only be corrected afterwards. Clearly, this not only depends on the type of task, but also on the level of experience and expertise of the performer. So, in further research, it would be helpful to determine when tasks may be harmlessly performed on automatic pilot relying on underlying (tacit) knowledge, and when controlled performance and deliberate learning should be preferred. Better knowledge on this issue would allow one to specify when there are real dangers of too strong an adaptation to familiar routines and how they might be overcome.

For all activities it would be interesting to know in what way they most contribute to the development of knowledge and skills in a domain. In what way should one best prepare a task, receive and give feedback, structure experiences by reflection and organise these activities in a working setting? And in addition, how may motivation to learn best be promoted both on an individual and team level in an organisation? The framework of research on deliberate learning in the professions as outlined in this chapter provides a basis for investigating the interplay between organisational environment, deliberate practice and self-regulated learning activities, motivational goals, knowledge development and effective personal and organisational performance. Clear analyses of the tasks being performed in different domains are necessary to determine in what way expertise development is specific to a domain or may exceed the specific domain.

REFERENCES

Adelson, B. (1984). When novices surpass experts: The difficulty of a task may increase with expertise. *Journal of Experimental Psychology: Learning, Memory, and cognition, 10,* 483-495.

Alexander, P. A. (1995). Superimposing a situation-specific and domain-specific perspective on an account of self-regulated learning. *Educational Psychologist, 30,* 189-193.

Ames, C. (1992). Classrooms: goals, structures, and student motivation. *Journal of Educational Psychology, 84,* 261-271.

Anderson, J. R. (1996). ACT: A simple theory of complex cognition. *American Psychologist, 51,* 355-365.

Anderson, J. R. (1999). *Cognitive psychology and its implications* (5th ed.). New York: Freeman.

Anderson, J. R., & Lebiere, C. (1998). *The atomic components of thought.* Mahwah: Erlbaum.

Bielaczyc, K., Pirolli, P. L., & Brown, A. L. (1995). Training in self-explanation and self-regulation strategies: Investigating the effects of knowledge acquisition activities on problem solving. *Cognition and Instruction, 13,* 221-252.

Bloom, B. S. (Ed.). (1985). *Developing talent in young people.* New York: Balantine.

Boekaerts, M. (1997). Self-regulated learning: A new concept embraced by researchers, policy makers, educators, teachers, and students. *Learning and Instruction, 7,* 161-186.
Boshuizen, H. P. A., & Schmidt, H. G. (2000). The development of clinical reasoning expertise; implications for teaching. In J. Higgs & M. Jones (Eds.), *Clinical reasoning in the health professions* (rev. ed., pp. 15 – 20). Oxford: Butterworth-Heinemann.
Boud, D., Cohen, R., & Walker, D. (Eds.). (1993). *Using experience for learning.* Bristol: The Society for Research into Higher Education and Open University Press.
Boud, D., & Garrick, J. (Eds.). (1999). *Understanding learning at work.* London: Routledge.
Boud, D., Keogh, R., & Walker, D. (Eds.). (1985). *Reflection: Turning experience into learning.* London: Kogan Page.
Charness, N., Krampe, R., & Mayr, U. (1996). The role of practice and coaching in entrepreneurial skill domains: An international comparison of life-span chess skill acquisition. In K.A. Ericsson (Ed.), *The road to excellence: The acquisition of expert performance in the arts and sciences, sports and games,* (pp. 51-80). Mahwah: Erlbaum.
Chi, M. T. H., Glaser, R., & Farr, M. J. (Eds.). (1988). *The nature of expertise.* Hillsdale: Erlbaum.
Davies, S. P. (1993). The structure and content of programming knowledge: Disentangling training and language effects in theories of skill development. *International Journal of Human Computer Interaction, 5,* 325-346.
Dunn, T. G., & Shriner, C. (1999). Deliberate practice in teaching: What teachers do for self-improvement. *Teaching and Teacher Education, 15,* 631-651.
Eraut, M. (2000). Non-formal learning and tacit knowledge in professional work. *British Journal of Educational Psychology, 70,* 113-136.
Ericsson, K. A. (Ed.). (1996). *The road to excellence: The acquisition of expert performance in the arts and sciences, sports and games.* Mahwah: Erlbaum.
Ericsson, K. A. (1998). The scientific study of expert levels of performance: General implications for optimal learning and creativity. *High Ability Studies, 9,* 75-100.
Ericsson, K. A., & Krampe, R. T., & Tesch-Römer, C. (1993). The role of deliberate practice in the acquisition of expert performance. *Psychological Review, 100,* 363-406.
Ericsson, K. A., & Lehmann, A. C. (1996). Expert and exceptional performance: Evidence of maximal adaptations to task constraints. *Annual Review of Psychology, 47,* 273-305.
Ericsson, K. A., & Smith, J. (1991). *Toward a general theory of expertise: Prospects and limits.* Cambridge: Cambridge University Press.
Ertmer, P. A., & Newby, T. J. (1996). The expert learner: Strategic, self-regulated, and reflective. *Instructional Science, 24,* 1-24.
Ettenson, R. Shanteau, J., & Krogstad, J. (1987). Expert judgement: Is more information better? *Psychological Reports, 60,* 227-238.
Howe, M. J. A. (1999). *Genius explained.* Cambridge: Cambridge University Press.
Kanfer, R., & Ackerman, P. L. (1989). Motivation and cognitive abilities: An integrative/aptitude-treatment interaction approach to skill acquisition. *Journal of Applied Psychology, 74,* 657-690.
Kolb, D. A. (1984). *Experiential learning: Experience as the source of learning and development.* Englewood Cliffs: Prentice Hall.
Merriam, S. B., & Caffarella, R. S. (1991). *Learning in adulthood: A comprehensive guide.* San Francisco: Jossey-Bass.
Mezirow, J. (1990). *Fostering critical reflection in adulthood: A guide to transformative and emancipatory learning.* San Francisco: Jossey-Bass.
Perrow, C. (1970). *Organizational analysis; A sociological review.* Belmont: Wadsworth.

Pintrich, P. R. (2000). The role of goal orientation in self-regulated learning. In M. Boekaerts, P. R. Pintrich, & M. Zeidner (Eds.), *Handbook of self-regulation* (pp. 451-502). San Diego: Academic Press.
Quote Professionals (2002-2003) *Strategy and HRM*. Amsterdam: Quote Publishing.
Rambow, R., & Bromme, R. (1995). Implicit psychological concepts in architects' knowledge: How large is a large room. *Learning and Instruction, 5*, 337-355.
Rogers, R. R. (2001). Reflection in higher education: A concept analysis. *Innovative Higher Education, 26*, 37-57.
Schmidt, H. G., Norman, G. R., & Boshuizen, H. P. A. (1990). A cognitive perspective on medical expertise: Theory and implications. *Academic Medicine, 65*, 611-621.
Schön, D. A. (1983). *The reflective practitioner: How professionals think in action*. New York: Basic Books.
Schön, D. A. (1987). *Educating the reflective practitioner: Toward a new design of teaching and learning in the professions*. San Francisco: Jossey-Bass.
Simon, H. (1977). *The new science of management decision*. Englewood Cliffs: Prentice Hall.
Smith, M. C., & Pourchot, T. (Eds.). (1998). *Adult learning and development: Perspectives from educational psychology*. Mahwah: Erlbaum.
Sonnentag, S. (1995). Excellent software professionals: Experience, work activities, and perceptions by peers. *Behaviour and Information Technology, 14*, 289-299.
Sonnentag, S. (1998). Expertise in professional software design: A process study. *Journal of Applied Psychology, 83*, 703-715.
Sonnentag, S., & Kleine, B. M. (2000). Deliberate practice at work: A study with insurance agents. *Journal of Occupational and Organizational Psychology, 73*, 87-102.
Starkes, J. (2000). The road to expertise: Is practice the only determinant? *International Journal of Sport Psychology, 31*, 431-451.
Starkes, J. L., Deakin, J. M., Allard, F., Hodges, N. J., & Hayes, A. (1996). Deliberate practice in sports: What is it anyway? In K. A. Ericsson (Ed.), *The road to excellence: The acquisition of expert performance in the arts and sciences, sports and games*, (pp. 81-106). Mahwah: Erlbaum.
Sternberg, R. J. (1999). *Cognitive psychology*, (2nd ed.). Fort Worth: Harcourt Brace.
Sternberg, R. J., & Horvath, J. A. (Eds.). (1999). *Tacit knowledge in professional practice: Researcher and practitioner perspectives*. Mahwah: Erlbaum.
Van de Wiel, M. W. J., Boshuizen, H. P. A., & Schmidt, H. G. (2000). Knowledge restructuring in expertise development: Evidence from pathophysiological representations of clinical cases by students and physicians. *European Journal of Cognitive Psychology, 12*, 323-355.
Van Lehn, K. (1996). Cognitive skill acquisition. *Annual Review of Psychology, 47*, 513-539.
Walsh, J. P. (1995). Managerial and organizational cognition: Notes from a trip down memory lane. *Organization Science, 6*, 280-321.
Warner Weil, S., & McGill, I. (Eds.). (1989). *Making sense of experiential learning: Diversity in theory and practice*. Philadelphia: The Society for Research into Higher Education and Open University Press.
Weggeman, M. C. D. P., & Berends, J. J. (1999). Facilitating knowledge sharing in non-hierarchical work relations. In J. Schreinemakers & J. P. Barthès (Eds.), *Advances in knowledge management* (pp. 57-69). Würzburg: Ergon.
Winne, P. H. (1995a). Inherent details in self-regulated learning. *Educational Psychologist, 30*, 173-187.
Winne, P. H. (1995b). Self-regulated learning is ubiquitous but its forms vary with knowledge. *Educational Psychologist, 30*, 223-228.

Zimmerman, B. J. (1998). Developing self-fulfilling cycles of academic regulation: An analysis of exemplary instructional models. In D. H. Schunk & B. J. Zimmerman (Eds.), *Self-regulated learning: From teaching to self-reflective practice* (pp. 1-19). New York: Guilford.

Zimmerman, B. J. (2000). Attaining self-regulation: A social cognitive perspective. In M. Boekaerts, P. R. Pintrich, & M. Zeidner (Eds.), *Handbook of self-regulation*, (pp. 13-39). San Diego: Academic Press.

Chapter 11

LEARNING PROFESSIONALS: TOWARDS AN INTEGRATED MODEL

P. Robert-Jan Simons[1] and Manon C. P. Ruijters[2]
[1]*IVLOS, Department of Education, Utrecht University, The Netherlands,* [2]*Twynstra Gudde Management Consultants, Amersfoort, The Netherlands*

1. WHAT IS A LEARNING PROFESSIONAL?

1.1 First thoughts on professionalism

In order to give a definition of a learning professional, we should of course also define what professionals are and what learning is. The definition of a professional relates closely to professions and professional associations. Professions are mostly defined as fields of work that have an explicit body of knowledge described in handbooks and official (scientific) journals, have standards of quality and professional associations (Thijssen, 1987). Professional associations bring these people together, define the standards of quality, help to develop the body of knowledge and certify education and training that guarantee the quality of the learning outcomes.

Then, what is a professional? Are you a professional? Why or why not? Maybe it is easier to explain what a professional is *not*. A professional is *not* a recognised member of a self-protective association of professionals defining standards of professionalism in terms of levels and kinds of education and training the person involved has completed. Thus, the medical doctor who did his medical training and was accepted as a member of the professional association of doctors is not yet a professional, in our opinion. We sympathise with the Dutch educationalist Lievegoed (cited in Germans, 1990) who already in the nineteen forties defined a professional in terms of

vision, methodology and tools and techniques. In our view, a real professional should meet the following criteria.
1. Have an explicit vision about the profession and its contribution to society;
2. developed a unique methodology (way of working);
3. be able to work with a set of tools and techniques that fulfil quality criteria of the professional association mentioned before;
4. and there should be alignment between the vision, methodology and tools and techniques.

A professional can now be defined as someone working in a professional field having an aligned combination of an explicit vision, a unique methodology and a set of high quality tools and techniques. In our experience in working with professionals we discovered that many "official" professionals do not meet these criteria. Few are even aware of their total body of knowledge or their vision, and alignment is not very often a criterion in the decision to embrace or reject specific tools or methodology. Perhaps the very existence of the professional bodies mentioned before refrain them from developing these ideas. They probably have the implicit idea that their education has equipped them with a complete and aligned package of professionalism. And perhaps this strong belief (we encounter this too often) that learning and professionalism result from following training courses, keep people from becoming professionals in the sense described above.

1.2 From professional to learning professional

Bodies of knowledge as well as the standards of quality change rapidly. Training was not enough to become a professional in the past, it certainly will not be in the future. In our view, the concept of a professional as developed so far is too static. Let us look into this a little more closely.

More and more, we realise that tacit knowledge and skills developed while working cannot be trained easily because they originate in daily practice in the working with clients. Tacit knowledge and skills are therefore being revalued. It has become clear that knowledge and skills have a social life (Brown & Duguid, 2000): They originate in and can be distributed only in social interactions. Which leads to new emphasis on the need for collective learning.

Furthermore, we observe fading boundaries between professions. New developments emerge at the boundaries of disciplines, professions and perspectives (Engeström, 1999). Multiperspective learning between communities of practice is needed as much as within-community learning (Lehtinen, 2001). Finally, innovation is an important characteristic of present-day work. The question is how professionals can contribute to the innovation of the profession. For all these reasons, we need a more dynamic concept of a professional. We have called this the "learning professional".

It is again Lievegoed (1977), who shows us the way. Already a long time ago, he wrote that there are three main activities to be performed: Working in practice, being connected with or carrying out research, and teaching others. (1) One can only be and remain a professional when working in practice with clients. For a doctor this means "working with patients", for a manager this means "working with employees", and for a researcher this means being oneself involved in experimentation. (2) A professional needs to be connected to the research in the disciplines connected to his work. (3) She/He has an important role in transmitting professional experience to others and contributing to the professional field of expertise.

In thinking about and working with these ideas of Lievegoed's and Germans's we have extended and changed them a bit in order to make them fit better into current theories. We have mainly added the learning experiences to it. Take the first element; it is not only working in practice, but also learning from it: experiential learning, which includes not only learning from experience, but also making the outcomes of this learning explicit. Secondly, it is not only being connected with research or being involved in research, but also learning from research. Therefore we have redefined the second step into three ways of learning explicitly: critical, inquiry and theoretical learning (see below). Finally, it is not only teaching others which is important, but it is more: helping the profession develop and by doing so learning yourself. This can be done through teaching, but also through writing books and articles, coaching, tutoring, lecturing at conferences, developing tools for others, being involved in discussions with other professions, etc. This contribution to the outside world can, in our view, also be at the team or organisational level: contributing to team learning or to organisational learning.

A learning professional is thus (Figure 1):
1. elaborating on his or her work-competences by learning from and in practice (elaboration);
2. expanding his theoretical knowledge and insights by learning explicitly from and in research (expansion) ;
3. externalising his practical and theoretical insights, which means contributing to the development of the profession (externalisation) and / or to team and organisational learning.

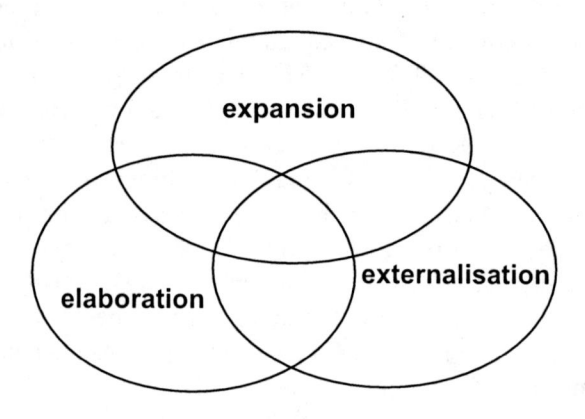

Figure 1. Professional learning of learning professionals

1.3 Then, what is learning?

These three ways to be a learning professional will be discussed more detail in the sections that follow. Let us first define learning (see Bolhuis & Simons, 1999, for the argumentation): "Learning, in our view, refers to implicit or explicit mental and / or overt activities and processes leading to changes in knowledge, skills or attitudes or the ability to learn of individuals, groups or organisations. These can under certain conditions also lead to changes in work processes or work outcomes of individuals, groups or organisations." A few remarks:

This definition starts with acknowledging that learning can be both implicit and explicit. While explicit learning has for a long time been the focus of attention, more and more it becomes clear that a large part of learning isn't so conscious, let alone, planned or directed. Professionals learn from and in the context of their daily work. So in talking about the learning professional, the implicit learning processes are of great relevance.

Next we argue that learning comprises both mental and overt activities and /or processes, at the group, team or organisational level. This distinction between activities and processes comes from Willems (1987). He convincingly argued that learning is sometimes organised (by persons themselves or by outsiders) and sometimes not at all. Then it is "just happening as a side product of working, playing or problem solving". We can only conclude afterwards that these learning processes must have taken place from changes we notice.

Sometimes learning can lead to changes in work processes and outcomes. Outcomes of learning can be knowledge, skills or attitudes, but also the ability to learn can be an important result of learning.

All of this can occur at three levels: individual, team and organisation. We want to underline the differences between these three levels. Team learning (or collective learning) is not the same as effectively organized learning processes of a group of individuals. Collective learning has its own characteristics and worth in the context of organizational change.

1.4 Distinguishing learning, development and change

In talking about professionalizing, it is not only learning, but also development and change, which are relevant. So for the sake of a clear discussion we will define both of them.

When the focus is on *long term* learning processes (mostly implicit) we can also call this learning "development". When the focus is on changes *in work processes or work outcomes*, the term "change" may be preferred. Because we have defined learning at three levels, there can thus also be group development and change and organisational development and change. We thus use the term learning in a broad sense encompassing development and change. In a more restricted sense learning focuses on changes in skills, knowledge, attitudes and learning abilities. Table 1 summarises these levels of learning on the one hand and differences of learning, development and change on the other hand. The same is pictured in Figure 2.

Table 1. The various ways and levels of learning and their outcomes (within the cells)

Levels of learning Ways of learning (broad sense)	Individual	Team	Organisation
Learning (restricted sense)	Skills, knowledge, attitudes, learning abilities of individual	Skills, knowledge, attitudes, learning abilities of group	Skills, knowledge, attitudes, learning abilities of organisation
Development	Long term skills, knowledge, attitudes, learning abilities of individual	Long term skills, knowledge, attitudes, learning abilities of group	Long term skills, knowledge, attitudes, learning abilities of organisation
Change	Work processes or outcomes of individual	Work processes or outcomes of group	Work processes or outcomes of organisation

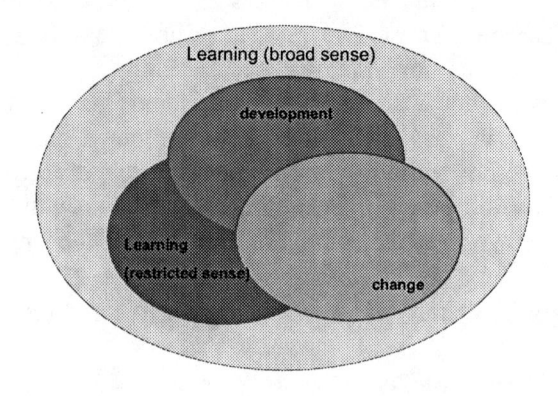

Figure 2. The various ways of learning and their interrelationships

Now that we have defined learning professionals, the three ways to learn (elaboration, expansion and externalisation) will be discussed in more detail.

2. ELABORATION

One important characteristic of a professional is, in our view, that (s)he is working in practice and is learning *implicitly* from and in that practice. We believe however, that this is not enough, but that it is important for professionals to become aware of the outcomes of their implicit learning. Why is this the case?

Mini-case: Anna, age 44, scientific degree, H R-manager

Anna is impressing people by her enormous body of knowledge. There seems no book she hasn't read and no theory she doesn't know about. In being confronted with a problem or assignment (in her line of work, as well as outside), almost the first step she takes is 'researching'- what is the best model to fit this problem and where can I find directions who lead me to a well-founded solution. In choosing her 'right'-solutions, she is very strict; no compromises, she follows the idea to the end. So although she is very concerned with the usability of ideas (they may not be to scientific), at the same time huge gaps between her knowledge-world and her real working-environment can come into being. Correction or feedback by colleagues on these issues do not occur often, because of her robust nature and self-confidence, and the knowledge that she will always have clear arguments to support her actions.

This case shows that although she put learning-effort into expansion, there is still room for improvement. Anna focuses her energy on theoretical learning, and leaves her critical learning untouched. Researching more into her values and norms, she would come to know that her desire to work 'clean' within one model conflicts with her desire to stay practical.

2.1 Why should professionals become aware of implicit learning?

More and more, it has become clear of late (again) that there are many implicit ways of learning (Bolhuis & Simons, 1999; Doornbos & Krak, 2001; Eraut, 2000). Here, we call this experiential learning. Both the processes and the outcomes of learning can be implicit or explicit to the learner (as well as to outsiders), determining four possibilities of awareness of processes and outcomes. Table 2 presents these possibilities and examples of all four. When learning processes are implicit, people do not realise that activities they are undertaking or processes they are involved in, can or will lead to changes in knowledge, skills, attitudes and / or learning ability. Awareness of learning *processes* (thus explicit learning processes) can arise before, during or after the activities and processes. Sometimes this awareness does not arise at all. When learning outcomes are implicit, people do not realise what they (have) learn(ed) during activities such as working, playing or problem solving. Awareness of learning *outcomes* can also arise before, during or after the activities or processes mentioned. And again sometimes this awareness of learning outcomes does not arise at all. Learning remains fully implicit in that case.

Table 2. Examples of implicit and explicit learning processes and outcomes

Outcomes Processes	Implicit	Explicit
Implicit	II: without knowing how a person learned to recognise visual expressions and (s)he is not aware that (s)he can do it	IE: a person knows that (s)he is able to recognise emotions in a face but does not know how (s)he has learned this
Explicit	EI: A person tries to learn to ride a bicycle but does not know that (s)he is already able to do it	EE: A person intentionally learns to drive a car and knows that (s)he can do it.

Research shows that many work related learning processes as well as learning outcomes remain implicit (Doornbos & Krak, 2001; Eraut, 1998). This becomes clear when people try to talk about their job-related learning. When Doornbos and Krak (2001) interviewed police officers about their work-related learning, they reported hardly any learning outcomes or learning processes. They discovered, however, that just asking them about learning was not the right approach. The word "learning" puts people into the wrong mode: they start looking for courses they attended, books they read, coaching they received and so on. Only when the word "learning" was not used and instead they were asked about changes in competences (see next paragraph), people started to realise that they had learned a lot in and from their work. By focusing on concrete changes in work processes or outcomes, they could become aware of their learning processes. When they realised *what* they had learned they started to talk about *how* they had learned. The study showed that police officers learned many new competences at work, ranging from new social competences to juridical, ethical and self-regulatory competences. Most of these competences were acquired through implicit ways of learning. The policemen were not aware of the learning and did not even call it learning. Most of their learning processes were combinations of experiential learning with some kind of support from colleagues. These could hardly be called coaches, however, because they were just imitated, just gave some feedback, or gave some hints. Self-directed learning and guided forms of learning were almost non-existent. Instead there was a lot of (implicit) learning with and from colleagues. Sometimes learning started implicitly and became somewhat more explicit after a while. In other cases learning started explicitly, but became a much more implicit form after a period of time.

Experiences in these studies as well as in advisory work in organisations show, that there are good reasons for professionals (as well as other workers) to develop more awareness of learning processes and outcomes. First, when people realise what they have learned implicitly they develop a sense of pride, and a shift in their mental model: from learning-is-only-for-the-IQ-smart to learning-can-take-place-every-moment-in-my-work (Claxton, 1999). "Geeh I did not know that this job gives me so many opportunities to learn" or "I thought I wasn't such an egghead, but I learned quite a lot in such a short time, and not only being lectured or reading things". It is important, according to our experience, to start by focussing on what one has learned, not about what is lacking.

A second reason to create awareness of learning processes and outcomes, lies in the fact that people can only share the outcomes of learning when they do recognise them.

Learning Professionals 215

And third, how can people improve their *ways* of learning when they do not know that, what and how they learn?

Hypothesis 1: On the basis of this we developed the following hypothesis. Making implicit learning results more explicit
1. leads to job-related pride,
2. makes outcomes of learning sharable,
3. makes it possible to reflect on implicit *ways* of learning.

A further hypothesis we propose relates to the willingness for extended forms of learning (learning in more conscious and explicit ways).

We believe that extended forms of learning presuppose a certain awareness of previous learning processes and outcomes. When people realise that and how they are learning all the time, they also start to realise, so says our experience, that there are things that they do not learn implicitly and automatically and that certain outcomes will only be realised when there is more explicit (self)regulation and direction.

Hypothesis 2: Therefore our second hypothesis is: Becoming aware of implicit learning outcomes and the processes leading to them, leads to increased willingness towards more explicit forms of learning.

In the next paragraph, we will first discuss ways to make implicit learning outcomes and processes explicit. Also, we will discuss some of its potential dangers. Next, we will return to the more explicit forms of learning.

2.2 How can one become aware of one's implicit learning outcomes and processes?

Because such a huge percentage of our learning takes place implicitly (Simons, Van der Linden, & Duffy, 2000), we are intrigued by the idea of improving implicit learning. In studying experiential learning and in our consultancy practice, we have been exploring how to act on implicit learning outcomes (and consequently on their learning processes). We have found six issues:

First, it is important to realise that it is neither possible nor desirable to make all implicit learning outcomes and processes explicit.

Moreover, sometimes it is better not to make implicit learning explicit. As Nonaka and his colleagues (Von Krogh, Ichijo, & Nonaka, 2000) made clear, there can be an implicit kind of exchange. And it is within informal activities and settings, and without explicitness, that people develop a feeling of shared competences (Nonaka, Reinmoeller, & Senoo, 1998).

When one does want to make learning outcomes and processes explicit, there are a couple of possibilities, and thus a couple of choices to make. The first choice lies between reflection-in-action and reflection-on-action. *In action* our implicit competences are, although not conscious to our selves, of course visible to others. By observing people in action, a trained observer can infer these underlying competences. By using pre- and post-action interviews, for example, people can learn to reflect-in-action, and become aware of their implicit competences and reflect on their knowledge, skills and attitudes themselves. In our experience, reflective practicum's as described by Schön (1987) can be a very powerful methodology. And Klarus (1998) devised and studied for this purpose an effective method consisting of a combination of pre- and post-action interviews with observations.

Reflection on action is probably less accurate, but nevertheless very informative. For this, you can either ask others to reflect on your learning, or do it yourself. Clients or colleagues may often have very good ideas of the specific competences they encounter in interactions with the subject we want to help become aware of their implicit learning. One can just ask clients for feedback: "What, in your experience, is my specific way of working?" Besides this, three hundred and sixty degree feedback methods can be a powerful tool. Probably more feasible however, is it to use reflective methods (both individual and collective ones). Then we help people to reflect on the outcomes of their learning. We will talk about them, more in depth in the next paragraph. Let us first give a short recapitalisation. Thus there are six ways to act on implicit learning outcomes (Figure 3).

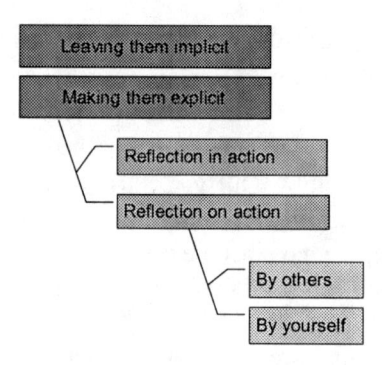

Figure 3. Six ways to act on implicit learning outcomes

2.3 Self-reflection

There are different methods to use in order to make learning outcomes explicit. Because they can add so much to professionalization and are not widely known yet, we will describe some of them in the next paragraph.

The first technique for making learning outcomes explicit through individual reflection came from Eraut (1998) and his colleagues. Instead of asking for learning outcomes directly, they asked (semi-)professionals (in their study: health care assistants, radiographers, and nurses) what had changed in their work. "In what ways is your current work different from one, two or five years ago?", "What does this tell you about what you know now and are now able to do that you were not able to at that time?" Another technique used is asking people to describe an ideal professional or worker. For example: "How does an ideal train conductor or an ideal human resource manager do his work?" In our experience, people have quite concrete ideal models. The next question can be "In what respect are you yourself already an ideal worker / professional?" This leads, almost automatically, to explicating learning outcomes and differences between ideal and practice. And sometimes this leads to on the spot discoveries of disconnections between current ways of working and ideals, and thus to new learning opportunities. For example, we met a human resource manager describing the ideal HR-manager as someone who is constantly networking with all line managers in the organisation in an informal way. On the spot, he himself discovered that he was not practicing this at all. Thus, asking people to reflect on the difference between their picture of an ideal practitioner and their own explicit and implicit competences may help them become aware of learning outcomes reached so far and needs for more explicit learning afterwards. A third technique often used is the critical incidents method. People try to think of practical situations that were critical. From there they start to think of the underlying competences. This technique resembles the "pretty good practices" approach described by Marsick (2001), in which people talk about examples of situations where they performed pretty well. Marsick notes that it is important not to ask for "best practices" because then we put too much pressure on people to excel. In our experience, we found that it is even important to avoid talking about failures and focus in the first place on positive incidents. By positive critical incidents or pretty good practices, there is a greater willingness and there are less defence mechanisms to do some "research" into details of the learning outcomes and processes. Related is also the "story telling"-technique, where people tell anecdotes and stories from their practices. The difference here is in the "story telling mindset" which activates a certain amount of detail in describing circumstances and events from a certain distance (talking about yourself in the third person).

Again another technique, described by Marsick (2001) is "Walking in the shoes of the client". People are asked to take the perspective of one of their clients and look at their own competences through the eyes of the client. A final example of a technique method described by Marsick is the "multiple intelligences approach". In this approach, people try to use pictures, drawings, metaphors, movements, etc. to make clear to themselves what they have learned implicitly.

Many other techniques could be thought of, to name a few more: Teaching others, looking into the future, working in heterogeneous groups, thinking of changes and improvements.

In these examples, we can easily recognise the connection to the other two fields of professionalizing. Teaching others is, as we will see later on a way to externalise, but in teaching others we do learn a lot about our implicit learning outcomes, and in thinking of changes and improvements, we are quite often inspired by models and articles of well-known thinkers in our field. In these concepts and ideas lies the overlap with "expansion".

A common underlying general feature of all of these methods is that they start from concrete situations or experiences and go from there to learning outcomes and competences.

Hypothesis 3: So a third hypothesis is: Professionals and other workers need to think of concrete situations and experiences in order to become aware of their implicit learning outcomes.

2.4 Putting the explication of implicit learning into perspective

From the previous discussions one might have gained the impression that we want professionals to learn in more explicit ways, both with reference to the outcomes and to the processes of learning. We call this educationalising. This is, however, contrary to our intention. Educationalising, meaning replacing implicit learning with explicit learning, is often a mistake. It is trying to pre-plan and pre-organise learning where it had better occur spontaneously in the context of work. This can, in our view, be a mistake for several reasons.
1. A large part of the existing work related learning is (as we mentioned before) implicit.
2. Often people enjoy finding new solutions and like to start new actions (and so learning implicitly) in their work, but resent learning in more explicit ways.

3. Educationalizing may focus people's attention too much on learning instead of on working.

Moreover, the possibility of ruining people's motivation is quite real. So, before educationalising, we propose to pose the following three questions.
1. What are the consequences of educationalizing specific working situations?
2. What is gained by replacing implicit learning with more explicit learning?
3. Can we reorganise working environments to increase the chances of implicit learning?

In many instances, we think it better to find ways to help people and their managers to reorganise work in such a way that the chances of implicit learning grow and increase.

2.5 Increasing implicit learning without making it explicit

This brings us to the following questions: Is it possible to (re)organise workplaces without making learning more explicit and to increase the chances of implicit learning? How can we do that? Based on the studies of Onstenk (1997) and Kwakman (1999), we think this is possible by focussing on six features of work processes and work environments, being (1) variation, (2) responsibilities, (3) feedback, (4) reflection, (5) innovation/experimentation, and (6) vision building.

These six can be organised by managers (giving time for reflection, organising feedback, giving autonomy, planning innovation and experimentation, and so on), but they can also be organised by the people themselves. They can try to look for feedback, reserve time for reflection, look for variation, be open to innovation, etc. All of these features of work environments can be organised individually as well as in collaboration with others: with colleagues, coaches, managers and clients. Each of these categories of actors may bring in different perspectives and contributions to implicit learning. Concluding this section again with hypotheses:

Hypothesis 4a: Before trying to educationalize working situations, first try to reorganise them in such a way that implicit learning is given better chances.

Hypothesis 4b: Implicit learning increases if working environments are organised in such a way that instances of variation, responsibility, feedback, reflection, vision building and innovation increase.

Hypothesis 4c: Reorganising work from the perspective of implicit learning, can improve (implicit as well as explicit) learning results.

3. EXPANSION

Although we have been focussing so far on the advantages of implicit learning processes, it seems clear that in some cases, implicit learning (processes) will not be enough. For instance, when a coherent system of new concepts has to be learned, when there are security risks involved, when intensive and guided practice of skills are needed or when people have to look critically at their work or life, more explicit learning processes are needed. Sometimes, implicit learning is too inefficient or not effective enough; for some kinds of learning conscious attention to learning itself may be needed; sometimes implicit learning is just too difficult or too time-consuming. Then, it is more effective or more efficient to use explicit learning. Parts of these will take place off the job in training courses or in educational institutes with special responsibilities for learning. Other parts can, it is our conviction, be organised on or near the job (on the job training, coaching, mentoring, etc.). Moreover, people can also organise these more explicit ways to learn on their own, both on and off the job: self-directed learning.

Trying to improve learning on the job by making learning more explicit can involve: formulating learning goals, planning learning activities and strategies, testing learning results, monitoring learning, judging and rewarding learning and/or placing learning processes and learning outcomes at the centre of attention. This can be done by professionals / workers themselves or by others (teachers, coaches, managers, books, computers).

Mini-case: Robert Martin, age 37, management consultant

Robert Martin strikes one as a creative person. He has been consultant ever since he left the university, and he published three books and several articles. Behind his impressive resume, you would expect a man of wide reading. But quite the opposite is true. He is gazing at you whenever you mention a theory, name or title of related literature. He isn't interested in someone else's ideas, he rather elaborates on theories of his own. By reflecting on his professional learning he characterizes his own learning as trial and error, immediately putting ideas to practice and awaiting what happens. Whatever he read was only in order to support his own thinking, and would take place during the writing of a new book. His ambitions don't include becoming a senior consultant. He rather becomes well known by his writings.

This case made us realize once more that learning could not be cyclic. Whatever expansion Robert Martin uses is always following his externalizations and being instrumental to it.

3.1 Explicit learning is not so obvious

Studies of learning on the job by Doornbos and Krak, and Eraut mentioned above, all show that, compared to the occurrence of implicit learning, only few people tend to organise explicit learning themselves. This, probably, has to do with the emotional states related to the occurrence of explicit learning. One needs some confidence before getting into (implicit) learning in the first place, and one needs some curiosity in order to be motivated to get into explicit learning (even if it concerns on the job learning). When one is learning explicitly, confidence in one's own, thus far implicit, theories and competences will increase. Moreover, learning explicitly can even create increased curiosity: The more one knows, the more one wants to know.

3.2 Three ways of learning explicitly

We tend to distinguish three ways of learning explicitly: Theoretical learning, inquiry learning, and critical learning (Bolhuis, 1995). In *theoretical learning* the learner (or trainer) decides to learn new concepts and ideas and to connect pre-existing concepts and ideas with those of others or with existing theories and research outcomes from the profession or discipline. This is a way of learning focussing on concepts, ideas, research outcomes, theories as developed by others, sometimes in scientific research, sometimes in thinking based on experience. In essence, it is connecting ones' own concepts, ideas, theories and research outcomes with those of others inside and outside the profession. One does this, for instance, through reading books, attending conferences, being involved in discussions and comparisons.

Inquiry learning is a form of (action) research: Learners (and or trainers) decide to find out whether hypotheses arising from experiential learning remain valid under varying conditions or can be tested (semi-)systematically on the job or in more scientific research. Hakkarainen et al. (2000) described a useful inquiry learning model for educational situations, that can also be used on the job.

In *critical learning*, people look critically at their norms and values. It concerns questions like "Are we walking the talk?", "Don't we have to adjust our way of working or learning in a more fundamental way?", "Is our way of working still in line with our norms and values?", etc. Although this form of expansion is closely related to elaboration, for this our learning should already be explicit in order to be an element of research. Besides this the central question is always partly one of theoretical ideas and concepts: Are the ones we choose (espoused) in harmony with what we show (in actions)?

Hypothesis 5: The hypothesis underlying this section is the following: Explicit individual learning will occur and will be needed when people want / need to
1. expand and test their action theories (inquiry learning);
2. compare these with other theories (theoretical learning); and
3. check whether they are walking the talk or still working in line with fundamental assumptions (critical learning).

4. EXTERNALISATION

The third part of our learning model, externalisation, refers to the need we see for professionals to connect their learning to concrete and public milestones. These milestones can be in the profession (publications, lectures, workshops, teaching activities, etc.) or in the workplace, both at the team (plan for group actions; contributions to team learning) and the organisational level (contributions to company policies or to organisational learning). Common in these milestones is that they are concrete and related to (learning) activities of other people. Moreover, these milestones can be made visible and connected to a date and a place, for instance, "I will write an article in that journal before the end of this year", "I will make a checklist for my organisation before Christmas and publish this on the company web" or "I feel the need to restate our vision and collective ambitions (due to new insights I need to share). Let's plan a date at short notice." Concrete milestones make the outcomes of explicit as well as implicit learning visible and easy to share and plan. Milestones can bring the necessary challenge that helps the learner to keep up motivation to continue and to learn, and to put personal learning outcomes in relation to the learning and working of other people. Colleague professionals and team members can co-profit from one's learning and the learner has something to look forward to. Reaching a milestone can provide an extra form of reward when reached. It is exciting to see that people use what you have learned and developed. It is rewarding to see that one's article is accepted for publication in a journal, etc. But most of all it is the learner who in searching for the right words or explicating ideas necessary for teaching others or making concrete applications, again profits in learning.

Learning Professionals

Mini-case: Bereta, age 35, university teacher

Bereta is a friendly and sociable type of person, committed to both his work as researcher-teacher and "his students". He is a quick learner. In order to become acquainted with, for example, a new computer program, or a new way of teaching, he only sits down and observes. You don't even realize he is learning, until the time he will come back to you and asks a detailed question. The next thing you'll notice is his strive for perfection. The results show. His students like him and reward his attempts to be the 'best teacher'. His perfectionism hides the fact that he really wasn't into expansion, until he changed profession, and became advisor for personnel and finance. Although this was a old dream come through, he wasn't at all prepared, and didn't realize he didn't have to sit back and wait for his 'education'. The possibility of actively searching for information on the net and in books, asking for coaching, and so on didn't cross his mind.

Bereta's learning power lies clearly into elaboration. And although his profession is teaching – this shouldn't be confused with externalization. Teaching is his primary process, not a way to externalize his thinking and insights on teaching. In his switch to another job it would be very helpful if he could extend on his learning power to expand and become a professional on his own strength.

Hypothesis 6: The hypothesis we propose: Determining externalised milestones helps people to intensify and sustain their implicit and explicit learning on and near the job.

5. THE COMPLETE MODEL OF ELABORATION, EXPANSION AND EXTERNALISATION

Figure 4 presents the full model where all of the ways of learning are distinguished.

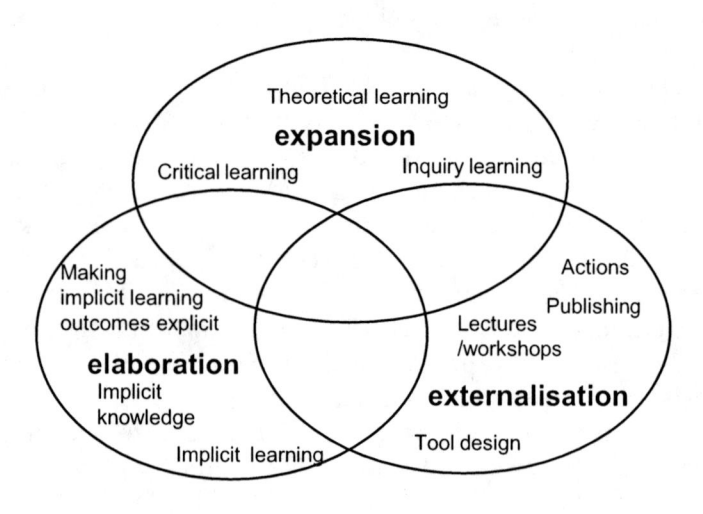

Figure 4. All forms of learning together in one view

6. THE ROLE OF EMOTION IN LEARNING AND PROFESSIONALISATION

Learning is not only about cognition, but most of the learning-models and theories are. As learning becomes more complex, and more challenging, more emotions come into play.

We believe that safety is a necessary and fundamental emotion involved in all kinds of learning. Therefore we have placed this in the centre of the model. The feeling of safety is not something static, but evolves from the "family of emotions" being interest/anxiety/excitement (Claxton, 1999). The interplay between these basic components causes a readiness for learning, and "resilience" as Claxton calls it.

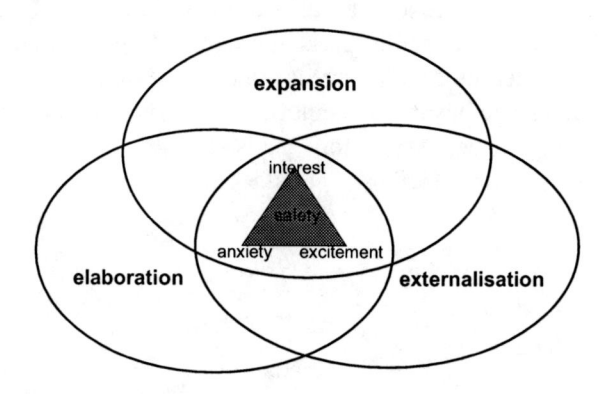

Figure 5. The basic family of emotions related to learning

Elaborating on learning, as we do in our theory of the learning professional, we detect more specific emotions connecting the different stages: Elaboration, expansion, and externalisation.

In the previous paragraphs we have already implicitly mentioned several emotional states, such as pride, confidence and curiosity that we considered to be important in themselves.

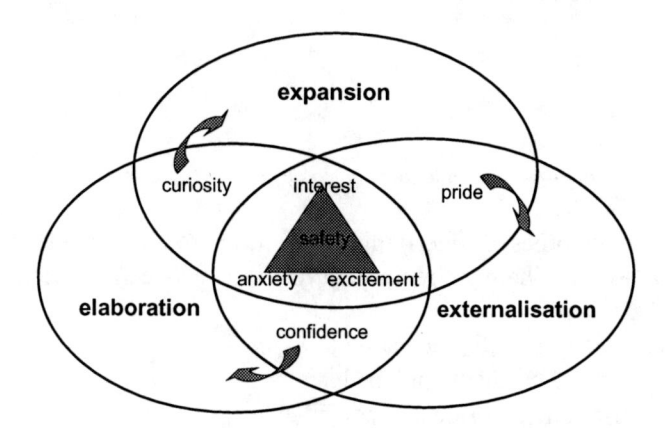

Figure 6. The family of emotions related to elaboration, expansion and externalisation

Moreover, we think that there are reciprocal relations between the emotional states and learning, meaning that the pre-existence of the emotion makes the kind of learning more probable and that the emotional state increases after learning has been successful. Take for example curiosity. This is needed for explicit learning and by expanding on your knowledge, insights and skills, the level of curiosity may increase. Equally, having confidence increases the willingness for explicating implicit learning and having explicated learning may increase one's confidence.

Finally, each stage has its own emotional outcome. Elaboration leads to a feeling of competence, expansion leads to a feeling of mastery and externalisation leads to a feeling of satisfaction.

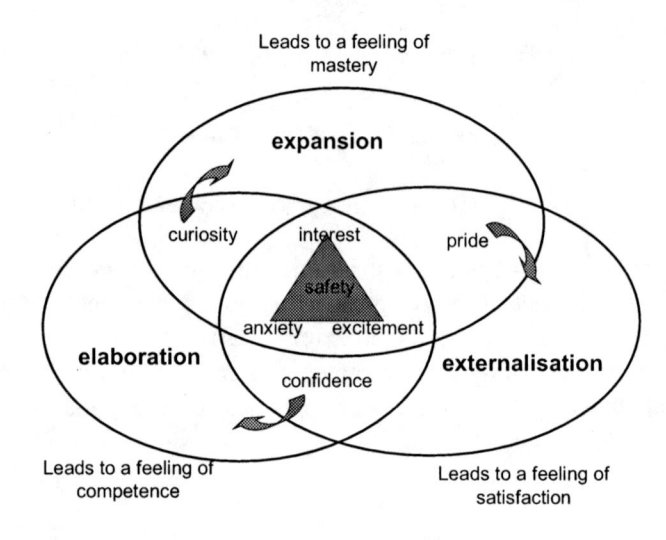

Figure 7. The emotional outcomes related to the three stages

The two hypotheses underlying this section are the following.

Hypothesis 7: There are reciprocal relations between emotional states and ways of learning:
1. elaboration and confidence and curiosity;
2. expansion and curiosity and pride;
3. externalisation and pride and confidence;
4. all three ways of learning and safety.

Hypothesis 8: Each stage has its own emotional outcome. Elaboration leads to a feeling of competence, expansion leads to a feeling of mastery and externalisation leads to a feeling of satisfaction.

7. COLLECTIVE LEARNING

So far, we have treated learning as if it would occur with individual professionals only. But collective learning is gaining importance. The accelerating developments in our society make it necessary but not enough to have excellent professionals in a work force. More and more, these professionals need to be able to work together in solving problems and innovating more accurately and quickly.

So, more and more professionals are working in teams, both interdisciplinary or monodisciplinary. The consequence of this, namely that professionals should also learn collectively, has not been discussed much so far. In our view, in the future professional learning needs to be extended to collective learning. Two forms of collective learning are to be distinguished: organisation-related collective learning and profession-related collective leaning.

Organisation-related collective learning refers to processes and intended outcomes of learning of a working team or an organisation. Teams of professionals or teams including professionals decide to collaborate in learning, focusing on common learning activities and processes or on common outcomes. "Communities of practice" (Wenger, 1998), sharing a common interest in the organisation, learn in and from their work and share this. This kind of collective learning has been described more fully elsewhere (Simons & Ruijters, 2001). There we distinguished collective elaboration, collective expansion and collective externalisation, which lead to different types of collective outcomes for example: balanced primary process, collective quality standards, gained and shared new insights, and collective visions, innovations and action plans for the team and/or organisation.

Profession-related collective learning consists of professionals, working in different organisations, but sharing the same profession and deciding to learn together from their different practices. They don't have a common interest in one organisation. They may be even competing for the same clients. Their common interest is in learning. Therefore we call these "communities of learners" and not "communities of practice". Collective outcomes can be partly the same as those of communities of practice, but in addition, collective professional outcomes relate to contributions to the professional field publications, lectures, tools, etc.

8. CONCLUSION

Our new model of professional learning defining professionalism in a dynamic way, as continuously working on vision, methodology and tools and techniques, and the alignment between these three components by
1. elaborating on his or her work-competencies;
2. expanding his theoretical knowledge and insights;
3. externalising his practical and theoretical insights, which means contributing to the development of the profession and / or to team and organisational learning.

We realise that this, including the various ways to learn at these three stages, is in a sense a normative model of professionalism. It specifies that professionals should be continuously involved in different kinds of learning and how they can organise this. We argue that every kind of learning, be it by elaboration, expansion or externalization has his own value for lifelong learning of a professional.

We also argue that confidence, curiosity and pride are emotions bridging these three stages, for example; there is a need for curiosity in order to expand – and expansion leads at a certain point to pride, which stands on the basis of externalizing, and so on. The different stages of learning add to the feelings of competence, mastery and satisfaction.

Finally we indicated that nowadays a model of professional learning cannot rely only on individual learning. Collective learning needs to be part of it. We find the three stage model of professional learning equally useful on a collective level, but did not get into this here.

Although parts of the model are based on empirical research, these hypotheses still await further empirical testing. We hope that researchers and practioners will take up the challenge to test these hypotheses and that we will be able to do that research ourselves in the years to come.

REFERENCES

Bolhuis, S. M. (1995). *Leren en veranderen bij volwassenen. Een nieuwe benadering.* Bussum: Coutinho.

Bolhuis, S. M., & Simons, P. R. J. (1999). *Leren en werken* (1st ed.). Deventer: Kluwer.

Brown, J. S., & Duguid, P. (2000). *The social life of information.* Boston: Harvard Business School Press

Claxton, G. (1999). *Wise up: the challenge of life long learning.* London: Bloombury.

Doornbos, A. J., & Krak, A. J. A. (2001). *Learning processes and outcomes at the workplace: A qualitative study.* Paper presented at the Conference on HRD Research and Practice Across Europe, Enschede.

Engeström, Y. (1999).Innovative learning in work teams. In Y. Engeström, R. Miettinen, & R. Punamaki (Eds.), *Perspectives on activity theory* (pp. 377-404). Cambridge: Cambridge University Press.

Eraut, M. R. (1998). *Development of knowledge and skills in employment.* Brighton: University of Sussex Institute of Education, Education Development Building.

Eraut, M. R. (2000). Non-formal learning and tacit knowledge in professional work. *British Journal of Educational Psychology, 70*, 113-136.

Germans, J. (1990). *Spelen met modellen.* Unpublished Ph.D. thesis, University of Tilburg.

Hakkarainen, K., Ilomaki, L., Lipponen, L., Muukkonen, H., Rahikainen, M., Tuominen, T., Lakkala, M., & Lehtinen, E. (2000). Students' skills and practices of using ICT: Results of a national assessment in Finland. *Computers and Education, 34*, 103-117.

Klarus, R. (1998). *Competenties erkennen. Een studie naar modellen en procedures voor leerwegonafhankelijke beoordeling van beroepscompetenties.* Nijmegen: Katholieke Universiteit Nijmegen, Velp.

Kwakman, C. H. E. (1999). *Leren van docenten tijdens de beroeploopbaan.* Unpublished Ph.D. thesis, Katholieke Universiteit Nijmegen.

Lehtinen, E. (2001, July). *Organisational learning and networked expertise.* Paper presented at the workshop "Changes in the Workplace and their Implications for Education", Regensburg.

Lievegoed, B. C. J. (1977). *Organisaties in ontwikkeling, zicht op de toekomst.* Rotterdam: Lemniscaat.

Marsick, V. (2001). *Informal strategic learning in the workplace.* Paper presented at the Second Conference on HRD Research and Practice Across Europe, Enschede, The Netherlands.

Nonaka, I., Reinmoeller, P., & Senoo, D. (1998). The 'ART' of knowledge: Systems to capitalize on market knowledge. *European Management Journal, 16*, 673-684.

Onstenk, J. H. A. M. (1997). *Lerend leren werken. Brede vakbekwaamheid en de integratie van leren, werken en innoveren.* Nijmegen: Katholieke Universiteit Nijmegen.

Schön, D. A. (1987). *Educating the reflective practitioner: Toward a new design for teaching and learning in the professions.* San Francisco: Jossey-Bass.

Simons, P. R.-J., Van der Linden, J., & Duffy, T. (2000). New learning: Three ways to learn in a new balance. In P. R.-J. Simons, J. Van der Linden, & T. Duffy (Eds.), *New learning* (pp. 1-20). Dordrecht: Kluwer.

Simons, P. R.-J., & Ruijters, M. C. P. (2001). Work related learning: Elaborate, expand, externalise. In L. Nieuwenhuis (Ed.), *Dynamics and stability in VET and HRD* (pp. 101-114). Enschede: Twente University Press.

Thijssen, J. (1987). *Bedrijfsopleidingen als werkterrein.* Den Haag: Vuga.

Von Krogh, G., Ichijo, K., & Nonaka, I. (2000). *Enabling knowledge creation.* Oxford: Oxford University Press.

Wenger, E. (1998). *Communities of practice.* Cambridge: Cambridge University Press.

Willems, J. (1987). *Studietaken als instructiemiddel.* Unpublished Ph.D. thesis, Katholieke Universiteit Nijmegen.

Chapter 12

FROM INDIVIDUAL COGNITION TO COMMUNITIES OF PRACTICE
Theoretical underpinnings in analysing professional design expertise

Anneli Eteläpelto[1] and Kaija Collin[2]
[1]*Research Centre for Educational Psychology, University of Helsinki, Finland,* [2]*Institute for Educational Research, University of Jyväskylä, Finland*

1. EXPERTISE: THE ROLE OF COGNITION AND SOCIAL CONTEXT

In recent discussion, cognitive and knowledge-based approaches have been criticised for their basic belief that knowledge and expertise are located in the heads of individual subjects. The situated and social learning approach, which has challenged the assumptions of cognitive and knowledge-based approaches, suggests that knowledge and expertise are primarily present in the discursive interactions of practical communities. In these approaches which use the participative metaphor, knowledge is understood as ways of relating to and participating in the world. Learning and acquiring professional expertise is conceived as a process of identity formation within practical communities. In empirical studies, identity formation is analysed in terms of the negotiation of meaning as part of the authentic practices of such communities, for example in work organisations.

The social theory of learning has given due emphasis to the contextual nature of professional expertise. However, radical situationism is open to the criticism that it neglects the subjectivity and thus also the developmental continuities that exist at the level of individual subjects. When applied to questions of the nature and development of professional expertise, the situated cognition approach may lead to professional expertise being reduced to mere workplace discourse, with no roots in the participants' experiential learning histories. At worst, this can lead to a form of theorising in which individuals are treated as if they themselves had no history or context. What is neglected in this perspective is the continuity of an individual's experience and sense-making, a continuity that includes developmental achievements which have a bearing on a broad spectrum of human activities.

Taking up the challenge of analysing some recent approaches to professional design expertise, the present paper critically reviews some mainstream notions in analysing design expertise. In so doing we shall focus on cognitive and knowledge-based approaches on the one hand, and social theory of learning approaches on the other. In addition to discussing the main theoretical underpinnings, we shall also summarise results of empirical studies addressing the nature of design expertise. On the basis of our studies which analyse systems analysts' expertise in terms of contextual and strategic knowledge (Eteläpelto, 2000) and development engineers' conceptions of learning at work (Collin, 2003), this paper goes on to seek answers to the question of how to analyse professional design expertise in a way that recognises the context-sensitive nature of expertise, without neglecting professional subjects and their developing skills and knowledge.

2. EXPERTISE IN SEMANTICALLY RICH DOMAINS: A KNOWLEDGE-BASED APPROACH

Expert-novice comparisons made in knowledge-rich domains have mainly addressed the relationships between expertise and experience. In the first place, these studies have operationalised expertise as a certain length of professional work experience; thus novices are those who have the domain education but little or no work experience, whereas experts are subjects who have in addition to their domain education a considerable amount of work experience. In determining the limit of minimum experience, there is variation depending on the domain. Two years is the minimum length most often adopted, since this is usually the period during which subjects become familiar with their work organisation and working conditions. Some professional associations demand a certain minimum length of experience before professionals can apply for membership of the association. For example, in the legal profession, this minimum length is usually four years.

The minimum length of necessary work experience will naturally vary, depending on the task domain and, for example, the amount of practical experience which has been built into the student curriculum. In systems design as well as in other design tasks, it is considered important that subjects should have a minimum period of training during which they complete at least one authentic project, including feedback from clients and users. The working conditions of designers do not always allow them to get proper feedback from their work (Collin, 2003; Rambow & Bromme, 1995; also Strasser & Gruber, this volume); this is often the case, for example, with architects. Nevertheless, the length of projects would normally be considered when setting minimum requirements for the length of experience.

With regard to professional tasks, there are few studies which have analysed the qualitative aspects of experience. Wang and Horng (1992) compared education-based and experience-based experts in business management. They found that experience-based expertise, observed in managers and novices, was characterised by a solution-focused and heuristic cognitive strategy. By contrast, education-based expertise, observed from students with higher levels of education, was characterised by a systematic and knowledge-based cognitive strategy.

Schmidt and Boshuizen (1993) compared two kinds of medical experts in their use of medical knowledge: Those with clinical experience and those with research experience. The authors found that those physicians who had experience as researchers were similar to students in their use of biomedical knowledge. By contrast, those experts who had had actual clinical experience used their clinical knowledge: This clinical knowledge is regarded by the authors as an encapsulated form of biomedical knowledge (see also Van de Wiel, 1997).

The interpretation of findings regarding expert-novice differences in semantically rich domains has mainly followed the trends of knowledge-based approaches to expertise (Greeno, Collins, & Resnick, 1996). The superiority of experts in their problem solving domain is believed to depend on the experts' possession of an extremely rich knowledge base, acquired through extensive experience. Such a knowledge-based approach has also appeared to offer a fruitful theoretical framework in analysing expertise in design tasks. With this approach, however, findings are often presented as a list of separate attributes whose relationships are not clearly specified. For example, it has not been specified how selectivity in perceiving relevant information would be related to the perception of large meaningful patterns. The lack of a relationship between different attributes has meant that findings have not really been used as a basis for constructing more coherent theoretical models of expertise development. When one merely lists expert-novice differences, one tends to include findings derived from descriptions at very different levels of human activity.

Despite the limitations of expert-novice comparisons made within the framework of a knowledge-based approach, these studies have significantly contributed to our understanding of how to differentiate between beginners and more advanced performers; they have also helped us to understand better the kind of changes that take place as a consequence of learning from practical experience. Nevertheless, it is clear that there has been much confusion through a failure to distinguish between experienced and high-performing subjects. Bereiter and Scardamalia (1993) have suggested that we should make a distinction among experienced subjects by differentiating between experienced experts and experienced non-experts. According to this differentiation, experts are high-performers; the non-experts could be experienced subjects, but their performance would be relatively poor.

In studies focusing on top-performances, expertise is operationalised as high-performance (Ericsson, 1996; Sonnentag, 1995). These studies have usually started with the selection of research subjects in a way that reflects their position on a ranked scale. In most domains of professional activity, however, this kind of ranking is hard to obtain, due to the contextual and normative character of professional expertise.

In general, a knowledge-based approach to expertise research can been considered fruitful and capable of contributing to a more realistic understanding of the nature of human expertise and its learning conditions. It has produced many new findings so that many aspects of cognition of expertise can now be characterised fairly well (see also Feltovich, Ford, & Hoffman, 1997). However, the limitations of a knowledge-based approach should be considered when evaluating generalisations based on findings derived from this approach.

3. LIMITATIONS IN THE KNOWLEDGE-BASED APPROACH, AND THE IMPORTANCE OF CONTEXT

The limitations of cognitive science approaches and the knowledge-based approach to expertise research have recently been discussed in various connections (Bereiter & Scardamalia, 1993; Engeström, 2001; Eraut, 1994; Gruber, 1994; Rambow & Bromme, 1995). Expert-novice comparisons which operationalise expertise mainly as a certain length of experience have been criticised, in that they tend to overestimate the role of practice as the main source of expertise. It is well known from daily life that despite having worked at something for many years, some people are still not very skilful.

Cross-sectional expert-novice comparisons have also been criticised for giving a static and uniform picture of professional expertise. Indeed, studies in knowledge-rich domains have shown that there is a lot of qualitative variety in the nature of subjects' solutions, and that such variety can tell us a great deal about the nature and quality of learning which produced the expertise. Studies addressing open and ill-defined tasks have shown that the nature and variety of subjects' experience explains the high performance of experts better than the length of their work experience (Sonnentag, 1995; Waltz, Elam, & Curtis, 1993). After a certain minimum length of experience, the scope and versatility of experience seem to be more important than the length of it.

In professional learning, the need for a redefinition of expertise has emerged from the rapid changes in working life and social conditions which have taken place within information societies. As a consequence of these changes, it is less common for people to work at the same task for long periods. This has resulted in a constant need to learn the use of new tools, methods and technical facilities; this in turn involves a continuous challenge to professionals' prior knowledge and competencies. In this context, there have been definitions of expertise which emphasise the need for continuous learning. Bereiter and Scardamalia (1993), who approach expertise from the perspective of a career, suggest as the central determinant of high-level expertise the subject's continuous surpassing of his or her previous level of knowledge and competence. This kind of "surpassing oneself" means that subjects are continuously working close to the limits of, or at the developing edge of their competence.

Other recent approaches of expertise research also emphasise contextual and social aspects (Engeström, 2001; Lave & Wenger, 1991; Wenger, 1998). Although different schools of thought have understood these contextual aspects differently, discussion on the role of context in the determination of expertise has gradually led to the adoption of a wider perspective; this involves the organisational, cultural and social aspects of the working and learning environment. The increased emphasis on social aspects of professional expertise has also led to an increased use of colleague or peer-evaluation in operationalising expertise. Indeed, the recognition of the social group has been considered as the primary determinant of expertise in these definitions. In the domain of service production, where customer and client perspectives are important, these perspectives can in fact be used in the definition of high-level expertise. The emphasis on contextual aspects in expertise research has also led to a move away from laboratory environments to field studies and authentic study settings (Symon, 1998).

In previous studies on design expertise, the external validity of the findings has also been limited by the selection of research subjects. In many expert-novice comparisons, research subjects have been chosen in such a way that the novices are students at the initial stages of their studies, and the experts are students who have studied considerably longer. Professional subjects have not always been used, even if the findings are supposed to be generalisable to professional expertise.

The limitations of research tasks and study settings have not allowed subjects to use their various knowledge domains, especially those connected with contextual and situational knowledge. It is thus understandable that these knowledge domains, even if they would have had central importance for professional problem solving, have not been manifested as expert knowledge. This is one important reason why we should re-conceptualise expertise in a way that incorporates contextual and strategic aspects. And indeed, following on criticism of previous expert-novice studies, much recent research has attempted to use approaches which would capture human expertise in its authentic contexts.

4. FROM THE EMPHASIS ON CONTEXTUAL KNOWLEDGE TO THE SOCIAL THEORY OF LEARNING

The need for re-conceptualising professional expertise has been increasingly discussed during the 90s. The central theme in this discussion has been that the role of context should be seriously considered when expertise is addressed. Many researchers now take the position that the analysis of expertise should not separate itself from the context of the expertise, context being seen an essential component of the expertise. The general theme of emphasising the role of context has been common to different theoretical approaches (Agnew, Ford, & Hayes, 1997; Brown & Duguid, 1994; Gruber, Law, Mandl, & Renkl, 1995; Hoffman, Feltovich, & Kenneth, 1997; Stein, 1997; Wenger, 1998). However, there are also considerable differences between schools concerning what is to be understood by the concept of context (Van Oers, 1998). Thus, anthropologically oriented approaches have defined context as socially and culturally conditioned aspects of practical communities, whereas cognitive science approaches have seen the context as constituted by environmental circumstances and also by the characteristics of tools and artefacts which determine the nature of human activities.

Although there has been active theoretical discussion on the role of context, there is not much empirical research on how the context becomes present as subjects reason on problems within their domains. Those few studies which deal with this issue have supported the suggestion that contextual issues have different roles at different stages of acquiring expertise. Expert-novice comparisons made in knowledge-rich domains have shown that the role of context is more important for experts' decision-making than for that of novices. Among novices, context has a minor role and is thus more or less separated from decision-making activities. Schmidt and Boshuizen (1993) found that in a recall task, expert physicians were able to recall more of their patients' contexts than novices; moreover, in diagnostic tasks, expert physicians made more use of the contextual knowledge they had of their patients than novices. A lack of such knowledge also seemed to have a greater effect on the quality of the diagnosis among experts than among novices. Beyond these studies, there has so far been relatively little research on the role of context and how it is connected with subjects' development of expertise. At present it is true to say that the issue of context has generated more theoretical interest than empirical investigation.

The situated learning approach, which has challenged cognitive science assumptions, suggests that knowledge and expertise are primarily present in the discursive interaction of practical communities (Lave & Wenger, 1991). In these approaches which use the participation metaphor (Sfard, 1998), knowledge is understood, not as static schematic structures, but rather as ways of relating to and participating in the world (Ackerman, 1996). Taken to its extreme, the situated approach concludes that the very idea of individual knowledge is totally inappropriate and that cognitive approaches which assume such knowledge should be thrown out (Lave & Wenger, 1991). Such a radical approach rejects the notion of human learning as the individual construction of knowledge, replacing it with the social construction of identities. In any case, within situated approaches, learning and the development of expertise are understood as the construction of identities through participation in practical communities of work organisations, teams, or social networks ranging across organisational boundaries (Greeno, 1997; Sfard, 1998).

Wenger (1998) regards learning as fundamentally social. The social nature of learning arises from the basic assumption that participation and engagement in social practices are the processes by which we learn and so become who we are. In the social theory of learning suggested by Wenger (1998), the primary unit of analysis is neither the individual nor social institutions but rather the informal "communities of practice" that people form as they pursue shared enterprises over time. Communities of practice define what forms of competence are considered relevant and valid. Learning is taking place through participation and negotiation of identities in such communities.

Wenger (1998) suggests a broad conceptual framework for thinking about learning. In this framework learning is perceived as an ongoing and integral part of our lives, not a special kind of activity separable from the rest of our lives. While asking what essentially defines learning as learning, Wenger suggests that whatever forms learning takes, it changes what we are by changing our ability to participate, to belong, to negotiate meaning. Wenger further adds that this ability is configured socially with respect to practices, communities, and economies of meaning where it shapes our identities. Learning is also first and foremost understood as an ability to negotiate new meaning; it involves our whole person in a dynamic interplay of participation and reification. Learning is not seen as reducible to its mechanics (information, skills, behaviour), and focusing on the mechanics at the expense of meaning tends to render learning problematic.

In the social theory of learning, the developmental aspect is inherent in the emergent structures of communities created by learning. Wenger (1998) suggests that learning requires enough structure and continuity to accumulate experience and enough perturbation and discontinuity to continually renegotiate meaning. In this sense, communities of practice are seen as constituting elemental social learning structures.

Wenger (1998) regards learning as experiential in the sense that it involves our own experience of participation and reification. As a consequence of the participation and negotiation of meanings within communities of practice, the transformation of subjects' identities takes place. Individual development is perceived in terms of subjects' personal histories, in relation to the histories of communities. In this sense, learning constitutes trajectories of participation, building personal histories that connect our past and our future in a process of individual and collective becoming (Wenger, 1998).

To sum up, critical discussion on the limitations of cognitive approaches has rightly acknowledged the socially and culturally mediated nature of learning and expertise. The radical perspective can be criticised in that it unduly neglects the individual learner as a constructor of expert knowledge, perceiving learning as a mere temporary and local discourse taking place in work organisations. Perceiving expertise fundamentally as a matter of social attribution does not mean that one should neglect the role of the individual learner as the constructor of professional identity. Furthermore, understanding expert knowledge as contextually imbued and socially determined (Eteläpelto & Light, 1999) is not in contradiction with analysing expertise in terms of developmental processes manifested, for example, in perceived learning challenges (Collin, 2002; Eteläpelto, 1999).

5. THE NATURE OF DESIGN AND PLANNING AS PROFESSIONAL TASKS

Professional tasks of design and development are ill-defined and complex activities whose aim is to construct social and technical artefacts for prospective users and clients. By their nature, design tasks always require redefinition and specification of the task in ways that take into account the constraints which users and clients impose or under which they operate. Indeed, recent discussion on design expertise has suggested that a primary characteristic of high-level expertise consists precisely of the consideration and management of a multitude of overall constraints, including those involving clients and prospective users.

In a field study, Curtis, Krasner and Iscoe (1988) analysed professional software development projects to identify the characteristics of those professionals who were considered exceptional designers. The authors found three main characteristics of high performers. Firstly, they knew the application domain of the software extremely well and were able to integrate their knowledge of the application domain with their computer knowledge. Their knowledge of the application domain was mainly acquired through experience, not by training. Secondly, exceptional designers showed exceptional communication skills. They educated other team members about the application domain and its relationships with computational knowledge. Thirdly, they had a high degree of identification with the project and its success. The study thus demonstrated in addition to cognitive aspects the importance of motivation, social involvement and communication skills for professional designers (Sonnentag, 1995).

In line with the general discussion on learning and expertise, contemporary approaches to professional design expertise emphasise the importance of context and contextual knowledge for design expertise (Brown & Duguid, 1994). It is emphasised that design products should serve the needs of the prospective users (Schuler & Namioka, 1993). Furthermore, recent socio-cultural approaches have suggested that end-users and customers should be conceived not as isolated individuals but rather as members of a broader contextual system with users embedded in teams, organisations and environments: the user must be understood as a part of his or her organisational context (Nardi, 1996; Winograd, 1995).

If these results are interpreted in terms of the social theory of learning, we can ask whether experts' use of contextual knowledge means more intensive participation by them in professional communities of practice. At the other end of the spectrum, at the novice level, professional subjects are still members of the educational community, the relevant context being e.g. the university where they acquired the competence needed in the academic community of practice. From this perspective, we can ask what takes place at the stage of transition from one community to another. At the transition stage, when novices participate in working-life oriented project learning courses, they can have a multimembership within university and working life contexts (Collin & Tynjälä, in press; Eteläpelto, 2000). Such multimembership is addressed by Wenger (1998), who considers learning in terms of dealing with boundaries. Bridging and creating boundaries has been considered useful, especially for the production of innovations in organisations.

6. LEARNING FOR DESIGN EXPERTISE AS THE ACQUISITION OF CONTEXTUAL AND STRATEGIC KNOWLEDGE

In our analyses of professional designers' knowledge structures and problem-solving strategies, we tried to capture the qualitative variation in professional design expertise and analyse the main sources of this variation. We used a combination of expert-novice comparisons and longitudinal methods to focus on the changes that occurred across a problem-based course of seven months. During this course students were making the transition to working life. The aim here was to investigate developmental continuities in the acquisition of the strategic and contextual knowledge necessary for professional design expertise.

The expert-novice comparisons revealed that experts tended to perceive the task of design and development on a much more comprehensive and abstract level than novices. The great majority of professional designers with abundant work experience perceived the development of an artefact at the level of an organisation. By contrast, the novices, who had very limited work experience, mainly perceived it at the level of an individual user (Eteläpelto, 1998, 2000).

The longitudinal dimension of the study showed that at the initial level of acquiring design expertise, the strategic component of professional knowledge formed the central focus of learning. Later, a more balanced combination of contextual and strategic knowledge was evident. In our study, the professional designers who had a great deal of work experience suggested more versatile strategies and ways of taking customer perspectives into account than did the novices. The experts also identified more with customers, and considered the customer's situation in a more comprehensive way. At the highest level of expertise, contextual constraints were sometimes considered from a meta-level perspective, with participants questioning the meaningfulness of the entire task assignment (Eteläpelto, 2000).

Our results indicate that designers who have been exposed to formal knowledge in the university context will not be able to take adequate account of the perspectives and organisational contexts of their customers until they have acquired strategic competence in the domain in question, and become involved in the practical communities of working life. Consideration of contextual factors in relation to both the professionals' own organisational context and that of their customers represents a major learning target at the initial stage of entering working life. In the later stages of a professional's career, the contextual knowledge of organisations plays a more minor role, whereas questions of professional goals and values are at the core of their continuing learning (Eteläpelto, 1998, 2000).

When interviewed about the origins of their solution strategies, some 90 % of both experts and novices judged that their solutions originated from recent experience in their work or in a practical training setting. This was confirmed by systematically comparing the approaches they adopted in problem-solving with the roles that they had occupied in their prior work or practical training contexts. (Eteläpelto, 2000). These results point to the importance of subjects' functional roles in work organisations as the determinants of the nature and quality of their professional design expertise.

From the findings of our studies, it can be suggested that the central constituent of design expertise consists of constraint management (Collin, 2002, 2003; Eteläpelto, 2000). The empirical findings indicate that high-level expertise in design and development is primarily characterised by the consideration and management of a multitude of high-level constraints relating to (product) users. In our subjects' perception of information systems development, high-level constraints were described in terms of the work organisations in which the information systems were developed. In design solutions, a high-level solution was characterised in terms of multiple and comprehensive client constraints, such as the economic and social conditions of the clients. The solution might further include a questioning of the second-order rationale of the design task in terms of the meaningfulness of the entire task assignment.

Another characteristic typical of high-level design expertise manifested itself in the ability to perceive alternative strategic ways of solving the problem. While lower-level solutions were characterised by the perception of only one strategy or method of problem-solving, the highest-level solutions typically included more than one way of solving the problem. Different kinds of strategies were seen as alternatives whose advantages and defects were considered. The alternatives were critically evaluated, considering for example the client's economic situation and the professional's role. In discussion concerning reflective professionals, this kind of competence has been characterised as the ability to make comparisons of different alternative solutions (Pirttilä-Backman, 1997). The knowledge and competence to use alternative strategies would also represent a necessary condition for the successful employment of the metacognitive monitoring, controlling and evaluation of one's own working strategies (Volet, 1991).

7. THE DEMANDS OF CONTINUOUS LEARNING AND THE NORMATIVE CHARACTER OF PROFESSIONAL EXPERTISE

From the perspective of current working life and social conditions - which are characterised by rapid changes and increased demands for professional competencies - the need for a redefinition of professional learning and expertise has become evident. As a consequence of continuous changes in subjects' work settings, it is less common for people to work at the same task for long periods. In an information society there is a constant need to learn about new tools, methods and technical facilities, and this in turn involves a continuous challenge to professionals' prior knowledge and competencies (Simons, 1997; Smith, Ford, & Kozlowski, 1996).

In work settings where intensive use of information technology is combined with constructive and creative tasks of design and development, continuous learning is a necessity if one is to maintain professional expertise. Designers represent a group of professionals who have to be disposed to continuous learning because of constant changes in their working conditions. The tools and methods available to designers are constantly under development. Thus, the specialised methodological knowledge acquired during basic education soon becomes obsolete when students enter working life. As well as this, designers must continuously make themselves acquainted with the application field and clients for which the artefacts are developed. The constantly changing needs of clients must therefore also be considered by designers. In addition, new economic and organisational notions have an impact on the theories and practices of design and development professionals.

One central point emerging from our research into design engineers' learning at work was the importance of continuous informal learning in the workplace (Collin, 2002). The design engineers' conceptions of learning were based on their own experience and ranged from learning as something that took place through actually doing the work, to learning as something occurring in external contexts such as family life and free time. However, learning was most frequently described in terms of evaluating one's own work experiences, and also as taking place though collaboration and interaction with colleagues. Our results confirmed prior notions suggesting that the demands and challenges of the work task itself, plus the social interactions one has with one's colleagues, clients and customers, are the factors that play a dominant role in continuous learning and the development of professional expertise (Eraut, Alderton, Cole, & Senker, 1998; Gerber, 1998; Gerber, Lankshear, Larsson, & Svensson, 1995).

The contextual knowledge involved in professional design expertise can be discussed in terms of the general characteristics of working life and the normative character of required expertise. In the first place, recent discussion of the normative characterisation of professional expertise emphasises the need for changes in education and training deriving particularly from the requirements of flexibility and the continuous need for innovations and increased productivity. Arising from lively discussions of the changes taking place in working life, the required expertise has been characterised using a variety of concepts. Desirable expertise has been characterised, for example, in terms of adaptive (Hatano & Inagaki, 1992; Smith et al., 1996), reflective (Rowland, Fixl, & Yung, 1992; Schön, 1987), creative (Akin, 1990; Christiaans, 1992; Winograd, 1995), innovative (Achtenhagen, 1995; Nijhof & Streumer, 1994) and expansive (Engeström, 2001; Kuutti, 1996) expertise. These are terms used to characterise the general nature of professional expertise needed in modern production life.

In the discussion of required expertise, it usually happens that one single, specific aspect is over-emphasised. As a consequence of this, basic foundations, such as domain-specific strategic knowledge may be disregarded. For example, in the extreme emphasis on reflective expertise, strategic domain knowledge and the need for practical experience has been largely forgotten. This brings about misconceptions leading to very limited or one-sided notions of what is involved in advanced expertise. It has also been very common for the normative definitions of desirable expertise, which emerge from observations on working life to be rapidly generalised - without modification - to every level of schooling and to all educational contexts. However, studies concerning the relationships of expertise and metacognition have shown, for instance, that the metacognitive monitoring that seems so successful among experts is not successful among novices, since they have not yet acquired the necessary preconditions to utilise it (Eteläpelto, 1998). The broader implication is that those procedures and phenomena that seem important for promoting expertise among professionals are not so simply transferable to another level of expertise. Accordingly, when we are discussing a certain normative definition characterising a desirable nature of expertise, the limits of its generalisation should always be considered.

One recent notion of what professional expertise should be, especially in rapidly changing workplaces, addresses the definition of adaptive expertise. In their specification of the adaptive expertise needed in present-day working life, Smith et al. (1996) suggest that adaptive expertise involves a high quality and content of knowledge structures, together with metacognitive awareness and regulation. The authors suggest that in constructing well-integrated, high-quality knowledge structures and in developing metacognitive awareness and regulatory processes such as skills in planning, the monitoring and evaluation of one's own activity is the prerequisite for adaptive expertise.

For our part, if asked to characterise adaptive expertise in design and development, we would suggest that the adaptiveness of professionals in these domains is manifested in relation to the product users and their contexts. If this kind of adaptiveness exists, it means that professionals have a comprehensive conception of the target domain and are therefore able to take into account users and customers as well as their organisational constraints. Furthermore, adaptive design expertise involves the comprehensive use of strategic knowledge and the contextual knowledge of users and customers. This means that there is fluency in utilising domain-specific strategies, and that they are applied flexibly, considering the specific context of users and customers. The results of our study suggest that the development of such expertise is not obvious until adequate domain-specific strategic knowledge has been acquired, and after a lengthy period of domain-related work experience.

To sum up, the good quality of professional expertise is always a normative issue. This normative conception of expertise has important consequences for how such expertise is to be acquired. The relationships of learning outcomes and learning strategies have recently received well-deserved attention in the learning sciences. The notion of learning as being contextual and situative is particularly important, suggesting that "what is learned" is determined by the situations "where it is learned" and "how it is learned" (see also Ropo, this volume). In expertise research, the question of "what is learned" can be analysed in terms of the normative character of high-quality expertise.

8. CONCLUSIONS

What, then, do these results suggest for our understanding of design expertise and the need for its re-conceptualising? On the basis of recent approaches, professional knowledge and expertise can be understood as related, in the sense that professional knowledge and expertise are first and foremost determined and imbued by subjects' functional roles in their work communities. These may consist of traditional work organisations with their working cultures, power relationships, divisions of responsibilities, and so on. In tasks producing services such as information technology artefacts for clients, they can be regarded as important determinants of the professionals' functional roles. However, the nature of software tools and hardware facilities also has an influence on the nature of the professional activities needed for systems design. Thus, the professional's work organisation, nature of tools, and clients together constitute the important social context for the expertise and professional knowledge that is applied when a domain task is perceived and solved. In this sense we can argue that professional expertise has a context-sensitive nature - and that this is manifested in professionals' socially conditioned functional roles.

However, in the case of professional expertise this is only part of the truth. Despite being influenced by their functional roles in their work organisations, professional subjects also seem to be affected by their developmental backgrounds, which involve their domain learning. The findings of knowledge-based approaches to expertise research have shown that the expertise of professionals does not seem to be determined only by their context, but rather that they seem to utilise their subjective experiences in reaching conclusions derived from these contexts.

An extreme domain-specific emphasis of expertise - as well as an extreme emphasis on the contextual and normative aspects of professional expertise - would tend to neglect the general characterisation of high quality in expertise. If an extreme domain-specific approach is taken as the starting point, we could come to the conclusion that a high level of expertise is identical with the most recent conceptions and models prevalent in domain literature. By contrast, an extreme emphasis on mere contextual and normative aspects would suggest that a high level of expertise is to be characterised in terms of performance in working life and work organisational demands, and is in fact identical with them.

Although both these aspects are necessarily involved in the characterisation of a high quality of expertise, they are not sufficient as such. At their extremes, both domain-specific and working-life-based definitions share the defect that they do not recognise the autonomous role of the subject and his or her development. Yet in creative work - which consists of ill-defined and open tasks - there is an increasing emphasis on the individual subject's skills and competencies and thus on his or her expertise. In tasks of an open and constructive nature, professional subjects have a great deal of freedom in defining their tasks as well as their functions and positions in organisations. As a consequence of this, subjects' expertise and competencies may even play a part in determining the profile of organisations. In this situation, it seems legitimate to ask what a high level of expertise at an individual level consists of.

Figure 1 suggests an agenda for future needs to re-conceptualise our theoretical framework for research on the nature and learning of professional design expertise in terms of developing professional subjectivities in practical communities.

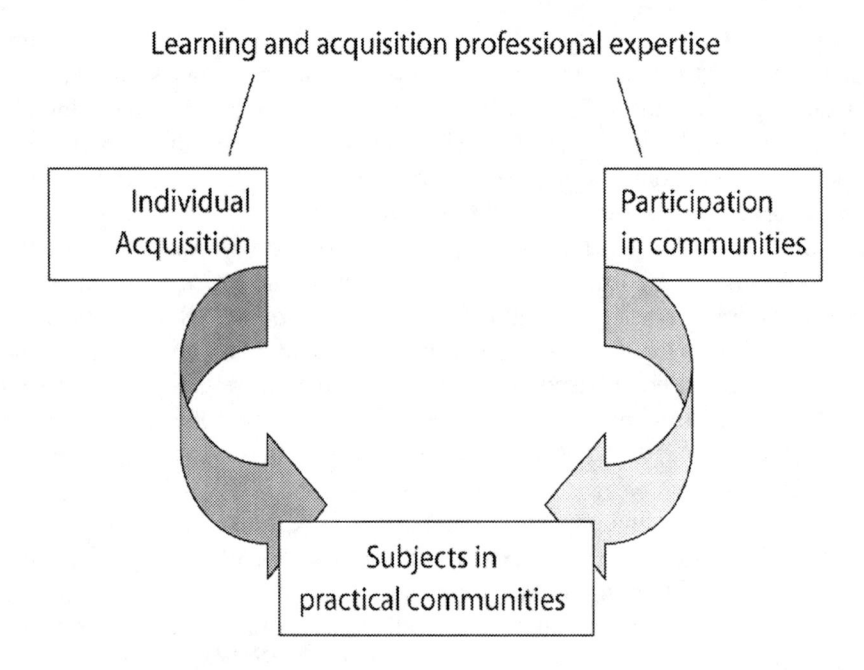

Figure 1. Suggestion for the need to re-conceptualise a framework for studying professional design expertise in practical communities

As a methodological implication concerning the relationship between the nature of expertise and subject's background experience, we would suggest that expertise cannot be characterised without characterising the nature and quality of the subject's background experience, which may involve, for example, his or her discourse of that experience. This is due to the fact that we cannot understand why a subject has a certain kind of representation, or how the components of this representation make sense in relation to each other, without reference to the subject's experience. In the empirical findings of our study, the integral nature of subjects' experiences was manifested to the extent that the nature of their experience was present in all their conceptual models and problem solutions.

The discussion of the cognitive and situative paradigms has led to the conclusion that both paradigms can offer useful starting points in researching different kinds of problems, and can also promote educational practices of various kinds. In line with Sfard (1998) one can conclude that the cognitive and situative paradigms seem not so much to be in contradiction, but rather to focus on different aspects of human life and activity. Rather than arguing about which of them has more relevance for deepening our understanding of the nature and development of professional expertise in ill-defined and creative tasks, such as design, we should ask how the social and cognitive aspects of expertise interact and relate to each other in authentic work contexts.

REFERENCES

Achtenhagen, F. (1995). Fusing experience and theory – Sociopolitical and cognitive issues. *Learning and Instruction, 5*, 409-417.

Ackerman, E. (1996). Perspective-taking and object construction - two keys to learning. In Y. Kafai & M. Resnick (Eds.), *Constructionism in practice: Designing, thinking, and learning in a digital world* (pp. 25-35). Mahwah: Erlbaum.

Agnew, N. M., Ford, K. M., & Hayes, P. J. (1997). Expertise in context: Personally constructed, socially selected, and reality-relevant? In P. Feltovich, K. M. Ford, & R. R.. Hoffman (Eds.), *Expertise in context: Human and machine* (pp. 219-244). Menlo Park: MIT Press.

Akin, O. (1990). Necessary conditions for design expertise and creativity. *Design Studies, 11*, 107-113.

Bereiter, C., & Scardamalia, M. (1993). *Surpassing ourselves - An inquiry into the nature and implications of expertise.* Chicago: Open Court.

Brown, J. D., & Duguid, P. (1994). Patrolling the border: A Reply. *Human-Computer Interaction, 9*, 137-143.

Christiaans, H. H. C. M. (1992). *Creativity in design; The role of domain knowledge in designing.* Utrecht: Lemma.

Collin, K. (2002). Development engineers' conceptions of learning at work. *Studies in Continuing Education, 24*, 133-152.

Collin, K. (2003, August). *The role of experiences in development engineers' work and learning.* Paper presented at the 9th EARLI Conference, Padova, Italy.

Collin, K., & Tynjälä, P. (in press). Integrating theory and practice? Employees' and students experiences of learning at work. *Journal of Workplace Learning.*

Curtis, B., Krasner, H., & Iscoe, N. (1988). A field study of the software design studies for large systems. *Communications of the ACM, 31*, 1268-1287.

Engeström, Y. (2001). Expansive learning at work: Toward an activity theoretical reconceptualization. *Journal of Education and Work, 14*, 133-156.

Eraut, M. (1994). *Developing professional knowledge and competence.* London: Falmer.

Eraut, M., Alderton, J., Cole, G., & Senker, P. (1998). *Development of knowledge and skills in employment.* Final report of a research project funded by 'The Learning Society' Programme of the Economic and Social Research Council. Sussex: University of Sussex.

Ericsson, K. A. (Ed.). (1996). *The road to excellence. The acquisition of expert performance in the arts and sciences, sports, and games.* Mahwah: Erlbaum.

Eteläpelto, A. (1998). *The development of expertise in information systems design.* Jyväskylä: University of Jyväskylä.

Eteläpelto, A. (1999). Challenges for professional learning as an indicator of expertise. *Lifelong Learning in Europe, 2*, 245-251.

Eteläpelto, A. (2000). Contextual and strategic knowledge in the acquisition of design expertise. *Learning and Instruction, 10*, 113-136.

Eteläpelto, A., & Light, P. (1999). Contextual knowledge in the development of design expertise. In J. Bliss, P. Light, & R. Säljö (Eds.), *Learning sites: Social and technological resources for learning* (pp. 155-164). Amsterdam: Pergamon.

Feltovich, P. J., Ford, K. M., & Hoffman, R. R. (Eds.). (1997). *Expertise in context; Human and machine.* Menlo Park: MIT Press.

Gerber, R. (1998). How do workers learn in their work? *The Learning Organization,* 5, 168-175.

Gerber, R., Lankshear, C., Larsson, S., & Svensson, L. (1995). Self-directed learning in a work context. *Education and Training,* 37 (8), 26-32.

Greeno, J. G. (1997). On claims that answer the wrong questions. *Educational Researcher,* 26 (1), 5-17.

Greeno, J. G., Collins, A. M., & Resnick, L. (1996). Cognition and learning. In D. C. Berliner & R. C. Calfee (Eds.), *Handbook of educational psychology* (pp. 15-46). New York: Macmillan.

Gruber, H. (1994). *Expertise. Modelle und empirische Untersuchungen.* Opladen: Westdeutscher Verlag.

Gruber, H., Law, L.-C., Mandl, H., & Renkl, A. (1995). Situated learning and transfer. In P. Reimann & H. Spada (Eds.), *Learning in humans and machines: Towards an interdisciplinary learning science* (pp. 168-188). Oxford: Elsevier.

Hatano, G., & Inagaki, K. (1992). Desituating cognition through the construction of conceptual knowledge. In P. Light & G. Butterworth (Eds.), *Context and cognition. Ways of learning and knowing* (pp. 115-133). New York: Harvester Wheatsheaf.

Hoffman, R. R., Feltovich, P. J., & Kenneth, M. F. (1997). A general framework for conceiving of expertise and expert systems in context. In P. J. Feltovich, K. M. Ford, & R. R. Hoffman (Eds.), *Expertise in context: Human and machine* (pp. 544-580). Menlo Park: MIT Press.

Kuutti, K. (1996). Activity theory as a potential framework for human-computer interaction research. In B. A. Nardi (Ed.), *Context and consciousness. Activity theory and human-computer interaction* (pp. 17-44). Cambridge: MIT Press.

Lave, J., & Wenger, E. (1991). *Situated learning: Legitimate peripheral participation.* Cambridge: Cambridge University Press.

Nardi, B. A. (1996). Studying context: A comparison of activity theory, situated action models, and distributed cognition. In B. A. Nardi (Ed.), *Context and consciousness. Activity theory and human-computer interaction* (pp. 69-102). Cambridge: MIT Press.

Nijhof, W. J., & Streumer, J. N. (1994). Flexibility in vocational education and training: An introduction. In W. J. Nijhof & J. N. Streumer (Eds.), *Flexibility and training in vocational education* (pp. 1-12). Utrecht: Lemma.

Pirttilä-Backman, A. M. (1997). Miksi asiantuntijan tulee kyetä reflektiivisiin arviointeihin? [Why an expert should be able to make reflective evaluations?] In J. Kirjonen, P. Remes & A. Eteläpelto (Eds.), *Muuttuva asiantuntijuus* (pp. 218-224). Jyväskylä: University of Jyväskylä, Institute for Educational Research.

Rambow, R., & Bromme, R. (1995). Implicit psychological concepts in architects' knowledge – How large is a large room? *Learning and Instruction,* 5, 337-356.

Rowland, G. A., Fixl, A., & Yung, K. (1992). Educating the reflective designers. *Educational Technology,* 32 (12), 36-44.

Schmidt, H. G., & Boshuizen, H. P. A. (1993). On acquiring expertise in medicine. *Educational Psychology Review,* 5, 205-221.

Schön, D. A. (1987). *Educating the reflective practitioner.* San Francisco: Jossey Bass.

Schuler, D., & Namioka, A. (Eds.). (1993). *Participatory design: Principles and practices*. Hillsdale: Erlbaum.

Sfard, A. (1998). On two metaphors for learning and the dangers of choosing just one. *Educational Researchers, 27* (2), 4-13.

Simons, P. R.-J. (1997). From romanticism to practice in learning. *Lifelong Learning in Europe, 2*, 1-20.

Smith, E. M., Ford, J. K., & Kozlowski, S. W. J. (1996). Building adaptive expertise: Implications for training design strategies. In M. A. Quinones & A. Ehrenstein (Eds.), *Training for rapidly changing workplaces: Applications of psychological research* (pp. 89-118). Washington: American Psychological Association.

Sonnentag, S. (1995). Excellent software professionals: Experience, work activities, and perception by peers. *Behaviour & Information Technology, 14*, 289-299.

Stein, E. W. (1997). A look at expertise from a social perspective. In P. Feltovich, K. M. Ford, & R. R. Hoffman (Eds.), *Expertise in context: Human and machine* (pp. 181-194). Menlo Park: MIT Press.

Symon, G. (1998). The work of IT system developers in context: An organizational case study. *Human-Computer Interaction, 13*, 37-71.

Van de Wiel, M. (1997). *Knowledge encapsulation. Studies on the development of medical expertise*. Maastricht: Universiteit Maastricht.

Van Oers, B. (1998). From context to contextualizing. *Learning and Instruction, 8*, 473-488.

Volet, S. E. (1991). Modelling and coaching of relevant metacognitive strategies for enhancing university students' learning. *Learning and Instruction, 1*, 319-336.

Waltz, D., Elam, J., & Curtis, B. (1993). Inside a software design team. *Communication of the ACM, 36*, 63-77.

Wang, C. W., & Horng, H.-Y. (1992, July). *Experience-based vs. education-based expertise in management*. Paper presented at the 25th International Congress of Psychology, Brussels, Belgium.

Wenger, E. (1998). *Communities of practice. Learning, meaning and identity*. Cambridge: Cambridge University Press.

Winograd, T. (1995). From programming environments to environments for designing. *Communications of the ACM, 38*, 65-74.

Chapter 13

COMPETENCE-SUPPORTING WORKING CONDITIONS

Christian Harteis and Hans Gruber
Institute for Education, University of Regensburg, Germany

1. DO EDUCATIONAL AND ECONOMICAL CONCEPTS CONVERGE?

During the last decade a number of concepts of personnel and organisational development that share a common goal have become popular: "Lean organisation", "learning organisation", "success res Harteis ource development", "improving performance", and "customer focus" all intend to transfer decision competence and responsibility to lower hierarchical levels of working organisations. Employees receive the opportunity to participate in decisions during their daily working practice. Thus, an increase in effectiveness of the value-adding process is expected. The new concepts of personnel and organisational development therefore follow goals of economical rationality.

Employees are provided with opportunities to acquire appropriate competencies and apply them in their daily work in order to improve the working organisation. Efforts of personnel and organisational development include the development of individual competencies and, therefore, they also follow goals of educational rationality.

Taken together, personnel and organisational development has the dual purpose to increase both effectiveness and humanisation. Based on this argument, educationalists started to proclaim, investigate, and controversially discuss the convergence of economical and educational rationality. It is still unresolved, however, under which conditions convergence or divergence are likely to occur. Few empirical studies exist, and there is no standard research methodology in this field. Therefore, convincing empirical evidence supporting the convergence assumption is still lacking.

This chapter presents the results of an empirical study, which tried to close this gap. In a Delphi study, employees' individual perception of their working field was investigated under different perspectives: How do employees experience their daily work in companies, which call themselves "learning organisations"? Do employees experience their working conditions as competence-supporting? The rationale behind our approach is to go beyond merely programmatic discussions, which are prominent in business organisation, and to survey the employees' interpretation of their enterprises' organisational culture. Both views can contribute to the assessment of convergence or divergence.

The argumentation in this chapter is as follows. After a brief survey of the development of business organisation in the 20th century, theoretical and empirical deficits concerning employees' individual competencies are analysed, which exist even in the most recent concepts of learning organisations. Resulting research questions are answered in a Delphi study conducted in German industrial enterprises. As a consequence, desiderata both for business practice and for further research are outlined.

2. DEVELOPMENT OF BUSINESS ORGANISATION IN THE 20TH CENTURY

2.1 Precursors of modern concepts of business organisation

At the beginning of the 20th century, Taylor (1911/1998) developed "scientific management", the classical concept of organisations. The entire organisation was tuned for stability, strictly based on a rigid separation of executive and directing work. With the machine-assisted production of the Model-T-Car, Ford optimised that principle of working organisation and became a pioneer of mass production. The crucial feature was not – contrary to public belief – the assembly line, but rather the complete exchangeability of all components and the simplicity of the assembly (Womack, Jones, & Roos, 1990).

Thus, skill trade production was replaced. It had been the dominating form of production in former periods. The master's competence no longer was of outstanding importance. The main paradigm in taylorism stressed simple tasks, which could be repeated with high frequency. Labour as well as machines became exchangeable and lost individuality. This formalisation aimed to delete uncertainties in the production process. If it was possible to anticipate the behaviour of all parts of the organisation, a kind of enterprise would emerge, which (according to Harold Geene, former Central Executive Officer of the company ITT) could be directed by Mickey Mouse (Kühl, 1998). Obviously, anonymity was a major goal in this kind of business organisation: Labour was conceived as a factor of production like raw materials, so that employees' individual competence was completely neglected.

2.2 Modern concepts of business organisation

Modern concepts of working organisation demand working structures that enable one to cope with increasing fierce competition. Time and flexibility are crucial criteria for competition, when swift and low-cost reactions to changing requirements are needed (Picot, Reichwald, & Wigand, 2003). The approaches that have been developed and discussed since the late eighties offer solutions for these problems on different abstraction levels.

These concepts demand concrete steps and understand themselves as concepts that break with tayloristic production processes. Examples are the concepts "lean organisation" (Womack et al., 1990) or "Business Process Reengineering" (Hammer & Champy, 1993). These organisation concepts are based on a limitation of the number of tasks that should be fulfilled within companies. This leads both to outsourcing of certain jobs and to redistribution of remaining jobs between the employees in a way that can be described as job enrichment including planning and disposal tasks even for those employees, who were until then purely considered as workers. Responsibilities were transferred to the production level to take care of smooth production processes and of prompt reactions to market changes. As a result, middle hierarchical levels became superfluous, because their supervision work was no more needed. The extent to which decision-making competence is conceded to employees, is simultaneously a measure of increasing demands: Employees now have to recognise and evaluate a number of action alternatives and side effects, before decisions are made. If different alternatives exist, employees take over the responsibility. Those in the hierarchy who delegate responsibility also have to provide more degrees of freedom for employees in decision-making situations (Heid, 1999b).

The conceptions of "Customer Focus" and "Boundless Enterprise" (Picot et al., 2003) emphasise different aspects. They take a systemic perspective and interpret companies as networks of organisation units within the context of other organisations (e.g. suppliers, customers). The most essential component of the firm network is customer relationship. Thus, these conceptions differ from the former ones, as they do not take an inside-view, but increase the company's responsibility towards outward areas. From a radical point of view, the new perspective is an interface conception, which strives to improve exchange processes between internal and external systems. Here employees play an important role, because they represent interfaces. This increases the demands placed on employees, because on the one hand they have to represent their company in an appropriate way, on the other hand they have to recognise customers' inquiries and to appropriately adjust their own organisation of work. Whereas concepts such as "learning organisation" and "business process reengineering" demand concrete changes for example job enrichment or job enlargement through the delegation of decision authority, customer oriented concepts only analyse organisational development in an abstract way.

Concepts such as "Human Resource Management" (Hilb, 1998) or "learning organisation" (Argyris, 1996; Senge, 1990) are even less concerned about concrete requirements for employees. They express rather diffuse ideas of collective learning processes through naïve models of an increase of knowledge within organisations.

All approaches outlined in this section stress the employees' importance in all necessary change processes. In order to cope with these increased requirements, employees need more individual competencies than was expected in administration or production companies organised on conservative lines. The use of the terms "human capital" and "human resource" indicates that modern concepts of personnel and organisational development highly appreciate the employees' individual development of competencies. At least on a programmatic level, competent employees are considered to be an important strategic factor for the future success of companies.

2.3 The importance of employees' individual competencies

In companies that consider their employees to be the main factor for successful organisational development and change, employees have to cope with a variety of new demands. In such companies, fostering employees' competence is much more important than in companies with tayloristic structures. In traditional working structures, workers were expected to follow orders, but not to reflect on them. In modern concepts of working organisation, a new paradigm was established which is based on key aspects (Appelbaum & Gallagher, 2000). (1) Workers have some degree of autonomy and control over job tasks and methods; thus, jobs are redesigned to enable employees to make work-related decisions. (2) Workers are expected to participate in problem-solving and in improving production techniques; thus, they need professional expertise to identify problems and to communicate solutions to colleagues. (3) The workplace is organised both around self-directed teams that are directly involved in the working process, and around offline problem-solving and quality-improvement teams that are not directly involved with regular working processes.

2.4 Discourse in business education: The assumption of convergence of economical and educational rationality

The increasing importance of employees' competence led a number of researchers in the field of business education to the assumption that economical and educational considerations converge in the modern workplace. This assumption is questioned by others. Both theoretical and empirical deficits can be identified in this discourse.

Achtenhagen (1990) claims "coincidence of economical and educational ratio" (p. 7), because "in particular, leading enterprises emphasise the importance of learning processes". The argument of integration of educational goals of individual development and efforts of personnel and organisational development appears attractive and plausible both for managers and researchers. This is one reason for the increasing popularity of the convergence assumption. However, an empirical inquiry into this assumption requires precise definitions and operationalisations of relevant aspects. The practice of working organisation and vocational training is a suitable field for investigating economical and educational aspects, because the system of making use of qualifications (system of employment) can be distinguished from the system of development of individual qualification (educational system). In the first system, suppliers and buyers of vocational qualifications are active. In the second system, educational staff is involved in the development of appropriate qualifications. Both systems depend on each other. The educational system cannot neglect major economical principles of the system of employment, and the system of employment cannot neglect the principles of the educational system (Heid, 1999a). Employees have to make use of their competencies and qualifications, and thus they have to take into consideration economical conditions by planning their individual curriculum vitae. On the other hand, companies have to make use of working power and competencies, and thus they have to take into consideration educational principles by structuring the working organisation in an appropriate way in order to foster educational development processes.

Obviously, companies that depend to a larger degree on making use of employees' individual competencies, more explicitly have to provide working organisations that support individual competence. Thus, companies following modern concepts of personnel and organisational development aim at employees' individual competencies. Such companies should seek the convergence of economical and educational rationality. Work should be organised in such a way, that employees are given many opportunities to acquire individual competencies. According to the employees' point of view, the workplace should be perceived as an opportunity and as a challenge to increase one's competencies. As a consequence, three roles of inner-firm actors can be distinguished: (1) Employees, who want to develop and utilise competencies; (2) employers, who want to grab employees' competencies; and (3) teachers, who support the development of individual competencies.

In such working organisations, interfaces exist between employers, employees, and teachers, whose links are based on abstract terms of competence. The mutual understanding of these terms is crucial, because it has to be translated into shared concepts of working and learning. The organisation of work has to meet learning requirements in order to produce convergence conditions (Seufert, Back, & Von Krogh, 2000).

3. THEORETICAL AND EMPIRICAL DEFICITS

It can be argued that the discourse in business education on convergence or divergence of economical and educational rationality suffers both from theoretical and from empirical deficits. Four main criticisms can be distinguished:

1. Almost no empirical evidence exists that substantiates the debate about competence-supporting working conditions. Much effort is expressed in theoretical discourses about competence-supporting working conditions, but it is not substantiated by empirical research activities. As a consequence, most arguments are still hypothetical. Hypotheses, however, are preliminary statements, which require empirical investigation.
2. Most debates about competence-supporting working conditions remain on a programmatic level. Programmatic statements, however, include expressions about desirable outcomes rather than about real ones. They stem from normative decisions, which neglect unbiased alternatives. Such normative expressions cannot be empirically true or wrong, but rather simulate versatile weight, with conditions for realising them often being blanked out. A critical aspect is that programmatic statements are frequently misunderstood as facts; from a theoretical point of view, this misunderstanding is a not acceptable transformation of normative statements into descriptive ones.

3. Modern concepts of business organisation include the employees' perspective, but they do so in terms of an unilateral connection: The connection is expressed as management's appeal to employees to behave as they are expected. Instead of considering employees' individual needs, functional aspects of management concepts prevail. Participation, employees' needs and trust serve their purpose by increasing effectiveness of the production processes (Becker & Langosch, 1995). Arguments lack this unilateral thinking and neglect the antipodal relation, which includes the question of how to accomplish employees' needs.
4. Concepts of business organisation describe qualification demands on employees only on a highly abstract level. The resulting wide range of interpretations leads to many difficulties when employees try to realise these demands in practice.

The deficits in the discussion about convergence or divergence of economical and educational rationality identified in this section clearly show that empirical investigation is needed to aid comprehension of whether theoretical accounts tally with empirical reality in companies.

4. RESEARCH QUESTIONS

The deficits in the educational debate about competence-supporting working conditions pose a number of research questions.

1. Do those who are responsible for education within companies succeed in creating socially shared cognitions about core competencies? Do subjects on different hierarchical levels agree in their interpretations of the role of core competencies like flexibility, leadership, responsibility, and independence? Does the co-existence of management-steered and member-steered groups affect the comprehension of core competencies? Answers to these questions require data from subjects from different hierarchical groups.
2. How does a working organisation convince its employees that their individual competencies are needed and appreciated in their daily work? Answers to this question help to understand employees' assessment of the workplace and to take the individual perspective that is neglected so far in the debate about competence-supporting working conditions.
3. To what degree do programmatic statements refer to the reality of daily practice? Do employees of modern companies perceive their workplace as competence-supporting? Do employees know concrete cases in which strong individual competencies have led to difficulties in daily work? Answers to these questions will help to analyse potential deficits in the daily practice.

In the remaining parts of this chapter, we describe an empirical study using the Delphi technique in which we tried to answer these research questions.

5. A DELPHI STUDY: METHOD

The Delphi technique is a method used to develop group-judgements (Clayton, 1997). It has a number of advantages compared with other empirical methods: (1) The influence of the researcher is low, because all inputs are given by subjects. (2) The anonymity of employees helps to avoid undesirable group dynamic distortions. (3) The technique allows the generation of qualitative and quantitative data in fields that lack empirical evidence. All in all the Delphi technique is well-suited for explorative studies.

In particular, the Delphi technique facilitates scientific inquiry within the context of group interactions by generating information and seeking a consensus through a series of interactive probes. Using the Delphi technique, personal attitudes and opinions can be investigated through written group interviews that are realised in postal form. In successive steps, each subject receives all other subjects' answers. Thus, the topic under discussion is perceived from multiple perspectives including feedback of intermediate results.

5.1 Sample

Thirty-two employees were investigated, differing in hierarchical level: 16 superiors vs. 16 working staff members. Subjects were recruited by the companies' educational staff.

5.2 Procedure

In the beginning, all participants received comprehensive information about the theoretical scope of the project, the goals of the investigation, and the Delphi method. The Delphi study included a four-step investigation.

Step 1: "Express your comprehension of core competencies!" Four core competencies were selected: Flexibility, leadership, responsibility, and independence. Subjects had to express their comprehension of these topics as an answer to the following instruction: "Please describe a personal definition of flexibility [leadership, responsibility, independence] as exactly as possible. Explain your definition by mentioning three concrete examples from your inner-firm daily work." In addition, subjects had the opportunity to mention further core competencies, which they considered important regarding their vocational qualifications. The individual perception should determine the answers, because subjects referred to their daily work experience. Aiming at the generation of a socially shared cognitions, the answers were distributed among all subjects in step 2.

Step 2: "Give examples of competence support! Offer suggestions how to improve this support!" Subjects had to describe examples from their workplace, which demonstrated appreciation of their individual competencies and/or support of the development of these competencies. Subjects also had to suggest ways how to improve their own workplaces in order to support the development of individual competencies. Both requirements were asked as open questions in order to receive the widest possible range of answers. The answers were sampled and returned to subjects without any interpretation in step 3.

Step 3: "Evaluate the examples given by other subjects!" Statements emerging from step 2 were evaluated by all subjects. Subjects received all statements from step 2. First, they had to judge all examples for competence support on a 10-point rating scale that indicated how correct they were with respect to one's own individual working field. In another 10-point rating scale, subjects evaluated how realistic the suggestions for improvement were. Secondly, subjects had to choose the ten most important citations in both lists and to bring them into a ranking order. The result was a group judgement of the individual answers from step 2.

Step 4: "Give examples for negative effects of competence!" In contrast to step 3, subjects had to express examples from their working experience, in which their individual competence led to difficulties either with colleagues, with the management or with inner-firm philosophies. These indicators of negative actions and appreciations of individual competencies again were sampled through open questions.

5.3 Analysis

Research question (1): Socially shared cognitions. Content analysis was used to deal with the answers to open questions. Similar answers were merged into categories in order to allow further quantitative analyses. "Socially shared cognitions" was operationalised by the parameter "ratio". Ratio means "proportion of data compression" and is computed by dividing the number of categories after condensing by the number of original statements. The data are on nominal level, so Chi^2 significance tests were used to analyse differences in ratio between subgroups.

Research question (2): Characteristics of competence-supporting working conditions. All ratings of correctness of statements and all suggestions for improvement were aggregated over subgroups. After z-transformation of the estimations of correctness, differences between subgroups were tested using a two-tailed t-test for independent samples.

Research question (3): Look beyond programmatic statements. Data analysis in this part was the same as with research question (2). Additionally, qualitative analysis was used to interpret the results of the answers to open questions.

6. RESULTS

6.1 Socially shared cognitions

The open questions stimulated a large number of responses, resulting in extensive data concerning definitions and examples of the four core competencies. A total of 714 statements were collected. These statements were summarised and categorised. Table 1 presents an overview of the most frequent answers.

Table 1. Overview of the most frequent answers concerning definitions and examples of the four core competencies "flexibility", "leadership", "independence", and "responsibility". Numbers ("f") indicate the frequency, i.e. the number of subjects that mentioned the respective category. (Maximum: 32)

Definitions	f	Examples	f
Core competence 1: Flexibility			
Adaptation	24	Variety of tasks	22
Readiness for mobility	12	(Temporary) Mobility	15
Rapidity	9	Time flexibility	14
Core competence 2: Leadership			
Social competence	13	Personnel development / being coach	15
Specialised knowledge	10	Support of social climate	9
Strategic competence	6	Motivation	9
Core competence 3: Independenc			
Fulfilment of tasks	21	Taking the initiative	12
Planning of tasks	13	Ordering targets	10
Making decisions	7	Planning the working organisation	10
Core competence 4: Responsibility			
Bearing action consequences	13	Quality consciousness	11
Making decisions	13	Engagement	9
Having success	7	Making decisions	8

According to the definition of "socially shared cognitions" by the parameter "ratio", a value of .25 or less was defined as a substantial amount of socially shared cognitions. Substantial agreement is present in those patterns of answers, which can be compressed to at least a quarter of the original quantity. Table 2 presents the "ratio" for both definitions and examples.

Table 2. Total numbers of statements and "ratio" as operationalisation of "socially shared cognitions" for definitions and examples. Data of the entire sample and of groups. def = definitions. ex = examples

	Number of statements		Ratio	
Core competencies (total sample)	def	ex	def	ex
Flexibility	83	92	.21	.25
Leadership	70	123	.37	.41
Independence	70	100	.26	.41
Responsibility	75	101	.24	.37
Core competencies (separated by subgroups)				
Superiors: Flexibility	36	45	.33	.40
Working staff members: Flexibility	47	47	.30	.32
Superiors: Leadership	37	70	.41	.56
Working staff members: Leadership	33	53	.61	.47
Superiors: independence	36	51	.28	.47
Working staff members: Independence	34	49	.38	.51
Superiors: Responsibility	40	48	.30	.54
Working staff members: Responsibility	35	53	.46	.49

Socially shared cognitions were found only within the total sample, concerning examples for "flexibility", definitions of "flexibility", and definitions of "responsibility". All other ratio measures are larger than .25. Chi^2 tests showed no significance between the two groups (Table 3).

Table 3. Chi^2 test of ratio values shown by groups referring to the first Delphi-step (df = 1). n.s.: not significant

	Chi^2	Significance
Definitions "flexibility"	0.56	n.s.
Examples "flexibility"	0.78	n.s.
Definitions "leadership"	0.27	n.s.
Examples "leadership"	0.21	n.s.
Definitions "independence"	0.35	n.s.
Examples "independence"	0.01	n.s.
Definitions "responsibility"	0.40	n.s.
Examples "responsibility"	0.46	n.s.

6.2 Characteristics of competence-supporting working conditions

One task in steps 2 and 3 of the Delphi study was to provide examples from daily working practice that support competence development. All statements were returned as feedback to all subjects in order to generate a group judgement. This group judgement is an aggregate score for importance and correctness of the statements. Table 4 shows the statements with highest group judgements of importance and the z-transformed figures for the group judgements of correctness.

Table 4. Statements with highest group judgements of importance and the z-transformed figures for the group judgements of correctness. SUM = sum of points of importance; z = z-transformed value of correctness

	SUM	z
Supporting problem solutions by superiors and colleagues	88	0.27
Project work	84	1.90
Degrees of freedom in decision processes	80	1.26
Participation in vocational education and training	75	0.20
Transfer of staff responsibility	72	0.84
High work demands as result of different tasks	68	1.60
Systematic training and integration of new colleagues	67	-0.44
Strategic orientation of the entire working organisation	64	-0.15
Exchange of experience between colleagues and superiors	61	-0.44
Variety of work demands	53	1.05
Regular feedback talks between superiors and colleagues	52	0.48

t-tests for independent samples revealed no significant differences between superiors and working staff members.

6.3 Look beyond programmatic statements

Looking beyond programmatic statements, subjects were asked to present suggestions as to how their working field could be improved so that this would contribute to an increase in support of competence development. Again, all statements were returned as feedback to all subjects in order to generate a group judgement. This group judgement is an aggregate score for importance and feasibility of the statements. The resulting suggestions for improvement are documented in Table 5.

Table 5. Statements with highest group judgements of importance and the z-transformed figures for the group judgements of feasibility. SUM = sum of points of importance; z = z-transformed value of feasibility

	SUM	z
More courage to change structures and well-known routines	103	2.12
Superiors should spend more time on assessing staff members' strengths and weaknesses	83	-0.01
Job rotation and enrichment of working tasks	78	1.74
Well-organised communication processes between colleagues and feedback talks	69	1.35
Elimination of the discrepancy between responsibility and freedom for decision-making	59	0.28
Orientation according to commonly shared values	55	0.91
More influence in the arrangement of higher goals	49	-0.35
Support and appreciation of creativity	49	0.33
Publicity of long-term planning	48	-0.06

t-tests for independent samples reveal a significant difference between superiors and working staff members concerning the importance of "orientation according to common shared values" ($t(16) = 2.71$; $p < .05$).

Additionally, subjects had to give examples from their working experience, when individual competence led to difficulties. Tables 6 and 7 show the results. Only those statements are listed that were mentioned by more than three subjects. Twelve subjects mentioned examples associated with their colleagues, 14 subjects mentioned examples associated with their superiors.

Table 6 Reasons why individual competence led to difficulties between colleagues. Frequencies of responses are given for groups and the entire sample

Reason	Superiors	Staff members	Total
Differences between persons and interests	5	0	5
Feeling of neglect	4	3	7

Table 7. Reasons why individual competence led to difficulties between superiors and working staff members. Frequencies of responses are given for groups and the entire sample

Reason	Superiors	Staff members	Total
Hierarchical differences	1	5	6
Differing judgement of situations	4	0	4

Almost all examples given by working staff members, in which individual competence led to difficulties with superiors, refer to hierarchical differences, not to factual reasons.

7. DISCUSSION

The discussion mainly focuses on the employees' individual perspective, because this perspective is neglected in the controversies about convergence and divergence of economical and educational rationality.

7.1 About the question of "socially shared cognitions"

The results show that appropriate grounding processes and as a consequence socially shared cognitions concerning core-competencies occur infrequently. Vast differences exist when interpreting the competence demands "independence" and "leadership".

These differences are to be seen as indicators of unfavourable prerequisites for competence-supporting working conditions. Without a commonly shared interpretation of working demands, compliance is barely conceivable.

Our subjects define "responsibility" in a way, which suffices the criteria for commonly shared cognitions. However, the large variance of the examples provided indicates a discrepancy between theory and practice. On the one hand there is substantial agreement on an abstract theoretical level, on the other hand the heterogeneous answers indicate individual experiences at the workplace.

Broad agreement exists concerning the definitions of flexibility and the examples provided for flexibility. The prerequisites for competence-supporting working conditions which are postulated by modern concepts of business organisation like "learning organisation" are probably fulfilled. It cannot be discerned from the data, however, whether this coherence is a consequence of some kind of a secret company curriculum (Heid & Lempert, 1982).

7.2 Characteristics of competence support

Altogether the findings show favourable conditions for realising competence-supporting working conditions:
1. Subjects highly rate the importance of examples for competence support, which are related to parts of modern concepts of business organisation.

These concepts fit with the economical rationality of guaranteeing future business success as well as with the educational rationality of appreciating and supporting the development of competencies.
2. The subjects' judgement of correctness provides an empirical confirmation that particularly these parts were rated as high.

7.3 Look beyond programmatic statements

Whereas the results mentioned so far only partly leave the programmatic level, the answers about obstacles for competence development leave it explicitly. They refer to subjects' working experience and are less distorted by desires and norms. Suggestions for improvement (Table 5) in most cases are criticisms of insufficient realisations of modern organisation concepts. Three aspects of daily work are mentioned: (1) formal procedures, (2) behaviour and interpersonal relations, and (3) basic suggestions for improvement.
1. *Formal procedures*. Aspects of modern concepts of business organisation are included in demands to intensify job rotation, to provide enlarging working tasks, and to increase within-firm communication and feedback. If these features are already realised in the subjects' working field, then implimentation is insufficient.
2. *Behaviour and interpersonal relations*. Subjects frequently appealed to superiors to spend more time on identifying their staff members' strengths and weaknesses. Only then can an orientation towards commonly shared values emerge. These suggestions reveal deficits in the leading behaviour which are a serious restriction of competence-supporting working conditions, because adjusting to employees' competencies is a crucial component of educational theories of learning motivation (Deci, Koestner & Ryan, 2001; Prenzel, Kramer & Drechsel, 2002). As mentioned above, the urge for commonly shared values is the only criterion, which revealed a significant difference between superiors and working staff members. Superiors stress that aspect much more than working staff members.
3. *Basic suggestions for improvement*. A basic suggestion concerns the major contradiction with modern concepts of business organisation, this being the gap between responsibility and freedom to act. Other elementary suggestions include the wish for more courage to change established structures and routines. This is related to the suggestion to appreciate creativity more intensively. The impression of daily work depicted in this suggestion leaves some doubts: If there is little freedom to act, how can inner-firm hierarchies be broken? If many stick to established routines, how can enterprises deal with changing markets and

customer demands? If there is little appreciation of creativity, how can innovation occur?

All three groups indicate serious constraints in realising competence-supporting working conditions. They can be interpreted as leadership problems. One may suspect that (deficits in) leading behaviour is one of the main causes for insufficient realisation of competence-supporting working conditions. A brief glance at the results of Delphi step 4 helps to support this hypothesis. When subjects discussed circumstances under which individual competencies lead to difficulties (Tables 6 and 7), more specific leading problems could be identified: While working staff members relate competence problems between superiors and working staff members to superiors' clinging to their hierarchical position, superiors suggest that such problems emerge from varying interpretations of facts and cases.

7.4 About hierarchy specifications

Systemic approaches of working organisations rate arrays (also hierarchical ones) within a company as highly important. This importance did not emerge in the present study. It was shown that deficits in competence-supporting working conditions were positively related to deficits in leading behaviour.

8. OUTLOOK

At the beginning of this chapter we argued that modern concepts of working organisation are based on assumptions, that have barely been tested empirically. We conducted an empirical study in order investigate some basic assumptions. A sample of 32 employees participated in a four-step Delphi study, which focused on three aspects from the employees' individual perspective, namely their understanding of core competencies (in order to investigate the notion of socially shared cognitions), their experience of competence-supporting working conditions, and their suggestions for improvement of the working field (in order to go beyond the level of programmatic statements). The main results of this study, favourable and unfavourable conditions for competence-supporting working conditions, can be summarised as follows.

1. Subjects experienced several aspects of modern concepts of business organisation as supporting their competencies in principle. They also indicated that these aspects occur in their own working field.
2. Referring to the definition of "flexibility", subjects showed socially shared cognitions.

3. A number of deficits in realising competence-supporting working conditions were identified which could be explained by (deficits in) leading behaviour.
4. Socially shared cognitions about "leadership", "independence", and "readiness for responsibility" could not be identified.

These findings lead to a number of conclusions for educational practice. The subjects were selected from enterprises, which undertake big efforts to recruit and develop broad competencies. Findings of positive conditions for competence-supporting working conditions underscore that business programs caring for human resources work to some degree. The study also revealed that according to the employees' individual perspective, certain aspects did not only motivate to work but were also interpreted as development of one's own competencies. However, negative conditions for competence-supporting working conditions were also mentioned. They show that the mere existence of business programs does not guarantee their effective realisation. Individual behaviour, not only that of superiors, can often be an obstacle for competence-supporting working conditions. Interventions and further development of organisational concepts should take this into consideration.

NOTE

The authors gratefully acknowledge the Deutsche Forschungsgemeinschaft (DFG) for a supporting grant.

REFERENCES

Achtenhagen, F. (1990). Vorwort [Foreword]. In Senatskommission für Berufsbildungsforschung (Ed.), *Berufsbildungsforschung an den Hochschulen der Bundesrepublik Deutschland* (pp. VII-VIII). Weinheim: VCH.

Appelbaum, S. H., & Gallagher, J. (2000). The competitive advantage of organisational learning. *Journal of Workplace Learning: Employee Counselling Today, 12*, 40-56.

Argyris, C. (1996). *Organisational learning. Theory, method, and practice.* New York: Addison Wesley.

Becker, H., & Langosch, I. (1995). *Produktivität und Menschlichkeit. Organisationsentwicklung und ihre Anwendung in der Praxis.* [Productivity and humanity. Organisational development applied.] Stuttgart: Enke.

Clayton, M. J. (1997). Delphi: A technique to harness expert opinion for critical decision-making tasks in education. *Educational Psychology, 17*, 373-386.

Deci, E. L., Koestner, R., & Ryan, R. M. (2001). Extrinsic rewards and intrinsic motivation in education. Reconsidered once again. *Review of Educational Research, 71*, 1-28.

Hammer, M., & Champy, J. (1993). *Reengineering the corporation.* New York: Harper Collins.
Heid, H. (1999a). Der Wirtschaftspädagoge im Spannungsfeld ökonomischer und pädagogischer Rationalität [The economical educationalist in the flash-point of economical and educational rationality]. In T. Tramm, D. Sembill, F. Klauser, & E. G. John (Eds.) *Professionalisierung kaufmännischer Berufsbildung* (pp. 292-299). Frankfurt am Main: Lang.
Heid, H. (1999b). Über die Vereinbarkeit individueller Bildungsbedürfnisse und betrieblicher Qualifikationsanforderungen [On the compatibility of individual needs for education and employment-related qualification requirements]. *Zeitschrift für Pädagogik, 45,* 231-244.
Heid, H., & Lempert, W. (Eds.). (1982). *Sozialisation durch den heimlichen Lehrplan des Betriebs* [Socialisation by secret curricula in companies]. Stuttgart: Steiner.
Hilb, M. (Ed.). (1998). *Management der Human-Ressourcen. Neue Führungskonzepte im Praxistest* [Management of human resources. New leading concepts tested in practice]. Neuwied: Luchterhand.
Kühl, S. (1998). *Wenn die Affen den Zoo regieren. Die Tücken der flachen Hierarchien* (5th ed.). [When apes reign the zoo. Perfidies of flat hierarchies.] Frankfurt am Main: Campus.
Picot, A., Reichwald, R., & Wigand, R. T. (2003). *Die grenzenlose Unternehmung. Information, Organisation und Management* (5th ed.). [The boundless enterprise. Information, organisation, and management.] Wiesbaden: Gabler.
Prenzel, M., Kramer, K., & Drechsel, B. (2002). Self-determined and interested learning in vocational education. In K. Beck (Ed.), *Teaching-learning processes in vocational education. Foundation of modern training programs* (pp. 43-68). Frankfurt: Lang.
Senge, P. M. (1990). *The fifth discipline. The art and practice of the learning organisation.* New York: Currency Doubleday.
Seufert, A., Back, A., & Von Krogh, G. (2000). Wissensnetzwerke: Vision – Referenzmodell – Archetypen und Fallbeispiele. [Knowledge networks: Vision – reference model – archetypes and case examples.] In K. Götz (Ed.) *Wissensmanagement. Zwischen Wissen und Nichtwissen* (2nd ed., pp. 133-156). München: Hampp.
Taylor, F. W. (1998). *The principles of scientific management.* New York: Harper. (Original published 1911).
Womack, J. P., Jones, D. T., & Roos, D. (1990). *The machine that changed the world.* New York: Rawson.

Chapter 14

NETWORK TIES, COGNITIVE CENTRALITY, AND TEAM INTERACTION WITHIN A TELECOMMUNICATION COMPANY

Tuire Palonen[1], Kaj Hakkarainen[2], Jaana Talvitie[3] and Erno Lehtinen[3]
[1]*Centre for Learning Research, Turku University, Finland,* [2]*Department of Psychology, University of Helsinki, Finland,* [3]*Department of Teacher Education, University of Turku, Finland*

1. NETWORKED EXPERTISE

The purpose of the chapter is to analyse networked expertise, i.e. expertise that arises from social interaction, knowledge sharing, and collective learning within a community of professionals. Since utilization of the experiences of others is an important resource of learning, it is reasonable to examine how members of an organisation share their experiences and knowledge, how knowledge flows, and innovation and ideas get distributed within the organisation. We have examined patterns of knowledge sharing and distribution within and between teams of 120 workers at a Finnish telecommunication company by applying social network analysis and interviewing key actors. Networking practices between the participants are studied by examining the extent to which persons provide pieces of advice and new information to each other or engage in informal interaction or mutual collaboration. The perspective is enriched by interviews that are focused on key actors, e.g., team members who are frequently asked for advice. These actors are traced by social network techniques.

The cognitive concept of expertise does not necessarily entail a special social status as a recognized expert. An actor may be an expert in his or her community even if he or she does not have a very important formal position in the organisation in general (Krackhard, 1990; Stein, 1997, on studying expertise as a social role in a community). Further, expert performance repeatedly incorporates as tacit knowledge, represented in various social practices, methods, and tools. Such knowledge, in general, cannot be taught directly, but newcomers adopt it through participating in expert culture (Feltovich, Spiro, & Coulson, 1997; Nonaka & Takeuchi, 1995). Techniques like social network analysis provide a reasonable approach, by studying knowledge exchange that cannot be explained through formal position, or official and formal interaction among members in the expert culture or workplaces.

Several theorists have emphasized the importance of context in which the expertise is embedded. Sfard (1998) and Wenger (1998) argued that the development of expertise is not only related to the nature of an individual's knowledge structures but also to that person's access to relevant formal and informal cultural knowledge through participation in an expert community or network. The dynamic development of expertise is fundamentally dependent on participation in an expert culture ("community of practice", Lave & Wenger, 1991; Wenger, 1998; "activity theory, Engeström, 1999) that carries the knowledge of the domain and provides effective tools and practices of cognitive activity. As a consequence, the focus of cognitive research on expertise has moved from examining how individual experts process knowledge to investigating how collaborative activities within an expert community facilitate the development of expertise (Bereiter & Scardamalia, 1993).

In a knowledge-based approach to organisation, learning has often been viewed as the process through which intellectual capital is combined and exchanged to create new knowledge (Ylirenko, 1999). Speaking in terms of "learning organisations" or "intelligent organisations", knowledge can be built by assimilating it from outside, or by creating new knowledge through reinterpretation and reformulation of existing and recently acquired information. Learning does not occur simply through obtaining additional data and information (Mason, 1995). It has been characterized in terms of creating routines and standard procedures or as the accumulation of production skills, the process of organisational renewal, and improved accuracy in problem solving. Organisational learning does not only take place through changing actions but also through changing internal structures and information processing procedures (Blanning & King, 1995).

In order to catch the optimal and multisided approach to knowledge, the team structure has become a familiar part of working-life in recent years. Teams are often composed of members with heterogeneous expertise so that the group can benefit from a larger knowledge pool than any individual member possesses. Further, there is a growing body of evidence that cognitive diversity and distribution of expertise promote knowledge advancement and cognitive growth, especially in complex working environments. Kitcher (1990) showed that the division of cognitive labour is an important prerequisite for the advancement of science. Distribution of cognitive efforts allows the community more flexibility and helps them achieve better results than would otherwise be possible. Moreover, groups, which consist of members with different but partially overlapping expertise, are more effective and innovative than groups with homogeneous expertise (Dunbar, 1995; Hutchins, 1995). In order to achieve high-level expertise, individuals in networks should complement each other's skills, yet there must be enough common ground to establish mutual understanding. Shared knowledge may help an organisation or its sub-units to reuse knowledge, avoid duplication of efforts or provide them complementary expertise. Such a group advantage can be best capitalized upon if individual members understand how expertise is distributed within the group.

Wegner (1986) argued that groups function more effectively as memory units when their members learn to know each other's domains of expertise. When new information is encountered, members presume that it will be processed and remembered by a participant who has special skills, interests, or knowledge in that domain. This kind of metaknowledge is an important determinant of effective problem solving. It is this knowledge of local knowledge resources that helps members in their information search, storage, retrieval, and management. Consequently, it is typically situated and embedded in the working environment and, as such, not useful outside the organisation.

With the metaknowledge, or local information, about who knows what, the overuse of shared information might be reduced. There is even an assumption that networks fill the gaps of unambiguous information. People use network structure as the best available information (Burt, 2000). Even in teams, much of the work is done in non-group settings. Individual workers can, however, call other members when needed, if group knowledge is openly expressed. Being aware of the limits of the team's expertise, group members can also seek knowledge outside the team or organisational borders (Austin, 2000). Knowledge about the structures of networks may replace knowledge as such by helping in finding relevant information.

So, only part of the information is available to all members, or it is only partially shared. The unshared information cannot be socially validated if a contributing member is not able to convince others that recall is accurate. A member who communicates unique information may be perceived as more competent, as better prepared for the task, and as having access to valuable resources, e.g. connections with important people outside of the group (Wittenbaum & Stasser, 1996). Moreland (1999) argued that groups and teams might have the potential benefit of having diverse and heterogeneous knowledge even when discussions are likely to be dominated by information that everyone already knows. Shared information thus dominates the discussions irrespective of whether it is the most significant or essential topic. Some groups focus primarily on exchanging member's knowledge and information so that they can establish a shared representation of the task at hand (Kameda, Otshubo, & Takezawa, 1997).

In our study, we analysed networking relationships among workers of a telecommunication company. The aim was to examine the density and distribution of interaction at individual and collective levels. We also assessed the relative importance of weak and strong ties within teams and among workers in order to find out how often knowledge is shared along strong (bi-directional) and weak network ties. Participating workers were asked to give some examples concerning joint learning in the team and to tell about their beliefs on expertise and the importance of knowledge sharing.

1.1 The nature of network connections

In order to understand how knowledge is embedded in organisations, we look at the way interaction is patterned among the workers. Network relations can be studied in several ways, ranging from an investigation of the overall network properties (like density) to dyad properties (such as symmetry and reciprocity). The essential aim is to reveal the importance of repeated exchange relations that form the basis of both dyadic (between individuals) and structural (in the company) embeddedness. One of the most consequential properties of repeated exchange relations is the strength of dyadic ties, that is, the intensity of exchange that reflects the degree to which a link is significant, stable and mutual.

The structure of knowledge exchange is often a nested one. Information circulates within a work group more than between groups, within a division more than between divisions and so on. At the individual level knowledge diffusion occurs among tightly linked workers. Thus, even if information would reach everyone, the fact that diffusion takes time means that individuals informed early or more broadly have an advantage (Burt, 1999, 2000; Friedman & Podolny, 1992). As knowledge facilitates the use of other knowledge, what can be learned is affected by what is already known (see Cohen & Levinthal, 1990, about "absorptive capacity"). Accordingly, knowledge gets transmitted to an individual or group that already has plenty of well-structured knowledge. In other words, knowledge appears occasionally to be "sticky" and sometimes "leaky" that can be explained by epistemological, cognitive and socio-cultural reasons (Brown & Duguid,

1999, 2001). Consequently, informal communities of practice have an essential role in knowledge exchange.

Hansen (1999) argued that efficient knowledge creation and sharing is characterized by tight coupling between people from different parts of an organisation. Intensive interaction between experts working in different organisational sub-units facilitates productive collaboration because of timely integration of knowledge across organisational boundaries. Granovetter's theory (1973) focuses on "strength of the weak ties". According to him, the distant or weak ties are efficient for knowledge sharing because they provide access to information by bridging otherwise disconnected groups and individuals in an organisation. Weak links are the key for crossing boundaries between various otherwise separated knowledge cultures. Table 1 presents a summary of characteristics of knowledge exchange associated with weak and strong ties.

Table 1. Nature of knowledge exchange and the strength of ties

CHARACTERISTIC OF KNOWLEDGE EXCHANGE	THE STRENGTH OF TIES	
	Strong	Weak
Information flow	Redundant and reciprocal	Nonredundant and often asymmetric
The nature of knowledge exchanged	Usually complex	Simple or well-defined
Form of knowledge	Often noncodified or tacit	Often codified and transferable
Relation to knowledge environment	Context-bound, i.e., a part of a larger knowledge structure	Often context-free and independently understandable
Type of communication	"Thick", including chunks, expert terms, and scripts	"Thin" and widely understandable
Management of network connections	Usually takes up a lot of resources	Not so much resources needed

Links between team members that frequently meet each other are typically strong. Strong ties tend to mediate redundant information because they usually occur among small groups of actors in which everyone knows what the others know. So, one obviously hears the same information several times though it may be abbreviated (Shanteau, 1992; Vicente & Wang, 1998) or allusive because of the tacit dimension. If tacit knowledge is highly shared (e.g. between two professionals from the same field) the communication can be abbreviated (Rikers, Schmidt, & Boshuizen, 2000;

Van de Wiel, Boshuizen, & Schmidt, 2000) but if the shared area is low (e.g. among multi-disciplinary scientists) the information has to be explained more carefully. Any shortcomings in the actors' willingness and ability to share their knowledge may also cause problems in transfer.

According to Nonaka and Takeuchi (1995), redundant connections are very important in the process of innovation because the sharing of tacit and informal knowledge is only possible through extended and intensive communication. The bi-directional interaction characteristic of strong ties is important for assimilating noncodified knowledge because the recipient is not likely to acquire the knowledge completely during the first interaction, but needs multiple opportunities to assimilate it. Knowledge that is not codified or fully documented, or that is dependent on its context, is often very difficult to transfer.

In contrast to strong links, weak links, in our view, support the functioning of a knowledge organisation by transmitting information to and from expert networks. This knowledge is additive, more than overlapping. Sparse networks usually have many weak links and nonredundant contacts. Networks with weak links are suitable for carrying out relatively simple, easily describable, and technical tasks (like formulas, detail information, etc.). Although weak ties may sometimes be reciprocal in nature, they tend to require less effort or energy to maintain than strong ties. Hansen's (1999) findings revealed that weak interunit ties help teams in searching for useful new knowledge but impede the transfer of complex knowledge, which tends to require a strong tie between the participants of the knowledge exchange (Uzzi, 1997).

Strong ties that start as nonredundant and weak contacts are likely to become redundant over time. The ties can also break down and reorganize under another structure and new ties may be formed. Transformation of network ties is not, however, a very well studied research area (Keister, 1999).

Further, results relying on social network analysis indicate that weak ties do not provide the same kind of socio-emotional support as strong ties. Networking linkages, which are based more on trust and personal relationships (Uzzi, 1997, calls this "embedded ties") than on exact contracts, tell about "doing more than is said in the contract." The economic importance of socially embedded links is not, however, clear and may have both positive and negative effects (Frank & Yasumoto, 1998). The concept of embeddedness has also arisen concerning "thick" information flows with tacit know-how (Larson, 1992), knowledge transfer and learning. Uzzi (1997) has described how information transfer in close ties is composed of "chunks" of information that are not only more specific but also more accurate than in other relations. Such transfer consists of composite chunks of information rather than of sequential pieces of dissimilar data (Ericsson & Lehmann, 1996; see also the concept of "script" in the theory of knowledge encapsulation Boshuizen & Schmidt, 1992; Schmidt & Boshuizen, 1993). Embedded relations may also be restrictive if they provide an access to resources while blocking activities outside the network. Overembeddedness is likely to reduce the flow of novel information into the network in case there are only a few links to actors outside the network (Burt, 1992, 2000).

The nature of the knowledge exchanged and the strength of ties among members of the network are very important considerations. Strong ties represent the reciprocal, redundant and specialized information flow, whereas weak ties guarantee an adequate number of ties with the result that new information can also be captured in the network. To conclude, neither weak nor strong links alone lead to efficient networking and knowledge sharing. Both have their respective strengths and weaknesses in relation to knowledge advancement or transfer of knowledge across organisation sub-units. The strong ties provide the best net effect in the case of complex knowledge whereas weak ties may be more effective in transmitting well-coded knowledge.

The informal network is usually larger than the organisation itself. Sparse networks that are characterized by weak links often have so-called *structural holes*, i.e., disconnections between actors that prevent the flow of relevant and meaningful information (Burt, 1992, 1999). Structural holes provide an opportunity for creating completely new links that can increase an organisation's intellectual capital by bringing together actors from parts nearby to the hole, and thereby helping people to become aware of the existence of knowledge and expertise relevant to their work. In such a process, "information gatekeepers," become important, having a crucial role both in intranetworks and internetworks. In many cases, they know how to find information that is relevant for solving problems (Brooking, 1999). The gatekeepers mediate information coming to the organisation from the surrounding environment. They provide an organisation with access to an extended network, (bridging a structural hole) which may be an important resource for learning and knowledge advancement.

The present project focuses on examining the role of the kinds of bridging of ties taking place between teams or within the networks of communities of practice. Special consideration will be given to identifying and examining the role of active and knowledgeable workers, who provide other workers with new information or good advice and know-how needed in their work. We rely on social network analysis for making visible the structure of the organisation's communication and the nature of information flow.

1.2 Research aims

We have simultaneously analysed both an individual's and a group's networking practices. Studying the relations among participants appears to help us to better understand and explain collaborative processes that affect the individual participants, as compared with individual assessment. The questions addressed at the organisational level were, how intensively did employees of the company engage in certain kinds of interaction (density of interaction) and, whether the participants' interactive activities were dominated by some particular workers or teams (centralisation of interaction). At the team level we asked how the knowledge is distributed within and between teams. We examined the role of each team within the organisation by assessing its cognitive centrality, i.e. to what extent other teams relied on knowledge produced by the given team, i.e. what was its "advice size"? We expected that a cognitively central group would play a pivotal role in the organisation more often than a cognitively peripheral one. We also assessed the relative importance of weak and strong ties within teams. Accordingly, we assessed how often knowledge is shared along strong (bi-directional links between workers in several questions asked) and weak (a great deal of asymmetric links only in some questions asked) ties. Further, team profiles were enriched by asking whether the teams were sharing diverse (non-overlapping) knowledge resources and work functions or if the action was based on homogeneous and shared (overlapping) expertise and work tasks. Team leaders are also asked to give some examples concerning joint learning in the team. Finally, we interviewed team leaders and certain key members (members who were in a central position of the participants' network of being asked advice) about their beliefs on expertise and the importance of knowledge sharing.

2. METHOD

2.1 Participants

The study took place in a Finnish telecommunication company. Out of the company's 500 workers, 120 participated. About 27 % ($n = 32$) of them were females. The participants represented 10 teams that belonged to three departments and formed one process delivering a particular kind of client service. About 65 % ($n = 78$) of the participants represented commercial and technical custom work, 13 % ($n = 16$) management services (administrative), and 22 % ($n = 26$) technologies.

The study was carried out as part of an organisational development project on facilitating teamwork. The intervention focused on educating teams and team leaders on issues, such as knowledge sharing, team work, intra- and inter-organisational networking and so on. The intervention aimed at developing between- and within-team interaction, as well as identifying various kinds of team competencies, increasing awareness of the competencies, as well as making them more well known for the other teams. The data were mostly collected near the end of the project. One main goal has been to utilize the results as a part of the project through discussing and asking the workers, and especially the team leaders, about knowledge sharing, as well as informing them of our findings.

2.2 Data collection

The data were collected as follows: We presented the respondent with a list of the names of all his or her fellow workers, and asked them to assess how intensively they are interacting with each of them. In other words, the questionnaire provided the participants with a matrix to be filled. The left hand column of the matrix consisted of the list of names of the participating workers ordered alphabetically, department by department. The participants were asked to assess (1) to whom they go for *advice*; (2) to whom they go for *new information*; (3) with whom they have *informal discussions* and, (4) with whom they carry out their most important *collaboration*. The response rate of the study was 88 %. The responses of the participants returning the questionnaire were, further, symmetrised, i.e., the networking connections of persons who did not, for one reason or another, return the questionnaire were assumed to correspond to the responses of participants who returned the questionnaire. Responses of a person who did not return the questionnaire were, in a sense, estimated by assuming that the responses would be symmetric to those of their fellow employees in networking connections with them. The response rate was high enough to allow this kind of operation.

2.3 Social network analysis

Social network analysis is a collection of techniques that are focused on uncovering the patterning of people's interaction and relational information on participation; i.e., patterned sets of connections (Scott, 1991; Wasserman & Faust, 1994). We studied information and knowledge exchange for its density (how often information flows between actors) and centrality or centralisation (whether there is an actor who is more important than the others or whether someone is not getting any information at all). So, the data consisted of the links between actors, indicating who engages in certain kinds of interaction with whom. The concepts of density and centralisation refer to the various aspects of a networked environment. *Density* describes the general level of cohesion, whereas *centralisation* describes the extent to which this cohesion is organised around particular actors (Scott, 1991).

We have used Freeman's degree to measure the network activity of individual actors. With this measure it is also possible to use asymmetric data (such as addressed versus received connections). Further, the QAP-correlation was used to analyse whether the four network dimensions examined (providing advice, new information, informal interaction, collaboration) could be combined or summed up for further analysis of strong and weak ties. Social network analyses were performed with the Ucinet 5 program (Borgatti, Everett, & Freeman, 1999).

2.4 Interviews

All team leaders (10) were interviewed, as well as the most central members of each team, selected by relying on the results of social network analysis. In addition, a long discussion session with the personnel manager was recorded on audiotape. Altogether, we conducted 21 interviews. The interviews focused on topics, such as collective learning, information seeking, and networking practices. However, the experts were also encouraged to describe the knowledge sharing practices of their teams outside the agenda. The tapes were then transcribed and the material was jointly studied. For the chapter, the interviews provide practical examples, explanations and confirm the analysis carried out with the social network analysis.

2.5 Results

2.5.1 Relations between teams

To begin the analysis, the density and centralisation of the knowledge exchange network were measured in the entire client-based process formed by the participating teams. We analysed the network regarding the providing of advice, the sharing of new information, informal communication, and collaboration.

The simplest way to measure the density of a network is to compare the observed interaction (who is connected to whom) to the most intensive interaction. So, the density of the network is the total number of ties divided by the number of possible ties, and it can vary from 0 to 1 in the case of a dichotomous matrix. The more actors are connected to one another, the denser the graph will be (Scott, 1991). It is also possible to examine the extent to which a whole graph has a centralised structure. The results can be interpreted so that if there would be one extremely central worker to whom everyone else would be connected, the graph centralisation would be 100 %; or if all of the workers had equal ties, the graph centralisation would be 0 %. Here the centralisation values are calculated separately for outgoing ties reported by the workers themselves (out-degree) and incoming ties reported by their fellow workers (in-degree). In Table 2 one can see the results of the density and centralisation analyses.

Table 2. Density of interaction among employees

	Density (Sd.)	Centralisation In	Out
Advice	0.24 (0.43)	34 %	67 %
New information	0.18 (0.38)	33 %	72 %
Collaboration	0.10 (0.30)	25 %	47 %
Informal communication	0.24 (0.43)	25 %	44 %

The results indicate that giving advice, together with the informal relations, is the most common way to interact among workers. A somewhat less dense network is observed as new information is mediated. As expected, the collaboration network is the thinnest of all. It is understandable that a long-standing and mutual co-operation takes more resources than, e.g. the occasional giving of advice. None of the networks of incoming ties (advice, new information, collaboration and informal communication) were especially centralised. Though, giving advice and sharing new information were more centralised than the maintaining of collaboration and friendship (informal) networks. On the contrary, the outgoing links (out-degree) were somewhat more centralised. This result indicates first of all that workers have different criteria for reporting their ties. For this reason we have used the more reliable in-degree values in the later analyses. The out-degree values are present when studying the reciprocal or symmetric ties. The asymmetric nature of relationships can particularly be seen in looking at the advice network: Some workers reported considerably more connections than other workers.

To examine whether the previous questions (advice, new information, informal relations and collaboration) can be seen as properties of the same dimension, the QAP-correlations were computed. The QAP-correlation procedure is principally used to test the similarity of networks. The algorithm first computes Pearson's correlation coefficient between corresponding cells of the two data matrices. Then, it randomly permutes rows and columns of one matrix and recomputes the correlation. The latter step was carried out 5000 times in order to compute the proportion of times that the correlation based on random permutations is equal to or larger than the observed correlation first calculated. The results indicated that the networks correlate very strongly, and thus, they can be seen as the properties of the same dimension. So, it is reasonable to add the matrices to examine the weak and strong ties among workers in later analyses. The mutuality and the value of the cell (how many times the relationship is confirmed in these 4 matrices) express the strength of the tie between two workers.

Using the density values inside each team and average centrality values of the team members, we get information concerning how often advice, new information and collaboration are provided to the rest of the organisation (Freeman's centrality measure) and how often knowledge is divided inside the team (density) (Figure 1). Although some of the teams do not densely share knowledge (e.g. Teams 2 and 5), others share but do not so eagerly provide knowledge to other teams, or the information is not greatly desired (e.g. Team 9). On the other hand, the knowledge exchange is measured at a low level with both of the aspects (sharing and providing, see Team 7), which indicates a weak team culture, and at a high overall level in the case of some teams (see Teams 6 and 10).

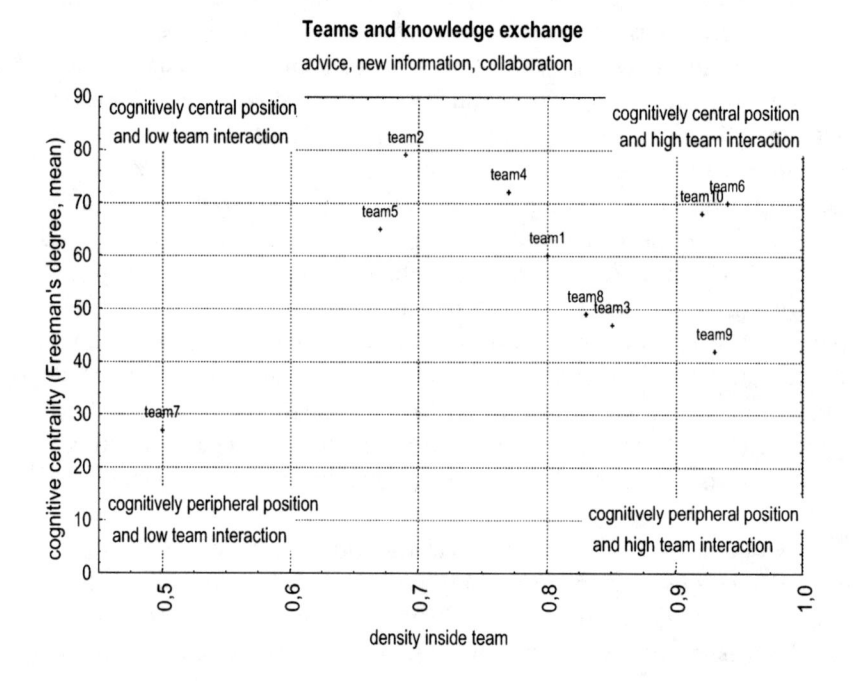

Figure 1. Teams and knowledge exchange: Advice, new information, and collaboration

Network Ties

We continued the results analysis by focusing on teams that diverged from each other in terms of cognitive centrality and density. These teams (Teams 5, 6, 7, and 9) represented the corners of Figure 1. Our aim was to examine more closely the team's strategies of building either on shared (homogenous) or distributed (heterogeneous, or multiple functional) expertise.

2.5.2 Strategies of sharing and distributing expertise inside teams

The four teams were compared in order to see their profile of networking practices. The average centrality values in providing advice and new information, as well as maintaining collaboration and informal ties are presented in Table 3. The centrality value of all incoming ties and all outgoing ties, likewise the average value of strong ties are presented in the table. The differences between the teams were analysed by using the one-way ANOVA test.

As expected, there are differences between the teams. The results indicate the characteristics of the teams with different profiles. The number of strong links is especially high in the case of Team 6; the number indicates the maximal team performance in terms of providing knowledge to the other teams. Team 6 also has a high *advice size*, indicating that it provides a high degree of knowledge to the rest of the workers. It also has cohesive team culture (compare Table 3 with Figure 1).

Table 3. Centralisation of knowledge sharing network

Team (n)	Advice (in) M	sd	New info (in) M	sd	Collab-oration (in) M	sd	Informal (in) M	sd	Total in M	sd	Total out M	sd	Strong links M	sd
Team 7 (11)	12	4.8	9	4.0	7	3.6	16	4.3	43	14.9	58	22.2	10	3.4
Team 5 (7)	32	14.1	22	10.7	12	7.0	26	16.3	91	46.1	79	30.6	15	6.8
Team 9 (7)	21	7.5	13	4.7	8	3.3	12	3.6	54	16.8	49	20.9	8	4.1
Team 6 (9)	34	14.1	21	8.6	15	7.6	23	8.3	93	36.9	144	99.1	21	13.2
F value	$F(3,30)$ = 9.04***		$F(3,30)$ = 6.92***		$F(3,30)$ = 3.93*		$F(3,30)$ = 4.0*		$F(3,21)$ = 3.41*		$F(3,30)$ = 6.46***		$F(3,21)$ = 2.78	

Average value among team members in the selected teams

The in-degree values are calculated by using a symmetrised matrix (n = 34) whereas the out-degrees and strong links are calculated based upon the original matrix where the number of cases is lower (n = 25). This procedure was selected because symmetrisation would have provided a biased description of the role of strong links. ***: $p < .001$; *: $p < .05$.

The differences are lowest in cases of informal ties and collaboration. The relative importance of providing advice and new information appears to distinguish Teams 5 and 6 from the others. Team 9, however, provides more advice and new information throughout the organisation than Team 7, whereas Team 7 has more informal ties and collaboration partners than Team 9.

The results indicate that teams' own networking activities have an outstanding role in the organisation. Teams 5 and 6 which were often regarded as important partners in networking activity, were also themselves engaged in their own networking activities (out-degree values). They were not just popular and frequently mentioned by other teams (in-degree values). The results, thus, equally emphasize the role of activity and popularity.

2.5.3 Participants' beliefs in teamwork and knowledge sharing

The interviews with team leaders provided evidence that supported the above results regarding the nature of differences between the teams. The leader of Team 6 (with a high degree of shared and distributed knowledge) described the knowledge sharing (not knowing about the results reported here):

> Our team is a very collaborative one, and everyone is, by and large, able to do a share of each other's work, so that if needed ... everyone should be able to do everything ... Is everyone able to master all kind of things? ... ...I don't think there is any who wouldn't do it. The other can do it better than the others. This is not so difficult. We are using only two technical environments ... it is not at all too difficult to learn them both ...it is more a question of the time -- that we have not had an opportunity to teach more. This has been the most important thing.

The leader of Team 5 (with little shared and much distributed expertise), in contrast, saw the situation in a different light. He explained why the work was distributed rather than shared in the following way:

> It would be a pretty amazing person who would be able, truthfully, to tell us he can master anything ... I say that here, one is confused [at a loss] all the time, so you need to educate yourself all the time just so you could keep up [in your own field], and know where we are going. We have quite a strict division of labour because in our team there are professionals of certain fields; so, in principle, work tasks cannot be shared. If one person represents a certain field, another does not have mastery of these issues and cannot deal with them. Only this customer

service [has less strict division], in that we can be a little bit flexible so that one can take care of another person's work.

...we have so many workers who have come into the 'house' in the 1970s. They are so fixated on the routines that it is very difficult to make it [the work process] different, to change direction. If they have told you that they are going to do certain kinds of things [work activity or tasks] or that it is not their business to do something, then it is so [in their view, and one can't argue with them]. *Why do you think that it is so?* It is an attitude, old habits ... They just cannot be flexible because previously they did only that [routine] sort of thing and did not have to do anything else.

The multiple functions and distributed tasks of the team were described in a similar way by another professional of the team who was frequently asked for advice:

We don't really explore anything together in the team. I am a lone wolf and work with my own tasks. The other members of the team are not aware of what I am doing ... This does not bother me and it is not going to. I work and do things alone, so that we are not really working together as a team. Otherwise it [the team] is working well, but I don't understand what they mean by the concept of team! We have always had one ... I guess that they know me mostly by my own name rather than as a member of this team.

The leader of Team 7 reported on his work as "a foreman". He could not see the difference between collaborative teams and the old idea of working together. Yet, he saw it as a problem that his team does not meet often enough:

I have, I have ... a great deal of experience as a foreman. I have been a foreman more than 30 years. I have only worked in this position ... It is not a new idea to ... that people work together in a group and be jointly responsible of the work. We [members of my team] have the problem that, [in general], we do not see each other very often; as a consequence our communication takes mostly place via email.

All of the teams were also asked to tell about their workplace communities, whether they have joint habits, a special kind of language or other cultural practices of their own. One of the team leaders recounted:

Yep, we have shared ways of speaking and our own special terms. Many customers are so-called regulars, and we have certain nicknames for them, so that only we know about whom or what we are talking.

For most of the workers, the team culture was taken for granted: One person said, "I suppose that every team has its special characteristics, its own sense of humour and system. What [team] would not have it?" But all of the participants did not understand the question [about team culture]. One of the less interacting team leaders asked:

> No, I don't understand what it [team culture] could be, a hug for everyone in the morning, or what?

Another expert commented, "There is nothing peculiar or special in the way we talk to each other. Just normal talk." Nevertheless, team culture was mentioned several times during the interviews. Having team spirit was, for example, was said to be shown in providing help and correcting mistakes without someone having to ask you whether you would mind doing it: "It is self-initiative, providing help when needed."

A densely or tightly connected team is, however, not always a good team. Neither does the "spirit of the team" necessarily facilitate learning: Strict norms and control may also cause anxiety for some members. Being outside of the in-group is harder in a densely connected team than in a loosely coupled team. One professional who felt herself to be an outsider in spite of her strong expertise, said:

> Our team's sense of belonging together is not the best possible. Sometimes a picture is presented [by someone] that we have always been a team and it goes well, but it is not so. People are given that sort of impression, and many persons in our workplace believe so, but it is not true…For example, people are not taking responsibly for work where there is the pile of unfinished tasks. When you try to guide, there is no willingness to learn. Even if we are organising some kinds of recreational activities, not all members of the team are always informed. Sometimes if you happen to be on a lunch break, and they chat about something together, agree about something, you might be completely left outside when you come back. Oh what, See what we've decided we're going to do, they say. This has [already] been agreed ... we suffer, we others in there. It is not personal, it is only the team. It is not workplace teasing or anything like that.

The loud and noisy way of talking between team members was not experienced negatively by the members. About the good spirit of Team 1, one of the members said:

> It is so that if an outsider listens to us [conversing], there is terrible screaming and noise, commotion, and it may sound like we are barking at each other. But everything is like that, it [noise] is a part of it [our work

process]. Maybe our way of using language may sound hard to a woman's ear. Everyone knows, however, that it is never at the personal or individual level, it is just general way of mouthing off.

A special characteristic of Finnish culture is to have joint "sauna" (bath) evenings among the team members. As soon as a person has participated in a sauna evening, then he is accepted/admitted to the group, as often stated in the participants' interviews. The participants proposed a "sauna indicator" of team spirit according to which a team was working well when 75 % of members participated in sauna evenings.

To enrich our perspective concerning expert performance, we examined the individual level with a help of some more questions during the interviews.

2.5.4 Individual expertise and personal networks

By interviewing key members of the teams we sought to deepen our understanding of the nature of the participants' expertise. We selected to interview 10 most frequently chosen (i.e. the highest advice size) employees, one from each team. They were asked about the practices of teamwork and knowledge sharing in their own teams. They were also asked about the education and work experience they had, and requested to give an assessment on whether it had turned out to be adequate. The participants were not told why they were selected for the interview. The qualities needed in expert work were frequently reported to be cognitive characteristics such as the memory and somewhat broader learning skills.

Cognitive memory load pressures frequently reported by the participants appeared at least partially to arise from the high proportion of noncodified information. The employees explained that because of manifold information and variations, it is difficult to create any procedures and the work is "just to play with lots of paper slips hanging all around."

Social skills were mentioned frequently. An expert stated that it is important that "an employee ... is able to co-operate and willingly works well with the other workers ... is a person who does not seclude themselves from others ..." Moreover, he or she should be "eager to inquire after information, it is just the interaction ..." Concerning other personal qualities, being alert or eager to always catch the newest information and self-help were described as useful. However, the experts thought that social skills and personal qualities were only little or not at all developed during education. Knowledge sharing was seen to be akin to such skills: If you don't have the personal characteristics that support social skills and co-operation, then there is not much that can be done to facilitate knowledge sharing. There is always someone who has "the knowledge in a drawer" or "the files on locked shelves."

The relation between education and work was seen by the participants as an intricate question. It was not a meaningless one, even though "the technology has changed in the data sector about 120 %. There are not even memories left about how it was done [before]."

The producers and other corresponding companies were often mentioned as an essential information source. The importance of the Internet and certain web pages was emphasized as well as the informal long-standing contacts with other experts, inside and outside of the company. "The information seeking or mining has become a daily routine," they told us. One of the experts characterized the way he himself finds the newest relevant information needed, as well as the learning process connected to the problem-solving situations in joint work situations:

> You just have to look for information ...the Net is a pretty good information source and the producers ... if you have something to do with them so you just keep on asking about matters and things. It is the activity that is needed... There is only one place inside the house that provides information for me. There is very little that we need or can get inside the house. We communicate more with the producers ...of course, every team member has their own links along which the information flows ...they are calling, discussing things with people, with the ones who make these things...you know the certain fellows and then you just call them and talk this and that. I also have certain passwords to load the stuff directly from the net. If you cannot get it there, then you just have to find something else. I also have other kinds of channels...informal contacts. You have to use your own links. I take the information direct where it is. I want to have it fresh. Others use my contacts as well. I know to whom to turn to. It is the interaction...you speak informally about this and that to make it work.

The informal communication channels were mentioned often, though no one described the issue in a very detailed way. The two useful places for employees to hear informal news that were "pretty often correct," became familiar to the researcher, too. People mentioned that "the social hatch area, of the equipment storage room is the best place to get news." Someone said that "news often has wings on its back"; thus, they do not need to get news from the official channels. The results are supported by *"grapevine"* studies suggesting that informal networks transmit messages faster than the formal ones. Most information transmitted by "grapevine" has been shown to be accurate but the part of the information that is inaccurate can cause severe problems. Yet, the "grapevine" fulfils a social function (Crampton & Hodge, 1998). Beneath formal ties there is the sea of informal relations.

2.6 Discussion

The results of the study indicate that social network analysis can productively be applied to analyse interaction among the workers. The methods of SNA helped us to examine relations between weak and strong links in various teams. Patterns of relations and social structure direct attention and dictate the information focusing onto essential issues. By providing explicit information on the networking practices of the organisation, we guided the company to examine its formal and informal network structures.

The study indicated that knowledge within the company is still centralised in certain critical experts rather than distributed among a large group of employees, although it was not centralised all over the field but for certain kinds of technical, expert knowledge that represents the core competence in the field. The experts on these fields cannot go for advice to other members of the organisation because those persons do not have sufficiently deep expertise. They have their own expert cultures, but these networks appear to extend beyond the boundaries of the company, in this case among the producers and, perhaps, to some competitor companies, either directly or indirectly via some third actor, such as clients. There appeared to be a need for the experts to keep up their own personal network, a phenomenon that fits closely with the idea of intentional networks (Nardi, Whittaker, & Schwarz, 2000).

Consequently, the experts who were frequently asked questions, appeared to function as information gatekeepers, who capitalise intellectual resources that arise from bridging structural holes (Burt, 2000). These kinds of boundary spanners play an important role in intergroup relations. It has been shown that some broker socio-emotional ties while some broker task oriented ties, measured e.g. by flows of advice. The persons with the best ideas are not always the most liked ones. The boundary spanning function is actually a composite entity, comprising multiple types of relations (Friedman & Podolny, 1992).

We also examined the extent to which knowledge sharing occurred within the teams and how the knowledge of the teams was distributed across the organisation. Strong ties were examined in relation to all incoming and all outgoing connections in order to assess the importance of redundant and mutual knowledge-sharing versus non-overlapping information resources. The actual performance measures (such as earnings, bonuses, goals achieved, and so on) were not available to us. These measures may not, however, have been meaningful because some of the teams only supported the functions inside the company, while others were responsible for functions outside the company (such as client work). However, the advice size - the amount of information and knowledge that an individual or a team provides for the other workers - could be treated as a rough estimate of cognitive centrality. Previous studies show a clear association between team performance and the importance of non-redundant sources of networks of advice and information (for a review of this issue, see Burt, 2000). Our results appear to be consistent with Austin's study (2000) indicating that the density of within-team ties alone does not determine a team's cognitive centrality. The frequency of diversified connections - such as multiple weak links - is a better indicator of a good team performance. The weak links appear, so to speak, to feed the strong links by updating the knowledge base. Presumably, the absence of weak links makes the working environment suffer deficiencies in information and knowledge updating, and perhaps even encourages biased *groupthink* where the action only depends upon information inside a cohesive group (Janis, 1982; Kameda & Sugimori, 1993).

The participants' interviews suggested that collective learning took place through interactive processes, such as shared inquiry and negotiations, as well as through developing a collective repertoire of behavioural routines - appropriate ways of thinking and acting. Teams' collective cognition appears to facilitate and guide team members' learning and open up new perspectives (Wong & Sitkin, 2000). It was noticeable that cohesive teams reported practices and experiences of collective learning. Maintaining and building expertise requires long-term relationships in which knowledge exchange can take place within a learned and shared code. Yet the quality or rigidity of the routines and practices should be taken into consideration: The most distributed practices are not necessarily the best ones.

Tacit knowledge cannot replace the codified conceptual and factual knowledge, but rather both of them are needed, especially in complex environments based on co-operation of several actors with distributed, work tasks and diversified expertise. Although expertise cannot be directly taught in education, formal and codified knowledge has an important role in working-life contexts. If codified information is not available, routines appear to serve as memory units as they are repeated sufficiently ("new things become routines", as one of the team members told us in the interview). However, knowledge is more easily transferable and changeable if it can be explicated. A knowledge-intensive and technical environment cannot be based on bare rituals and noncodified knowledge. In the present case, there were strong demands to get more assistance provided by written codes ("helps") to facilitate practical work. Similar results have been reported by some other studies (Vartiainen, Hakonen, Simola, Kokko, & Rantamäki, 1999). For deeper collaborative knowledge to be produced, explicit but uncodified knowledge would have to be more widely shared, not merely held by a few "gatekeepers".

It is suggested that information diversity is more likely to lead to improved performance when tasks concern nonroutine (Jehn, Northcraft, & Neale, 1999). Yet, knowledge sharing is extremely important for coping with complex environments and creating new solutions, and in dealing with other affairs that one person would not be able to manage alone. Having an appropriate relationship between shared and distributed human resources is the key to optimal collaborative outcomes, although quite difficult to assess. The highly centralised communication structure is certainly familiar to many working places acting in a field of rapid change: Conventional tasks can be handled by most of the workers, as the newest techniques and know-how are in the hands of only a few workers. In this kind of situation expertise is not sufficiently shared so as to obtain the best collaborative results. It takes a great deal of resources to codify or distribute even the most urgent pieces of the core knowledge. For all that, it appears that the individuals who possess superior analytical skills, task specific knowledge, or social skills (e.g., narrative techniques) are likely to enhance the collective learning processes. They are likely to become central actors notwithstanding how knowledge is otherwise organised in the company.

The relation between expertise and experience is often highlighted. Comparing novices and newcomers with expert workers having long work careers has been a common way of examining the nature of expertise. Long experience does not, however, necessarily make one an expert; there are many people who may be characterized as experienced non-experts (Bereiter & Scardamalia, 1993). It appears that, while dealing with a rapidly changing field, the versatility of experience is more important than the duration of experience as such, although a certain minimum length of practical experience is needed. The employees are typically working for several years in the same company (sometimes even 30 or 40 years). The youngest may, however, in some areas provide the knowledge concerning the newest technique. In our study, a relatively long and rich experience of working life appeared to be characteristic of almost every person invited to be interviewed on the basis of cognitive centrality among the social network of the company. Yet, we do not know why only some of the workers with long experience achieved an exceptional level of expertise.

REFERENCES

Austin, J. R. (2000). *Knowing what and whom other people know: Linking transactive memory with external connections in organizational groups.* Best Paper Proceedings (CD). Briarcliff Manor: Academy of Management.

Bereiter, C., & Scardamalia, M. (1993). *Surpassing ourselves: An inquiry into the nature and implications of expertise.* Chicago: Open Court.

Blanning, R. W., & King, D. R. (1995). An overview of organizational intelligence. In R. W. Blanning & D. R. King (Eds.), *Organizational intelligence* (pp. 1-9). Los Alamos: IEEE Computer Society Press.

Borgatti, S. P., Everett, M. G., & Freeman, L. C. (1999). *UCINET 5.0 Version 1.00.* Natick: Analytic Technologies.

Boshuizen, H. P. A., & Schmidt, H. G. (1992). On the role of biomedical knowledge in clinical reasoning by experts, intermediates and novices. *Cognitive Science, 16,* 164-184.

Brooking, A. (1999). *Corporate memory: Strategies for knowledge management.* London: International Thompson Business Press.

Brown, J. S., & Duguid, P. (1999). *The social life of information.* Harvard: Business School Press.

Brown, J. S., & Duguid, P. (2001). Knowledge and organization: A social practice perspective. *Organization Science, 12,* 198-213.

Burt, R. S. (1992). *Structural holes: The social structure of competition.* Cambridge: MIT Press.

Burt, R. S. (1999). Entrepreneurs, distrust, and third parties: A strategic look at the dark side of dense networks. In L. L. Thompson, J. M. Levine, & D. M. Messick (Eds.), *Shared cognition in organizations: The management of knowledge* (pp. 213-243). Mahwah: Erlbaum.

Burt, R. S. (2000). The network structure of social capital. *Research in Organisational Behavior, 22,* 345-423.

Cohen, W. M., & Levinthal, D. A. (1990). Absorptive capacity: A new perspective on learning and innovation. *Administrative Science Quarterly, 35,* 128-152.

Crampton, S. M., & Hodge, J. W. (1998). The informal communication network: Factors affecting grapevine activity. *PublicPersonnelManagement, 27,* 569-585.

Dunbar, K. (1995). How scientists really reason: Scientific reasoning in real-life laboratories. In R. J. Stenberg & J. Davidson (Eds.), *The nature of insight* (pp. 365-395). Cambridge: MIT Press.

Engeström, Y. (1999). Activity theory and individual and social transformation. In Y. Engeström, R. Miettinen, & R.-L. Punamäki (Eds.), *Perspectives on activity theory* (pp. 19-38). Cambridge: Cambridge University Press.

Ericsson, K. A., & Lehmann, A. C. (1996). Expert and exceptional performance: Evidence of maximal adaptation to task constraints. *Annual Review of Psychology, 47,* 273-305.

Feltovich, P. J., Spiro, R. J., & Coulson, R. L. (1997). Issues of expert flexibility in contexts characterized by complexity and change. In P. J. Feltovich, K. M. Ford, & R. R. Hoffman (Eds.), *Expertise in context* (pp. 125-146). Menlo Park: AAAI Press.

Frank, K., & Yasumoto, J. Y. (1998). Linking action to social structure within a system: Social capital within and between subgroups. *American Journal of Sociology 104,* 642-686.

Friedman, R. A., & Podolny, J. (1992). Differentiation of boundary spanning roles: Labor negotiations and implications for role conflict. *Administrative Science Quarterly 37,* 28-48.

Granovetter, M. S. (1973). The strength of weak ties. *American Journal of Sociology, 78*, 1360-1380.

Hansen, M. T. (1999). The search-transfer problem: The role of weak ties in sharing knowledge across organization subunits. *Administrative Science Quarterly, 44*, 82-102.

Hutchins, E. (1995). *Cognition in the wild.* Cambridge: MIT Press.

Janis, I. (1982). *Groupthink. Psychological studies of policy decision.* Boston: Houghton Mifflin.

Jehn, K. A., Northcraft, G. B., & Neale, M. A.(1999). Why differences make a difference: A field study of diversity. Conflict and performance in workgroups. *Administrative Science Quarterly, 44*, 741-763.

Kameda, T., Otshubo, Y., & Takezawa, M. (1997). Centrality in sociocognitive networks and social influence: An illustration in a group decision-making process. *Journal of Personality and Social Psychology, 73*, 296-309.

Kameda, T., & Sugimori, S. (1993). Psychological entrapment in group decision making: An assigned decision rule and a groupthink phenomenon. *Journal of Personality and Social Psychology, 65*, 282-292.

Keister, L. A. (1999). Where do strong ties come from? A dyad analysis of the strength of interfirm exchange relations during China's economic transition. *International Journal of Organizational Analysis, 7*, 5-25.

Kitcher, P. (1990). The division of cognitive labor. *The Journal of Philosophy, 87*, 5-22.

Krackhard, D. (1990). Assessing the political landscape: Structure, cognition, and power in organisations. *Administrative Science Quarterly 35*, 342-369.

Larson, A. (1992). Network dyads in entrepreneurial settings: A study of the governance of exchange relationships. *Administrative Science Quarterly, 37*, 76-104.

Lave, J., & Wenger, E. (1991). *Situated learning: Legitimate peripheral participation.* Cambridge: Cambridge University Press.

Mason, R. M. (1995). Strategic information systems: Use of information technology in a learning organization. In R. W. Blanning & D. R. King (Eds.), *Organizational intelligence. AI in organizational design, modeling, and control* (pp. 218-227). Los Alamos: IEEE Computer Society Press.

Moreland, R. L. (1999). Transactive memory: Learning who knows what in work groups and organizations. In L. L Thompson, J. M. Levine, & D. M. Messic (Eds.), *Shared cognition in organizations: The management of knowledge* (pp. 3-31). Mahwah: Erlbaum.

Nardi, B., Whittaker, S., & Schwarz, H. (2000). It's not what you know, it's who you know: Work in the information age. *First Monday,* 5, 5. URL: http://firstmonday.org/issues/issue5_5/nardi/index.html

Nonaka, I., & Takeuchi, H. (1995). *The knowledge-creating company: How japanese companies create the dynamics of innovation.* New York: Oxford University Press.

Rikers, R. M. J. P., Schmidt, H. G., & Boshuizen, H. P. A. (2000). Knowledge encapsulation and the intermediate effect. *Contemporary Educational Psychology, 25*, 150-160.

Schmidt, H. G., & Boshuizen, H. P. A. (1993). On acquiring expertise in medicine. *Educational Psychology Review 5*, 205-221.

Scott, J. (1991). *Social network analysis. A handbook.* London: Sage.

Sfard, A. (1998). On two metaphors of learning and the dangers of choosing just one. *Educational Researcher 27* (2), 4-13.

Shanteau J. (1992). How much information does an expert use? Is it relevant? *Acta Psychologica, 81*, 75-86.

Stein, E. W. (1997). A look at expertise from a social perspective. In P. J. Feltovich, K. M. Ford, & R. R. Hoffman (Eds.), *Expertise in context* (pp.181-194). Menlo Park: AAAI Press.

Uzzi, B. (1997). Social structure and competition in interfirm networks: The paradox of embeddedness. *Administrative Science Quarterly, 42*, 35-67.

Van de Wiel, M. W. J., Boshuizen, H. P. A., & Schmidt, H. G. (2000). Knowledge restructuring in expertise development: Evidence from pathophysiological representations of clinical cases by students and physicians. *European Journal of Cognitive Psychology 12*, 323-355.

Vartiainen, M., Hakonen, M., Simola, A., Kokko, N., & Rantamäki, T. (1999, July). *Learning project model and transfer of experience*. Paper presented at the 6th EIASM International Product Development Conference, Cambridge, UK.

Vicente, K. J., & Wang, J. H. (1998). An ecological theory of expertise effects in memory recall. *Psychological Review, 105*, 33-57.

Wasserman, S., & Faust, K. (1994). *Social network analysis. Methods and applications*. Cambridge: Cambridge University Press.

Wegner, D. M. (1986). Transactive memory: A contemporary analysis of the group mind. In B. Mullen & G. R. Goethals (Eds.), *Theories of group behavior* (pp. 185-248). London: Kogan Page.

Wenger, E. (1998). *Communities of practice: Learning, meaning and identity*. Cambridge: Cambridge University Press.

Wittenbaum, G. M., & Stasser, G. (1996). Management of information in small groups. In J. L. Nye & A. M. Brower (Eds.), *What's social about social cognition? Research on socially shared cognition in small groups* (pp. 3-28). Thousand Oaks: Sage.

Wong, S., & Sitkin, S. B. (2000). Shaping collective cognition and behavior through collective learning. *Academy of Management Proceedings* (MOC:B1). Location: Publisher.

Ylirenko, H. (1999). *Dependence, social capital and learning in key customer relationships. Effects on performance of technology-based new firms*. Espoo: Acta Polytechnica Scandinavica.

Index

Aarons, E. J. 122, 137
Abelson, R. P. 75, 94
absorptive capacity 274
academic knowledge 4, 5
Achtenhagen, F. 243, 247, 255, 268
Ackerman, E. 237, 247
Ackerman, P. L. 187, 204
Ackermann, W. 74, 93
ACNielsen 98, 117
action knowledge 58
active learning 125, 136
activity theory 272
adaptive expertise 50, 243, 244
Adelson, B. 182, 203
Agnew, N. M. 173, 176, 236, 247
Akin, O. 243, 247
Albanese, M. 116, 117
Alberdi, E. 36, 46
Alberts, G. M. 12, 25
Alderton, J. 242, 247
Al-Diban, S. 33, 46
Alexander, P. A. 187, 203
Allard, F. 189, 205
Allwood, C. M. 74, 93
Ames, C. 185, 194, 202, 203
Anderson, J. R. 161, 165, 176, 187, 191, 203
anxiety 126, 224, 286
Appelbaum, S. H. 254, 268
Apple, M. W. 175, 176

Areglado, R. J. 144, 149, 154
Argyris, C. 254, 268
Arocha, J. F. 110, 118
Arts, J. A. R. 97, 102, 108, 109, 110, 111, 112, 116, 117
assessment 14, 115, 128, 136, 148, 252, 278, 287
Atkinson, R. K. 61, 69
Auerbach, A. H. 12, 25
Austin, A. E. 146, 154
Austin, J. R. 273, 290, 292
authentic learning environment 115

Back, A. 256, 269
backwards reasoning 110
Baets, W. 100, 117
Baldwin, R. G. 146, 154
Barbichon, G. 74, 93
Barrows, H. S. 76, 94, 111, 117, 124, 125, 137
Barthès, J. P. 205
basic research 51
basic science 92, 121, 124, 126, 130, 135, 136
Bassok, M. 54, 68
Beck, K. 269
Becker, H. 257, 268
Becker, U. 47
Bédard, J. 74, 93
beliefs 13, 57, 59, 68, 90, 91, 141, 142, 143, 144, 145, 146, 147, 148, 149,

150, 151, 152, 153, 155, 160, 186, 190, 274, 278, 284
Bennett, N. 143, 154
Bennett, S. N. 178
Bereiter, C. 33, 46, 170, 171, 174, 176, 234, 235, 247, 272, 291, 292
Berends, J. J. 192, 205
Bergin, A. E. 25
Berliner, D. C. 159, 162, 163, 166, 168, 176, 177, 248
Beutler, L. E. 13, 25
Biddle, B. J. 159, 176
Bielaczyc, K. 188, 203
Bigelow, J. D. 97, 98, 117
Billett, S. 14, 24, 25
biomedical reasoning 84
biomedical science 135
Blanning, R. W. 272, 292, 293
Bliss, J. 248
blocked practice 128
Bloom, B. S. 74, 93, 181, 183, 203
bodies of knowledge 83, 208
Boekaerts, M. 186, 187, 188, 204, 205, 206
Bogg, J. 122, 137
Bolhuis, A. M. 133, 137
Bolhuis, S. M. 210, 213, 221, 228
Bonner, S. E. 161, 176
book-keeping 50, 53, 56, 57, 61, 63, 64, 67
Boothe, B. 25
Borders, L. D. 15, 26
Borgatti, S. P. 280, 292
Boshuizen, H. P. A. 3, 16, 24, 25, 27, 73, 74, 75, 77, 81, 82, 83, 84, 86, 87, 89, 91, 92, 93, 94, 95, 98, 102, 103, 108, 109, 112, 115, 117, 118, 119, 121, 122, 126, 127, 128, 133, 137, 138, 160, 174, 176, 178, 182, 204, 205, 233, 236, 248, 275, 276, 277, 292, 293, 294
Boud, D. 91, 93, 189, 204
Bowden, J. 98, 117
Bower, G. H. 27, 178
Boyatzis, R. E. 97, 117
Bradley, R. C. 144, 154
Bransford, J. D. 98, 117, 123, 137
Bresinsky, A. 30, 47
Breuer, F. 12, 25

Broadbent, D. 90, 94
Broder, L. J. 74, 93
Bromme, R. 3, 29, 34, 47, 160, 176, 182, 205, 233, 234, 248
Brooking, A. 277, 292
Brooks, L. R. 128, 131, 132, 137
Brooks, L. S. 137
Brophy, J. 164, 177
Brower, A. M. 294
Brown, A. L. 51, 61, 68, 69, 123, 137, 164, 178, 188, 203
Brown, J. D. 173, 176, 236, 239, 247
Brown, J. S. 33, 46, 54, 69, 208, 228, 274, 292
Bruner, J. S. 164, 179
Buchman, M. 144, 154
Bundred, P. 122, 137
Burt, R. S. 273, 274, 277, 289, 290, 292
business organisation 252, 253, 265
Business-Higher Education Forum 97, 98, 117
Butterworth, G. 69, 248

Caffarella, R. S. 190, 204
Calderhead, J. 142, 153, 154, 177
Calfee, R. C. 177, 248
Calman, K. C. 122, 137
Campbell, A. 142, 143, 154
Carre, C. 143, 154
Carretero, M. 178
Carter, K. 166, 176
case-based learning 22, 30, 32, 34, 43
Caspar, F. 13, 25
Catrambone, R. 54, 55, 68
Champy, J. 253, 269
Chandler, P. 54, 69
Charness, N. 129, 137, 181, 184, 204
Chase, W. G. 160, 176
Chi, M. T. H. 54, 68, 74, 93, 102, 117, 118, 160, 166, 168, 169, 176, 181, 204
Christensen, C. R. 110, 117
Christiaans, H. H. C. M. 243, 247
Clark, R. E. 24, 26
Claxton, G. 153, 154, 214, 224, 228
Clayton, M. J. 258, 268
Clegg, S. R. 101, 118
clerkships 83, 88, 91, 121, 122, 126, 127
clinical judgement 13, 14

Index

clinical reasoning 74, 75, 76, 82, 83, 87, 127, 131, 135
Cockburn, J. 122, 138
Cocking, R. R. 123, 137
Cognition and Technology Group at Vanderbilt 52, 69, 123, 137
cognitive apprenticeship 33, 44, 45, 55, 61, 62
cognitive flexibility theory 33, 43, 45, 57
cognitive load 52, 53, 60, 89, 92
Cohen, R. 189, 204
Cohen, W. M. 274, 292
Colbert, J. 155
Cole, G. 242, 247
collaboration 146, 219, 242, 275, 279, 280, 281, 282, 283, 284
collaborative teams 285
collective learning 208, 211, 227, 228, 254, 280, 290, 291
Collin, K. 24, 174, 177, 231, 232, 233, 238, 239, 241, 242, 247
Collins, A. 33, 46, 54, 55, 61, 69
Collins, A. M. 173, 177, 233, 248
Collison, J. 143, 154
communities of learners 227
communities of practice 208, 227, 237, 238, 239, 275, 277
competence 11, 12, 13, 24, 29, 73, 74, 76, 89, 91, 92, 103, 108, 123, 135, 171, 183, 184, 185, 186, 189, 194, 200, 202, 214, 215, 216, 217, 218, 221, 226, 228, 235, 237
complex tasks 17, 59, 136
conceptual knowledge 24, 49, 58, 59, 64, 66
conceptual understanding 59, 142
confidence 221, 225, 226, 228
constraint management 241
consultant 134, 192, 193, 194, 200, 201
continuous learning 235, 242
Cooke, N. J. 161, 176
Cooper, G. 56, 69
co-operative learning 67
Coulson, R. L. 33, 47, 54, 70, 272, 292
counselling 11, 12, 13, 14, 15, 17, 18, 19, 23, 24
Covell, A. J. 14, 26
Cowen, S. S. 97, 117
Crampton, S. M. 289, 292

Curtis, B. 171, 178, 235, 239, 247, 249
Cushing, K. 166, 176
Custers, E. J. F. M. 82, 87, 93, 131, 137, 160, 176

Darling-Hammond, L. 159, 177
Davidson, J. 292
Davies, S. P. 182, 204
Dawes, R. R. 12, 14, 25
De Corte, E. 178
De Grave, W. S. 112, 118
De Groot, A. D. 74, 93, 160, 177
De Jong, T. 58, 69, 93
De Leeuw, A. C. J. 101, 118
De Volder, M. L. 94
De Vries Robbé, P. F. 89, 94
Deakin, J. M. 189, 205
Deci, E. L. 266, 268
decision-making 6, 13, 17, 37, 89, 101, 163, 236, 253
declarative knowledge 16, 22, 24
deliberate practice 16, 17, 23, 26, 129, 182, 183, 184, 185, 187, 188, 189, 190, 192, 193, 195, 196, 200, 201, 202, 203
delphi method 258
delphi study 252, 258, 262, 267
delphi technique 258
Dent, T. H. 122, 137
Desberg, P. 155
design engineer 242
design experiments 52, 67
design expertise 232, 235, 239, 240, 241, 243, 244, 245
diagnosis 74, 76, 79, 84, 85, 89, 103, 104, 105, 108, 110, 127, 129, 131, 132, 135, 191, 237
diagnostic accuracy 103, 109
Dillon, R. F. 119
DiSessa, A. 153, 154
Doane, S. M. 161, 177
Dole, J. 142, 143, 154
domain-specificity 14, 18
Donaldson, M. 122, 137
Doornbos, A. J. 213, 214, 221, 228
Dörr, G. 47
Drechsel, B. 266, 269
Dreyfus, H. 162, 169, 177
Dreyfus, S. 162, 169, 177

Drukker, J. 138
Duffy, T. 215, 229
Duguid, P. 173, 176, 208, 228, 236, 239, 247, 274, 292
Dunbar, K. 273, 292
Dunn, T. G. 184, 200, 204
Dunwoody, S. 36, 46
Durlak, J. A. 12, 25
Dweck, C. S. 59, 69

economical rationality 251
Edelstein, B. A. 12, 25
educational rationality 251, 256, 257, 265
educationalising 218, 219
Edwards, A. 143, 154
Ehrendorfer, F. 30, 47
Ehrenstein, A. 249
elaboration 54, 55, 56, 57, 58, 61, 62, 63, 66, 85, 123, 124, 128, 136, 212, 222, 225, 226, 227, 228
Elam, J. 171, 178, 235, 249
Elshout, J. J. 36, 47
Elstein, A. S. 74, 94, 118
Emmer, E. 164, 177
employee 209, 251, 252, 253, 254, 255, 256, 258, 265, 267, 268, 278, 279, 287, 288, 289, 291
encapsulation 16, 75, 81, 82, 83, 87, 88, 89, 277
enculturation 6, 7, 8
Engeström, Y. 145, 153, 154, 208, 229, 234, 235, 243, 247, 272, 292
Eraut, M. 14, 25, 91, 94, 105, 118, 189, 204, 234, 242, 247
Eraut, M. R. 213, 214, 217, 221, 229
Ericsson, K. A. 15, 16, 26, 35, 36, 46, 73, 94, 118, 129, 137, 161, 177, 181, 182, 183, 184, 191, 200, 204, 205, 234, 247, 277, 292
Ertmer, P. A. 186, 187, 204
Eteläpelto, A. 24, 174, 177, 231, 232, 238, 239, 240, 241, 243, 247, 248
Ethington, C. A. 15, 26
Ettenson, R. 182, 204
Eva, K. W. 128, 132, 137
evaluation 12, 34, 50, 57, 61, 65, 78, 89, 147, 152, 182, 184, 186, 187, 190, 193, 196, 200, 202, 235, 241, 244
Evans, D. A. 94

Eveland, W. P. 36, 46
Everett, M. G. 280, 292
Evertson, L. 164, 177
expansion 212, 218, 222, 225, 226, 227, 228
experience 3, 5, 6, 7, 11, 13, 14, 15, 16, 17, 19, 20, 21, 22, 23, 24, 25, 32, 35, 36, 64, 68, 73, 75, 81, 82, 83, 84, 85, 87, 88, 89, 90, 91, 92, 102, 104, 106, 107, 108, 109, 110, 122, 126, 127, 129, 130, 132, 133, 134, 136, 141, 143, 144, 146, 152, 153, 160, 161, 163, 164, 165, 166, 167, 168, 169, 170, 171, 182, 183, 185, 186, 187, 188, 189, 190, 191, 192, 193, 194, 197, 199, 200, 201, 202, 203, 208, 209, 214, 215, 216, 217, 218, 221, 232, 233, 234, 235, 238, 239, 240, 241, 242, 243, 244, 245, 246, 252, 259, 264, 265, 266, 267, 286, 287, 290, 291
experiential learning 90, 91, 92, 133, 134, 183, 189, 190, 209, 213, 214, 215, 221, 232
expert 4, 5, 6, 7, 8, 15, 17, 18, 19, 21, 23, 33, 34, 35, 36, 39, 46, 52, 73, 74, 81, 82, 83, 87, 90, 99, 102, 108, 110, 116, 121, 131, 160, 161, 162, 163, 165, 166, 167, 168, 169, 170, 171, 172, 173, 174, 175, 181, 182, 183, 184, 186, 189, 191, 192, 193, 199, 201, 202, 236, 237, 238, 271, 272, 276, 286, 287, 289, 291
expert culture 272, 289
explicit learning 24, 136, 210, 213, 217, 218, 220, 221, 223, 225
externalisation 212, 222, 225, 226, 227

fading procedure 61
Fairbairn, G. J. 24, 26
Farr, M. J. 102, 117, 118, 160, 176, 181, 204
Fasse, B. B. 114, 118
Faust, K. 279, 294
feedback 23, 24, 32, 34, 43, 44, 55, 56, 116, 147, 184, 188, 203, 214, 216, 219, 233, 258, 263
Feiman-Nemser, S. 143, 153, 154

Index

Feltovich, P. J. 33, 47, 54, 70, 74, 76, 93, 94, 160, 176, 234, 236, 247, 248, 249, 272, 292, 294
Fenstermacher, G. D. 143, 153, 154
Ferguson-Hessler, M. G. M. 58, 69
Ferrier, B. M. 130, 139
Fessey, C. 92, 94
Fessler, R. 143, 154
field research 51
Finkelstein, M. 113, 118
Fischer, F. 112, 118
Fischer, K. 46
Fixl, A. 243, 248
Floden, R. E. 144, 154
Flora of North America Association 46
Fong, M. L. 15, 26
Ford, J. K. 242, 249
Ford, K. M. 173, 176, 234, 236, 247, 248, 249, 292, 294
forwards reasoning 110
Frank, K. 276, 292
Freeman, L. C. 280, 282, 292
Friedman, R. A. 274, 289, 292
Friedrich, H. F. 178

Gage, N. L. 162, 177
Gallagher, J. 254, 268
Galton, M. 122, 137
Garb, H. N. 13, 24, 26
Garfield, S. L. 25
Garrick, J. 189, 204
Ge, X. 114, 116, 118
Gerber, R. 242, 248
Germans, J. 207, 209, 229
Gibbs, T. 122, 137
Giddens, A. 174, 177
giftedness 171, 172, 173
Gijselaers, W. H. 97, 98, 102, 111, 117, 118
Gillard, J. H. 122, 137
Glaser, R. 54, 68, 74, 93, 102, 117, 118, 160, 165, 166, 176, 177, 181, 204
Globerson, T. 50, 69
Goethals, G. R. 294
Gore, J. M. 142, 154
Götz, K. 269
Granovetter, M. S. 275, 293
grapevine 288, 289
Gräsel, C. 112, 118

Gray, J. T. 114, 118
Greene, T. R. 17, 27, 160, 178
Greeno, J. G. 51, 69, 162, 165, 173, 177, 233, 237, 248
Griffey, D. C. 166, 177
Grimmett, P. 142, 156
Grob, A. 118
Groen, G. J. 102, 103, 109, 118, 131, 138
Groen, M. G. M. 36, 47
Groothuis, S. 75, 94
groupthink 290
Gruber, H. 3, 11, 14, 15, 16, 22, 26, 49, 55, 56, 69, 70, 129, 233, 234, 236, 248, 251
Gunzelmann, T. 12, 26
Gurman, A. S. 25

Hakkarainen, K. 221, 229, 271
Hakonen, M. 291, 294
Halford, G. S. 94
Hamilton, M. L. 142, 144, 146, 154
Hammer, M. 253, 269
Hanninen, G. 168, 177
Hansen, M. T. 275, 276, 293
Hargreaves, A. 143, 155
Harré, R. 174, 178
Harrington, H. 144, 155
Harteis, C. 251
Hatala, R. 128, 129, 137
Hatano, G. 50, 69, 243, 248
Hayes, A. 189, 205
Hayes, N. 90, 94
Hayes, P. J. 173, 176, 236, 247
Heid, H. 253, 255, 265, 269
Held, S. 33, 46
Helminger, A. 25
help functions 34, 44, 45
Hess, C. 33, 34, 46
Higgs, J. 77, 93, 137, 138, 204
Hilb, M. 254, 269
Hinds, P. J. 35, 46
Hinkofer, L. 49, 56, 66, 69, 70, 129
Hirsig, R. 25
Hodge, J. W. 289, 292
Hodge, N. J. 189, 205
Hofer, B. K. 142, 143, 153, 155
Hoffman, R. R. 161, 176, 177, 234, 236, 247, 248, 249, 292, 294
Holt-Reynolds, D. 143, 155

Hölzenbein, S. 34, 46, 47
Horng, H.-Y. 233, 249
Horvath, J. 118
Horvath, J. A. 169, 170, 171, 178, 191, 205
Housner, L. D. 166, 177
Houston, W. 154
Howe, M. J. A. 181, 204
Hoz, R. 154, 155, 156
Hutchins, E. 273, 293
Hylkema, N. 138

Ichijo, K. 215, 229
identity 7, 133, 142, 173, 174, 231, 238
illness scripts 16, 75, 76
ill-structured domains 17, 18
ill-structured problem 17, 32, 100, 116, 192
Ilomaki, L. 229
implicit learning 90, 210, 212, 213, 215, 216, 218, 219, 220, 221, 222, 226
Inagaki, K. 50, 69, 243, 248
incomplete example 61, 62, 63
inductive reasoning 115
inert knowledge 33, 50, 51, 131
informal learning 133, 134, 136, 242
inquiry learning 221
instructional explanations 56, 57, 58, 59, 60, 61, 62, 67
integrative research paradigm 51, 52, 66, 67, 68
interaction 37, 39, 58, 63, 113, 116, 134, 149, 150, 163, 171, 186, 189, 208, 216, 231, 237, 242, 258, 272, 274, 275, 276, 278, 279, 280, 287, 289
interactive learning environment 30, 34, 46
intermediate 22, 35, 75, 77, 81, 83, 106, 107, 108, 109, 258
Iscoe, N. 239, 247
Isenberg, D. J. 102, 118

Jacobson, M. J. 33, 46, 47, 54, 70
Janis, I. 290, 293
Jehn, K. A. 291, 293
Jennings, L. 14, 26
John, E. G. 269
Johnson, M. 12, 25
Jones, A. 122, 137

Jones, D. T. 252, 269
Jones, M. 77, 93, 137, 138, 204
Joyce, B. R. 144, 155
Jungermann, H. 46
Jungk, S. 175, 176
Jüngst, K. L. 47

Kafai, Y. 247
Kagan, S. 113, 118
Kalyuga, S. 54, 69
Kameda, T. 274, 290, 293
Kane, I. 142, 143, 154
Kanfer, R. 187, 204
Katzenbach, J. R. 154, 155
Kauchak, D. 143, 156
Kaufman, D. R. 110, 118, 130, 138
Keil, F. C. 47
Keister, L. A. 276, 293
Kenneth, M. F. 236, 248
Keogh, R. 91, 93, 189, 204
Keravnou, E. 94
Kiffe, K. 34, 46, 47
King, D. R. 272, 292, 293
Kirjonen, J. 248
Kitcher, P. 273, 293
Klahr, D. 88, 94
Klarus, R. 216, 229
Klatzky, R. L. 161, 177
Klauser, F. 269
Kleine, B. M. 184, 185, 193, 195, 200, 205
Kleinmuntz, B. 177
Knoblich, G. 32, 46
knowledge diffusion 274
knowledge exchange 272, 274, 275, 276, 277, 279, 280, 282, 290
knowledge integration 83
knowledge networks 269
knowledge sharing 24, 271, 274, 275, 277, 278, 279, 280, 284, 287, 289, 291
knowledge structure 20, 22, 24, 40, 75, 88, 89, 102, 108, 161, 167, 173, 191, 192, 240, 243, 272
Koestner, R. 266, 268
Kokko, N. 291, 294
Kolb, D. A. 24, 26, 91, 94, 97, 117, 190, 204
Kolodner, J. 76, 94
Kolodner, J. L. 16, 26, 114, 118

Index

Korpi, M. 36, 46
Korthagen, F. 91, 94
Kozlowski, S. W. 242, 249
Krackhard, D. 272, 293
Kraemer, I. 119
Kraemer, K. I. 114
Krak, A. J. A. 213, 214, 221, 228
Kramer, K. 266, 269
Krampe, R. 181, 204
Krampe, R. T. 16, 26, 181, 204
Krasner, H. 239, 247
Kremer Hayon, L. 144, 155
Krogstad, J. 182, 204
Kühl, S. 253, 269
Kuutti, K. 243, 248
Kwakman, C. H. E. 219, 229

Ladany, N. 15, 26
Lakkala, M. 229
Lambert, M. J. 15, 26
Land, S. M. 114, 116, 118
Lane, P. S. 144, 154
Langosch, I. 257, 268
Lankshear, C. 242, 248
Larson, A. 276, 293
Larsson, S. 242, 248
Lash, F. B. 99, 100, 102, 118
Lave, J. 123, 137, 142, 155, 173, 177, 235, 237, 248, 272, 293
Law, H. 236, 248
Lawrence, J. A. 113, 118
laypersons 6, 35
lean organisation 251, 253
learning by worked-out examples 53, 67
learning environment 30, 34, 43, 44, 45, 46, 51, 52, 59, 67, 97, 115, 122, 126, 128, 136, 202, 235
learning organisation 251, 252, 254, 265, 272
learning processes 34, 61, 63, 73, 74, 76, 92, 134, 210, 211, 213, 214, 215, 220, 255
learning professional 207, 208, 209, 210, 212, 225
learning skill 7, 88, 90, 92, 187, 188, 287
Lebiere, C. 187, 191, 203
LeBlanc, V. R. 131, 137
Lehmann, A. C. 15, 26, 161, 177, 181, 204, 277, 292

Lehtinen, E. 208, 229, 271
Leiner, T. 130, 138
Leinhardt, G. 162, 165, 177
Lempert, W. 265, 269
Leprohan, J. 161, 177
Lester, H. 122, 126, 138
Levin, B. 144, 155
Levine, J. M. 292, 293
Levinthal, D. A. 274, 292
Lewis, M. W. 54, 68
Lichtenberg, J. W. 16, 26
Lievegoed, B. C. J. 207, 209, 229
Light, P. 69, 238, 248
Lipponen, L. 229
Lloyd, B. 178
Locke, T. F. 14, 26
Lohman, M. C. 113, 118
Louden, W. 145, 146, 154, 155
Loughran, J. 142, 155
Lundeberg, M. A. 144, 145, 148, 155

Machado, P. P. P. 13, 25
Maier, U. H. 61, 69
Malakuti, R. 24, 26
management education 97, 98
Mandl, H. 49, 55, 56, 69, 70, 112, 118, 129, 178, 236, 248
Marotta, S. 15, 26
Marsick, V. 217, 218, 229
Martin, A. K. 159, 177
Marton, F. 98, 117
Mason, R. M. 272, 293
mathematics teacher 164
Mayer, R. E. 54, 69
Mayer-Smith, J. 142, 156
Mayer-Smith, J. A. 142, 155
Mayr, U. 181, 204
Mc Gilly, K. 137
McArdle, P. J. 122, 137
McGill, I. 189, 205
McKibbin, L. 98, 118
McManus, I. 126, 137
medical education 122, 124, 126, 127, 128, 129, 134, 135
Meier, B. 25
Merriam, S. B. 190, 204
Messic, D. M. 292, 293
metaknowledge 273
Metz, J. C. M. 93, 94

Mezirow, J. 189, 204
Miettinen, R. 229, 292
Miller, S. L. 102, 119
Milter, G. M. 118
Mintzberg, H. 100, 101, 118
Mitchell, I. J. 142, 155
Monchner, F. J. 13, 26
Montgomery, H. 74, 93
Moon, B. 142, 156
Moreland, R. L. 273, 293
Morrison, L. 122, 137
Moss, F. 126, 137
Mullen, B. 294
multiple perspectives 52, 56, 57, 58, 59, 61, 63, 67, 68, 145, 258
Munby, H. 159, 177
Murphy, C. 144, 155
Murphy, J. 144, 155
Muse-Burke, J. L. 15, 26
Müsseler, J. 46
Muukkonen, H. 229

Namioka, A. 239, 249
Nardi, B. 289, 293
Nardi, B. A. 239, 248
Neale, M. A. 291, 293
negotiation of meaning 231, 238
network tie 274, 276
Neufeld, S. A. 13, 25
Neville, A. J. 128, 137
Newby, T. J. 186, 187, 204
Newman, S. E. 33, 46, 54, 69
Nichols, M. W. 122, 137
Nieuwenhuis, L. 229
Nijhof, W. J. 243, 248
Nix, D. 155
Nonaka, I. 215, 229, 272, 276, 293
noncodified knowledge 276, 290
Norman, G. R. 74, 94, 102, 119, 124, 127, 128, 130, 131, 132, 137, 138, 182, 205
Northcraft, G. B. 291, 293
Northfield, J. 142, 155
novice 4, 6, 8, 15, 17, 18, 19, 21, 22, 23, 24, 25, 26, 32, 34, 35, 45, 46, 73, 74, 81, 83, 87, 91, 97, 99, 102, 103, 105, 107, 108, 109, 110, 111, 123, 128, 160, 161, 162, 163, 164, 165, 166, 167, 168, 169, 170, 171, 172, 176, 178, 182, 232, 233, 235, 236, 237, 239, 240, 241, 243, 291
novice-expert research paradigm 99
Nye, J. L. 294

O'Neill, P. 122, 137
O'Rourke, B. K. 101, 118
O'Byrne, K. 24, 26
Onstenk, J. H. A. M. 219, 229
Oosterheert, I. 142, 144, 155
organisational development 211, 251, 254, 255, 256
Otshubo, Y. 274, 293

Paas, F. 76, 95
Paas, F. G. W. C. 52, 70
Palincsar, A. S. 61, 69, 164, 178
Palonen, T. 271
participating 57, 115, 123, 136, 173, 231, 237, 272, 274, 279, 280
participation 92, 113, 123, 134, 237, 238, 239, 272, 279
Patel, V. L. 94, 102, 103, 109, 110, 112, 118, 130, 131, 138, 161, 177
Patterson, M. 35, 46
PBL 110, 111, 112, 113, 114, 115, 116, 117, 122, 123, 124, 125, 126, 127, 128, 130, 135
Pell, T. 122, 137
Pellegrino, J. W. 161, 177
Penner, B. C. 17, 27, 160, 178
Pennington, N. 161, 176
Perrig, W. J. 118
Perrow, C. 191, 204
personal network 287, 289
personnel development 251, 254, 255, 256
Peters, T. 100, 118
Pfeffer, J. 35, 46
Pfister, H. 46
Picot, A. 253, 269
Pieschl, S. 29, 34, 47
Pinnegar, S. 166, 176
Pinsonneault, A. 114, 119
Pintrich, P. R. 142, 143, 153, 155, 185, 186, 194, 200, 202, 205, 206
Pirolli, P. L. 188, 203
Pirttilä-Backman, A. M. 241, 248
PISA 175, 178

Index

Pitts, J. H. 15, 26
Podolny, J. 274, 289, 292
Pope, M. 178
Porter, L. 98, 118
positioning theory 174
Post, T. A. 17, 27, 160, 178
postulant 166
Pourchot, T. 190, 205
Pozo, J. I. 178
practice 4, 7, 12, 14, 15, 16, 17, 20, 24, 32, 43, 45, 49, 50, 51, 52, 53, 67, 68, 76, 77, 88, 89, 90, 98, 100, 107, 108, 110, 113, 116, 121, 122, 123, 125, 126, 127, 128, 129, 130, 131, 132, 133, 134, 135, 136, 141, 142, 143, 144, 145, 146, 150, 151, 152, 153, 160, 169, 172, 175, 181, 182, 184, 187, 188, 190, 191, 201, 202, 208, 209, 212, 215, 217, 220, 227, 231, 234, 237, 238, 239, 242, 246, 251, 252, 255, 262, 265, 268, 272, 278, 280, 283, 285, 287, 289, 290
Prenzel, M. 266, 269
pride 214, 225, 228
Prince, K. J. A. H. 87, 89, 94, 115, 121, 122, 126, 127, 128, 130, 131, 132, 134, 138
Prinz, P. J. 13, 26
Prinz, W. 46
prior knowledge 54, 55, 56, 58, 64, 111, 123, 124, 127, 128, 136, 186, 235, 242
problem solving 6, 32, 36, 59, 81, 102, 109, 110, 121, 123, 166, 210, 213, 233, 236, 272, 273
problem space 100, 109, 110
problem-based learning 122, 123, 124
procedural knowledge 6, 24, 32, 58, 64, 66
professional knowledge 4, 5, 6, 11, 18, 22, 23, 143, 144, 147, 152, 153, 160, 240, 244, 245
professional learning 6, 7, 45, 141, 146, 151, 183, 189, 227, 228, 235, 242
psychotherapy 13
Punamaki, R. 229
Punamäki, R. L. 292

QAP-correlation 280, 281
Quilici, J. L. 54, 69

Quinones, M. A. 249
Quote Professionals 183, 191, 192, 201, 205

Radcliffe, C. 122, 126, 138
Rahikainen, M. 229
Rambow, R. 182, 205, 233, 234, 248
Rantamäki, T. 291, 294
Razin, A. M. 25
reciprocal teaching 61, 62, 63, 67, 164
Rees, E. 166, 176
reflection on action 141, 216
Regehr, G. 131, 137
Reichwald, R. 253, 269
Reimann, P. 54, 68, 93, 248
Reinecker, H. 12, 26
Reinmoeller, P. 215, 229
Remes, P. 248
Renkl, A. 49, 52, 54, 55, 56, 61, 67, 69, 70, 236, 248
research paradigm 52, 160
resilience 224
Resnick, L. 233, 248
Resnick, L. B. 46, 69, 173, 177
Resnick, M. 247
retention 124, 127, 152
Revans, R. 100, 119
Richardson, V. 142, 143, 144, 155, 156, 177
Rikers, R. M. J. P. 275, 293
Roche, A. M. 122, 138
Rogers, R. R. 190, 205
Ronnestad, M. H. 14, 26
Roos, D. 252, 269
Ropo, E. 159, 164, 165, 166, 167, 168, 169, 178, 244
Rosch, E. 170, 178
Ross, G. 164, 179
Rosson, M. B. 161, 178
Ross-Smith, A. 101, 118
routine 15, 23, 24, 50, 88, 91, 92, 129, 133, 134, 165, 166, 182, 191, 203, 272, 288, 290
Rowland, G. A. 243, 248
Ruijters, M. C. P. 51, 189, 202, 207, 227, 229
Russell, T. 159, 177
Ryan, R. M. 266, 268

Sabers, D. 166, 176
Säljö, R. 248
Salomon, G. 50, 69
Sanson Fischer, R. W. 122, 138
Scardamalia, M. 33, 46, 170, 171, 174, 176, 234, 235, 247, 272, 291, 292
Schaie, W. 177
Schank, R. C. 75, 94
Schaper, N. C. 81, 95, 127, 128, 130, 138
Scherpbier, A. J. J. A. 24, 27, 88, 89, 91, 93, 94, 95, 122, 128, 133, 138
Schiefele, U. 52, 57, 69
Schiepek, G. 12, 26
Schmeck, R. R. 119
Schmidt, H. G. 16, 25, 74, 75, 77, 81, 82, 83, 86, 92, 93, 94, 95, 102, 109, 112, 117, 118, 119, 121, 123, 124, 127, 130, 137, 138, 160, 174, 176, 178, 182, 191, 204, 205, 233, 236, 248, 275, 276, 277, 292, 293, 294
Schön, D. A. 24, 26, 91, 94, 134, 138, 191, 205, 216, 229, 243, 248
Schooler, C. 177
Schreinemakers, J. P. 205
Schuler, D. 239, 249
Schunk, D. H. 145, 156, 206
Schwartz, D. L. 98, 117
Schwarz, H. 289, 293
Scott, J. 279, 280, 281, 293
Seel, N. M. 33, 46
Segers, M. S. R. 97, 111, 117
self concept 57
self-directed learning 80, 133, 148, 149, 150, 152, 214, 220
self-reflection 217
Sembill, D. 269
Senge, P. M. 254, 269
Senghas, K. 31, 36, 47
Senker, P. 242, 247
Senoo, D. 215, 229
Seufert, A. 256, 269
Seybold, S. 31, 36, 47
Sfard, A. 237, 246, 249, 272, 293
Shanteau, J. 182, 204, 275, 293
shared information 273, 274
shared representation 274
Shohov, S. P. 137
Shorrock, S. B. 142, 153, 154
Showers, B. 155
Shriner, C. 184, 200, 204
Shuell, T. J. 153, 155
Shulman, L. 142, 155
Shulman, L. S. 74, 94, 103, 118, 159, 178
Sikula, J. 155
Silberstein, M. 154, 155, 156
Simola, A. 291, 294
Simon, H. 191, 205
Simon, H. A. 32, 35, 36, 46, 47, 100, 119, 160, 176
Simon, T. J. 94
Simons, P. R.-J. 51, 133, 137, 178, 189, 202, 207, 210, 213, 215, 227, 228, 229, 242, 249
Sinatra, G. 142, 143, 154
Sitkin, S. B. 290, 294
Sitte, P. 30, 47
situated approach 237
situated cognition 51, 231
situated learning 54, 123, 237
situational knowledge 58, 64, 66, 236
Skovholt, T. M. 14, 15, 16, 26
Sleeman, D. H. 36, 46
Smith, D. G. 154, 155
Smith, E. M. 242, 243, 249
Smith, J. 118, 161, 177, 181, 204
Smith, M. C. 190, 205
Smyth-Pigott, P. J. 122, 137
social network 171, 173, 174, 237, 272, 276, 277, 279, 280, 289, 291
social theory of learning 171, 231, 232, 237, 238, 239
socialisation 122, 126
Sommer, W. 47
Sonnentag, S. 171, 178, 182, 184, 185, 193, 195, 200, 205, 234, 235, 239, 249
Spada, H. 248
Spiro, R. J. 33, 46, 47, 54, 57, 70, 154, 155, 272, 292
Sprafka, S. A. 74, 94, 103, 118
Stahl, E. 29, 34, 47
standards 4, 145, 146, 182, 188, 189, 202, 207, 208, 227
Stanley, R. 61, 69
Stark, R. 49, 54, 55, 56, 69, 70, 129
Starkes, J. 184, 205
Starkes, J. L. 189, 205
Stasser, G. 273, 294

Stein, D. M. 15, 26
Stein, E. W. 236, 249, 272, 294
Stenberg, R. J. 292
Sternberg, R. 118, 176
Sternberg, R. J. 169, 170, 171, 172, 173, 178, 186, 191, 205
Stinson, J. E. 118
Stokes, D. E. 51, 70
Strasser, J. 11, 22, 26, 233
strategic knowledge 116, 232, 240, 243, 244
stress 14, 78, 87, 92, 122, 126, 132, 136, 175, 188, 254
Streumer, J. N. 243, 248
Stuyt, P. M. J. 89, 94
Sugimori, S. 290, 293
Svensson, L. 242, 248
Sweller, J. 52, 53, 54, 56, 69, 70, 76, 89, 95
Symon, G. 235, 249
Szegedi, K. H. P. 181

tacit knowledge 118, 145, 146, 191, 204, 205, 208, 229, 272, 275, 290
Takeuchi, H. 272, 276, 293
Takezawa, M. 274, 293
Talmon, J. L. 75, 94
Talvitie, J. 271
Tamblyn, R. M. 111, 117, 124, 125, 137
Taylor, F. W. 252, 269
Tesch-Römer, C. 16, 26, 181, 204
The Holmes Group 159, 178
theoretical learning 209, 221
theories of learning 266
Thijssen, J. 207, 229
Thompson, L. L. 292, 293
Tillema, H. 160, 176
Tillema, H. H. 141, 143, 144, 149, 153, 154, 155
tools 57, 75, 114, 191, 208, 209, 227, 228, 235, 236, 242, 244, 245, 272
training 4, 5, 11, 12, 14, 15, 16, 17, 23, 24, 25, 54, 55, 56, 58, 61, 66, 67, 68, 73, 74, 75, 82, 88, 89, 92, 100, 103, 104, 106, 108, 110, 121, 122, 123, 126, 129, 133, 136, 144, 148, 159, 171, 182, 184, 207, 208, 220, 232, 239, 241, 243, 255
Tramm, T. 269

transfer 33, 50, 51, 54, 66, 113, 114, 116, 128, 136, 160, 251, 276
transfer of knowledge 116, 128, 277
transition 7, 37, 87, 98, 103, 104, 109, 122, 123, 126, 127, 132, 135, 136, 141, 187, 239, 240
Trimble, K. 155
Tuominen, T. 229
Tuovinen, J. 54, 69
Tyler, S. W. 105, 119
Tynjälä, P. 239, 247

U.S. Department of Education 159, 178
Uzzi, B. 276, 294

Van de Wiel, M. W. J. 75, 81, 89, 92, 93, 94, 95, 122, 126, 127, 128, 130, 138, 160, 176, 181, 182, 191, 205, 233, 249, 276, 294
Van der Linden, G. 100, 117
Van der Linden, J. 215, 229
Van der Meer, J. W. M. 89, 94
Van der Vleuten, C. P. M. 24, 27, 89, 91, 93, 94, 95, 122, 128, 130, 133, 138
Van Fossen, P. J. 102, 119
Van Langenhove, L. 174, 178
Van Lehn, K. 70, 187, 205
Van Mameren, H. 130, 138
Van Manen, M. 142, 155
Van Merriënboer, J. J. G. 52, 70, 76, 92, 95, 123, 138
Van Oers, B. 236, 249
Van Someren, M. W. 93
Vartiainen, M. 291, 294
Veenman, M. V. J. 36, 47
Vicente, K. J. 275, 294
vision 3, 208, 219, 222, 227, 228
Volet, S. E. 241, 249
Volkart, R. 25
Von Krogh, G. 215, 229, 256, 269
Voss, J. F. 17, 27, 105, 119, 160, 168, 169, 178

Wagenaar, A. 24, 27, 91, 95, 126, 133, 134, 138
Walker, D. 91, 93, 189, 204
Wallace, J. 145, 146, 154, 155
Walsh, J. P. 102, 119, 182, 192, 205
Waltz, D. 171, 178, 235, 249

Wanders, A. 130, 138
Wang, C. W. 233, 249
Wang, J. H. 275, 294
Ward, M. 53, 70
Warner Weil, S. 189, 205
Wasserman, S. 279, 294
Weggeman, M. C. D. P. 181, 192, 205
Wegner, D. M. 273, 294
Wenger E. 248
Wenger, E. 92, 95, 123, 137, 142, 155, 173, 177, 179, 227, 229, 235, 236, 237, 238, 239, 249, 272, 293, 294
Whittaker, S. 289, 293
Wickelgren, W. A. 100, 119
Wideen, M. 142, 156
Wierzbicki, M. 14, 27
Wigand, R. T. 253, 269
Willems, J. 210, 229
Williams, S. M. 111, 119
Wilson, R. A. 47
Winitzky, N. 143, 148, 156
Winne, P. H. 187, 188, 205
Winograd, T. 239, 243, 249
Wittenbaum, G. M. 273, 294
Womack, J. P. 252, 253, 269

Wong, S. 290, 294
Wood, D. J. 164, 179
Woodward, C. A. 130, 139
work related learning 214
workplace 3, 4, 5, 7, 20, 91, 92, 97, 98, 99, 102, 103, 104, 108, 110, 133, 136, 219, 222, 232, 242, 243, 255, 256, 259, 265, 272, 285

Yasumoto, J. Y. 276, 292
Yengo, L. A. 105, 119
Ylirenko, H. 272, 294
Youngs, P. 159, 177
Yung, K. 243, 248

Zeichner, K. M. 142, 154
Zeidner, M. 205, 206
Ziegler, H. 30, 47
Zimmerman, B. J. 145, 156, 186, 187, 188, 200, 202, 206
Zorga, S. 23, 27
Zuzowsky, R. 144, 156

Innovation and Change in Professional Education

1. M. Segers, F. Dochy and E. Cascallar (eds.): *Optimising New Modes of Assessment: In Search of Qualities and Standards.* 2004
   Hb ISBN 1-4020-1260-8; Pb 1-4020-1357-4
2. H.P.A. Boshuizen, R. Bromme and H. Gruber (eds.): *Professional Learning: Gaps and Transitions on the Way from Novice to Expert.* 2004
   Hb ISBN 1-4020-2065-1; Pb 1-4020-2066-X

KLUWER ACADEMIC PUBLISHERS – DORDRECHT /BOSTON / LONDON

Printed in the United States
100909LV00002B/15/A